Microsoft® Works 4.5 For Windows® For Dummies® Cheat Sheet

W9-AHO-354

Navigating in Almost Any Document

To Do This ...	Do This ...
Scroll up/down	Use vertical scroll bar
Scroll sideways	Use horizontal scroll bar
Right, left, up, down	Press arrow key
End of column/next paragraph	Press Ctrl+down arrow
Start of column, paragraph	Press Ctrl+up arrow
One screen up/down	Press PgUp / PgDn keys
Beginning/end of line or row	Press Home / End keys
Beginning/end of document	Press Ctrl+Home / Ctrl+End keys

Starting, Saving, Printing, Closing

To Do This ...	Do This ...
Start Works	Double-click on Works Shortcut icon
Exit Works	Choose File⇨Exit
Start a new document	Press Ctrl+N
Save a document	Press Ctrl+S
Open a document	Press Ctrl+O
Close a document	Press Ctrl+W
Choose an open window	Choose Window, then 1 or 2 or 3 ...
Print Preview	Choose File⇨ Print Preview
Print	Press Ctrl+P

Editing Almost Everywhere

To Do This ...	Do This ...
Select something	Click on it or drag across it
Select with keys	Press Shift+navigation key
Delete	Press Delete key or Backspace key
Cut selection to Clipboard	Press Ctrl+X
Copy selection to Clipboard	Press Ctrl+C
Paste from Clipboard	Press Ctrl+V
Move	Select, drag to position
Copy	Select, Ctrl+drag to position
Insert file into document	Drag file from My Computer window

For more information about IDG Books Worldwide's books, call 1-800-762-2974.

IDG BOOKS WORLDWIDE

...For Dummies: #1 Computer Book Series for Beginners

Microsoft® Works 4.5 For Windows® For Dummies®

Cheat Sheet

Miscellaneous Spreadsheet Stuff

To Do This ...	Do This ...
Sum at end of column or row	Press Ctrl+M, or click Sigma in the toolbar
Change column width	Drag edge to the right of column letter
Change row height	Drag edge below row number
Insert row above	Choose Insert⇨Row
Insert column to left	Choose Insert⇨Column

Number Formats in Spreadsheets and Databases

To Do This ...	Press This ...
Dollars	Ctrl+4 ($ key)
Percent	Ctrl+5 (% key)
Comma at thousands	Ctrl+, (comma)

Quick Formatting in the Word Processor

To Do This ...	Press This ...
Add or Remove space before paragraph	Ctrl+0 (zero)
Indent	Ctrl+M
Un-indent	Ctrl+Shift+M
Hanging indent	Ctrl+Shift+H
Un-hang indent	Ctrl+Shift+T
Bullet on/off	Click bullets button on toolbar

Quick Formatting Almost Everywhere

To Do This ...	Press This ...
Bold	Ctrl+B, or click **B** on toolbar
Italic	Ctrl+I, or click *I* on toolbar
Underline	Ctrl+U, or click U on toolbar
Center	Ctrl+E, or click center align on toolbar
Left-align	Ctrl+L, or click left align on toolbar
Right-align	Ctrl+Shift+R, or click right align on toolbar
Remove font styles	Ctrl+spacebar
Insert page break	Ctrl+Enter
Change margins, page	Choose File⇨Page Setup

Inserting Date and Time Almost Everywhere

To Insert This ...	Press This ...
Today's date	Ctrl+; (semicolon)
Time now	Ctrl+Shift+; (semicolon)
Date or time, any format	Choose Insert⇨Date and Time

...For Dummies: #1 Computer Book Series for Beginners

MICROSOFT® WORKS 4.5 FOR WINDOWS® FOR DUMMIES®

by David Kay

IDG Books Worldwide, Inc.
An International Data Group Company

Foster City, CA ♦ Chicago, IL ♦ Indianapolis, IN ♦ New York, NY ♦ Southlake, TX

Microsoft® Works 4.5 For Windows® For Dummies®

Published by
IDG Books Worldwide, Inc.
An International Data Group Company
919 E. Hillsdale Blvd.
Suite 400
Foster City, CA 94404
www.idgbooks.com (IDG Books Worldwide Web site)
www.dummies.com (Dummies Press Web site)

Library of Congress Catalog Card No.: 97-81224

ISBN: 0-7645-0231-X

Printed in the United States of America

10 9 8 7 6 5 4

1O/SZ/QU/ZY/IN

Distributed in the United States by IDG Books Worldwide, Inc.

Distributed by Macmillan Canada for Canada; by Transworld Publishers Limited in the United Kingdom; by IDG Norge Books for Norway; by IDG Sweden Books for Sweden; by Woodslane Pty. Ltd. for Australia; by Woodslane Enterprises Ltd. for New Zealand; by Longman Singapore Publishers Ltd. for Singapore, Malaysia, Thailand, and Indonesia; by Simron Pty. Ltd. for South Africa; by Toppan Company Ltd. for Japan; by Distribuidora Cuspide for Argentina; by Livraria Cultura for Brazil; by Ediciencia S.A. for Ecuador; by Addison-Wesley Publishing Company for Korea; by Ediciones ZETA S.C.R. Ltda. for Peru; by WS Computer Publishing Corporation, Inc., for the Philippines; by Unalis Corporation for Taiwan; by Contemporanea de Ediciones for Venezuela; by Computer Book & Magazine Store for Puerto Rico; by Express Computer Distributors for the Caribbean and West Indies. Authorized Sales Agent: Anthony Rudkin Associates for the Middle East and North Africa.

For general information on IDG Books Worldwide's books in the U.S., please call our Consumer Customer Service department at 800-762-2974. For reseller information, including discounts and premium sales, please call our Reseller Customer Service department at 800-434-3422.

For information on where to purchase IDG Books Worldwide's books outside the U.S., please contact our International Sales department at 650-655-3200 or fax 650-655-3295.

For information on foreign language translations, please contact our Foreign & Subsidiary Rights department at 650-655-3021 or fax 650-655-3281.

For sales inquiries and special prices for bulk quantities, please contact our Sales department at 650-655-3200 or write to the address above.

For information on using IDG Books Worldwide's books in the classroom or for ordering examination copies, please contact our Educational Sales department at 800-434-2086 or fax 817-251-8174.

For press review copies, author interviews, or other publicity information, please contact our Public Relations department at 650-655-3000 or fax 650-655-3299.

For authorization to photocopy items for corporate, personal, or educational use, please contact Copyright Clearance Center, 222 Rosewood Drive, Danvers, MA 01923, or fax 978-750-4470.

is a trademark under exclusive license to IDG Books Worldwide, Inc., from International Data Group, Inc.

About the Author

Dave Kay is a writer, reformed engineer, and aspiring naturalist and artist, combining professions with the same effectiveness as his favorite business establishment, Acton Muffler, Brake, and Ice Cream (now defunct). Dave has written more than ten computer books, by himself or with friends, including *Web Publishing with WordPerfect 8 For Dummies, VRML and 3D on the Web For Dummies,* and various editions of *Works For Windows For Dummies, WordPerfect For Windows For Dummies, MORE WordPerfect For Windows For Dummies,* and *Graphics File Formats.*

In his other life, as the Poo-bah of Bright Leaf Communications, Dave creates promotional copy, graphics, and Web sites for high-tech firms. He and his wife, Katy, live in the wilds of Massachusetts where, in his spare time, he studies human and animal tracking and munches edible wild plants. He also has been known to make strange blobs from molten glass, sing Gilbert and Sullivan choruses in public, and hike in whatever mountains he can get to. He longs to return to New Zealand and track kiwis and hedgehogs in Wanaka. He hates writing about himself in the third person like this and will stop now.

ABOUT IDG BOOKS WORLDWIDE

Welcome to the world of IDG Books Worldwide.

IDG Books Worldwide, Inc., is a subsidiary of International Data Group, the world's largest publisher of computer-related information and the leading global provider of information services on information technology. IDG was founded more than 25 years ago and now employs more than 8,500 people worldwide. IDG publishes more than 275 computer publications in over 75 countries (see listing below). More than 60 million people read one or more IDG publications each month.

Launched in 1990, IDG Books Worldwide is today the #1 publisher of best-selling computer books in the United States. We are proud to have received eight awards from the Computer Press Association in recognition of editorial excellence and three from *Computer Currents'* First Annual Readers' Choice Awards. Our best-selling *...For Dummies®* series has more than 30 million copies in print with translations in 30 languages. IDG Books Worldwide, through a joint venture with IDG's Hi-Tech Beijing, became the first U.S. publisher to publish a computer book in the People's Republic of China. In record time, IDG Books Worldwide has become the first choice for millions of readers around the world who want to learn how to better manage their businesses.

Our mission is simple: Every one of our books is designed to bring extra value and skill-building instructions to the reader. Our books are written by experts who understand and care about our readers. The knowledge base of our editorial staff comes from years of experience in publishing, education, and journalism — experience we use to produce books for the '90s. In short, we care about books, so we attract the best people. We devote special attention to details such as audience, interior design, use of icons, and illustrations. And because we use an efficient process of authoring, editing, and desktop publishing our books electronically, we can spend more time ensuring superior content and spend less time on the technicalities of making books.

You can count on our commitment to deliver high-quality books at competitive prices on topics you want to read about. At IDG Books Worldwide, we continue in the IDG tradition of delivering quality for more than 25 years. You'll find no better book on a subject than one from IDG Books Worldwide.

John Kilcullen
John Kilcullen
CEO
IDG Books Worldwide, Inc.

Steven Berkowitz
Steven Berkowitz
President and Publisher
IDG Books Worldwide, Inc.

**Eighth Annual
Computer Press
Awards ≥1992**

**Ninth Annual
Computer Press
Awards ≥1993**

**Tenth Annual
Computer Press
Awards ≥1994**

**Eleventh Annual
Computer Press
Awards ≥1995**

IDG Books Worldwide, Inc., is a subsidiary of International Data Group, the world's largest publisher of computer-related information and the leading global provider of information services on information technology. International Data Group publishes over 275 computer publications in over 75 countries. Sixty million people read one or more International Data Group publications each month. International Data Group's publications include: **ARGENTINA:** Buyer's Guide, Computerworld Argentina, PC World Argentina; **AUSTRALIA:** Australian Macworld, Australian PC World, Australian Reseller News, Computerworld, IT Casebook, Network World, Publish, Webmaster; **AUSTRIA:** Computerwelt Osterreich, Networks Austria, PC Tip Austria; **BANGLADESH:** PC World Bangladesh; **BELARUS:** PC World Belarus; **BELGIUM:** Data News; **BRAZIL:** Annuário de Informática, Computerworld, Connections, Macworld, PC Player, PC World, Publish, Reseller News, Supergamepower; **BULGARIA:** Computerworld Bulgaria, Network World Bulgaria, PC & MacWorld Bulgaria; **CANADA:** CIO Canada, Client/Server World, ComputerWorld Canada, InfoWorld Canada, NetworkWorld Canada, WebWorld; **CHILE:** Computerworld Chile, PC World Chile; **COLOMBIA:** Computerworld Colombia, PC World Colombia; **COSTA RICA:** PC World Centro America; **THE CZECH AND SLOVAK REPUBLICS:** Computerworld Czechoslovakia, Macworld Czech Republic, PC World Czechoslovakia; **DENMARK:** Communications World Danmark, Computerworld Danmark, Macworld Danmark, PC World Danmark, Techworld Danmark; **DOMINICAN REPUBLIC:** PC World Republica Dominicana; **ECUADOR:** PC World Ecuador; **EGYPT:** Computerworld Middle East, PC World Middle East; **EL SALVADOR:** PC World Centro America; **FINLAND:** MikroPC, Tietoverkko, Tietoviikko; **FRANCE:** Distributique, Hebdo, Info PC, Le Monde Informatique, Macworld, Reseaux & Telecoms, WebMaster France; **GERMANY:** Computer Partner, Computerwoche, Computerwoche Extra, Computerwoche FOCUS, Global Online, Macwelt, PC Welt; **GREECE:** Amiga Computing, GamePro Greece, Multimedia World; **GUATEMALA:** PC World Centro America; **HONDURAS:** PC World Centro America; **HONG KONG:** Computerworld Hong Kong, PC World Hong Kong, Publish in Asia; **HUNGARY:** ABCD CD-ROM, Computerworld Szamitastechnika, Internetto online Magazine, PC World Hungary, PC-X Magazin Hungary; **ICELAND:** Tolvuheimur PC World Island; **INDIA:** Information Communications World, Information Systems Computerworld, PC World India, Publish in Asia; **INDONESIA:** InfoKomputer PC World, Komputek Computerworld, Publish in Asia; **IRELAND:** ComputerScope, PC Live!; **ISRAEL:** Macworld Israel, People & Computers/Computerworld; **ITALY:** Computerworld Italia, Macworld Italia, Networking Italia, PC World Italia; **JAPAN:** DTP World, Macworld Japan, Nikkei Personal Computing, OS/2 World Japan, SunWorld Japan, Windows NT World, Windows World Japan; **KENYA:** PC World East African; **KOREA:** Hi-Tech Information, Macworld Korea, PC World Korea; **MACEDONIA:** PC World Macedonia; **MALAYSIA:** Computerworld Malaysia, PC World Malaysia, Publish in Asia; **MALTA:** PC World Malta; **MEXICO:** Computerworld Mexico, PC World Mexico; **MYANMAR:** PC World Myanmar; **NETHERLANDS:** Computer! Totaal, LAN Internetworking Magazine, LAN World Buyers Guide, Macworld Netherlands, Net, WebWereld; **NEW ZEALAND:** Absolute Beginners Guide and Plain & Simple Series, Computer Buyer, Computer Industry Directory, Computerworld New Zealand, MTB, Network World, PC World New Zealand; **NICARAGUA:** PC World Centro America; **NORWAY:** Computerworld Norge, CW Rapport, Datamagasinet, Financial Rapport, Kursguide Norge, Macworld Norge, Multimediaworld Norge, PC World Ekspress Norge, PC World Nettverk, PC World Norge, PC World ProduktGuide Norge; **PAKISTAN:** Computerworld Pakistan; **PANAMA:** PC World Panama; **PEOPLE'S REPUBLIC OF CHINA:** China Computer Users, China Computerworld, China InfoWorld, China Telecom World Weekly, Computer & Communication, Electronic Design China, Electronics Today, Electronics Weekly, Game Software, PC World China, Popular Computer Week, Software Weekly, Software World, Telecom World; **PERU:** Computerworld Peru, PC World Profesional Peru, PC World SoHo Peru; **PHILIPPINES:** Click!, Computerworld Philippines, PC World Philippines, Publish in Asia; **POLAND:** Computerworld Poland, Computerworld Special Report Poland, Cyber, Macworld Poland, Networld Poland, PC World Komputer; **PORTUGAL:** Cerebro/PC World, Computerworld/Correio Informatico, Dealer World Portugal, Mac*In/PC*In Portugal, Multimedia World; **PUERTO RICO:** PC World Puerto Rico; **ROMANIA:** Computerworld Romania, PC World Romania, Telecom Romania; **RUSSIA:** Computerworld Russia, Mir PK, Publish, Seti; **SINGAPORE:** Computerworld Singapore, PC World Singapore, Publish in Asia; **SLOVENIA:** Monitor; **SOUTH AFRICA:** Computing SA, Network World SA, Software World SA; **SPAIN:** Communicaciones World España, Computerworld España, Dealer World España, Macworld España, PC World España, PCactiv, Windows World España; **SRI LANKA:** Infolink PC World; **SWEDEN:** CAP&Design, Computer Sweden, Corporate Computing Sweden, Internetworld Sweden, it.branschen, Macworld Sweden, MaxiData Sweden, MikroDatorn, Nätverk & Kommunikation, PC World Sweden, PCaktiv, Windows World Sweden; **SWITZERLAND:** Computerworld Schweiz, Macworld Schweiz, PCtip; **TAIWAN:** Computerworld Taiwan, Macworld Taiwan, NEW ViSiON/Publish, PC World Taiwan, Windows World Taiwan; **THAILAND:** Publish in Asia, Thai Computerworld; **TURKEY:** Computerworld Turkiye, Macworld Turkiye, Network World Turkiye, PC World Turkiye; **UKRAINE:** Computerworld Kiev, Multimedia World Ukraine, PC World Ukraine; **UNITED KINGDOM:** Acorn User UK, Amiga Action UK, Amiga Computing UK, Apple Talk UK, Computing, Macworld, Parents and Computers UK, PC Advisor, PC Home, PSX Pro, The WEB; **UNITED STATES:** Cable in the Classroom, CIO Magazine, Computerworld, DOS World, Federal Computer Week, GamePro Magazine, InfoWorld, I-Way, Macworld, Network World, PC Games, PC World, Publish, Video Event, THE WEB Magazine, and WebMaster; online webzines: JavaWorld, NetscapeWorld, and SunWorld Online; **URUGUAY:** InfoWorld Uruguay; **VENEZUELA:** Computerworld Venezuela, PC World Venezuela; and **VIETNAM:** PC World Vietnam.   3/24/97

Dedication

This edition is dedicated to Rusty (the Wonder Dog), the most loving, beautiful, funny, dignified and well-behaved dog anyone ever had, and to Yankee Golden Retriever Rescue who made Rusty's life with us possible.

Author's Acknowledgments

I would like to acknowledge the support and tolerance of my wife Katy and of my friends and family, from whose company I am sadly removed while writing these books. Thanks also to Matt Wagner and the rest of the folks at Waterside, and to the congenial editors at IDG Books Worldwide, including:

- Project editor Ryan Rader, who faints not, though the hour draws near
- Copy editor Andrea Boucher, for tolerating my tormented sentence structure
- Technical editor Michael Young, for keeping me as honest as I can stand

Publisher's Acknowledgments

We're proud of this book; please register your comments through our IDG Books Worldwide Online Registration Form located at http://my2cents.dummies.com.

Some of the people who helped bring this book to market include the following:

Acquisitions, Development, and Editorial

Project Editor: Ryan Rader

Acquisitions Editor: Michael Kelly

Copy Editor: Andrea C. Boucher

Technical Editor: Michael C. Young

Editorial Manager: Elaine Brush

Editorial Assistant: Paul E. Kuzmic

Production

Project Coordinator: Valery Bourke

Layout and Graphics: Steve Arany, Lou Boudreau, Angela F. Hunckler, Drew R. Moore, Heather N. Pearson, Brent Savage, Deirdre Smith

Proofreaders: Kelli Botta, Vickie Broyles, Rachel Garvey, Nancy Price, Rebecca Senninger, Janet M. Withers

Indexer: Sherry Massey

Special Help

Rowena Rappaport, Copy Editor; Stephanie Koutek, Proof Editor

---

General and Administrative

IDG Books Worldwide, Inc.: John Kilcullen, CEO; Steven Berkowitz, President and Publisher

IDG Books Technology Publishing: Brenda McLaughlin, Senior Vice President and Group Publisher

Dummies Technology Press and Dummies Editorial: Diane Graves Steele, Vice President and Associate Publisher; Mary Bednarek, Director of Acquisitions and Product Development; Kristin A. Cocks, Editorial Director

Dummies Trade Press: Kathleen A. Welton, Vice President and Publisher; Kevin Thornton, Acquisitions Manager

IDG Books Production for Dummies Press: Beth Jenkins Roberts, Production Director; Cindy L. Phipps, Manager of Project Coordination, Production Proofreading, and Indexing; Kathie S. Schutte, Supervisor of Page Layout; Shelley Lea, Supervisor of Graphics and Design; Debbie J. Gates, Production Systems Specialist; Robert Springer, Supervisor of Proofreading; Debbie Stailey, Special Projects Coordinator; Tony Augsburger, Supervisor of Reprints and Bluelines; Leslie Popplewell, Media Archive Coordinator

Dummies Packaging and Book Design: Patti Crane, Packaging Specialist; Kavish + Kavish, Cover Design

◆

The publisher would like to give special thanks to Patrick J. McGovern, without whom this book would not have been possible.

◆

Contents at a Glance

Cartoons at a Glance

By Rich Tennant

page 9

page 213

page 365

page 279

page 149

page 323

page 77

Fax: 978-546-7747 • E-mail: the5wave@tiac.net

Table of Contents

Introduction

Congratulations! You have already proven your superior intelligence. Rather than blowing several hundred bucks on the biggest and most muscle-bound word processor, database program, spreadsheet program, graphics, and communications software you can find, you're using Microsoft Works 4.5 — a program that can do probably everything you need for a lot less trouble and money. Heck, you're so smart that you may have bought a PC with Works already installed.

So then why, exactly, should you be reading a book for Dummies? Because Dummies are an underground group of people smart enough to say, "Okay, so I'm not a computer wizard. So sue me. Call me a dummy if you will. I still want to use this stuff." The ... *For Dummies* books are for people who:

- Want to learn about their software without being bored silly.
- Feel like there should be a manual to explain the software manual.
- Actually want to get some work done. Soon. Like today.
- Don't want to wade through a lot of technical gibberish.
- Don't think like computer software engineers seem to think.

What's in This Book

This book describes how to use all the tools of Microsoft Works 4.5, separately and together, plus some introductory things on Windows, disks, and other basics, plus instructions for using Microsoft Internet Explorer. In this book, you learn about the following topics:

- Window basics (opening, closing, and painting them shut).
- Word processing (like food processing, only messier).
- Spreadsheets (for soft, comfortable naps on your spreadbed).
- Databases (for storing all your baseless data).
- Graphics (for charting uncharted waters and general doodling).
- Web browsing (for shmoozing the Internet's World Wide Web).
- Communications (for teaching your computer to talk).

What's Different about This Book

Unlike software manuals, this book doesn't have to deliver a positive message about the software, so it doesn't breathlessly try to show you everything you could possibly do. Nor does it describe, as a manual does, every button and command. Instead, it focuses on the everyday things you have to do, gives you some background, points you toward shortcuts, and steers you around some of the stuff you probably don't need.

This book doesn't assume that you already know about software. Heck, it doesn't even assume that you know much about Windows. If you are already comfortable with your PC and Windows, that's great, and this book won't bore you to tears. But if — like a lot of new PC users — your soundest PC skill so far is finding the ON switch, there's a whole introductory section to get you going. Plus, this book tries not to rely on special terms to describe how to do something. It uses the terms so that you get to know them, but it doesn't force you to go look them up in the manual.

Who Do I Think You Are, Anyway?

Apart from thinking that you are a brilliant and highly literate person (evidenced by the fact that you have bought or are considering buying this book), here's what I assume about you, the esteemed reader:

- ✔ Your PC has Works 4.5 installed on it. (See the next section, "How To Choose the Right ...*For Dummies* Book.")

- ✔ You don't necessarily have great familiarity with Works, Windows, or mice, except perhaps that you know that it Works to put screens on Windows to keep mice out.

- ✔ You don't really give a gnat's eyebrow about Windows except for what you absolutely need to do your work.

- ✔ Heck, you may even have thought that Works was part of Windows, if it came with your PC. (It's not.)

- ✔ If you're on a computer network, you have a computer and network guru available — an expert whom you can pay off in cookies or pizza to solve network problems.

- ✔ You're not one of those people who is secretly hoping that Works, a fifty-buck program, will let you do desktop publishing, relational databases, multilevel spreadsheets, and 3-D graphics. (You people know who you are.)

Apart from that, you could be darn near anybody. I know of mathematicians, computer scientists, business people, and daycare center managers who use Works quite happily.

How to Choose the Right ...For Dummies Book

Microsoft Works has been around awhile, and many older versions are still in use. The same is true for the *...For Dummies* books about Works. (Heck, the same is true for authors.) For best results, you need to match the book to the software.

If you have Microsoft Works 4.5, introduced in the fall of 1997, this book is the one written for you. It covers new features, such as *Internet Explorer,* and offers additional material on existing Works features such as Easy Calc, a feature that simplifies calculations.

If you have Microsoft Works 4.0 for Windows (originally known as *Works For Windows 95* because it was the first version of Microsoft Works to run under Windows 95), most of this book will apply to you — but *Microsoft Works For Windows 95 For Dummies* is the book that was written specifically for you. (We're making the title say *Works 4 ...* in new printings to make things clearer.) Works 4.5 is exactly like Works 4.0 except that Works 4.5 comes with Microsoft's Internet Explorer, a new and expanded ClipArt Gallery, and Microsoft-supplied templates.

You might even have Microsoft Works 3.0 for Windows, which was designed for Windows 3.1, but which also runs under Windows 95 if you ask it to. In that case, you want *Microsoft Works 3 For Windows For Dummies,* not this book. The following table sums it all up:

Table I-1	Choosing *...For Dummies* Books for Dummies	
Your Software	*Your Operating System*	*What Book to Buy*
Works 4.5	Windows 95	This book
Works 4.0	Windows 95	This book or *Microsoft Works For Windows 95 For Dummies*
Works 3.0	Windows or Windows 95	*Microsoft Works 3 For Windows For Dummies*

How to Use This Book

Nobody, but nobody, wants to sit down and read a book before they use their software. So don't. Instead, just look something up in the index or table of contents and "go to it." Don't just read, though. Follow along on your PC, using this book as a tour guide or road map. I use pictures where necessary, but I don't throw in a picture of everything because you have the pictures right there on your PC screen, and they're even in color.

If you're already fully fenestrated (Windows-cognizant), just march right along to the part on your favorite tool. Since Works is an integrated package of several tools, you'll find that they have a lot in common. If you're still figuring out what the heck all this stuff is on your computer screen, check out Part I, Survival Skills.

This is mainly a reference book, so you don't have to read it in any particular order. Within each part, though, the earlier chapters cover the more fundamental stuff. So if you want, you can just read the chapters in order (in each part) to get from the simple to the more complex.

How This Book Is Organized

Unlike some computer books, which seem to be organized alphabetically by gadget, this book is organized by what you are trying to learn. It doesn't, for example, explain each command as it appears on the menu. Unless you are one of those compulsive people who, say, actually learns all the buttons on their VCR remote control before using it, that sort of organization is pretty useless.

No, what this book does is break things down into the following useful parts, including one part for each tool. In each tool's part, there's something for everyone, whether you've never used a similar tool before or you're an old hand who just needs to learn how Works does it.

Part I: Survival Skills

If you're currently beating your head against Windows, files, directories, mice, or disks, or you're just trying to get under way with Works, Part I is the place to turn. Here's how to start Works, make your various windows behave, and get basic keyboard and mouse skills.

Part I is also the place to go for things that work pretty much the same everywhere in Works: opening and closing files, getting help, cutting and pasting, and changing the appearance of things.

Part II: The Wily Word Processor

The one tool that nearly everyone uses — the word processor — can also be rather elusive. In this part, you discover its wiles and ways. This part covers everything from basics, such as how to use the keyboard, to subtle and elusive facts, such as where paragraph formatting hides. Learn how to get the document you want and save work by avoiding old-fashioned typewriter habits. Later chapters introduce editing techniques and essential bells and whistles like page numbers, tables, borders, lines, headers, footers, and footnotes.

Part III: Setting Sail with Spreadsheets

Yo, ho, ho! Stay the mizzen! Batten down the poop deck! Here's how to put the wind in your spreadsheets and computerize your calculations. Even if your feelings for calculation are more "oh, no" than "yo, ho!", Part III shows you how to have a nice cruise. From the basics of entering stuff in cells and navigating around, to the secrets of creating and copying formulas, to the subtleties of date and time arithmetic, Part III is your port of call.

Part IV: Doing Active Duty at the Database

As some old soldier once said, "There's the right way, there's the wrong way, and there's the Army way." Well, in Works there's the Works database way. If you've never used a database before, Part IV will give you your basic training. If you've already done a hitch with other database software, Part IV will help you understand the slightly quirky Works way of doing and talking about databases. This part explores fields, records, data entry, different views, making changes, filtering, and creating basic reports.

Part V: Exploring the Internet Wilderness

There's an information highway out there, and it winds through a vast digital wilderness called the Internet. Sometimes, however, the route to this information highway is a bumpy and twisted road. Part V of this book paves the potholes and gets you on the road. (The ride is not free, however. You will have to lay out a few bucks every month to an Internet Service Provider.)

The most exciting way to get online is through Microsoft's Internet Explorer, a separate program bundled with Microsoft Works 4.5. Part V of this book tells you how to get connected to the Internet and use Internet Explorer to read information published on the World Wide Web. Once you're on the Web, you can even download additional Internet software such as electronic mail programs.

Works does provide a Communications tool, but for most people this tool will not provide the communications they want (such as electronic mail) on the Internet. The Communications tool lets you turn your PC into a computer terminal for two-way communication with certain types of remote computers. If you have access to such a computer at your school or work, Part V tells you how to make the connection.

Part VI: Creating Great Works of Art: Graphics

A mercenary artist friend of mine says, "A picture is worth a thousand bucks." Well, your pictures might be worth that, but with Works they'll cost a lot less. Works provides easy charting and other forms of graphics, from "blob art" with the Draw tool, to WordArt and ClipArt. Part VI first shows how to quickly transform a spreadsheet into a bar, pie, line, area, or other kind of chart, complete with labels and legends and charty stuff like that. Then it shows you how to use Works' drawing tool for creating your own diagrams and other works of art. Finally, it takes you on a brief tour of Works' ClipArt Gallery and the swoopy, loopy world of the WordArt tool.

Part VII: The Part of Tens

The Part of Tens? Why not the part of eights? Who knows, but thanks to the perfectly ridiculous act of fate that gave humans ten fingers, every ...*For Dummies* book has a Part of Tens. Here are Ten Nifty Tricks, Ten Things NOT to Do, and other suggestions and recommendations that will make your life easier.

Icons Used in This Book

You'd think we were in Czarist Russia from the popularity of icons in the computer world. Everything from toasters to VCRs has icons instead of words now, which is no doubt responsible for all those sleepy folks sticking bread into the tape slot at breakfast time. (That's not a problem at your house?) Anyway, not to be left behind, this book uses icons, too — only ours are much cuter than the ones on your toaster. Here's what they mean:

If there's an easier or faster way to do something, or if there's something really cool, you'll find one of these target-thingies in the margin.

If there's something that you really shouldn't miss, this icon lets you know about it.

This icon reminds you that you shouldn't forget to remember something — something that was said earlier but is easily forgotten.

This icon cheerfully tells you of something that might go wrong, with consequences ranging from mild indigestion to weeping, wailing, and gnashing of teeth.

You won't see too much of Mr. Science (alias the Dummies guy) in this book. When he does appear, he indicates that here's a little inside information on how things work that you just might want to know. But, if you ignore him, you won't be much worse off.

If there's something important somewhere else in the book, this icon lets you know about it. Because a lot of Works tools work alike, you see a bunch of these guys.

The One Shortcut Used in This Book

This book always uses genuine English words to describe how things work! Well, almost always (sorry). There's one important exception. When you see an instruction that looks something like this,

"Choose Blah⇨Fooey from the menu bar . . ."

it means, "Click Blah in the menu bar, and then click Fooey in the menu that drops down." (If you don't know what *click, menu bar,* or *menu* mean, that's okay — see Chapters 1 and 2.)

This sort of instruction crops up so often that, if we didn't use that shortcut, you'd be bored silly by Chapter 3 — and IDG Books would have to slaughter another forest worth of trees to get the extra paper to print the book!

(You may also notice another very minor typographic habit of this book. This book capitalizes first letters of certain Works features, even though Works itself doesn't. That habit makes sentences like, "Click the check box labeled Center Across Connection" readable, whereas, "Click the check box labeled Center across connection" would be gibberish.)

Where to Go from Here

If Works is already installed on your PC, you probably have tried to do something with it. You are probably already perplexed, annoyed, or intrigued by something you've already seen. Look it up in the table of contents or the index and see what this book has to say about it. If you're just trying to start a document in Works, see Chapter 1. If you're trying to master some of the basics, such as controlling windows and moving around, see Chapter 2.

Otherwise, drag a comfy chair up to your PC, bring along a plate of cheese for your mouse, and thumb through the book until you find something fun. Feeling whimsical? Check out Part VI, "Creating Great Works of Art: Graphics." Need to create your own marketing junk mail? Turn to the Appendix, "Wisdom and Wizardry for Common Tasks." You may end up with something useful, and — in any event — it beats the heck out of working!

All authors enjoy hearing from readers, and I'm no different. If you have comments or questions, you can send me e-mail at works45@gurus.com. (Attach your Works file if you're reporting a beginner's-level problem with a document that this book doesn't seem to solve.) I'm just one guy, not Microsoft, so I can't promise to reply to your message or to solve your problems; but your mail will help make future editions of this book better! After you have gone "online" to the Internet with Internet Explorer as Chapters 16 and 17 describe, you can fill out the online registration form at http://www.dummies.com/register.html on the World Wide Web!

Part I
Survival Skills

The 5th Wave — By Rich Tennant

"IT'S NOT THAT IT DOESN'T WORK AS A COMPUTER, IT JUST WORKS BETTER AS A PAPERWEIGHT."

In this part . . .

The old recipe for bear stew read: "First, catch a bear." This was great advice as long as the reader was pretty well informed about bears. Otherwise, the prospective stewer became the stewee more often than not.

If you think most computer books, like that recipe, leave out some pretty important fundamentals, Part I of this book is where you want to start. Here's where you can find out how to use and control the windows on your PC; how to start programs like Works; what all those weird keys are on your keyboard; what your mouse or trackball is all about; how to create folders on your computer; and all those other fundamentals that other books assume you know all about.

"Though this be madness, yet there is method in't."

Hamlet, Wm. Shakespeare

Chapter 1

Starting

● ●

In This Chapter

▶ Getting comfortable with your keyboard

▶ Moving around with your mouse or trackball

▶ Starting Works

▶ Using and losing the Task Launcher

▶ Starting new documents

▶ Navigating files, disks, folders, and directories

▶ Starting with an existing document

▶ Finding documents

● ●

*L*ots of software books jabber away about keyboards, mice, files, disks, folders, and directories as if you had spent your childhood with a mouse in your hand and had used a keyboard for a pillow. (If you were born before about 1980, the only way that this circumstance could have happened is if you had lived in a rodent-infested typewriter shop. If you were born after 1980, you are probably genetically hardwired to use a computer and need only a quick refresher.)

This book does things a little differently. Here you can start at the beginning, if starting at the beginning is what you need to do. This chapter talks about some things that few software books ever tell you, such as what's what on your keyboard, how to use your mouse, and what icons, files, disks, folders, and directories are.

If you're already keyboard-qualified, rodent-ready, and file-familiar, thumb ahead in this chapter to the section on starting Works. If you've already managed to get Works started, read on about Works' Task Launcher, which helps you create new documents and find where your existing ones are hiding in that vast expanse of your disk drive.

Using Your Keyboard

Take a look at your keyboard. I bet it looks something like Figure 1-1. If you're using a laptop computer, all bets are off. The laptop manufacturers put stuff where they feel like putting it, so you have to check your manual.

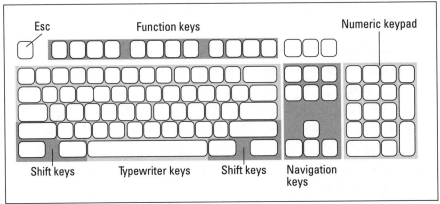

Figure 1-1:
Interesting
keys, most
of which
weren't on
your Smith-
Corona.

- Esc
- Function keys
- Numeric keypad
- Shift keys
- Typewriter keys
- Shift keys
- Navigation keys

✔ **Function keys:** These keys are usually located along the top of the keyboard and are labeled F1 through F10 or F12. The function keys carry out one set of commands when you use them by themselves; these same keys carry out other commands when you use them with the *shift keys:* Alt, Ctrl, and Shift. Pressing F1 is especially useful: It causes a window of Help information to be displayed.

✔ **Typewriter keys:** Your old Royal typewriter had most of the same characters, numbers, and punctuation keys. The computer people added a few new ones to jazz things up. You use these keys mostly to type stuff in, but you can also use them with the Alt, Ctrl, and Shift keys to issue commands.

✔ **Navigation keys:** These keys are to the right of the typewriter keys. Four of the keys have arrows on them and move the cursor when you're typing or move the highlight that appears when you're using Windows menus or scroll bars. The others, marked Home, End, PgUp (or Page Up), and PgDn (or Page Down), are keys that move you around in a document in large gulps. Nearby are a Delete key (which deletes stuff) and an Insert key (which doesn't actually insert anything). Try not to hit the Insert key. If you do, it makes you type over existing text; hit the Insert key again to type normally.

✔ **Numeric keypad:** The keys on this keypad duplicate the number keys and useful math symbols that are across the top of your keyboard. On many computers, the numeric keypad also contains a duplicate of the Enter key. The keypad can alternatively perform the function of the navigation keys if you press the Num Lock button, located somewhere nearby.

✔ **Enter key:** This key is generally labeled Enter, or it is marked with a funny L-shaped arrow. The Enter key is used mostly to signal that you've finished typing a paragraph or some data. You generally *do not* use the Enter key the way that you do on a typewriter, to end every line.

✔ **Esc key:** Called the Escape key, this little guy lets you back out of commands you didn't mean to get into. Pressing Esc does the same thing as clicking the Cancel button that Works sometimes displays during commands.

✔ **Shift keys:** The keys in this shifty bunch don't do anything by themselves — they work only in combination with other keys, sort of like the pedals on a piano. When the Shift, Alt, and Ctrl (pronounced Control) keys are held down, they impart new meanings to other keys.

When you use shift keys, use them in the right sequence, as shown in these steps:

1. **Press a shift key (Shift, Alt, or Ctrl, as directed) first and hold it down.**

2. **Press the other key (the F6 key, for example).**

3. **Finally, release both keys.**

    If your fingers don't work well together, release the shift key last.

These types of combinations are written as Shift+F6, for example, or Ctrl+F6 or Alt+F6 (if F6 is the other key being pressed).

Sometimes, you must press more than two keys. Such an instruction is written as Ctrl+Shift+F6, for example; but the instruction may as well be written Shift+Ctrl+F6 because the order in which you press the Ctrl and Shift keys doesn't matter. Just get both of 'em down before you press the last key and release 'em all at once.

Using Your Mouse or Trackball

That strange rodent-shaped object with push buttons on the top, plugged into your computer by its tail, is probably a *mouse*. If you have something with a ball on the topside, you probably have a *trackball*. If you don't seem to have a mouse or trackball, check the manuals that came with your computer and find out how to install one or the other. Using Windows or Works without a mouse or a trackball is practically impossible.

Mouse anatomy and behavior

The mouse or trackball is the modern, polite, and mature way to do what you did as a toddler: point at what you want. Now, however, you point by moving a *mouse pointer* or *mouse cursor* (typically an arrow, although the symbol changes) that appears on your screen. You move the mouse pointer by moving the mouse around on your desk (preferably on a mouse pad) with your hand. With a trackball, you move the cursor by spinning the ball of the trackball with your fingers. After the pointer is over the thing you want, you *click* — that is, you press a button on the mouse/trackball.

The mouse (or trackball) generally wears two buttons. Really snazzy dressers may sometimes sport three. If you have a third, middle button, consider it a vestigial remnant of the days when giant, Jurassic-era mice roamed the countryside and intimidated each other with their vast arrays of buttons.

In Works and all other Windows programs, the left button is the most important one. (If you're left-handed, you can ask your computer guru to make the right button the most important one.)

The right mouse button, in Works, brings up a menu of commonly used editing commands such as Copy and Paste. You can find the same editing commands elsewhere in Works, but this feature puts these commands conveniently at your fingertips.

TIP

Really basic basics

If you have a mouse, it goes on a pad on your desk, not on the floor. You operate the mouse with your hand, not your foot. The curved, button side goes up.

If you have a trackball, it also goes on your desk and needs to be kept from sliding around. The ball side goes up. Operate the ball and buttons with your fingers, not any other extremity. (If a ball is protruding from the surface of your laptop, it's probably the trackball, and its buttons are next to it.)

Any other modes of operation require a level of dexterity not known to exist in Earth fauna and are probably illegal between consenting adults in several states. This is not to say that otherwise intelligent people have not tried them.

Mouse skills

The first mouse skill you need in order to control a Windows program is the ability to *point and click,* so here's exactly what this term and related terms mean:

- ✔ **To point:** Move the mouse pointer or cursor by pushing your mouse around or spinning the trackball. Move the pointer so that its tip is anywhere on top of, or very near, the thing that you're pointing at.

- ✔ **To click something (also called clicking "on" something):** Point to it and then press and release the button (traditionally the left one) on the mouse.

- ✔ **To double-click:** Press and release the button twice in rapid succession. Discovering just how fast you need to click may take a bit of time.

- ✔ **To click and drag (sometimes simply called *dragging*):** Press the mouse button down and hold it down. Then move the mouse while holding down the button; this action *drags* something, such as the edge of a highlighted area, around on the screen. When you're done dragging, release the button.

Understanding Files, Disks, Folders, and Directories

Besides keyboards and mice, another subject that lots of beginners are in the dark about is "What are the basic lumps of stuff that software is made of?" Well, here's an overview of the fundamental atoms and molecules that make up that mysterious substance called *software*:

- ✔ *Files* are how your computer stores programs, your documents, and other forms of information. Each file has a *filename,* given either by you or by the program that created the file, so that you and the PC can both identify it. In Windows, when you see a file listed somewhere, you can almost always double-click the file to open it.

- ✔ A *hard disk* is where your PC keeps files that live permanently in your PC. You can also keep copies of files on a removable *diskette* (a little flat plastic thing that is often simply called a *disk*), also called a *3¹/₂ inch floppy* by Windows. Diskettes are used either for backup (in case your hard disk breaks) or to give files to other people. The diskette drives (the places you put diskettes) are called *A:* and sometimes *B:* (you may have only *A:*). The hard disk is called *C:*. If you have a second hard disk or a CD-ROM drive, it's drive is usually called *D:*. (Why the colons? It's ancient PC tradition.) If your computer is on a network, you can store things on disk drives on someone else's computer; talk to the person who manages your network in order to find out how you can do this task. To see what hard disk drives and floppies you have available, look for a symbol labeled My Computer on your Windows screen and double-click it.

✔ *Folders* help you organize your files into groups. Folders are analogous to file folders in a file cabinet, so they appear as yellow file folders. These computer file folders (sometimes called *directories* or *subdirectories*) have names, too. Some folders are created and named automatically by Windows — other folders you have to create and name yourself. Works lets you create a new folder at the same time that you save a file, so that you can easily organize your documents. Folders are usually within folders within folders on your PC — a hierarchy of folders. To go *up* the hierarchy is to open the folder that contains the currently open folder. To see the folders on your C: drive, double-click the My Computer icon on your Windows screen; then, in the window that opens up, double-click the symbol labeled (C:). To see what's in a folder, double-click it.

✔ Whenever you save your work in a file, you give your file a filename. In Works 4 or 4.5 and other programs that are designed for Windows 95, you can give files nice, readable filenames with spaces and punctuation in them, such as *Letter To Mom About Cookies.* (You can't, however, use any of these characters: * ? " < > | : / \.) If you have friends or colleagues who are still using earlier versions of Windows and you want to share your files with them, using filenames that are less than eight characters long is best (and use just letters and numbers — no spaces or punctuation).

✔ Files also have an *extension* to their names; an extension can be up to three characters long, preceded by a period. The extension is added by the program that you use, such as Works. When you click a file to open it, the extension tells Windows what program to use to open the file. When you save a file, you may, if you like, specify the extension yourself, but in general, letting Works or whatever program you are using take care of specifying the extension when you save a file is best.

✔ When you want to tell your computer in detail about a specific file in a specific location, you can put all the preceding information together into one line called a *path*. You start with the disk drive; then you add the directory (folder) name, any subdirectories' names (folders within that folder), filename, and finally the file extension. To separate each piece of information, you type a special slash mark called the *backslash*. (The backslash key is usually near the Backspace key.) A path is written something like this:

```
c:\letters\mom\cookies.wpd
```

Finding and Starting Works

First things first — you need to wake Works up and get it running. Finding and starting Works is very easy if, when it was installed, a *shortcut* icon was placed on your screen. Look on your screen for an *icon* (a tiny picture) labeled Shortcut to Microsoft Works, and double-click that icon. Figure 1-2 shows that icon and some of the other things that are probably on your screen.

Figure 1-2: The Start button, the Works shortcut icon, and some of the other icons that may be on your screen.

If you can't find a Shortcut to Microsoft Works icon, here's how to find and start Works:

1. **Click the Start button (shown in Figure 1-2).**

2. **In the menu that springs up, point with your mouse pointer to Programs and pause there.**

   Another menu appears next to the first one.

3. **Move your pointer horizontally until it's on the new menu. Then move the pointer vertically to point to a folder icon labeled Microsoft Works.**

   Yet another menu appears. At this point, your screen has begun to resemble Figure 1-3.

Figure 1-3:
Where
Works
lurks:
menus
within
menus
within
menus.

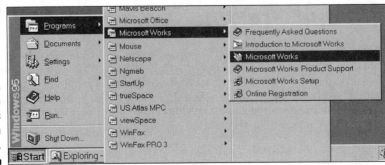

4. **Again, move your pointer horizontally until it's on the latest menu.
Then move your pointer down to point to another icon labeled
Microsoft Works. Click that icon.**

Hey, you did it! You got Works running, and the Works window appears on
your screen. You know that the window is the Works window if the title
Microsoft Works appears on the top line. (All windows have a top line like
this one, called the *title bar* of the window, that gives the name of the
program or file that appears in that window.)

Using and Losing the Task Launcher

As shown in Figure 1-4, when you first start Works, it displays a rectangular
area entitled Works Task Launcher. Works Task Launcher helps you find
files, choose the tool you need, or create a new document with a TaskWizard
(an automated program).

You can call up the Task Launcher at any time while you're using Works.
Simply choose File⇨New from the menu bar at the top of the screen or press
Ctrl+N.

This book uses a shortcut way to describe choosing something from the
menu bar, that list of words marching across your Works window just under
the title bar. When this book says, "Choose *Blah⇨Fooey* from the menu bar,"
it means, "Click the word *Blah* in the menu bar; then click the word *Fooey* in
the menu that drops down."

The Works Task Launcher gives you three ways to get going, represented as
three *index cards,* whose tabs you see in Figure 1-4, with the TaskWizards
card on top. Click one of the other tabs to see the contents of that card. The
three ways to get going are to:

- ✔ Have a TaskWizard create a new document for you.

- ✔ Choose a document from a list of recently worked-on documents or find an existing document.

- ✔ Go directly to one of the four main Works tools. (I usually choose this approach.)

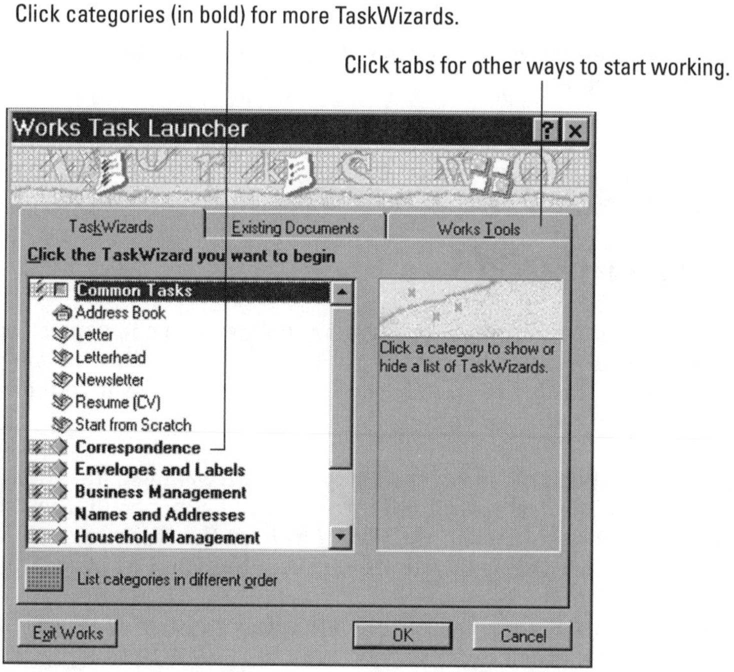

Click categories (in bold) for more TaskWizards.

Click tabs for other ways to start working.

Figure 1-4:
The
Works Task
Launcher,
displaying
Task-
Wizards —
one of three
ways to get
started on a
document.

Works Task Launcher	? X
TaskWizards | Existing Documents | Works Tools	
Click the TaskWizard you want to begin	

Common Tasks
Address Book
Letter
Letterhead
Newsletter
Resume (CV)
Start from Scratch
Correspondence
Envelopes and Labels
Business Management
Names and Addresses
Household Management

Click a category to show or hide a list of TaskWizards.

List categories in different order

Exit Works   OK   Cancel

The Task Launcher is a helpful feature when you are starting out, but later you may prefer to simply open the file that you need. To get rid of the Task Launcher, you can press the Esc key, click the Cancel button, or click the X button in the top-right corner of the dialog box.

If you don't use TaskWizards much, you would probably rather have Works display something other than the TaskWizards card when you start Works. To change the card that is initially displayed when you start Works, you use the Options tool. The following magic commands take you through the changing process:

1. **Press Esc to clear the Task Launcher.**

2. **Then choose Tools⇨Options from the menu bar and click the View tab in the Options dialog box.**

3. **In the lower right-hand corner of the Options dialog box, do one of the following:**

   Click Open E̲xisting Tab to choose the Existing Documents card for startup.

   Click Wor̲ks Tools Tab to choose the Works Tools card.

   Click Remem̲ber Last Tab to make Works remember the last card that you used.

4. **Press the Enter key or click the OK button in the dialog box when you're done.**

Starting New Documents with TaskWizards

TaskWizards are automated programs that ask you a few questions; they then automatically build (or at least begin to build) the document that you need. TaskWizards are great for keeping things simple, if you don't mind Works making some of your decisions for you.

Lots of TaskWizards, in several categories, are waiting to do your bidding. To use a TaskWizard, start from the Works Task Launcher. (If the Task Launcher is not on your screen, choose F̲ile⇨N̲ew from the Works menu bar or press Ctrl+N.) Choose the TaskWizards card and then do any of the following:

- To see what TaskWizards are in a category (in bold type), click the category. (Click the category again to close it.)

- To see a description of the task, click its TaskWizard.

- To start a TaskWizard, double-click it.

TaskWizards generally just get you started — you still have to make changes to the document afterward. Some of these changes can be tricky, so for more information on using TaskWizards to do some of the more common tasks, such as creating mailing lists and newsletters, see the Appendix.

Opening Existing Documents

If you have recently created or worked on a document in Works, Works remembers.

If you're using the Task Launcher when you get the urge to return to one of these recently created or recently worked-on documents, click the Existing Documents tab in the Works Task Launcher and you see a list, as shown in Figure 1-5. (To get the Task Launcher on your screen, choose File⇔New from the Works menu bar or press Ctrl+N.)

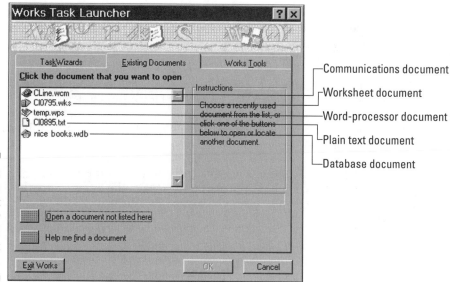

Figure 1-5:
Works lists
your most
recently
used
document
first.

Communications document
Worksheet document
Word-processor document
Plain text document
Database document

To choose a document from this list, click the document name and then click the OK button of the Task Launcher. Or you can just double-click the document name.

If you are already working on a document, you can find a short list of recently opened documents by clicking File in the Works menu bar. Click one of the documents listed to open it.

Opening Existing Documents Not Listed on the Task Launcher

It is possible to have a document on your PC but not have it show up on the Existing Documents card of the Task Launcher. This happens when you haven't used the document in a while or your copy of Works has never seen the document before, so Works doesn't know about it. For example, the document may have been created on another computer and brought over to your PC, the document may have been created by another program, or the document may have been created before you installed your current version of Works.

If you think that you know which folder your document is in, you can use the Existing Documents card of the Task Launcher to browse around and find the document.

If the Task Launcher is on your screen, click the Existing Documents tab; then click the Open a Document Not Listed Here button.

Clicking this button takes you to a dialog box called Open (short for *open a document*).

If the Task Launcher is not currently on your screen, choose File⇨Open from the Works menu bar or press Ctrl+O (that's the letter O, not the number 0). This procedure also takes you to the Open dialog box (shown in Figure 1-6).

Look in any higher-level folder or disk drive.

This is the folder you are looking in.

The Up One Level button.

Show filenames only.

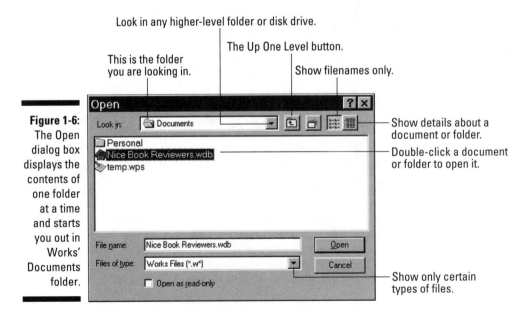

Figure 1-6: The Open dialog box displays the contents of one folder at a time and starts you out in Works' Documents folder.

Show details about a document or folder.

Double-click a document or folder to open it.

Show only certain types of files.

Browsing through the folders

The Open dialog box shows you the contents of whatever folder you looked in last. This dialog box displays the name of the folder at the top of the dialog box in the area marked Look In.

- ✔ If you see the document that you want, double-click it (or click it and click the Open button).

- ✔ To open a folder that is displayed, double-click it.

- ✔ To open the folder that contains the folder Works is currently showing you, click the Up One Level button at the top of the dialog box. (See Figure 1-6.)

- ✔ To go more than one level up the folder hierarchy, click the down-arrow button to the right of the Look In box. Click any folder in the list that appears.

- ✔ To look on a diskette (or to look at the very top of the folder hierarchy on your hard disk), click the down-arrow button to the right of the Look In box. In the list that appears, click disk drive *C:* for your hard disk and click *A:* or *B:* for your diskette. (*D:* is typically your CD-ROM drive if you have one, but you probably won't find any Works documents there.)

When you first start Works, it opens a folder called Documents and shows you what's inside the Documents folder. This Documents folder is within a folder called MSWorks, which is in another folder called Program Files.

Looking for different types of documents

Works creates four main types of *documents* (or *files*), one type of document for each of the four main tools. Different types of documents have different icons, and their names end in unique three-letter combinations called *extensions*. The Works document types and their extensions are:

- ✔ **Database:** wdb
- ✔ **Word processor:** wps
- ✔ **Worksheet:** wks
- ✔ **Communications:** wcm

The Open dialog box initially displays all of these file types. (In fact, the Open dialog box displays any file with an extension beginning with the letter *w;* some of these files may come from another program, and Works may or may not be able to read them.)

If you want to see any other type of file (or if you are interested only in, say, Works spreadsheets), click the down-arrow to the right of the Files of Type box and select one of the other types from the list that appears. If you are trying to open a file created by another program, your best choice is All files (*.*).

Finding Documents with the Task Launcher

It won't take too long before you're knee-deep in documents and folders and need a little help finding the document that you want. Your buddy, the Task Launcher, can come to your rescue. (If the Task Launcher is not displayed, choose File⇨New from the Works menu bar or press Ctrl+N.)

With the Task Launcher on your screen, click the Existing Documents tab and then click the button labeled Help Me Find a Document.

The Find dialog box springs into view. The Find dialog box may look familiar to you if you have used the Find tool in Windows 95 — they are both the same tool! (You get the Find dialog box directly from Windows by using Start⇨Find⇨Files Or Folders from the Windows Taskbar.) For the full, gory details of using the Find dialog box, see *Windows 95 For Dummies* by Andy Rathbone (IDG Books Worldwide, Inc.).

The Find dialog box has multiple cards like the Task Launcher has; click a named tab to select a card. Here are the most useful things to know, organized by card:

> ✔ **If you know part of the name:** Choose the Name & Location card.
>
> First, press the Del key to delete what's there and type the part of the name that you remember in the Named box. Substitute the * (asterisk) character for any other part that you don't remember. So, for example, if you're looking for an invoice, and you know that the file begins with *inv,* type **inv***. To look only for Works documents, add a Works three-letter extension to the end: .wps for a word-processing file, .wks for a worksheet file, .wdb for a database file, or .wcm for a communications file.
>
> ✔ **If you know when the file or folder was created or last modified:** Choose the Date Modified card.
>
> First, click Find All Files Created Or Modified. Then specify the date, either by clicking between and then double-clicking and typing over the dates shown or by clicking During The Previous and specifying a number of preceding months or days.

✔ **If you know any text that the file or folder contains:** Choose the Advanced card.

This selection is *really* useful because you don't have to remember anything about the document's name or location! If you wrote a letter to Mr. Smith about condominiums, just enter either Smith or condominium into the Containing Text box. Try to choose a unique word or phrase.

✔ **After you have specified something on any or all of these cards:** Press the Enter key or click Find Now.

A list of documents appears at the bottom of the Find dialog box — just double-click the document you want in order to open it!

Starting by Choosing a Tool

Some of us simpler-minded types prefer to skip all this helpful Task Launcher stuff — such as TaskWizards and lists of recently used files — and just start by choosing the tool that we want. If that's the way you work, too, just click the Works Tools tab on the Task Launcher and pick your tool. (To get the Task Launcher if it's not on your screen already, choose File⇨New from the Works menu bar or press Ctrl+N.)

Works has four main tools, and the Tools card gives you brief descriptions of what these four tools do. Click one of the four buttons to use a tool. For more details on each tool, see that tool's section in this book. For an overview of these tools, see Chapter 2.

Chapter 2
Getting Around

• •

In This Chapter

▶ Understanding the tools of Works

▶ Taking control of Works' Windows

▶ Moving around in your document

▶ Understanding menus and toolbars

▶ Using the keyboard command shortcuts

▶ Using dialog boxes

▶ Using and controlling Help

▶ Dealing with files and folders

▶ Exiting Works and shutting down your PC

• •

*I*f cars had as many gadgets and doodads as Windows software does, we'd all be taking the bus. Works 4.5 for Windows tries to be helpful about all of its doodads, but sometimes even the help can be a little bewildering. So this chapter tries to point out the stuff you need for day-to-day survival, including some Windows basics that nobody may have pointed out to you before.

The Tools of Works

Works is a program made up of smaller programs called *tools*. When Microsoft built Works, the programmers put in a bunch of tools that they thought most folks would be likely to need at some time. No matter how you start a document — even if you start it by using a TaskWizard — you are using one of these tools. These tools include:

- A word processor for writing letters and other documents
- A spreadsheet for creating tables and doing calculations
- A database tool for storing large amounts of information and helping you find it easily
- A communications tool that lets your computer talk to other computers (but is not generally used for Internet communications)
- A charting tool for making charts out of the information in spreadsheets and tables
- A drawing tool called Microsoft Draw
- A tool called WordArt for doing artistic things to words and letters
- A bunch of other little tools, such as a spell checker and a thesaurus

In addition, because to most people today "computer communications" means "Internet communications," and because Works' communications tool doesn't work with the Internet, Microsoft has now *bundled* (software marketing terminology for *included*) its Internet Explorer with Works. The Internet Explorer is, however, a completely separate program from Works.

The first four tools in the preceding list are what I call the Big Four; the others are sort of helper tools, like elves. I talk about each of the Big Four and the various elves in detail in Parts II through V. Right now, I show you what the tools have in common.

As with a Swiss Army Knife, you usually have only one tool in Works open at a time, although there's nothing to stop you from having several tools open at once. Sometimes, having more than one tool open at a time is helpful. You may, for example, want to create a drawing (using the drawing tool) to be inserted into a document that you're working on (using the word processor). You still *use* only one tool at a time, but you want to be able to switch back and forth between them quickly and easily. (See the section "Controlling Works' document windows" later in this chapter for more information on switching from one document to another.)

Each tool is a specialist: It works only on its own kind of thing. The drawing tool is for working on drawings; the spreadsheet tool is for tables and spreadsheets. But these tools do work together. For example, when you need to create a drawing in a document, the word processor calls in Microsoft Draw as a specialist. When you need to put a spreadsheet in a document, the word processor calls in the spreadsheet tool.

The things that these tools work on are all called *documents* by Microsoft, which therefore forces us to talk about word-processor documents, spreadsheet documents, database documents, and so on. What a bore. Most of the time in this book, I rebel and call the spreadsheet documents *spreadsheets* and the database documents *databases* and the graphics documents *graphics*. Radical, huh?

As with the Swiss Army Knife (and I promise to drop this analogy soon), the individual tools in Works are not the *best* — in the sense of being the most fully featured — of their kind. Just as a professional carpenter would probably prefer a solid screwdriver to the folding one in the knife, a professional financial analyst would probably prefer a more fully featured spreadsheet program, such as Excel, Quattro Pro, or Lotus 1-2-3, to the one in Works. Nonetheless, the Works tools are perfectly fine for most of what the vast majority of people want to do, and they cost less and need less memory and disk space on your computer. In a way, Works' tools *are* the best because they don't have a lot of extraneous features that you don't need and that would only trip you up.

Because all these tools are part of the same Works package, they look and work very much alike. When you go to print a spreadsheet, for example, you do it almost exactly the same way that you would print a word-processing document. Certain things may be different, but the similarities are very helpful. You don't have to relearn the basic commands for each tool.

Controlling Works' Windows

When you start working on a document, you're often confronted with a window full of confusing stuff. What's more, the window is probably an inconvenient size and is covering up something important on your screen.

Works' windows behave like those of every other program that runs under Windows 95. You can refer to *Windows 95 For Dummies* (IDG Books Worldwide, Inc.) for the full gory details on handling windows, but the basics are here.

Here's how to manage Works' windows:

Controlling Works' program window

To get your Works program window under control, belly up to the *title bar.* Every window in Windows has a bar (called the title bar) at the top that describes what that window is all about. Whenever you are working in a particular window, its title bar is colored (usually blue). Otherwise, it remains a sleepy, dull gray. To select a window, just click in that window's title bar (but not on a button or icon). To move a window, click that same area and drag. To change the size of a window, click any edge or corner (your mouse cursor turns into a double-headed arrow) and drag.

The title bar also contains (in the right-hand corner) buttons useful for controlling the size of your program window, as shown in Figure 2-1.

Figure 2-1:
The Works title bar heads your Works window and provides buttons to control window size.

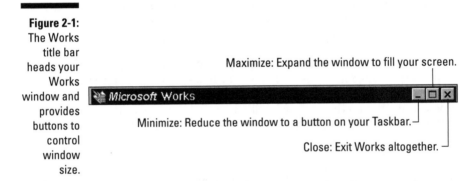

Maximize: Expand the window to fill your screen.

Minimize: Reduce the window to a button on your Taskbar.

Close: Exit Works altogether.

Figure 2-1 shows you how to minimize, maximize, and close Works, and it defines what those terms mean. Here are a few other things you can do with your program window:

- **To shrink a maximized Works window:** When you have expanded the window to its maximum, Windows replaces the "maximize" button with one that looks like this:

  Click this guy to restore your Works window to an intermediate size.

- **To enlarge/reduce the window's width or height:** Click an edge or corner of the window (where your cursor turns into a double-headed arrow) and drag the edge or corner in any direction.

▶ **To restore the window after it's been shrunk to a Microsoft Works button on the Taskbar:** Click that button. (The Works button has the Works icon on it; the Taskbar is that long [usually gray] bar in Windows 95 with the Start button on it.)

▶ **To move the Works window:** Click the title bar, but not any of the buttons or the Works icon at the far left. Hold down the mouse button, drag the window where you want it, and release the mouse button.

You can also control the Works window by clicking the Works icon at the far left of the title bar and then clicking a selection in the menu that drops down.

Controlling Works' document windows

Like one of those Russian dolls that's full of more dolls (a *Matroishka,* I think), the Works window contains even more windows. Whenever you create or open a document, or create a drawing or graph, that document, drawing, or graph gets its own window. (Most of the time, you have only one document open.)

If you open more than one document at a time, things may get a little more confusing. Look at the Works program window in Figure 2-2, which shows the Works window with four different document windows (plus the Help window) open at once.

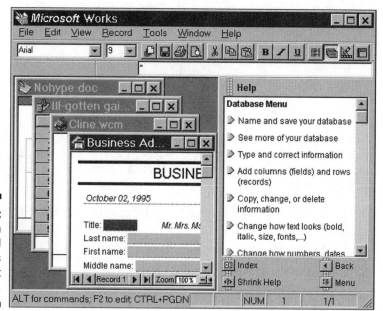

Figure 2-2: Works, with several documents open at once.

Here are the important facts to know about managing document windows:

- ✔ **Only one document can be active at a time:** The *active document* is the one whose title bar is in some exotic designer color, such as blue.

- ✔ **To make a document active:** Click anywhere on the document.

- ✔ **To bring any document window to the top:** Click any part of that document that you can see. If you can't see the document at all, click Window and then click the name of the document, which is listed in the bottom part of the menu that drops down.

- ✔ **Works automatically switches to the right kind of tool for a document when you choose that document:** In other words, the menu bar and the toolbar change subtly when you choose a different type of document.

- ✔ **To shrink or enlarge a document window:** You can control a document window the same way that you control the Works program window: Use the buttons in the upper-right-hand corner of the window. The buttons look the same as for the Works window.

- ✔ **When you minimize a document window:** The document window becomes a little rectangle in the bottom-left corner of the Works window. Click the little rectangle to reinflate the document window.

If your document window is maximized (and that's how documents usually start out), the tiny buttons that shrink and enlarge that window don't appear in the title bar (for reasons known only to Microsoft). Nope, they appear instead just under the minimize/maximize/close buttons for Works, on the Works *menu bar,* for cryin' out loud! They look like this:

See how nice and neat the document windows are in Figure 2-2? You don't think that *I* did that, do you? Not a chance. You should see my office. I can't even see my desktop. No, such neatness is a product of the Window menu in the Works menu bar. Here's how you can achieve the same effect:

- ✔ **To arrange documents neatly overlapping (as in Figure 2-2):** Choose Window⇨Cascade.

- ✔ **To arrange documents side by side, like tiles:** Choose Window⇨Tile.

- ✔ **For any other arrangement:** You have to do the arranging yourself by shrinking, enlarging, and moving windows. Whichever window is active is always displayed on top.

Zooming

"If you can't raise the bridge, lower the water." This saying has served many people well over the years, despite the fact that it is complete gibberish. Continuing in this vein, an alternative to making a window bigger so that you can see more is to make the document text smaller, known as zooming out. (Or is it zooming in? Never can remember, but never mind; it's *zooming*, anyway.)

The important thing to realize is that zooming has absolutely no effect on your document. Zooming just makes the text look bigger or smaller. Your document prints out the same.

Here's one way to zoom:

Choose View⇨Zoom: The Zoom dialog box zooms into view and lets you choose a magnification expressed as a percentage — the smaller the percentage, the smaller the document. You can either click one of the standard percentages listed there, such as 75%, or type a percentage in the Custom box. Click the OK button in this dialog box when you're done.

And here's another way to zoom:

Click the minuscule + or – buttons next to the Zoom button at the bottom-left corner of your document window. The + button enlarges your document; the – button shrinks it.

Taking a Stroll in Your Document

The smoothest way to get around in your document is to slide! At the side and bottom of each document window are scroll bars (which I think should be called "sliders") that let you move the document around within the document window.

To see farther up or down in your document, use the vertical scroll bar, which is shown in Figure 2-3:

Figure 2-3:
The vertical
scroll bar.

Click and drag down to divide the window.

Click to see farther up.

Click and drag to slide document up or down.

Click to see farther down.

✔ **To slide the document up or down in little increments:** Click the arrows at the top and bottom.

✔ **To slide the document with a lot more speed:** Click and drag the box in the middle up or down. (Or click above or below the box.) The position of this box on the scroll bar gives you a rough idea of how far down in the document you are. If the box is large, nearly filling the scroll bar, that means most of your document is visible in the window.

✔ **To slide the document horizontally (in case your window isn't wide enough to display the entire width of the document):** A horizontal scroll bar at the bottom of the window works the same way as the vertical one.

A little-known feature of the vertical scroll bar is the capability to divide the document window into two parts. This feature is great if, for example, you want to see two distant parts of your document at once. To perform this trick, click and drag the tiny bar at the top of the scroll bar downward; stop about halfway down the document window. When you release the mouse button, your document window divides into two parts. Each of these subwindows has its own scroll bars so that you can view two different parts of your document! To return to a single window, click and drag the bar back up to the top.

Another easy way to get around in your documents is to *navigate*. For this technique, use the *navigation keys* on your keyboard: the arrow keys plus the Page Up, Page Down, Home, and End keys. The navigation keys move the blinking cursor that defines where editing takes place, and your document slides around to keep that cursor visible in the window. The arrow keys move one step at a time, but the Page Up and Page Down keys move one window's worth at a time.

If you use the scroll bars to move around in your document, make sure that you click in the new location before you begin typing or editing. The scroll bars move your viewpoint around, but the scroll bars do not move the blinking cursor that defines where the editing action takes place. Before you press a key, put that blinking cursor where you want it by clicking where you want to type or edit. Otherwise, your cursor jumps back to its preceding location as soon as you press a key.

Ordering from the Menu Bar

The main way to place your orders in Works is to use the menu bar, shown in Figure 2-4. Click any of the words in the menu bar, and a menu of commands drops down. Then click one of these commands to execute it. Yet another menu may appear, or a dialog box may spring up.

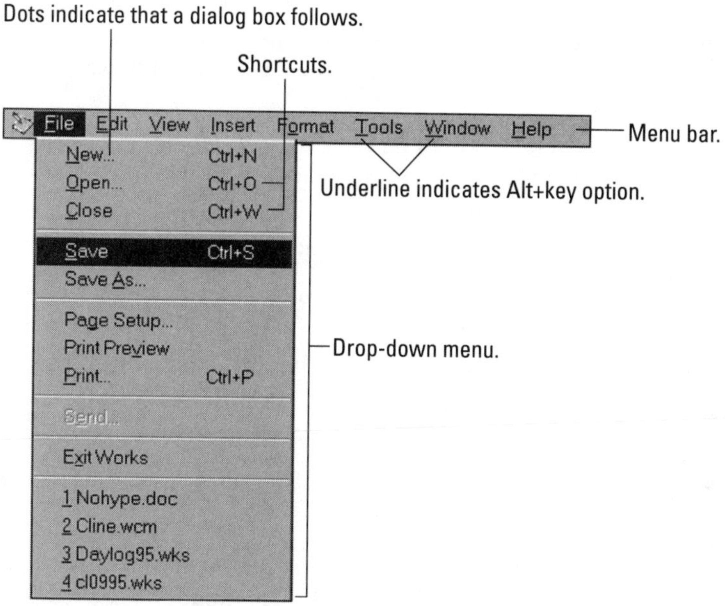

Dots indicate that a dialog box follows.

Shortcuts.

File	Edit	View	Insert	Format	Tools	Window	Help	— Menu bar.

New...   Ctrl+N
Open...   Ctrl+O —— Underline indicates Alt+key option.
Close   Ctrl+W

Save   Ctrl+S
Save As...

Page Setup...
Print Preview   —— Drop-down menu.
Print...   Ctrl+P

Send...

Exit Works

1 Nohype.doc
2 Cline.wcm
3 Daylog95.wks
4 cl0995.wks

Figure 2-4:
Clicking a word in the menu bar gets you a variety of yummy commands in a drop-down menu.

The sequential process of choosing things from menus is pretty boring to write about (and even more boring to read about) without using some kind of shortcut notation. I could say, "Click File on the menu bar; then click Save on the menu that drops down," but this kind of talk would drive you batty after awhile. So in this book (and in ...*For Dummies* books in general), I say the same thing using this kind of notation:

Choose File⇨Save.

Just like the menu in your local sandwich shop, a large portion of the Works menu bar always appears the same. This regularity is true no matter what tool you are using — the menu bar for each tool appears very much the same. However, each of the words on this menu bar leads to a set of commands, some of which change with different tools. So, if ever the commands on a menu look unfamiliar to you, it is probably because you have different types of documents open in Works, and you have switched from one type to another. This book goes into detail on the more important differences in the tool-specific Parts II through V.

Generally speaking, here's what you can do in each of these menu bar selections:

- ✔ **File:** Open, close, and save documents; set up the page layout; print.
- ✔ **Edit:** Copy text and numbers, move them, find them, replace them; also (and very important) undo whatever change you just made to the document.
- ✔ **View:** See things differently or otherwise change the way the screen looks (but without changing the document itself), such as by turning the toolbar on or off.
- ✔ **Insert:** Plug stuff into your document, such as illustrations from another document or file.
- ✔ **Format:** Change the appearance of text and numbers and how they line up.
- ✔ **Tools:** Use the spell checker or other little helpers to the Big Four tools.
- ✔ **Window:** Arrange the document windows or make a different window active.
- ✔ **Help:** Read help information about Works or turn the Help feature on or off.

Part I of this book deals with the commands that remain the same in each of these menus. For anything in these menus unique to a particular tool, see that tool's part later in this book.

Keep your eye on the bottom line!

If, before you choose any of the commands in a drop-down menu, you would like a reminder of what the command does, keep your eye on the Works status bar. No, the status bar is not some high-status watering hole in, say, trendy Foster City, California (one home of IDG Books) — the status bar is the bottom line of the Works window.

After you click File or any of the other words in the menu bar, a drop-down menu appears. Without clicking any buttons on your mouse, move your mouse slowly toward you. As you do this, you move the colored highlight down the drop-down menu. The status bar tells you what the highlighted command does. Click to choose the command that you need.

Command Shortcuts Using the Keyboard

If you don't want to take the time to order from a menu, here's a shortcut. Some commands in the drop-down menus have a key combination (such as Ctrl+S) shown on the same line. This means that you don't even have to make that menu drop down in order to use that command. Just press the key combination: Hold down the Ctrl key, in this example, and then press the S key. Ctrl+S, for example, saves your document as a file. You can find these shortcuts easily because they are listed in the drop-down menu whenever you click a menu selection. Refer to Figure 2-4 for examples.

If you're more comfortable using a keyboard than a mouse, Windows gives you another way to use menus. See all those underlined letters in the menu bar? Press the Alt key *and* the underlined letter key on the menu bar, and the drop-down menu springs cheerfully up (so to speak) under that word. To choose a command from the drop-down menu, just press the letter *without* the Alt key.

The Ctrl+key combinations work immediately, without going through the menu. The Alt+key combinations let you pick items off whatever menu is currently displayed so that you use the key combinations sequentially; for example, use *Alt+F* to open the File menu followed by *S* to save a file.

When commands go gray

One aspect of Windows that occasionally gives new users gray hairs is the "graying out" of certain commands on a drop-down menu or in a dialog box. An example of graying out is the Send command in Figure 2-4.

When commands are grayed out, they are temporarily inactive, not applicable, or otherwise unavailable for comment. Generally, you won't care, but sometimes, you really, really *want* Works to execute that command. Well, to do so, you have to figure out *why* that command is currently deactivated. Why doesn't it apply in this case? For example, the Send command in Figure 2-4 is inactive because I don't have networking on my PC, and I can't send the document anywhere. Generally, something is grayed out because the action that command is responsible for can't be done at the time or the item the command relates to just isn't present in your document (or in the area of your document that you have selected).

Toiling with Toolbars

The Works menu bar is lovely, full of genuine English words and lots of drop-down menus. Although the Works menu bar is quite nice, it's just a tad tedious to use sometimes. You click the menu bar, you click the drop-down menu, you click the dialog box . . . pretty soon your eyes glaze over and you just sit there and click . . . click . . . click — until you are found and revived, days later, by the *Mouse-Induced-Stupor (MIS) Patrol.*

After having had to resuscitate a few afflicted colleagues, the engineers at Microsoft did something about this grave problem. They employed the classic engineering technique of going to a bar. In this case, they went to a tool bar (known in Works parlance as the *toolbar*).

The toolbar, shown in Figure 2-5, is the line of stuff just under the menu bar; the toolbar is the one that's as full of icons as a Russian museum. If you find the toolbar aesthetically displeasing or just plain don't want it around, you can click View⇨Toolbar to remove it from the screen. If you later decide that you want it back, do the same thing.

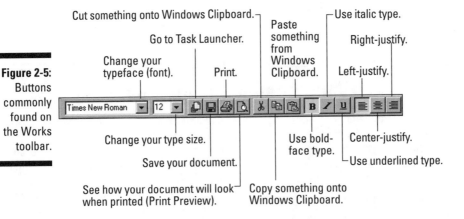

Figure 2-5: Buttons commonly found on the Works toolbar.

Each *icon* is a shortcut alternative to some command in the menu bar — a command that the folks at Microsoft thought that you may use a lot. Just click the icon once, and stuff happens: Your file gets saved, for example, or you print something out. No more click, click, click. Just click.

The selection of icons in the toolbar changes a bit. Some icons appear in all of the Big Four tools of Works; others appear only for a particular tool. For example, the Save icon appears in each toolbar because you always need to be able to save your work. On the other hand, the Insert Record icon appears only with the database tool. That icon makes no sense anywhere else. The toolbar changes along with your tool, so if you switch your active window from a database document to a spreadsheet document, the toolbar changes.

The icons that appear most frequently are shown in Figure 2-5.

If you forget what an icon is supposed to do, just move your mouse cursor over it (don't click). A tiny square (typically yellow) appears with a one-word description of the icon's function. The status bar at the bottom of the Works window gives you a few more words about the icon.

For more about the editing, formatting, and file operations that these buttons actually do, see Chapters 3 and 4.

For each tool in Works, as it turns out, you can customize which icons appear on your toolbar. I'm not going to fool with telling you how to customize your icons in this book. If you want to take matters into your own hands, the command for changing icons is Tools⇨Customize Toolbar.

Dealing with Dialog Boxes

Dialog boxes tend to crop up all over the place. A command that ends in three dots (. . .) warns you that you're about to have to deal with a dialog box. The dialog box's purpose in life is to let you specify important details about the command, such as what to name something you want to store and where to put it.

On the surface, dialog boxes look like windows, but you can't shrink or expand dialog boxes. (You can drag them around by their title bars, though, if they are in the way.) Internally, dialog boxes can look like darn near anything. Here, in Figure 2-6, is an example from Works. Fortunately, certain internal gadgets (I prefer the technical name, "thingy") reappear regularly.

The following is how this dialog box stuff works. Don't try to memorize all the names and distinctions of the thingies. I certainly don't use the names any more than I have to. Just refer back here if you get confused about a dialog box.

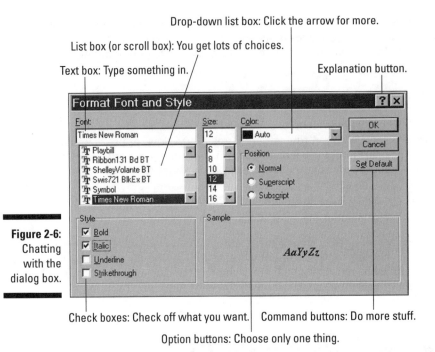

Drop-down list box: Click the arrow for more.

List box (or scroll box): You get lots of choices.

Text box: Type something in.

Explanation button.

Figure 2-6:
Chatting
with the
dialog box.

Check boxes: Check off what you want. | Command buttons: Do more stuff.

Option buttons: Choose only one thing.

Explanation button (question mark): Click this button in the title bar, and a question mark attaches itself to your mouse cursor. "Gee, how useful!" you say. But wait — the excitement is yet to come: If you *then* click a button or setting in the dialog box, you'll see an explanation of that item. Click in a plain area of the dialog box to clear the explanation off the screen.

Text box: You can type something in a text box, but often a quicker way (such as clicking something in a *list box* immediately underneath the text box) is available to accomplish the same task. When you open a text box, it usually has something in it as a suggestion. You can delete that suggestion by pressing the Delete key, or you can change the suggestion by clicking anywhere in the box to get a typing cursor. Type or press the Backspace or Delete keys to erase stuff. Do *not* press the Enter key when you're done typing unless you don't need to do anything else in this dialog box!

List or scroll box: List boxes or scroll boxes show you a list of choices. Click one of the choices, and your choice generally appears in a text box above the list. Double-click one, and the computer not only chooses that item, but it also tells the dialog box, "I'm done — go and do your thing!" If more text is in the list than fits in the box, a scroll bar appears alongside the list box. (Such scroll bars work like the scroll bars in your document window.)

Pinky finger alert!

Touch typists, keep your pinky fingers under control. Pinky fingers tend to want to press the Enter key or the Esc key, either of which can make a dialog box go away. When you press Enter, the dialog box goes off and does stuff, even if you're not ready for that stuff to be done. When you press Esc, the dialog box just goes away quietly, as if you never started the command. (Pressing Esc is the same as clicking the Cancel button.)

Drop-down list box: A drop-down list box is like a list box, but you have to act to make it appear. To make a drop-down list box reveal itself, click the down-pointing arrow alongside the box.

Check boxes: Check boxes are like tax forms, but even more fun. Check off one or more things by clicking them or the box next to them. A check mark appears when an item is selected. Click the item (or the box next to it) again to deselect it.

Option buttons: These buttons allow you to click only one thing in the list. The center of the button appears black when the button has been selected (is "on").

Command buttons: The most important command button is OK. Click the OK button when you're done with a task. If you want to back out of a command, click Cancel. Other command buttons may take you to yet more dialog boxes.

When this book discusses a feature in a dialog box (say, a checkbox labeled "No header on first page"), it uses initial capital letters for the feature's name. For instance, you see, "Click On The No Header On First Page checkbox" rather than "Click on the No header on first page checkbox," which looks like utter gibberish.

Hollering for Help

We all need a little assistance now and then. A *little* assistance, I say, not necessarily the squadron of very eager helpers that have been built into Works. The helpers are all very nice, but they can be a bit overwhelming if you don't know how to keep them under control. In this section, I try to sort them all out and make the Help features of Works a little more, um . . . helpful.

The Help feature is a little bit like having a manual in your computer. The nice thing is that Works can sometimes put you on the right page of Help automatically, based on what you're doing at the time. (This feature, called *context-sensitive help,* is found in most Windows programs.) Even when Works doesn't put you on the right page automatically, you can look through the equivalent of a table of contents or an index and zap yourself to the right page.

Kinds of help

Two basic kinds of help are available in Works:

- **Brief explanations of dialog box thingies:** When confronted with a dialog box that looks only slightly less complex than the cockpit of a jet fighter, here's how you can find out what the various buttons and settings do: Click the ? button in the upper-right-hand corner of the dialog box and then click the button or setting. A brief explanation appears. To make the explanation go away, click a blank area of the dialog box.

- **Detailed documentation on how to do things:** This form of help appears in the panel that pops up automatically in Works whenever you start a new document, and it sets up shop in the right-hand side of the Works window. I describe this type of help in the rest of this section.

Getting . . . and getting rid of . . . Help

One of the first things you may want to do with Help is put it away! If you don't need Help, its pop-up panel takes up valuable real estate on the right side of your Works window. To put Help away, click the ? button labeled Shrink Help at the bottom of the Help panel. This button then retreats to the lower-right edge of your Works window; click this button again to restore the Help panel. Alternately shrinking and restoring the Help panel is a good way to follow the Help instructions without the Help panel itself getting in your way.

You can call the Help squadron into action by doing any of the following:

- Press the F1 key to get help related to whatever you're currently doing.

- Choose Help⇨Contents from the menu bar to choose help for a particular tool.

- Choose Help⇨Index from the menu bar to get help on darned near anything.

- Click the button with the tiny book-like icon in the lower-right edge of the Works window (this icon, too, takes you to the Help Index).

These commands not only bring up the panel that displays the actual Help information (as shown in Figure 2-7), they also bring up the Help Topics dialog box. This dialog box is helpfully designed to help you find the help you need. (Oh, help!) See the section "Help on what? Using Help's Index and Contents," coming up soon in this chapter.

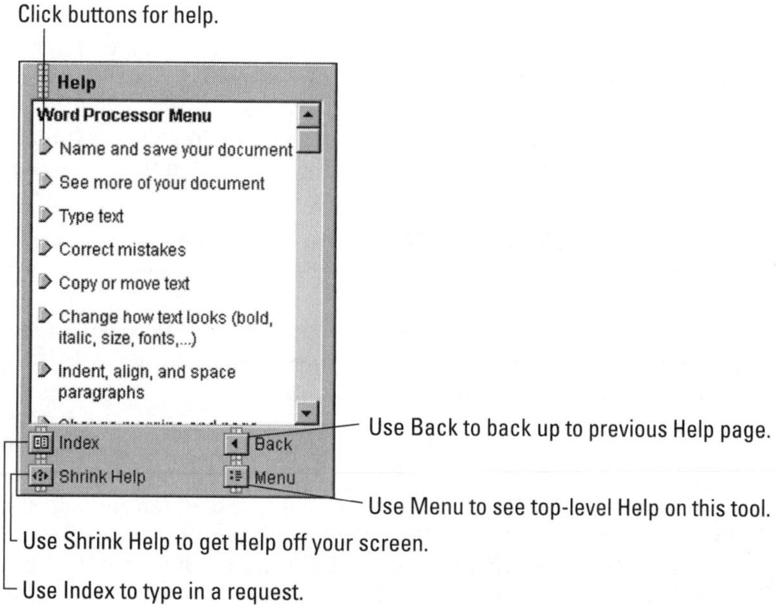

Click buttons for help.

Figure 2-7:
The Help
panel being
its helpful
self.

Help

Word Processor Menu

▷ Name and save your document
▷ See more of your document
▷ Type text
▷ Correct mistakes
▷ Copy or move text
▷ Change how text looks (bold, italic, size, fonts,...)
▷ Indent, align, and space paragraphs

Index   ◀ Back   — Use Back to back up to previous Help page.
Shrink Help   Menu

                                  — Use Menu to see top-level Help on this tool.
└ Use Shrink Help to get Help off your screen.

└ Use Index to type in a request.

Navigating Help

Works' Help feature has a series of levels that you navigate by clicking the arrow-like bullets next to each topic. Each bullet is a link to another page of Help. Your goal is to get a set of numbered instructions. The levels go as follows:

Menu of Help topics for a tool (word processor, spreadsheet, database, or communications). (To return here, click the Menu button at the bottom of the Help panel.)

 Subtopics, such as "To type text in the header or footer"

  Maybe more subtopics

   Your goal: step-by-step instructions and links to related topics or subtopics

Help on what? Using Help's Index and Contents

Works tries to use what you are currently doing to figure out what topic you are interested in. For example, when you start a new word-processing document, Works puts up the word processor Help information.

If you want help on something other than what's displayed in the Help panel, choose either the Help Contents or the Index.

- ✔ **To type in a subject you want help on or to select a subject from an amazingly long list:** Choose Help⇨Index from the menu bar or click the Index button at the bottom of the Help panel.

- ✔ **To choose Help for a different tool than the one you're currently using:** Choose Help⇨Contents from the menu bar.

Either command brings up the Help Topics dialog box, which has two tabbed *cards* like the Task Launcher has. One of these cards is the Index, and the other card is the Contents.

The Index is the most helpful Help helper (so to speak). When the Index appears, simply type in a word or phrase describing what you want help on. As you type, Works looks at what you've typed so far and scrolls the list of topics to match the letters that you have typed to a topic, if it can. When you see the subject that you want, just click it. (If the subject has a folder icon, the icon can open up and reveal subtopics.) The subject appears either in the Works Help window or in a separate dialog box.

Saving Files and Creating Folders

Existence is fleeting and fragile, especially for Works documents. They flicker into life when you create them, but they cannot survive when Works is not running or your PC is off. To preserve Works documents, you have to save them as files on a disk, whether that disk is your permanent *hard disk* or a removable *diskette* (or *floppy disk*). See the discussion of files, disks, folders, and directories in Chapter 1 for more on files and their residences.

Works won't let you exit the program without asking you whether you want to save your work as a file, so you don't have to worry about that, but you never know when someone's going to trip over the power cord to your PC, so save your work to a file often.

Works gives you three ways to save your document as a file. Choose your favorite:

- ✔ Choose File➪Save from the menu bar.
- ✔ Press Ctrl+S.
- ✔ Click the button with the diskette icon (on the toolbar).

When you use these commands to save a document for the first time, Works gives you the Save As dialog box, as shown in Figure 2-8, so that you can give the file a name and a location. After you have saved the document for the first time, Works subsequently saves it with the same name and to the same location.

To make a copy of the file and give it a different name, different location, or even a different *file type,* use the File➪Save As command to get to the Save As dialog box. This procedure is helpful if you need slightly different versions of the same file (for example, if you are sending the same letter to three different people).

The Save As dialog box is a close relative of the Open dialog box described in Chapter 1. A twin, in fact. These two dialog boxes work in almost exactly the same way: You need to tell Works where the file is to go and what its name should be.

Telling Works where the file should go

Unless you tell Works otherwise, it puts all your documents on your hard disk, in a single folder. (What a program does unless you say otherwise is called its *default.*) Putting your documents on your hard disk is fine, but having all your documents in the same folder is, however, like the extended-wear diaper — not a particularly good idea. Both of these storage solutions result in a rather full and untidy situation. I'm sure you wouldn't put all your documents in a single folder in your file cabinet (although I might). If you continually use this Works default, Works puts all your documents in its Document folder. (The Document folder is located within the MS Works folder, within the Program Files folder on your hard disk, in case you need to find it.)

You have the choice of putting your document in any existing folder or creating a new folder for your document. You can create folders with the Documents folder, if you like. Here's how to specify what folder the document should go into:

- ✔ **To put your document in any of the named folders displayed in the big white box:** Double-click that folder.

- ✔ **To open the folder that contains the current folder:** Click the Up-One-Level button, at the top of the dialog box (see Figure 2-8).

- ✔ **To go more than one level up the folder hierarchy:** Click the down-arrow button to the right of the Save In box. Click any folder shown.

- ✔ **To use a disk or to open the very top of the folder hierarchy on your hard disk:** Click the down-arrow button to the right of the Look In box. Click a disk drive: *C:* for your hard disk, *A:* or *B:* for your diskette.

- ✔ **To create a new folder in the folder that's currently open (shown in the Save In box):** Click the New Folder button (see Figure 2-8). A new folder, cleverly named New Folder, appears; just type a name to replace this clever, if obvious, name that Works initially gives the folder.

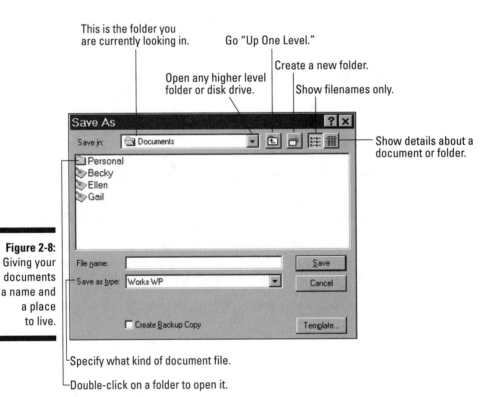

This is the folder you are currently looking in.

Go "Up One Level."

Open any higher level folder or disk drive.

Create a new folder.

Show filenames only.

Show details about a document or folder.

Figure 2-8:
Giving your documents a name and a place to live.

Specify what kind of document file.

Double-click on a folder to open it.

Naming your file

To name your file, put a name in the File Name box. Just click the box and type in a new name. (Leave off the three-letter extension; Works supplies it automatically, according to the file type displayed in the Save As Type box.)

You can choose to use the name of an existing file; just click the existing file's name in the big white area of the Save As dialog box. If you use a file that already exists, you overwrite the file, and its original contents are lost. Works warns you about this situation, however, and gives you a chance to change your mind.

For veterans of earlier Windows and DOS software, Windows 95 is cause to rejoice! You are no longer stuck with filenames of eight characters or less, with no spaces or funny characters! Now you can use filenames up to 255 characters long, with whatever you please for characters. Before you go wild, however, consider whether you're going to be giving files to some poor colleague still stuck in Windows 3.1 or DOS. If you are going to do that, stick to the old naming rules. Also, choose Works for Windows 3.0 — or whatever the name of the software is that your colleague is running — in the Save As Type box.

Works Stoppage

Why stop Works from running at all? Why not just minimize Works to a button on the Taskbar? Well, maybe you need to use some other program that takes a lot of memory. (You'd know that was the case because Windows would complain that it had insufficient memory when you tried to run the other program, or else all your programs would run very slowly.) Or, hey — maybe you even want to shut off your PC and go to bed! (What a concept!)

You can use any one of the following ways to exit Works:

- Shut down your computer (using the Windows Start➪Shut Down command on the Taskbar).
- Click File➪Exit Works.
- Click the button with the *X* in the upper-right-hand corner of your Works window.
- From the Task Launcher, click the Exit Works button.
- Press Alt+F4.
- Click with your right mouse button on Microsoft Works on the Windows Taskbar (where the Start button lives), and choose Close from the menu that drops down.

Works stops running, and the Works window disappears from your screen.

Except . . . if you've been working on something and haven't saved your work as a file, a dialog box pops up at this point. The dialog box asks whether Works should save changes to the file you're working on and gives you three choices: Yes, No, or Cancel.

✔ If you click Yes, whatever you've been doing in Works is saved with the filename you gave in the Save As dialog box. (If you never named this document, Works presents the Save As dialog box now so that you can do so.) If you've been changing an existing file, the changes overwrite the old contents of that file; the process is just like recording over a videotape.

✔ If you click No, whatever you've been doing in Works goes to that big bit-bucket in the sky and is lost forever. If you've been working on an existing file, that file goes back to the way it was before you started working on it. If you had created a new file, you end up with nothing.

✔ If you click Cancel (or press the Esc key), nothing happens to your document. You don't exit Works, and nothing is saved.

This dialog box may appear several times, once for each different document you are working on. Each time this dialog box appears, it asks only about a single file. When all the open documents are saved, Works disappears from your screen.

Chapter 3

Basic Editing and Formatting

. . . .

In This Chapter

▶ Selecting items in various Works applications

▶ Using styles (bold, italic, and underline)

▶ Choosing fonts from the toolbar

▶ Specifying fonts and styles with the Format Font and Style dialog box

▶ Undoing mistakes

▶ Catching spelling mistakes with the spell checker

. . . .

*Y*ou there, with the eyeshade and the ink stains. Yeah, you — you're an editor, believe it or not. In computerese (geek-speak), whenever you change a document, you have *edited* it. And, as it turns out, many of the basic editing operations are the same in the different tools of Works.

But before you whip out your blue pencil and go a-editing, you have to be able to do one really basic thing: tell Works exactly *what* text you want to edit — what to delete or move or underline, or whatever your editorial instincts induce you to do. This procedure of telling Works which text to edit is called *selecting,* or sometimes *highlighting,* text. Read on.

Selecting (Highlighting)

Selecting is pointing out to Works exactly what in your document you want Works to operate on: what text you want in bold, or what illustration you want to delete, or what cells in the spreadsheet you want to copy.

Selecting is really pretty simple. To select a bunch of stuff (text, spreadsheet cells, whatever) with your mouse, perform the following mouse-based highlighting process:

1. **Click at one end of the text that you want to select but keep your mouse button pressed down; don't let up.**

2. **Move your mouse pointer to the other end of the text that you want to select.**

   As you do this action, a black, rectangular area extends out in the direction you're moving, enveloping your text like an ominous fog. Incongruously, this fog is sometimes called the highlight. (In the word processor, the fog envelops one character at a time until you extend it beyond one word; then it hungrily envelops one word at a time!) If any illustrations are in the middle of your text, they're selected, too.

   When you select multiple lines of text, don't go to the end of the line and then back to the beginning of the next, and so on; you can drive yourself buggy doing that. Like driving in Boston, just go directly toward your final destination, ignoring all intervening pedestrians and other distractions.

3. **Release the mouse button.**

   The text is now selected, and your mouse cursor is free to do other stuff, like choose things from Works menus or click buttons on the toolbar. (If you're in the word processor, you may notice that the word *drag* attaches itself parasitically to your cursor whenever the cursor passes over your selected text. Ignore that for now.)

   If you didn't quite get the end point where you wanted it when you released the button, you can cleverly adjust the end point by using the arrow keys on your keyboard. (See the "Text selection without rodents" sidebar.)

Text selection without rodents

If you're working while skydiving or bungee-jumping, or doing other tasks where a mouse is impractical, inaccurate, or downright hazardous, a mouse-free way to select text or adjust your selection is available:

1. Use the navigation keys (arrow keys, plus Home, End, Page Up, and Page Down) to position the insertion point at one end of the text you want to select.

2. Then hold down the Shift key and again use any navigation key to move the end point of the selection. Keep the Shift key down and press navigation keys repeatedly until you've selected the text that you want.

In the word processor, this keyboard selection technique is useful in that — unlike selecting with the mouse — the highlight extends itself by only one character at a time. (If you want to extend it one word at a time, hold down both the Ctrl and Shift keys while you press navigation keys.)

This distinction lets keyboard selection serve as a clever trick for adjusting the end point of a selection you made with the mouse. Hold down the Shift key and press a navigation key, and you can adjust the end point of a selection you just made. Sorry, you can adjust only the end point, not the starting point.

Here are a few special cases you might encounter when selecting text. For more information on tool-specific special cases, see the chapter on that tool.

✔ **To select a word:** Double-click it. And the word processor has even more click-tricks that let you select lines and paragraphs. Check out Chapter 5 for more on the nifty word processor.

✔ **To select the entire document:** Click Edit in the menu bar and then click Select All in the menu that drops down.

✔ **To select an illustration or chart or some other solitary chunk of stuff in your document:** Just click it once.

✔ **In a spreadsheet, just click a cell to select it.** Use the highlighting process to select multiple cells, though; a border makes a little corral around the selected area.

✔ **Likewise, to select a single field in a database, just click the field.** Selecting stuff in List view works just like in a spreadsheet.

Being Bold (Or Italic): Quick Text Styles

B/<u>U</u>? Or be I not you? That is the question. And if I *were* you, I'd want to know what these **B**, *I*, and <u>U</u> buttons in the Works toolbar are all about. Here's the answer:

(Warning! The following text contains material that may be offensive to anyone with poetic sensitivities or other forms of good taste.)

> **B** is for bold, as all writers should be,
>
> *I* is for italic, from Italy across the sea,
>
> <u>U</u> is for underline, when emphasis is key, and
>
> ***<u>this</u>*** is what you get when you use all three!

(See what writing computer books does to your brain? You have been warned!)

Bold, italic, and underlining are three really basic ways you can change the appearance *(format)* of your text. This particular form of text formatting is called *character formatting,* or more specifically, *changing the font style.*

Changing the font style for text that you've already typed

Here are the incredibly complex and sophisticated instructions for making text bold, italic, underlined, or all three:

1. **Select some text. (See the section "Selecting (Highlighting),"earlier in this chapter.)**

2. **Click the B, *I*, and/or U button on the toolbar.**

You can turn this formatting on or off. Notice that after you click the button on the toolbar, it appears to be depressed. In a fit of perverse psychology, these buttons look depressed while they are *on*. This is the case whenever your current insertion point is amidst or upon bold, italic, or underlined text. Why the buttons should be so unhappy, I don't know. But if you later select that same text and click the depressed button, the formatting is undone, and the button no longer appears depressed (it's now *off*).

Changing the font style for text that you're currently typing

If, instead of typing first and then formatting as I just described, you prefer to type directly in bold, italic, or underlined text, follow these even more incredibly complex and sophisticated instructions:

1. **Click the B, *I*, and/or U button on the toolbar to turn on formatting.**

2. **Type.**

3. **Click the same button again to turn off formatting.**

Changing the font style without using the toolbar buttons

The preceding two highly complex procedures work whenever the **B**, *I*, and U buttons appear in the toolbar. (If the buttons don't appear, you don't need them. Trust the folks at Microsoft. They know what you need.) But if you don't like using the mouse, you can use the following key combinations rather than clicking the toolbar buttons:

- Press Ctrl+B for **bold.**
- Press Ctrl+I for *italic.*
- Press Ctrl+U for <u>underline</u>.

You can specify the font style yet another way (besides using buttons or key combinations). This other way requires a few more steps, involving the Font and Style command in the Format drop-down menu. I get into this procedure in the upcoming section, "Using the Format Font and Style dialog box."

Reading the toolbar buttons

Even if you don't use the buttons, they still continue to reflect the style of your text by looking depressed. Don't take it personally; it's their job. Their depressed look occurs whenever your current insertion point is amidst or upon bold, italic, or underlined text.

In the word processor, the buttons have yet another trick. If you have selected a bunch of text, and some of it has a style applied, but some does not, the appropriate button takes on a peculiar, hollow look, as if it were engraved, not depressed. (Wouldn't you be depressed, too, if you were engraved?) If you click the button, Works applies that style to all of the selected text. Click it again, and Works removes the style.

Removing font styles

If you want to get rid of any and all styles, you can use Ctrl+spacebar. To unformat a block of text, select the text first and then press Ctrl+spacebar. To begin typing with unformatted text, press Ctrl+spacebar; then start typing.

Ctrl+spacebar also changes the font and size back to the original, except in the word processor. The word processor offers no quick way to go back to the original font and size. You have to respecify the original font and size by using the font and size boxes; these boxes appear both on the toolbar and in the Format Font and Style dialog box.

Fooling with Fonts

You may have noticed a rather tedious consistency in Works. A lot of the type looks the same. The way type looks is called its *font*. (The way type looks used to be called the typeface, but the computer industry has transmogrified the terminology.) Works has a rather boring preference for using two fonts called Times New Roman (a truly dumbfounding name) and Arial (incorrectly calling to mind Disney's *The Little Mermaid*, if you're a parent). How can you bring a ray of sunshine into this dreary world of fonts?

Changing font and size with the toolbar

If you're using any of the Big Four tools except the communications tool (the word processor, database, or spreadsheet tools), take a gander at your toolbar. If you're not using any tools at the moment, redirect your gander — and any other waterfowl you may have lying around — to Figure 3-1, where you can see a piece of the toolbar with a drop-down menu.

Figure 3-1: Grab a more interesting font from the toolbar's font area.

The font box on the toolbar, together with its sidekick, the font size box (the one with the 12 in it in Figure 3-1), lets you brighten up your document with any font that's installed on your computer.

Here are two quick steps to change the font you're currently typing in:

1. **Click the down-arrow next to the font box.**

   Works shows you each font by name. The name is written in that font to give you an example of what it looks like.

   To see more fonts, use the scroll bar on the right of the menu. (See Chapter 2 for more on scroll bars.)

2. **Click any font in the drop-down menu.**

To change the font of text that you've already typed, select the text first and then do the preceding two-step.

Changing font size works the same way. To change the size you're currently typing in, click the down-arrow to the right of the font size box for a drop-down list of sizes. Click any size in the menu that drops down from the box. (Or you can click in the font size box, type a new size, and then press the Enter key.) To change the font size of text that you've already typed, select that text first and then change the font size box.

Using the Format Font and Style dialog box

The main command for changing font, style, and all other type-related stuff is Format⇨Font and Style, which brings up the Format Font and Style dialog box of Figure 3-2. The Format Font and Style dialog box does the same things as the font, size, and style features on the toolbar, plus a little bit more. You can choose the additional style ~~strikethrough~~ here; choose a color for your type (at least on the screen and on the printer, too, if you have a color printer); and if you're using the word processor, you can choose a *position*, either subscript or superscript.

Position options (word processor only).

Click on a
font here.　　Click on a size here.　Sample window　Make
　　　　　　　　　　　　　　　　shows the effect　settings
　　Click on a style here.　　　of your choices.　standard.

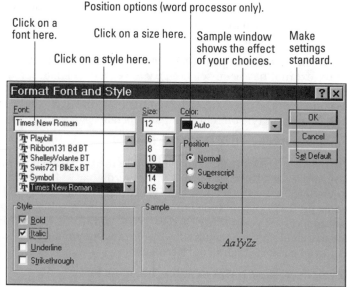

Figure 3-2:
The Format
Font and
Style dialog
box does it
all: font,
size, style,
and more.

The Format Font and Style dialog box also lets you save your font and style selections as the initial (or *default*) selections for certain types of new documents. See the next section, "Changing the font that Works uses for new documents."

In the spreadsheet tool and in the database tool, it's technically not the Format Font and Style *dialog box,* but the Font *card* of the Format Cells dialog box — but it looks and works basically the same as what I describe here.

Here's how to format characters using the Format Font and Style dialog box:

1. **If you're formatting text that you've already typed, select that text.**

   If you just want to start typing in a new font or style, skip this step.

2. **Choose Format⇨Font and Style.**

   The Format Font and Style dialog box arrives on your screen.

3. **Click the font and/or size that you want.**

   To see more fonts or sizes, click the arrows in the adjoining scroll bars.

4. **If you want a special style, such as Bold, click it.**

   The Style selections of bold, italic, and underline (the ones you get using the buttons **B**, _I_, and U in the toolbar) appear in the dialog box as check boxes in the lower left of the dialog box. (Another style, strikethrough, is also listed; strikethrough is used for editing and has a line through the middle. Weird, huh?)

   If a given style is currently _on_ (being applied to text that you're typing or to text that has been selected), you see a check mark in its check box. If the box is gray, as is the Bold selection in Figure 3-2, that means that some of the currently selected text has that style and some does not. To turn a style _off,_ click that style again.

5. **For colored type, click the Color box.**

   Zowie! Color! Click the color you want in the drop-down menu that appears. (Click the down-arrow in the scroll bar to the right of the menu for more colors.) But don't get too excited unless you have a color printer. Colored type comes out as black on a black-and-white printer. Even if your printer is only black and white, color can be useful for distinguishing certain parts of your document, such as changes or editorial comments, on your screen.

6. **If you need superscript or subscript, click it.**

   You can do superscript or subscript only while you're using the word processor. The area marked Position in Figure 3-2, where these selections hang out, doesn't appear with any other tool. Clicking Superscript raises text above the normal line, as is used for footnote numbers and exponents. Subscript lowers text below the normal line.

   To remove sub- or superscripting, click Normal.

7. **After you've set up everything the way that you want it, click the OK button.**

In the word processor toolbar, you can choose superscript or subscript right from the keyboard without using a dialog box. Press Ctrl and the = (equals) key for subscript, and press Ctrl+Shift and the = (equals) key for superscript.

Changing the font that Works uses for new documents

Okay, you now know how to change the font that you're working with in your current document. But what about the next time you create a document? Works is stuck on this Times New Roman/Arial shtick, so Times New Roman/Arial is what you get every time you create a new document. If you don't care for these fonts, you can change the font every time, but what a bore! Instead of changing the font every time you create a new document, however, you can change Works' *default* font and style (the font and style it starts a new document with).

To specify the default, do the following: Before you begin, make sure that you're working in a document of the same type for which you want to specify future default fonts. For example, if you want to specify the default font for, say, spreadsheet documents, you need to be currently working with a spreadsheet document. (That is, a spreadsheet document must be the *active* one in the Works window.)

1. **Summon up the Format Font and Style dialog box by choosing Format⇨Font and Style.**

2. **Specify your font, size, style, and other stuff in the dialog box. (See the section "Using the Format Font and Style dialog box," earlier in this chapter.)**

3. **Click the Set Default button in the dialog box.**

   An impertinent little dialog box crops up, asking in bold type whether you really, truly want to change the default font to whatever font, size, style, and color you specified in Step 2 (cryptically stated as something like Arial 10, Bold, Auto). Click the Yes button.

Now, the next time you create a new document of the same type you're currently working in, you'll start out using the font and style that you set as the default.

Cutting, Copying, and Pasting

Finally, this sentence was written. Subsequently, this sentence. First, this sentence was written. Paragraph sense make does this? No? Then you (or somebody) needs to edit it.

The particular editing features in Works that can make short work of such scrambled writing are the cut, copy, paste, and drag features. The first three features are practically universal among Windows programs. Employing, as they do, a Windows feature called the Clipboard, these features even let you transfer things *between* Windows programs, using that Clipboard as a vehicle.

The Windows *Clipboard* is a temporary storage area that holds only one thing at a time; text and illustrations and all kinds of things can be copied to the Clipboard. The contents of the Clipboard can then be pasted into any document in any Windows program.

Besides carrying things between Windows programs, this Clipboard also serves as a vehicle to move things around *within* a Works document or *between* Works documents. Works' drag feature does not use this Windows Clipboard, so the drag feature works only within Works — either to move something or to copy something.

Copy and paste

You can copy any text or illustration onto the Windows Clipboard and then insert it (*paste* it) somewhere else. In fact, after you have copied the text or illustration onto the Windows Clipboard, you can paste the text or illustration as many times as you like. This feature can be very useful if you are repeatedly typing something lengthy, such as Dinglehausen-Schneitzenbaum Furniture Prefabrication Company.

Here's the procedure for copying:

1. **Select the text or illustration that you want to copy.**

2. **Press Ctrl+C, or**

   Choose Edit⇨Copy, or

   Click the Copy button in the toolbar. (The Copy button is normally next to the button with the scissors, and the icon on the Copy button shows two overlapping documents.)

   This procedure copies the selected stuff onto the Windows Clipboard. These commands do the same thing in most other Windows programs, by the way.

3. **Click where you want a copy to appear.**

   This spot can be in the document that you're working on, in some other Works document, or even in something that you're working on outside of Works, in another Windows program that's currently running. You can take your time opening documents or whatever you need to do.

   Whatever you copy stays on the Clipboard only until you copy or cut something else or turn off your computer.

4. **Press Ctrl+V, or**

   Choose Edit⇨Paste, or

   Click the Paste button in the toolbar. (The Paste button shows a clipboard with a document.)

   This procedure copies stuff off the Windows Clipboard and pastes it into the new location. The Ctrl+V (paste) command is the same in most Windows programs.

You can repeat Steps 3 and 4 as many times as you like, until you put something new on the Clipboard. Dinglehausen-Schneitzenbaum Furniture Prefabrication Company. Dinglehausen-Schneitzenbaum Furniture Prefabrication Company. See, it works!

If you want to make only a single copy of some text or an illustration, you may find it easier to use the drag feature, coming up soon in the "Drag" section of this chapter.

Cut and paste

If you want to move something, one way to move it is to cut and paste it. This procedure is exactly like the copying and pasting just described, except that the original text is removed from your document and placed in the new location of your choosing. (Copying something leaves the original text in its original place because you *copied* it as opposed to *cutting* it.) The cut and paste method is particularly useful for moving something a long distance — over several pages or between documents. Within Works, you can also just drag something to move it, as I show you in a minute.

Here's the procedure for cutting and pasting:

1. **Select the text or illustration that you want to move.**

2. **Press Ctrl+X, or**

   Choose Edit⇨Cut, or

   Click the Cut (scissors) button in the toolbar.

   This procedure copies the selected stuff onto the Windows Clipboard and deletes it from your document. These commands do the same thing in most other Windows programs.

   The next two steps are the *paste* procedure, which is identical to the procedure you use in copying and pasting.

3. **Click where you want the text or illustration to appear.**

4. **Press Ctrl+V, or**

   Choose Edit⇨Paste, or

   Click the Paste button on the toolbar.

As with the copy procedure described previously, you can repeat Steps 3 and 4 as many times as you like until you put something new on the Clipboard.

Drag

As even Og the Caveman knew, dragging is often an easy way to move something. In Works, you can drag text or an illustration to a different place within a document, or even to another document, as long as the document to which you are dragging the text or illustration is open in a window.

If you have to move or copy something for a distance of many pages, to a document that you haven't opened yet, or to or from some program other than Works, the cut (or copy) and paste method is better.

Here's how to move or copy something by dragging it:

1. **Select the text or illustration that you want to move.**

2. **Place your mouse cursor over the highlighted area.**

   Note that the word *drag* attaches itself, lamprey-like, to your cursor. This word is merely a suggestion, but follow it.

3. **Press down the mouse button (don't let go) and drag the selected text or illustration to where you want to move it.**

   If you want to copy, not move, the selected text, press and hold the Ctrl key down at this point. The word *drag* changes to the word *copy*.

   If your destination is not visible in the document window, drag to the window's edge in the direction that you'd like to go. When your cursor hits the edge, the window scrolls.

   If your destination is in another Works document, that document has to be open in a window; just drag to your destination into that window.

4. **Release the mouse button at your final destination.**

Windows allows you to drag illustration (graphic) files from a My Computer window into a Works document. See Chapters 21 and 23 for more on putting illustrations in your documents. You might notice that you can drag text between Works and other Windows programs, too, but because the result is more complicated than it appears to be, I don't recommend this technique.

Yikes! Undoing What's Been Done

Yikes! You just accidentally pasted a double-cheesecake recipe into your non-dairy diet book! What now?

One way in which Works improves on real life is that Works lets you undo your mistakes. Works doesn't allow you to undo all mistakes, mind you, but you can undo most editing mistakes, such as changes that you make to the contents of an open document. But Works doesn't undo mistakes that you make with files, mistakes such as deleting, replacing, renaming, and file-ish stuff like that.

If you accidentally delete a file from your hard disk, you can undelete it using Windows (not Works). Find the Recycle Bin icon on your Windows screen, and double-click it to open the Recycle Bin window. In that window, find the file you deleted, click it, and choose File⇨Restore from the menu in that window.

Works also doesn't undo any more than the last thing that you did. If you made two mistakes, Works only undoes the last, or most recent, one. If you undo again, your undo gets undone (which sounds as if it would be your undoing, but it's not; you can just undo again). Typing or deleting a succession of characters counts as one single mistake, not a bunch of them. If you type a sentence and then undo it, the entire sentence goes away.

To undo, choose Edit⇨Undo *(something)*. The *something* is whatever you last did: typed, entered a number, deleted, formatted. A faster way to undo is to press Ctrl+Z.

If Works can't undo your mistake, it tells you so by graying out the Undo command line and displaying Can't Undo in the command's place.

Checking Your Spelling

One of the helpful little gnomes that scurry around in Works is the Spelling Checker (or *spell checker,* although the idea of checking a spell sounds more wizardish than gnome-like). Unlike the rest of the help squad described in this chapter, the spell checker actually does something instead of just informing you about things. Specifically, the spell checker helps you eliminate typographical errors (typos) and misspellings. Actually, what the spell checker does is make sure that your document contains 100 percent genuine words (or words that it thinks are genuine).

The spell checker does not, however, make sure that you use words write. Like just then — the word *write* is absolutely and indisputably a word; it just happens to be in the wrong place at the wrong time. The spell checker doesn't turn up anything wrong with that that sentence.

The spell checker, however, does catch the repeated word *that* in the last sentence of the preceding paragraph, which can be nice for people like me who pause in the middle of a sentence and often repeat articles such as *the* — repetitions that are hard to see. The spell checker also catches capitalization and hyphenation errors.

The Spelling Checker runs like this: The spell checker looks for words that it doesn't have in its dictionary. If the spell checker finds any such unrecognized words, it points out the word and lets you change it. If you know that the word is okay, you can just tell the spell checker to ignore the word and continue checking. You can also tell the spell checker to add this word to its dictionary so that it always ignores the word thereafter.

Here's the inside scoop on snaring misspellings:

1. **If you are just going to check a single word or block of text, select the word or text block by highlighting it.**

   Otherwise, to check your whole document starting where your insertion point or spreadsheet cursor is, go on to Step 2.

2. **Choose Tools⇨Spelling or press the F7 key on your keyboard.**

   In the word processor, you can alternatively click the Spelling Checker button on the toolbar (the check mark with ABC on it).

   If the spell checker doesn't find any words that it can't recognize, a little box tells you that the spell-checking process is done; click the OK button in that box.

   Otherwise, you get the Spelling dialog box shown in Figure 3-3.

3. **See whether the word that the Spelling Checker found is really incorrect.**

   The word is shown at the top of the Spelling dialog box, where it says Not In Dictionary. Works suggests a replacement in the Change To text box.

4. **If the word is okay, ignore it or add it to the dictionary.**

   If the word is okay this particular time but may be a typo or misspelling if it appears again in this document or any other document, click Ignore. If the word comes up again during this spell-checking session, it is flagged again.

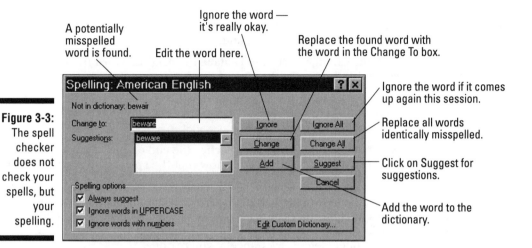

A potentially misspelled word is found.

Ignore the word — it's really okay.

Edit the word here.

Replace the found word with the word in the Change To box.

Ignore the word if it comes up again this session.

Replace all words identically misspelled.

Click on Suggest for suggestions.

Add the word to the dictionary.

Figure 3-3:
The spell checker does not check your spells, but your spelling.

If the word is okay in this document (as *Snark* may be in a document about sailboats) but may be a typo or misspelling in some other document, click Ignore All. The word is ignored until the next time that you use the Spelling Checker.

If the word is a real word (such as *uvula*) that you might use again and again, click Add. The word is then added to the spell checker's Custom Dictionary and is thereafter and forever ignored in any document that you check. Be certain that the word is really spelled correctly before you do this!

If you have acronyms such as *NAVCOM,* the Spelling Checker ignores them. If you want the spell checker to point out such uppercase-only words to you as errors, click the check box marked Ignore Words in UPPERCASE so that the check mark disappears from the check box.

If you have terms that have numbers in them, the Spelling Checker ignores them. If you want the spell checker to point out terms with numbers to you as errors, click the check box marked Ignore Words With Numbers so that the check mark disappears from the check box.

After you act on any of the preceding tasks, the Spelling Checker moves on to check the remainder of the document.

5. If the word suggested by Works in the Change To box is not correct, edit it.

If you know the correct word, click the Change To text box and edit the word. Or other suggestions may be in the Suggestions box; click one of these suggestions, and it fills the Change To box.

If you don't like this suggestion stuff, clear the check mark in Always Suggest by clicking that check box. Otherwise, Works lists suggestions for every misspelling that it finds.

6. **Click the Change button to replace the original word in your document with the one in the Change To box.**

You don't get to watch this replacement happen because the action happens so fast. The spell checker moves right along to your next apparent blunder, and you're back at Step 3.

Eventually, the spell checker reaches the end of your document and puts up a little box letting you know that the spell-checking process is done. Click OK in this box.

If you didn't start spell checking at the beginning of your document, Works asks whether the spell checker should go back to the beginning and do so. Click OK in this box if you would like to check the first part of your document. Click Cancel if you're done.

Where is this dictionary?

Works maintains yet another dictionary where it stuffs the words you add during spell checking. This second dictionary is called the Custom Dictionary. If you would like to add words to or remove words from that dictionary, click the Edit Custom Dictionary button in the Spelling dialog box. To add a word to the Custom Dictionary, type the word in the Word text box and click the Add button. To delete a word from the Custom Dictionary, find it in the big white list box, click it, and then click the Delete button. Whichever task you do, click the Done button when you've finished. Most dictionaries are hard to miss. The one in your PC is hard to see. (Oops, make that *the several* dictionaries in your PC.) In the U.S. of A., your copy of Works comes with a dictionary in good ol' A-Merican, plus another in that fancy British stuff, where they talk like they invented the language or something. (To change the language orientation of your dictionary, choose Tools⇨Options, click the tab labeled Proofing Tools, and then click the dictionary of your choice in the Choose Dictionary text box. Finally, press Enter.)

Chapter 4

Basic Printing

• •

• •

*A*ccording to some accounts, computers were supposed to lead to the age of the paperless office. No more of this cutting down forests, flattening them into paper, smearing ink all over them, and then dumping them into landfills where typos are preserved like mummies for the critical eye of posterity. Hah! As my fellow technology skeptic (and co-author on other books) Margaret Levine Young is fond of saying, "The paperless office of the future is just down the hall from the paperless bathroom of the future."

No, computers actually have increased paper consumption. And you, too, can join the parade with your own printer. Fortunately, features such as Works' Print Preview can at least minimize the amount of paper that you waste.

Printing is something that you can do in the word-processor, database, and spreadsheet tools, and printing proceeds roughly the same way in each one. In each tool, the commands that have anything to do with printing (including page setup, such as margins and orientation) have been forced by Microsoft to live with evil relatives in the File menu. Perhaps, someday, some handsome royalty from the kingdom of Microsoft will rescue them and give them their very own Print condominium on the menu bar.

The special world of envelopes

Unless you really like figuring out the nuts and bolts of how things work, you probably shouldn't attempt to print envelopes without help from Works. Works has a special envelope tool (which also serves as the envelope TaskWizard) that works with the word-processor tool and takes care of all your page setup and printing needs.

Because this special envelope tool uses the word processor to create the envelope, I've put the discussion of how to print a single, simple envelope in Chapter 7. For a discussion of using the envelope tool/TaskWizard to create multiple envelopes for mass mailing, see the Appendix.

Setting Up the Page

Ever since humankind moved from scrolls to pages, things have been going downhill. Now we have to worry about top and bottom margins as well as side margins. Even worse, now we can print the darn pages sideways! Back to scrolls, I say!

But, in the meantime, I suppose that we have to deal with all this stuff. Fortunately, the controls for page margins, page size, and orientation work the same for all the different Works tools.

You don't have to set up the page every time you print — just set up the page once for each document. Your page setup is saved as part of the document file. In fact, you may be quite happy with the margins and other page setup stuff that Works uses automatically (the default). In that case, you don't have to bother with setting up your pages at all! Skip ahead to "Previewing Coming Attractiveness," later in this chapter, which describes how to see what your document looks like before you print it. If you like the way your document looks, don't bother fooling with Page Setup.

Making marginal decisions

Margins in Works are defined as the spaces between the edge of the page and the regular body text and footnotes of the document. Headers and footers (including page numbers) go within these margins, and you specify their positions separately using the Header margins.

Choose File⇨Page Setup to get a Page Setup dialog box; then click the
Margins tab. The Margins card then graces you with its presence, as shown
in Figure 4-1:

Figure 4-1:
A place to
do your
marginal
thinking: the
Margins
card.

🡲 **To increase or decrease a margin:** Click the up-arrow or down-arrow
next to the value.

🡲 **To type in a specific margin value:** Double-click that margin's white box
and type in a new number. If you want inches (or whatever your default
units are), you can just type in the value and leave off the units (for
example, type **2.5** for 2.5 inches).You can type in other units, too, such
as **cm** for centimeters, **mm** for millimeters, **pi** for picas, and **pt** for points.

When you type a margin value into a box, the Sample doesn't show the
result until you click within some other margin box. Works then knows
that you have finished typing the value.

🡲 **To set header or footer margins:** *Headers* and *footers* are text that
appears in the margins on the top or bottom of every page. The header
distance is measured from the top edge of the page to the bottom of the
header text, so the header distance must be set to a value no larger
than the top margin. The footer distance is measured from the bottom
edge of the page to the top of the footer, so the footer distance must be
set to a value no larger than the bottom margin.

Hooked on metrics

Let's face it: Inches are silly, but that's what we grew up with here in the good old U.S. of A. If you live in a country where people have discovered that they have ten fingers and toes, you probably prefer the metric system. Or perhaps you've worked in the typing, publishing, or printing businesses, where they have really silly measurements, such as the pica. (Maybe the pica is a small and fuzzy measurement named after the small fuzzy alpine bunny, *Pica D'Amerique,* or *Pika.*)

If you want Works to use your favorite *metrics* (units of measure), do this:

1. **Click the Cancel button in any dialog box that's open, such as in the Page Setup dialog box.**

2. **Click Tools⇨Options. A somewhat intimidating Options dialog box springs up; click the General tab and then focus your attention on the upper-left corner marked Units.**

3. **Click whatever unit you want Works to use by default.** (That is, the unit you want Works to use when you don't specify a unit, just a number.)

4. **Click the OK button in this Options dialog box.**

Setting source, size, and orientation

You may print 99 percent of your work on standard-sized paper in the *normal,* or *portrait,* orientation. Still, for spreadsheets, signs, certain kinds of flyers, and other work, you may want your printer to print sideways, in the *landscape* orientation. (Note that landscape orientation does *not* mean that you put the paper sideways into your printer!) Also, many printers require you to manually insert the paper for special-sized paper. For this special printing to work, you should tell Works about it on the Source, Size & Orientation card of the Page Setup dialog box, shown in Figure 4-2.

Choose File⇨Page Setup to get a Page Setup dialog box; then click the Source, Size & Orientation tab.

✔ **To set page orientation:** Click the Source, Size & Orientation card. Then click either Landscape or Portrait in the lower-left corner. The page icon (with the letter A) illustrates how type will be printed on the page.

✔ **To tell Works that you are using a special paper source on your printer:** On the Source, Size & Orientation card, click the box marked Paper Source. If you need to use a special paper-feeding place on your printer, such as a single-sheet feed slot, you can click that source in the list that drops down. After you indicate the source, Works prompts you at the right time to put the paper in for manual feeding; for automatic feeding, Works tells the printer to use that special source.

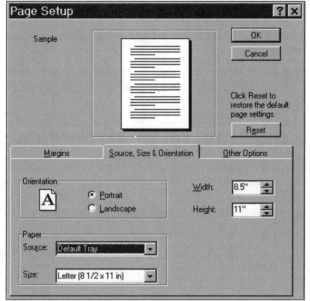

Figure 4-2:
Getting
sourced,
sized, and
oriented all
at once.

✔ **To tell Works that you're using a special paper size or an envelope:**
On the Source, Size & Orientation card, click the box marked Paper
Size. Click the paper size in the box that drops down. If you're using a
paper size that's not shown in the drop-down box, double-click the box
marked Width and type in a new value; then do the same for Height.
(Width always refers to the direction a line of text will run.) When
you're done, check the Sample to see whether things look roughly
correct. Click the Reset button to return to the default paper size.

Starting page number and other options

Each type of Works document has certain special options for page setup, so
see the individual tool sections in this book for more information on those
options. One "other option" that they all have in common is the capability to
specify what page number should appear on the first page of your document. The main use for this process is when you are writing a document
with lots of sections and chapters, and each Works document is a section. In
that case, you want to set the first page number to something other than 1.

Here's how:

1. **Choose File⇨Page Setup to get a Page Setup dialog box; then click the Other Options tab.**

2. **Either click the Starting page number box and type in a value, or click the adjoining up-arrow to increase the page number setting.**

Reusing the same setup all the time

Because your page setup only affects the current document, the situation can be a little frustrating if you want to use the same settings all the time. (You have to set the settings up each time that you want to use them.) One solution to the problem is to create a custom template. A *template* is a sort of prototype document that is all set up to do a particular type of document. After you have created a template, you can start a new document based on this template by choosing from User Defined Templates, a category that now appears on the list of TaskWizards in the Task Launcher. For more on templates, see "Creating and Using Templates" in the Appendix.

Previewing Coming Attractiveness

You've formatted your document, and you think that it will look quite attractive on paper. But how do you know? The time for a preview of coming attractiveness has arrived. Specifically, it's time for Print Preview, which shows you how Works thinks your document will look in print without wasting paper. (See Figure 4-3 for a preview of Print Preview.)

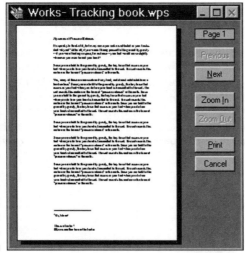

Figure 4-3:
Works shows you teeny-tiny print on a minuscule page. Click the page to zoom in.

You can get into Print Preview in any of three ways:

✔ **Click File⇨Print Preview in the menu bar.**

✔ **Click the button in the menu bar that looks like a document with a monocle.** (To see if you're on the right button, place your mouse cursor over the button without clicking, and Works puts up a tiny label saying Print Preview.)

✔ **In the word processor, press Ctrl+P and then click the Preview button in the Print dialog box that appears.**

Whichever way you use, you get a Print Preview dialog box that initially shows you a tiny, illegible picture of your document. (The picture may be illegible, but this initial bird's-eye view is actually helpful for checking margins and overall layout.)

Here are some of the things you can do in this dialog box:

✔ **To see other pages:** Click Next to see the next page or click Previous to see the preceding page. If no next or preceding page exists, the buttons are grayed out.

✔ **To enlarge the view of the document:** Position your mouse cursor over a location in the document you want to see; then click. Click a second time for greater magnification. Clicking the Zoom In button also enlarges the view of the document. Use the vertical and horizontal scroll bars to view parts of the document that extend beyond the window.

✔ **To shrink the document:** Keep clicking on it. The document returns to its original size after a total of three clicks. Or hold down the Ctrl button and click. Clicking the Zoom Out button also shrinks the view.

✔ **To actually print the document on paper (what a stunning concept!):** Click the Print button. (When you print, don't worry about how big the document looks in Print Preview. The document prints at normal size.)

✔ **To return to the document window:** Click the Cancel button or press the Esc key.

Printing on Actual Paper!

What will they think of next? Imagine being able to actually see words and graphics on paper rather than on a computer screen!

Printing is a little different for each tool in Works, and sometimes printing is even different *within* that tool, depending on exactly what you're doing (for example, printing a document with an envelope page). For some of the most important printing variations within each tool, see the chapter on that tool.

Printing is pretty simple when things go right:

1. **Turn on your printer.**

2. **Wait until it comes online**.

   Most printers have an indicator light somewhere that is marked On Line. If this indicator light lights up, the printer is telling you that it has had its morning coffee, has done its exercises, and is ready to roll.

3. **To print the whole document without further ado, click the Print button on the Works toolbar.**

   (The Print button has a picture of a printer on it.)

   At this point, you're essentially done. Read "Terminating Printing" later in this chapter if you've changed your mind about printing the document.

   Works may display a First-Time Help dialog box when you print, as it does for certain other commands. As with all First-Time Help dialog boxes, you can choose to either see a demo or receive step-by-step instructions (which means that Works displays its Help window). After your first experience with this dialog box, you may no longer need it. You can keep it from reappearing by clicking the check box labeled Don't Display This Message In The Future. You can turn off all First-Time Help dialog boxes by choosing Tools⇨Options, clicking the View tab on the Options dialog box that appears, and then clicking the check box labeled Show First-Time Help to remove its check mark.

4. **If you want to print only a part of the document or print multiple copies, click File⇨Print or press Ctrl+P. (Pressing Ctrl+P does the same thing.)**

   The Print dialog box comes to your aid.

5. **For multiple copies, click the Number Of Copies box (in the Print dialog box) and type the number of copies that you want (but don't press the Enter key).**

   Or you can click the up- or down-arrows next to that box to change the page count.

6. **To print a specific group of pages, click Pages (in the Print dialog box) and enter the starting and ending page numbers.**

7. **To print faster but with less quality, click Draft Quality Printing (still in the Print dialog box).**

8. **Click the OK button (or press the Enter key).**

   If all goes well, you can now just close your eyes and wait for your document to be printed. If you change your mind about printing — quick, read "Terminating Printing."

Terminating Printing

Stopping a document before it gets to the printer is like trying to catch a bus that's just left the bus stop. If you're really fast, you can flag the bus down. Otherwise, you have to run to the next bus stop.

Don't just turn off the printer. Your paper may get stuck halfway and need to be carefully extracted; your PC will get confused and start tossing complaints on your screen; and when you start the printer up again, your first page may be a mess.

The printing route has three bus stops. First, the document goes to the printing part of Works, which displays the Print dialog box. Then as that part of Works prepares each page for printing, the document goes to the Windows Print Manager. Finally, the Print Manager delivers each page, one at a time, to the printer. To stop printing, you can interrupt the process at any point.

> **Stop 1.** If you move fast enough, you can click the Cancel button in the Printing dialog box. This box disappears fairly quickly, though, and you may not be able to move fast enough to stop the first page or two.
>
> **Stop 2.** If you miss the opportunity to cancel printing in Works, you can still catch the bus at the next stop.
>
> Certain types of printers bring up their own bus stop: a dialog box where you can stop or pause printing. Check your printer manual for instructions.
>
> If your printer doesn't come with its own bus stop, use the Windows Print Manager. At the other end of the Taskbar from the Start button (near the time-of-day display), a printer icon appears. Double-click it to open a Print Manager window. Click on the name of your document in the list shown there and then click the Delete button. After a pause, the document name no longer appears. Click the X button at the top right of the dialog box to exit.
>
> **Stop 3.** If you know where the online/offline button is on your printer (not the power button), you can press that button. Your printer software or the Print Manager eventually discovers your action and displays a box complaining that `The printer on LPT1 is offline or not selected` or some such stuff. Click the Cancel button in this box. Next, follow the directions for Stop 2. Finally, press the online/offline button on your printer again.

Selecting or Installing a Printer

There's a good chance that Works already knows what printer you have and how you want that printer to work. No, Works hasn't been snooping in your credit card records. When you (or your friendly local software guru) installed Windows, you installed the printer there, too: You told Windows what printer or printers you would be using, and you loaded some software. If you said that you may use more than one printer, you may also have specified one printer as the standard (or *default*) printer. Unless you tell Works otherwise, it uses this default printer.

Here are the main circumstances under which you may need to tell Works or Windows something about a printer:

✔ If you just installed a new printer (or a fax modem), you need to tell Windows about it.

✔ If you are switching to another printer, or if you want to send a fax with your fax modem and fax software (which makes Works think that the fax modem is a printer), you need to tell Works about these actions.

Selecting a printer or fax modem in Works

After a printer has been installed (both physically and in software), Works can use it. If you have more than one printer installed and you want to switch to another printer, you have to choose the other printer from Works. Although you probably don't have more than one real printer, you may have a fax modem that transmits faxes; usually the fax modem and its program work like a printer. To send a fax in that case, you have to choose the fax selection in place of a printer, and then print.

Here's how to select an installed printer or fax modem:

1. **Choose File⇨Print in the menu bar or press Ctrl+P.**

   The Print dialog box winks into existence on your screen.

2. **In the Print dialog box, click the down-arrow on the Name box.**

   This action displays the list of installed printers or fax modem software.

3. **Click the printer or fax software of your choice in the list.**

   After a brief delay, you're done. Now proceed to print.

Before you print, you may want to check the document's appearance with Print Preview. Choosing a different printer or selecting fax software can affect the document's appearance.

When you print to a fax modem, your document will be automatically handed off to special fax modem software where you enter the fax number, perhaps create a cover sheet, and do other fax-specific tasks before the document is actually transmitted over the phone line.

Installing a new printer or fax software

Here's how to go about installing a new printer and telling Windows about it. You may need to have your Windows installation disks or CD handy; or if your printer came with a disk containing *printer drivers,* you may need that disk. If you are installing fax software, you need to follow the directions that came with it. To install a printer, do the following:

1. **Shut down Windows and turn off your PC.**

2. **Physically unpack and set up the printer.**

   Remove all the tabs, Styrofoam chunks, and rubber bands that the manufacturer tells you about. Read the instruction manual and do your best to follow the instructions. In the process, you'll plug the printer's cable into a *parallel port* or a *serial port* on your PC.

3. **Turn on your PC.**

4. **Choose Start➪Settings➪Printers from the Windows Taskbar.**

5. **In the Printers dialog box that appears, double-click the Add Printer icon.**

6. **An Add Printer Wizard appears; click the Next button and follow the directions.**

Now you are all set with your shiny new printer — probably color, too, you lucky person.

Part II
The Wily Word Processor

The 5th Wave   By Rich Tennant

"OK, TECHNICALLY, THIS SHOULD WORK. JUDY, TYPE THE WORD 'GOODYEAR' IN ALL CAPS, BOLDFACE, AT 700-POINT TYPE SIZE."

In this part . . .

So, you're ready to dash off that important report or write that long-awaited letter in the Works word processor? Well, Works makes it pretty easy — but as with all word- processing software, it's still a bit wild. Don't expect to just walk right up and pounce on it. It's a good idea to sidle up to it, nice and easy, and know what sort of interesting behavior to expect when you finally lasso it and put it to use.

This part covers everything from basics, like how to use the keyboard, to subtle and elusive facts, like where paragraph formatting hides. Learn about the word-processing habitat: why it's important to replace your old typing habits with new word-processing habits. Finally, learn how to teach your newly tamed word processor advanced tricks, like page numbers, tables, borders, lines, headers, footers, and footnotes.

Chapter 5

In Search of the Wily Word Processor

So, you're ready to hunt down the wily word processor? Well, pack up your safari gear and get to know the wiles and ways of this wacky wordivorous wonder. Soon, you, too, will be able to write such annoying alliterative allegories as this one — and then avoid embarrassment by quickly deleting them again, as I should have — without the trials of type-writer ribbons and whiteout.

What's the Big Deal?

Three being a magical number, there are, of course, three big deals about word processing:

> **Big Deal 1.** You can make documents that you would never even attempt to create with a typewriter, such as two-column newsletters or presentation transparency foils (those see-through thingies that you put on an overhead projector) using big type.

> **Big Deal 2.** Your documents look better and fancier, without pain and strain, when you use nice typefaces of different size and style, centered or indented text, borders, and graphics.

> **Third and Final Big Deal.** Playing around with things until you like the results — changing words or sentences, moving paragraphs, or changing margins and page breaks — is really easy in word processing.

In addition to the three big deals, word processing has some tiny little deals, such as copying text from one place to another, automatic spell-checking, sending documents over the phone lines, and being able to add word processing to your résumé. So word processing is a good deal all around.

What's different from a typewriter?

You can do lots of things with a word processor that you can't do with a typewriter. (Word processors don't make that cool clickety-clack sound, but what the heck?) But even for doing things that you're accustomed to doing on a typewriter, there are a few differences to be careful of:

✔ Do not, *absolutely* do NOT, use the Enter key like the carriage return key, pressing it at the end of every line of text. This habit, a carry-over from the old typewriter days, all but guarantees a bitter, contentious relationship with your word processor. A person who presses Enter after every line is like the old farmer who, upon buying his first car, hooks up his horse to pull it. He then spends his days cursing this newfangled means of transportation because his miles-per-bushel-of-hay went down.

✔ Think twice before using the Tab key and the spacebar to position text. There are a lot of cool automatic formatting features, such as automatic centering or justifying of a line of text, for example. Strange things can appear on the page when your tab-and-space formatting starts to interact with the automatic formatting. Works provides better ways to do the indentations and positioning that you want, as I describe in Chapter 7.

✔ Some keys, such as the Backspace key and Caps Lock key, work a bit differently. See the section "Keyboard tips and peculiarities" later in this chapter.

✔ Text flows around on your screen like spilled coffee on a desktop. (At least the text doesn't soak through to other documents.) When you add something or remove it, the remaining text moves away or flows in to fill the gap. For example, if you remove the special marks that keep paragraphs separate, the paragraphs merge together. Paragraphs are supposed to behave this way. You just have to go with the flow.

✔ Your screen doesn't always show you *exactly* what your document would look like if you printed it. You can work in two *views,* Normal and Page Layout; Normal view lets Works respond a bit more quickly as you type, and Page Layout view is closer to the final appearance. Print Preview, described in Chapter 4, is even more accurate.

✔ Do not use dashes and other symbols to make lines. Heavens, no — this way of making lines is far too tacky. There are lots of other, cleaner ways to do lines and borders.

What can you do with a word processor?

The Works word-processing tool lets you make documents, including simple letters and memos, newsletters, scholarly reports, or even things that need big letters, such as signs or transparency foils for presentations. Here are some of the things that this tool lets you do with documents:

✔ Automatically move text around as you type new text in or delete old text

✔ Move text and graphics, or copy them, from one place (or one document) to another

✔ Use any of a wide variety of typefaces, in sizes from barely legible to utterly humongous — even in color, if you have a color printer

✔ Automatically indent, center, left-justify, or right-justify your paragraphs

✔ Quickly set or change line spacing or spacing between paragraphs

✔ Automatically add bullets to lists (such as this one)

✔ Automatically put page breaks in the right places

✔ Automatically floss your teeth

✔ Put your socks in the correct drawer

✔ Use charts, tables, and illustrations

✔ Automatically number footnotes and keep them on the correct page as you move text around

✔ Automatically search for certain words or phrases — and even replace them with other text, if you want (For example, you may want to find all occurrences of "you pompous old windbag" and replace them with "Mr. Wiggins.")

✔ Automatically check your spelling

✔ Find synonyms for words using a built-in thesaurus

✔ Walk your dog

✔ Print envelopes

✔ Automatically put headers or footers on each page (as in this book, where each page has a header identifying the chapter number or part)

Just kidding about the teeth, the socks, and the dog, but the rest is true. And this is just the beginning.

Getting Started

Enough preamble. Time to gird your loins and stroll onto the word-processing wrestling mat.

To find out about starting Works and the different ways of starting a word-processing document or opening an existing one, see Chapter 1. Likewise, turn there if you're a little shaky on using the mouse or keyboard. For background on windows, menus, and dialog boxes, check out Chapter 2.

With Works running, either choose File⇨Open (to open an existing word-processor document), or start the Task Launcher by choosing File⇨New. From the Task Launcher, you can start a new word-processing document with a TaskWizard, if you like, or open or find an existing one. To start a new document, click the Works Tools tab of the Task Launcher; then click the Word Processor button on the Tools card. You are now gazing at the word-processing window, its toolbar, and other assorted paraphernalia.

The Word-Processing Window and Toolbar

Figure 5-1 shows you what's what in your *word-processing window.* ("Word-processing window" is my name for how the Microsoft Works window looks when you use the word processor.) A document with one of the dweeby sort of startup names that Works gives new documents, "Unsaved Document 3," is on the screen. (You'd think they'd baptize these documents or something, so that they would be saved.) Then there's the usual Works menu bar (with all the commands) near the top of the Works window, and the word-processing toolbar is underneath that.

You may also find a Help panel occupying the right-hand side of your Works window. If you find this panel helpful, leave it there. Otherwise, click the Shrink Help button in its bottom-left corner. For more on Help, see Chapter 2.

Don't try to memorize all the names in Figure 5-1. Stick a pencil here (or turn back the corner of the page) and come back here whenever you need to refresh your memory.

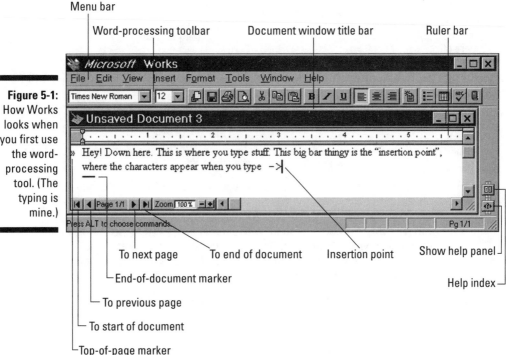

Figure 5-1: How Works looks when you first use the word-processing tool. (The typing is mine.)

Make a mental note that you're looking at one of two possible views of your document here; this view is called *Normal view,* and the other view is called *Page Layout view.* The Normal view doesn't waste space showing you your margins. The Page Layout view does, but it gives a somewhat more accurate picture of what your document really looks like. I get into these views more in the section "Seeing What Your Document Really Looks Like" later in this chapter.

The ruler bar and toolbar are optional. You can turn them off or on. To turn them off, click View in the menu bar and then click Toolbar or Ruler in the menu that drops down — click on whichever one of these bars you want to turn off. To turn that bar back on, do the same thing again. Everything else is pretty permanent.

The word-processing toolbar (shown in Figure 5-2) is similar to the toolbars in other Works tools. For more on the Works' toolbars, see Chapter 3.

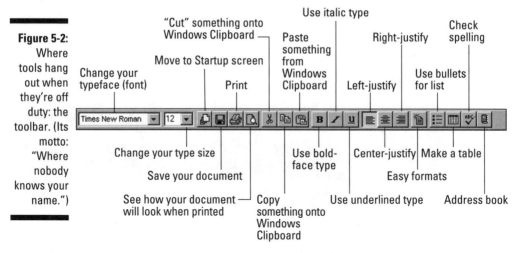

Figure 5-2: Where tools hang out when they're off duty: the toolbar. (Its motto: "Where nobody knows your name.")

Most of the toolbar buttons are the usual suspects mentioned in Part I for starting, saving, printing, doing basic cut-and-paste edits, changing fonts, and getting help. The remaining toolbar buttons are more specific to word processing and are discussed in the following places:

   ✔ **Align Left/Align Right, Center, Justify:** See Chapter 7.

   ✔ **Bullets for lists:** See Chapter 8.

   ✔ **Make a table:** See Chapter 8.

> ✔ **Check spelling:** See Chapter 6.
>
> ✔ **Easy formats:** See Chapter 7.
>
> ✔ **Address book:** See the Appendix.

Typing and Deleting

Typing and deleting are the big existential deals of word processing: existence and nonexistence; calling into creation and returning to the void. All else is illusion (or maybe illustration).

Typing

If you're now looking at a word-processing window, away you go. Just start typing. All the regular keys on the keyboard — the letters, numbers, and punctuation — put characters on the screen when you press them.

Keep on typing and do NOT press the Enter (or Return) key when you get to the end of the line. The text you type automatically starts on the next line, a phenomenon called *line wrap*. When you get to the bottom of the document window, the document *scrolls up,* like paper in your typewriter. Press the Enter key when you get to the end of a paragraph — NOT BEFORE!!!

If you want space between your paragraphs, you can press the Enter key twice at the end of the paragraph, but there's a better way, called *paragraph formatting,* that I get into in Chapter 7. For now, try this technique: If you want a line's worth of space above the paragraph that you're currently typing (and a line's worth of space above subsequent paragraphs), press Ctrl+0 (that's zero, not the letter *O*). If you want that space to go away, press Ctrl+0 again.

The insertion point

As you type, you start pushing around that big vertical bar, the *insertion point.* The insertion point's main function in life is to mark where the next character appears when you type or where a character disappears when you delete.

Beware the insidious Insert key

Works provides two ways for you to type with your keyboard: *insert mode* and *overtype mode.* (A third mode, *a la mode,* is when your ice cream cone drops onto the keyboard.) Normally, you are in the insert mode, which means that if you move the insertion point into the middle of text and type, the existing text scoots to the right to make room. If, however, you should accidentally press the Insert key (which lives over by your navigation keys, just waiting to be pressed accidentally), you find yourself transported to the parallel dimension of overtype mode. (A little OVR shows up in the bottom-right corner of your Works window.) Now if you move the insertion point into the middle of text and type, the existing text vanishes as you type over it. If you find you are typing over existing text, you have probably pressed Insert. Press the Insert key again to return to your home dimension.

You can nudge the insertion point up, down, or sideways by pressing the arrow and other navigation keys on your keyboard. Or you can teleport the insertion point: just click the mouse pointer at the place in your document where you would like to start typing. See "Getting Around in Your Document" later in this chapter.

Notice what happens to your mouse pointer when you move it into the white area where you type. The mouse pointer changes into a mouse cursor, an *I-beam* shape that's a little easier to fit in between characters than the pointer is.

Don't confuse your mouse cursor (where you're pointing) with the insertion point (where you're typing). The mouse cursor is the symbol that you move with your mouse. Clicking the mouse brings the insertion point to where the mouse cursor is.

Deleting

You can delete stuff with either the Backspace key or the Delete key. To delete a character you just typed, press the Backspace key (usually on the upper-right corner of the typewriter keys). Technically speaking (geek-speak), the Backspace key deletes the character *before* the insertion point, and the Delete key deletes the character *after* the insertion point.

To delete a character in the middle of a line of text, you can use either the Backspace key or the Delete key — your preference. If you click just after the character, you can use the Backspace key. If you click just before the character, you can use the Delete key (which hangs out near your navigation keys).

To delete a block of text, select the text by clicking and dragging your mouse cursor across it; pressing either the Backspace key or the Delete key deletes the selected text. The selected area can span as many words, lines, paragraphs, or even pages as you want. For more on selecting text, see Chapter 6.

To undelete (that's *un-delete,* not *undulate* — don't get excited) something that you deleted by accident, press Ctrl+Z. You have to do this immediately, like cardiopulmonary resuscitation, or you lose the patient. To untype something you just typed, you can also use Ctrl+Z.

Rapping about wrapping

If you've never used a word processor before, here's something about line wrapping that may catch you by surprise: Lines *unwrap* when you delete, just like they wrapped when you were typing. Try it. Type a couple of lines; then move the insertion point to somewhere in the second line and start deleting by pressing the Backspace key. When the insertion point gets back to the beginning of the line, don't let up. The insertion point jumps back up to the end of the first line and starts gobbling characters there. (The backspace key on your typewriter definitely did not work this way.)

The same thing happens when you move the insertion point with the arrow keys. If you're at the end of a line and go right, you wrap down to the beginning of the next line. If you're at the beginning of a line and go left, you wrap up to the end of the preceding line.

Typing spaces, tabs, and other invisible characters

You probably have already suspected that your document is haunted by powerful invisible beings. What you probably didn't know is that you're the one who put them there. Yes, indeedy. You pressed the keys that brought them into existence.

Some of these characters, such as the space character, are familiar and fairly innocuous. (You know, like Commander Data of *Star Trek: The Next Generation*. What a space character!) Other characters, such as the tab mark that you get when you press the Tab key, are somewhat more mysterious.

The spacebar puts a space mark (character) in your text. Unlike the space on a typewriter, the word processor's spacebar gives you a very skinny space (much thinner than most other characters you type). The space mark's width depends on the *font* (typeface and size) that you're currently using.

When you press the Tab key, you insert a tab mark. The tab mark creates space in your text starting from where the insertion point is and ending where the next *tab stop* is. See Chapter 7 for more on tabs.

The elite of these invisible beings, the paragraph mark that you get when you press the Enter key, is so powerful that it gets its own section in this chapter, "Paragraphs and paragraph marks," coming up soon.

"What tab mark? What paragraph mark?" you say. Well, these marks are *invisible,* of course, which is why they don't stand out in a crowd. They're easy to overlook when you format or delete. But they do affect the way your document looks and can cause weird, spooky, inexplicable things to appear, such as big gaps in your text (due to a tab mark or a line of spaces you didn't know was there) or a paragraph merging with another (when a paragraph mark gets deleted) or a font for your text that you didn't expect (when the insertion point gets plunked down next to an invisible character that has a different font attached to it).

For all these reasons, you need to be able to see these invisible characters, at least occasionally. Read on.

Seeing invisible characters

I discuss the why and how-not-to of these mysteries later, but for now just follow this simple step to see these creepy invisible guys:

Click <u>V</u>iew⇨<u>A</u>ll Characters.

AAAaaggghh! Your document is filled with nasty dots and funny marks! In fact, it looks almost as bad as the document shown in Figure 5-3! What a mess! Aren't you glad that these characters are normally invisible? Those dots between your words are spaces. The little backwards-P-looking thing is a paragraph mark, and it hangs out with the text that precedes it. If you have any tab marks, they look like arrows with a deodorant-failure problem (lots of space around them). Manually inserted page breaks are dotted lines.

relieve·its·internal·pressure. ··In·the·next·section,·we·will·explore·some·of·the·basic·
pressure·releases·for·different·types·of·motion.¶

Section·3¶
Pressure·against·the·side·of·the·track¶

Varying·pressures·against·the·side·of·the·track·result·in·the·pressure·releases·of·Table·3-1,·
below.¶

Table·3-1:·Lateral·pressures·and·their·indications¶

Pressure	→	Indication↵
Light	→	crest↵
Moderate	→	cave↵

Figure 5-3: Invisible characters are lurking in your document.

Now, if any of these invisible dudes are giving you trouble, just revoke their existence (delete them). Put the insertion point in front of them and press the Delete key. The visible text moves around to fill the gap.

To make these characters invisible again, click View⇨All Characters again. Frankly, however, until you get used to having these characters lurking around, your life may be easier if you leave the characters visible.

Paragraphs and paragraph marks

Your English teacher told you what a paragraph is, right? Topic sentence? Two or more related sentences? Well, Works has its own idea about paragraphs. A Works paragraph is created when you press the Enter key and create one of those secret, invisible paragraph marks that I talked about in "Typing spaces, tabs, and other invisible characters" earlier in this chapter.

That paragraph mark is very powerful, as invisible beings tend to be. Here are three extremely important and utterly critical things to know about the paragraph mark:

✔ **A paragraph mark tells Works, "Do not line wrap beyond this point; start a new line."**

A paragraph mark is the thing that keeps paragraphs apart.

✔ **The paragraph mark controls paragraph formatting for its paragraph.**

In other words, the mark affects all the text preceding it (up to the preceding paragraph mark).

Paragraph formatting is indentation, spacing between paragraphs, tab stops, alignment, justification, and other stuff that I talk about in Chapter 7. When you format a paragraph, all this formatting information is *owned* by the paragraph mark and applies to the text preceding it. (The paragraph mark does *not,* however, specify type: meaning the typeface [font] or any aspect of type, such as style or size.) So if you copy a paragraph mark and paste it somewhere else, *it brings its paragraph formatting with it!*

✔ **Every time that you press the Enter key (creating a new paragraph mark), the new paragraph mark inherits all the paragraph formatting of the paragraph you were just in.**

The indentation, the spacing, the tab stops, and all the other paragraph stuff will be the same. In other words, just type, and new paragraphs will look just like the first one. To change appearances of new paragraphs, adjust the final paragraph's formatting. Any new paragraphs you create from it will inherit its appearance.

What these points mean for you is the following:

✔ Don't press the Enter key at the end of every line; only press it at the end of your paragraph. Otherwise, your paragraph is actually a bunch of Works paragraphs. If you go to do something paragraphy, like indenting everything but the first line, the format won't work properly because (as far as Works is concerned) every line *is* the first line!

✔ Do press the Enter key at the end of short lines in a list, such as this one.

✔ To split one paragraph into two, put the insertion point where you want the split and press the Enter key. The two new paragraphs will have identical paragraph formatting.

✔ To create a new paragraph in front of the one that you're currently in, move your insertion point to the beginning of the current paragraph and press Enter.

✔ To create a new paragraph to follow the one that you're currently in, move your insertion point to the end of the current paragraph (click the last line and press the End key to be sure) and press Enter.

✔ If you delete text that includes a paragraph mark (for example, if you select and delete text crossing two paragraphs), the two paragraphs merge. The remaining single paragraph takes on the paragraph formatting of the bottom of the original pair. Try pressing Ctrl+Z to undo whatever you did. You can also take a look at Chapter 7 for more on formatting changes.

Unfriendly mergers and takeovers of paragraphs

The Backspace and Delete keys delete invisible characters in the same way that they delete visible characters. If your insertion point is at the beginning of a paragraph and you press the Backspace key, you delete the preceding character: the invisible paragraph mark at the end of the preceding paragraph! Likewise, if you press the Delete key at the end of a paragraph, you delete the paragraph mark. Without a paragraph mark to hold it back, the first paragraph spills into the following one and forms one humongous paragraph.

What's worse, if the two paragraphs were formatted differently — say that one paragraph was centered and the other paragraph wasn't — both of them are now formatted like the second paragraph.

You can get out of this mess by pressing Ctrl+Z (or clicking Edit⇨Undo) immediately. Another option is to reinsert the paragraph mark by clicking where you want the paragraph break and pressing the Enter key, but you still may need to reformat the first paragraph.

Keyboard tips and peculiarities

For the big picture on the keyboard, see Chapter 1. Here are a few tips and peculiarities of the keyboard that are important to word processing:

- ✔ The two Shift keys work just like they do on a typewriter.
- ✔ If you hold down a key long enough, it *autorepeats* — that is, it repeatedly and rapidly types the character.
- ✔ The Backspace key doesn't just backspace; it deletes at the same time.

- ✔ The Tab key inserts an invisible character that pushes your text around. (Flip on over to Chapter 7 for more on tabs.)

Getting Around in Your Document

Sometimes you just want to look around in your document and check things out. Other times you want to move the insertion point to do some work on your document.

Looking around

You can scroll around to look at one part of the document, maybe to review something you wrote earlier (which I never do, personally), while leaving your insertion point (that vertical bar) where you're typing. Leaving your insertion point in place is convenient because while you look around, you don't lose your place. To perform this trick, scroll the document with the scroll bar on the right side or bottom of the document window. (See Chapter 2 for information on the scroll bar.)

If you type a word or if you press Delete, however, your view suddenly returns to the insertion point, because that's where you just typed. Works figures that, if you're working somewhere, you ought to be looking at what you're doing.

Moving around

To work someplace different, you move your insertion point. To move your insertion point by using the mouse, just click somewhere in your document. To move to another page, click the arrow buttons (shown back in Figure 5-1) to the left of the scroll bar at the bottom of the document window. (Your view changes, too.)

To move your insertion point by using the keyboard, press the arrow or other navigation keys, like Page Up and Page Down. Table 5-1 shows you how to move the insertion point by using the keyboard. See "Rapping about wrapping," earlier in this chapter, to read about how the insertion point moves from one line to another.

Table 5-1	Navigating with Keys
Navigation Key	*Where It Moves the Insertion Point*
Left-arrow/right-arrow	One character's worth left or right
Up-arrow/down-arrow	One line's worth up or down
Page Up/Page Down	One window's worth up or down
Home	Beginning of the line
End	End of the line
Ctrl+Home	Beginning of the document
Ctrl+End	End of the document

Seeing What Your Document Really Looks Like

One of the weird things about word processors is that they're all a little reluctant to show you *exactly* what your document looks like. In the Works word processor, you have three main ways of looking at your document (apart from printing it).

When you first start up the word processor, it shows a view of your work that is pretty close to, but not exactly, what you see when you print. For example, this first view doesn't show any page margins. Your word processor considers this view to be *Normal.* Humph.

A second view, called *Page Layout,* is a bit more exact. You can see your page breaks and margins realistically; also, if you use page numbers, headers, or footers, Page Layout view shows them. Normal view doesn't. Page Layout view is a bit slow to use, however: Works takes longer to show your changes as you make them, and your text may jump around as Works tries to figure out where to put the page breaks.

Finally, the *Print Preview* feature lets you see something that's as close to the paper printout as Works can manage. You can't work on the document while looking at it in Print Preview, however. For more on this feature, see Chapter 4.

  ✔ To switch to the more realistic Page Layout view, choose View➪ Page Layout in the menu bar.
  ✔ To return to the Normal view, choose View➪Normal in the menu bar.

As you add and delete text in your document, the page breaks move fairly often. In the Normal view, the top of each page is marked by an unobtrusive little >> symbol. In the Page Layout view, your pages actually break. A gap and a dividing line appear between one page and the next. This gap makes working in the vicinity of the page break — doing things like selecting text across the break — rather awkward. You probably want to use Normal view for most of your composing and then switch to Page Layout for final editing.

Printing

Ahh, printing. Where the ink meets the paper. So visceral, so satisfying, so . . . confusing! At least it is sometimes. When everything works well, printing is fun. But getting everything to work the way that you want it to work can be a bit exasperating.

Fortunately, printing is pretty much the same for all the tools of Works. That's why the place to read all about printing is in Chapter 4, not here. Here, I just give a quick executive summary and point out what's different about printing a word-processing document. *p. 65*

The executive summary goes like this:

✔ You can print your whole document or any set of pages in it.

✔ The easiest way to print a single copy of the whole document is to click the Print button in the toolbar.

✔ To print a portion of your document, click File⇨Print, or press Ctrl+P, and specify (in the Print dialog box) the pages that you want to print.

The main peculiarity of printing using the word processor is the *envelope* tool (or TaskWizard). For information on the envelope tool, see Chapter 8.

Saving Your Document

Saving your word-processing document is just like saving any other Works document: Click the Save button on the toolbar (the one with the diskette icon), or choose File⇨Save from the menu bar, or press Ctrl+S. See Chapter 2 for detailed information about saving documents.

Exiting the Word Processor

To exit the word processor, all you have to do is close your word-processing document. Click the X at the top right corner of the document window. (Do not click the X in the top right corner of the Works window unless you want to exit Works completely.) If you prefer using menus, click File⇨Close, or if you like using the keyboard, press Ctrl+W.

If your current document is still unsaved, or if it has changed since the last time you saved it as a file on a disk, Works puts up a dialog box to ask you if you want to save changes to your document. Click the Yes button, unless you really want to throw away what you've done since the last time you saved your work. If that's the case, click No.

Chapter 6

Hacking through the Jungle of Your Text

. . . .

In This Chapter

▶ Selecting text

▶ Deleting, moving, and copying text

▶ Repeating words and phrases

▶ Finding words and phrases

▶ Replacing words and phrases

▶ Looking up alternative phurds and wrases

▶ Correcting white-space errors

▶ Using the thesaurus

▶ Checking your spelling

. . . .

*H*as your document become a tangle of misplaced paragraphs, wrong-headed words, and excessively long, lengthy, redundant, and duplicate descriptions? Time to sharpen up the old machete and cut an editorial swath through the underbrush.

Here's how to find and target such text and then move it, copy it, delete it, or replace it. Gird your loins, buckle your swash, and have at it.

Selecting Your Target

In order to do anything to the text you've typed, such as move it or copy it, you have to be able to tell Works exactly which text you're talking about. This process is called *selecting* or *highlighting* text; and because selecting works pretty much the same in all the Works tools, it is covered in detail in Chapter 3. Recall that the following two methods of selection work any-where in Works:

- **Mouse method:** Click and drag the mouse cursor across the text you want to select. Release the mouse button when all the text you want to select is highlighted (white text on a black background).

- **Keyboard method:** Position the insertion point at one end of the text, hold down the Shift key, and then press an arrow key or another navigation key to expand the highlight. Release the keys when all the text you want to select is highlighted. For example, to select big gobs of text, press Shift+Page Up or Shift+Page Down; then switch to Shift+arrow keys for precision. Or to select forward from the insertion point to the end of the line, press Shift+End.

The word processor offers some additional selection options not found in the other tools:

- When you use the mouse, you can select one individual character at a time within the first word, but after you have selected more than one word, you get one word at a time. Why? Go figure. If you like working this way, fine. But if not, you can fix it. Choose Tools⇨Options, and then click the tab labeled Editing in the Options dialog box that appears. Click the check mark in the box labeled Automatic Word Selection.

- To select a line, click in the white area to the left of that line; to select several lines, hold down the mouse button and drag.

- To select a paragraph, double-click anywhere in the white area to the left of the paragraph. To select several paragraphs, hold down the mouse button when you make the second click and drag up or down.

- Finally, to select the whole document, choose Edit⇨Select All.

Chopping Up Your Text: Moving, Copying, and Deleting

Remember the machete that you strapped on at the start of this chapter? Time to unbuckle it. And put on your pith helmet, because now's the time to cut that editorial swath through your pithy prose.

To aid you in this worthwhile endeavor, the Works word processor provides a variety of features that let you move text around, delete blocks of text, and copy text that is too tedious to retype every time it needs to appear.

These features are pretty much the same in every tool in Works. So rather than repeat them here, I just give you the executive summary of how to edit text. (For a more thorough discussion, check out Chapter 3.)

✔ To delete a block of text, select it; then press the Delete or Backspace key.

✔ To move text, select it; then click it again and drag it with the mouse.

✔ To copy text, do the same thing as for moving text, but hold the Ctrl key down while you drag.

✔ To make multiple copies, select text and then press Ctrl+C; click wherever you want a copy of that something to appear and press Ctrl+V.

✔ To remove text and put a copy of it elsewhere, select it and then press Ctrl+X; then click wherever you want a copy to appear and press Ctrl+V.

You can use the buttons on the toolbar in place of the key combinations:

Ctrl+C is Copy, the button that shows two documents overlapping.

Ctrl+V is Paste, the button that shows a clipboard.

Ctrl+X is Cut, the button with the scissors.

Or you can find Copy, Paste, and Cut on the drop-down menu that appears when you click Edit.

Using Easy Text: Works' Electronic Parrot

If you need to use the same phrase over and over again, get a parrot. But if you need to *type* the same phrase over and over again, try Works' Easy Text feature — a sort of electronic parrot. Easy Text lets you record text and then play it back whenever you need it, instead of typing it over and over again. If, for instance, you were writing a rave review of *Microsoft Works 4.5 For Windows For Dummies* and needed to use the title repeatedly, you could type the title once and then use Easy Text to insert it thereafter. You can record several chunks of text in Easy Text and then choose them from a list to insert them. Each document keeps its own list of Easy Text phrases.

To record text in Easy Text, do the following:

1. **If you have already typed the text you want to record, highlight (select) it. Otherwise, just go to Step 2.**

2. **Choose Insert⇨Easy Text⇨New Easy Text.**

   The New Easy Text dialog box appears.

3. **Type a one-word name for your text using only letters or numbers.**

   For instance, you could type **title** as a name for *Microsoft Works 4.5 For Windows For Dummies*. (The name can also be the same as the text you want to insert: using **orange** as the name for "orange," for example.)

4. **Click in the Easy Text Contents box and type the text that you want to record, if it's not already there.**

   If, in Step 1, you selected the text you wanted to record, that text will already be in the Easy Text Contents box.

5. **To format the Easy Text using the Easy Format dialog box, click the Format button. Otherwise, click the Done button.**

   See Chapter 7 for more information on Easy Formats.

Inserting Easy Text that you have recorded is easy. Choose Insert⇨ Easy Text; then click the name of your Easy Text in the short menu that drops down. If you don't see the name in the menu, choose More Easy Texts to view the Easy Text dialog box. Click on the name of the Easy Text in that dialog box, and then click the Insert button.

To delete Easy Text, choose Insert⇨Easy Text⇨More Easy Texts. In the Easy Text dialog box, click on the name of your text, and then click the Delete button. A warning dialog box ask whether you really intend to delete that text; click Yes. Then click the Close button to return to your document.

Finding Elusive Fauna (Or, Where's That Word?)

In the jungle of words that is the typical document, it's easy to lose track of important words and phrases. Perhaps way back somewhere in a 70-page tome, you had a discussion of the fauna of temperate transition zones (such as the Chicago suburbs). You'd like to cross-reference that discussion at this point, but you can't remember quite where it was.

Finding a word or phrase is no problem for your efficient and jungle-wise guide, the Find dialog box.

Here's how to give this trusty companion its marching orders:

1. **Press Ctrl+Home.**

   This action moves the insertion point to the beginning of the document. Because the Find feature starts looking at the insertion point, pressing Ctrl+Home ensures that Works searches the entire document.

   Or if you know that what you seek is in a certain area, you may highlight (select) that area instead of pressing Ctrl+Home. The Find feature then restricts its search to the selected area.

2. Choose Edit⇨Find or press Ctrl+F.

The Find dialog box springs into action and presents itself for duty, as shown in Figure 6-1.

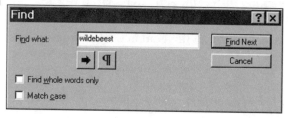

Figure 6-1:
Tell Find to
go forward
and seek a
word or
phrase.

3. Type the word or phrase that you want to look for in the Find What box.

If you know that the word or phrase you want has some capital letters, capitalize them here and turn on the Match Case feature. (Click the Match Case check box to enable the feature.) If, for example, you know that you are looking for a section of your document entitled *Wildebeest,* use the capital letter and enable the Match Case feature.

If the word or phrase you want to find includes a question mark, put the symbol ^ (Shift+6 on your keyboard) in front of the question mark. As it turns out, the ? symbol, when used in the Find dialog box, means "any character." By putting a ^ (pronounced "^") in front of the question mark, you tell Works, "No, stupid, I really mean a question mark. Sheesh."

4. Click Find Next or press Enter.

Find scurries forward into the underbrush, looking for *wildebeests* or whatever. When Find finds one, it highlights (selects) the *wildebeest* so that you can do stuff to it if you want to: delete it, format it, copy it, or just observe it in its habitat.

If Find can't find your word or phrase, it runs smack into the end of your document (or into the end of the text you selected for the search). Rubbing its forehead, Find puts up a little box to ask whether it should continue searching from the beginning of your document. Click Yes if you think that the *wildebeest* may be somewhere behind you. Other-wise, click No to return to the Find dialog box so that you can revise your marching orders.

If Find has searched the entire document (or all of the text that you had selected) without success, it puts up a box saying Works did not find a match, which is Workspeak for "Back to the drawing board." Click OK in this box to return to the Find dialog box.

5. **To find another instance of the word or phrase, click Find Next or press the Enter key again.**

   Remember that your document may be swarming with *wildebeest*s. Keep searching until you find the right one.

6. **To find something different, edit your search word or phrase in the Find What box.**

7. **Click the Cancel button in the Find box when you're done with your searching.**

Whole wildebeests or pieces?

Is it *wildebeest* or *wildebeast*? If you're not sure how to spell what you're searching for (or not sure that you spelled it right when you used it before), try typing in just the portion of the word or phrase that you are sure of. You can just type **wilde**, and you can be pretty certain of finding wilde-whatevers. This trick also works if you're simply lazy and don't want to type the beest/beast part. Sloth is not a sin in finding words. (Though when you're finding sloths — well, never mind.) This method also works if you want both singular and plural *wildebeest(s)*: Just leave off the *s*.

For any of these find-the-partial-word tricks to work, however, you have to make sure that the check box marked Find Whole Words Only (in the Find dialog box) does *not* have a check mark in it. Click that check box to clear the check mark if it is present.

Searching for wildebeests and finding Oscar Wilde

Sometimes it's not such a good idea to search for pieces of a word. The Find feature may return from the hunt with Oscar Wilde instead of a wildebeest. Very embarrassing. Alas, Find offers no way to tell it "Do not find dead playwrights."

Sticky boxes and words

The check boxes in the Find dialog box, such as Match Case, are *sticky*. No matter which way you leave them when you quit Find (checked or not checked), that's how they appear when you use Find again, later. Always look to be sure that the check box is marked correctly before you begin searching. The word that you type is also sticky (as are the words that you type when using the Replace dialog box).

So if there's a chance that your document includes both the fragment (*Wilde*) and the whole word (*wildebeest*), tell Find to search for whole words only. (A *whole word* is a bunch of characters set off by spaces or punctuation.) This whole-word option is very useful for short words, such as *an,* that crop up now <u>an</u>d again as fragments of other words.

To tell Find to search for whole words only, make sure that the check box marked Find Whole Words Only has a check mark in it. Click that check box if it does not.

Replacing Wildebeests with Whelks

If you've been typing along about wildebeests and suddenly realize that you meant *whelks,* not wildebeests, you have some personal problems that go beyond software, and I will not attempt to deal with them here. I can, however, tell you how to replace *wildebeest* with *whelk*.

Your companion on this environmentally dubious quest of replacing mammals with shellfish is not Find, but Find's twin, Replace. To use the Replace dialog box, you do exactly as you do with Find, giving a word or phrase to look for, except that you also give Replace something new to replace that word or phrase with. As Replace finds instances of the original word, you have the option of replacing each instance. You can also replace all instances.

Here's how to replace some text with other text:

1. Narrow the area for your search and replace, if you can.

Like Find, the Replace command starts searching from your insertion point and goes forward. Click just before the area in which you want to replace text. If you know what you seek is in a certain area, highlight (select) that area. Replace restricts its search to the selected area.

2. Choose Edit⇨Replace or press Ctrl+H.

The Replace dialog box springs into action and presents itself for duty, as shown in Figure 6-2.

3. Type the word or phrase that you want in the Find What box.

See "Finding Elusive Fauna (Or, Where's That Word?)" earlier in this chapter; the comments about capitalization, whole words, question marks, and invisible characters apply here as well.

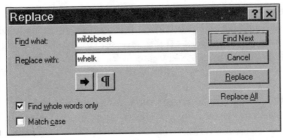

4. Type the replacement word or phrase in the Replace With text box.

Unless you specifically want the replacement word to always be capitalized, using all lowercase letters is best. If the original text is capitalized, Replace cleverly capitalizes the new text.

See "Finding Elusive Fauna (Or, Where's That Word?)" earlier in this chapter; the comments about invisible characters apply here as well.

5. Click the Find Next button or press Enter.

Replace scurries forward into the underbrush, looking for *wildebeest*s to replace. When Replace finds one, it highlights (selects) the *wildebeest* so that you can see whether this particular *wildebeest* is one that you want to replace.

If Replace can't find your word or phrase, it runs into the end of your document and, like its sibling, Find, asks if you want it to search from the start of the document. If this seems like a good idea, click Yes. If Replace has searched the entire document without success, it puts up a No Match Found box. Click OK in this box.

6. To replace the highlighted text, click the Replace button.

Poof! Your wildebeest is a whelk and happy as a clam.

Or to replace all instances of the search text, click the Replace All button. Replace All doesn't pause for each instance to ask your permission; it just does the replacement. If you selected a region of text back in Step 1, only that region is affected.

If you don't want to replace the particular instance that's currently highlighted, move on to Step 7.

7. To find another instance of the word or phrase, click the Find Next button or press Enter again.

Remember that your document may be swarming with *wildebeest*s. Keep searching until you find all the ones that you want to replace.

Replace lets you know when it has finished searching the whole document (or whatever text you selected).

8. When you're done with your replacing, click the Cancel button or the X in the upper-right corner of the Replace dialog box.

Here are a few tips and tricks for replacing:

✔ To replace a noun throughout your document, use the singular form (say, *wildebeest* or *whelk*) and make sure that the check box marked Find Whole Words Only does NOT have a check mark in it. (Click the check box, if it does.) Where you once had *wildebeests*, you now have *whelks*. (This trick doesn't work if you're changing *wildebeests* to *octopi*, however.)

✔ The Replace All button can be dangerous. Use it carefully and make sure that you are replacing only what you want to replace. If you want to change *days* to *weeks*, make sure that you're not changing *Sundays* to *Sunweeks*.

Finding and Replacing White-Space Characters

Many documents are teeming with invisible, microscopic life — tabs and paragraph marks, in particular — inserted by their authors to control the spaces within and between paragraphs. (See more about these invisible characters in Chapter 5.)

Finding and replacing these so-called *white-space characters* can sometimes be useful. For example, you may have long lists of items separated by commas (as in "apples, oranges, bananas, whale uvulas") and want to put the items on separate lines instead. If you replace the two separating characters "," (comma and space) with a paragraph mark, each item would appear on its own line.

An even more common task is replacing multiple tabs or paragraph marks with single ones. Newcomers to word processing often press the Tab key several times to indent, rather than using a single tab and setting the tab stop, or they press the Enter key multiple times to add space between paragraphs instead of changing the paragraph format. As newcomers get more familiar with word-processor formatting, they often want to change or get rid of some of these characters because the overabundant characters create more work.

In the Find or Replace dialog box, you can't simply press the Tab key to enter a tab character or press the Enter key to enter a paragraph mark. Works requires you to enter special codes to represent these characters. Because the tab and paragraph marks are so commonly used, Works provides buttons for entering their special codes in the Find and Replace dialog boxes. The buttons are marked with an arrow (for tab) and a backward P (for paragraph). If you click one of these buttons, it inserts a special code (^T for Tab and ^P for paragraph) wherever you have placed your insertion point (blinking cursor) in the Find What or Replace With text box. If you would rather type the codes yourself, you can do so. Type the ^ symbol by pressing Shift+6, and then type **T** (for tab) or **P** (for paragraph). You can also type ^**w** to find instances of repeated tab or space characters or type ^**d** to find manually-inserted page breaks.

Meeting the Mighty Thesaurus

Among the various critters roaming around in the word processor is a thesaurus. Although not quite as mighty as the brontosaurus, the thesaurus is, perhaps, superior in intelligence. Its basic job is to help you find alternative words. (Note, Star Trek fans, that I said alternative *words,* not alternative *worlds.* Stay with me here.) This thesaurus is nice and convenient, but it can't really hold a candle to a printed thesaurus (which is good, because they are generally flammable). Still, when you're stuck for a word, the Works thesaurus is good to have around.

The basic idea is to select (highlight) a word and then let the thesaurus look up alternatives. You can even select compound words, such as *blow up.* If the word can have several very different meanings (as the word *balloon* can have, for example), the thesaurus lists those and also lists alternative words within each meaning. You can explore alternatives for any of these words if you like. At any point, you can choose a word to replace the selected one.

Here's the click-by-click description of how to use the thesaurus:

1. **Select (highlight) the word you want to look up.**

2. **Choose Tools⇨Thesaurus (or press Shift+F7).**

   The Thesaurus dialog box of Figure 6-3 lumbers out of the wilderness and wants to be your friend.

3. **Click any likely looking word or phrase either in the Meanings box or in the list of synonyms just below the Replace With Synonym box.**

   Your substitute word can come from either list. If you click a *meaning,* you get a new list of synonyms to play with.

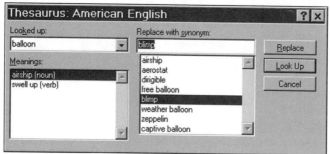

Figure 6-3:
The baby
thesaurus
in Works is
not purple,
but it still
wants to be
your friend.

4. **To look for synonyms to your synonyms, click anything in either list and then click the Look Up button.**

   You can keep up like this all day. From *balloon*, you can eventually float to almost anywhere. What fun! (If at any point you think "How the heck did I get here?" click the down-arrow next to the Looked Up window, and the whole list of what you've looked up so far drops down.)

5. **When, in either list, you see a good substitute word or phrase, click it and then click the Replace button.**

   Your original word or phrase in the document is replaced.

Your new word or phrase may not be any better than your old one, but what a good time you've had. Beats working!

Snaring Your Misspellings

Typos and misspellings sneak unnoticed into the undergrowth of any word-processing document. You may be amazed at how many errors you make that Works' spelling checker can discover and help you correct.

To start Works' spelling checker, press F7, or choose Tools⊅Spelling from the menu bar, or click the Spelling Checker button (the check mark with ABC) on the toolbar. Because the Works spelling checker is one of those helpful features that is available for several tools, you can find the details of using it in Chapter 3.

Chapter 7

Keeping Up Appearances

*E*ven when on safari in the world of word processing, one must keep up appearances. There's no excuse for frumpy fonts, untidy indentation, improper alignment, unkempt tab stops, and mismanaged margins. Indeed, those who format fastidiously can even print sideways and control page breaks.

In this chapter, I show you how to attain all those niceties of civilization — first-line indentation, line spacing, paragraph spacing, and more — automatically, without typing a bunch of tabs and blank lines. I work from the small to the large — from characters to paragraphs to documents — and explore how Works can help give your document a civilized and smart look.

Charming Characters

When your characters are losing their charm, it's time to look for a prettier face — typeface, that is (or *font,* as it is misnamed in the geeky world of computers). Works can put your type in any face (just what the world needs, more in-your-face typing) that you happen to have lying around on your PC, from stodgy Times New Roman to swirly Script. Not only that, but

Works can make the type large enough to see from across the room or small enough to be mistaken for flyspecks on your contracts. But wait! There's more! You can also easily change your font's style, making it **boldface**, *italic*, <u>underlined</u>, ^{superscript}, _{subscript}, or ~~strikethrough~~!

All told, you have three different kinds of formatting to play with: font, size, and style. These different aspects of type are sometimes called *character formatting*.

Changing the font, size, and style of your characters is one of those things that works the same way for all the tools of Works. So for full details, turn to Chapter 3. The executive summary goes like this:

Works offers three alternative techniques to change the way your type looks. To change the appearance of a particular chunk of text, first select (highlight) that text and then:

Alternative 1. Use the toolbar. The Font Name box is at the far left end of the toolbar, and the Font Size box is right next to it. The Bold, Italic, and Underline buttons (**B**, *I*, and <u>U</u>) are just right of the center of the toolbar. For the other styles, you have to use Alternative 2.

Alternative 2. Choose font, size, and style from something called the Font And Style dialog box. To get this dialog box, choose Format⇨ Font And Style.

Alternative 3. (To change style only) Press Ctrl+B for bold, Ctrl+I for italic, and Ctrl+U for underline.

To change the appearance of the text you are currently typing, use one of these alternatives with no text selected. In that case, you are changing the formatting of the insertion point. Any new characters that you type have the same formatting that the insertion point has. (To find out what the current formatting of the insertion point is, just look up at the toolbar.)

Pretty Paragraphs

There's no accounting for taste. (In fact, there's no Personnel, Purchasing, or any other department for taste.) Some folks like the first line of their paragraphs indented. Others, perhaps plumbing professionals, like them flush right. Some folks like their lines double-spaced, and maybe they like bigger spaces between paragraphs, too. All this stuff is called paragraph formatting, which all boils down to a few things you can fool with:

Spooky formatting changes

Sometimes you plunk your insertion point down, planning to do a little work in the middle of, say, Times New Roman text, and suddenly find yourself typing in, say, Oz Handicraft font. You recall having done a little Oz work the other day, but you had changed your mind and reformatted back to Times New Roman.

Most likely, your problem is that something invisible (like a space, tab, or paragraph mark)

follows your insertion point. You didn't reformat the invisible mark yesterday because you couldn't see it. The insertion point always takes on the formatting of the character that follows it, which is why your typeface is Oz. Press the Delete key to remove the invisible character. (Check out Chapter 5 for more on typing with these invisible characters.)

✔ **Indentations:** How far the paragraph's margins should be from the page's margins. Also how far from the left page margin the first line of the paragraph should be.

✔ **Alignments:** How the paragraph's text lines up with the margins.

✔ **Breaks:** Whether to split up a paragraph when it crosses over onto the next page or to keep the paragraph as one solid lump; also, sometimes you may want two paragraphs, like marriage partners, to stay with each other on the same page.

The big deal about using Works paragraph formatting is that you need to format only once if you want all your paragraphs to be the same. As you type, spawning new paragraphs from the original whenever you press the Enter key, the same paragraph formatting applies to those descendants.

In Works (a program that is trying, after all, to be all things to all people) you generally have two or three ways to do anything. Well, lots of ways are available to do paragraph formatting. Buttons, keystrokes, dialog boxes, the ruler bar, direct mind-to-chip control — you name it, it works. (Okay, I made one of them up.) Which ones you like may depend on whether you prefer pictures or lists, how picky you are about getting things to look just the way you want, your astrological sign, and so forth. So if in the course of this chapter you find yourself saying, "There's got to be an easier/more precise/ better way than that," keep reading. There probably is.

Alignments: Making your lines line up

Alignments are the simplest kind of paragraph formatting, so I get them out of the way first. Works has four kinds of alignment.

Left, left.

Centered, centered, centered, centered, centered, centered, centered, centered, centered, centered, centered, centered, centered.

Right, right.

Justified, justified.

There are two really easy ways to change alignment. First select the paragraphs you want to realign (or, for a single paragraph, simply click to place your insertion point anywhere within it), and then either:

✔ **Click one of the three alignment toolbar buttons.**

Toolbar buttons are above the ruler. The alignment buttons are at roughly the 4-inch mark, each showing a bunch of horizontal lines representing the lines of text in your paragraph. The buttons are, in order, Align Left, Align Right, and Align Center. For reasons best known to Microsoft, no Justify button is on the toolbar.

✔ **Or press the appropriate key on the keyboard.**

Ctrl+L for align left

Ctrl+Shift+R for align right

Ctrl+E for align centered

Ctrl+J for justified

If you happen to find yourself using the Format Paragraph dialog box for some other reason, you can alternatively click one of the four alignment buttons there. The Format Paragraph dialog box is explained later in this chapter and is shown in Figures 7-3 and 7-4.

Spaced-out paragraphs

Space is the final frontier of paragraph formatting. If you need a little air in your text, you can always ventilate your paragraph by double-spacing or adding space between paragraphs. But don't add spaces the way you did on your old Dumbrowski-Stanowitz steam-powered typing machine:

- ✔ Don't press the Enter key twice at the end of every line to double-space. (Don't even press it once.)
- ✔ Don't press the Enter key twice at the end of every paragraph to get spaces between your paragraphs.

The quick way to get space between paragraphs is by pressing Ctrl+0. (That's zero, not the letter O.) This puts one line's worth of space before the current paragraph if that space isn't there already. If one line's worth of space is already there, this action takes it away. You can also use keyboard commands to set the line spacing within a paragraph:

- ✔ Ctrl+1 single spaces the current paragraph (where your insertion point is).
- ✔ Ctrl+2 double spaces the current paragraph.
- ✔ Ctrl+5 imposes one-and-a-half-line spacing on the paragraph. Why 5? Well, in the strange math of Works, 5 = 1.5. Or at least it does here.

You can also do this stuff (and lots more) with the Format Paragraph dialog box. See "Having it your way: The Format Paragraph dialog box," later in this chapter.

Quick indenting and outdenting

If you're used to typing on a typewriter, you're probably accustomed to using the Tab key to indent stuff. In Works, the Tab key makes your text begin at the next tab stop. Unless you set things up differently, tab stops occur at every half-inch, starting at the left margin.

Using the Tab key is okay for the first line of a paragraph, but if you have to indent a whole paragraph or a series of paragraphs, tabbing gets pretty tedious. Here's a better way:

Select the paragraphs you want to indent (or, for a single paragraph, click anywhere in it), and then use Ctrl key combinations as follows:

✔ **To indent the left side:** Press Ctrl+M; the paragraph indents to the first built-in (so-called *default*) tab stop (normally at $^1\!/_2$ inch). Press Ctrl+M again, and your paragraph indents another half inch, and so on. (The *default* is the setting that Works uses until you tell it otherwise.)

✔ **To indent every line but the first line of the paragraph (called a *hanging* indent):** Press Ctrl+Shift+H.

✔ **To undo any left-side indentation:** Press Ctrl+Shift+M; this action *outdents* (reverses indentation) by one tab (moves the left edge of the paragraph left one default tab stop).

For more control over the indentation of a paragraph, you need to use something other than a Ctrl-key combination. Here are two ways to get fancier indentation:

✔ The fast way to do indentations at other than half-inch intervals is with the ruler bar. Check out "Indenting with the ruler" later in this chapter. The ruler also lets you indent the first line or the right edge of the paragraph.

✔ When you indent using Ctrl keys, Works uses the half-inch default indentation. You can change the default indentation by changing the default tab stops, which the "Setting, clearing, and changing tab stops with a dialog box" section in this chapter discusses.

The tab stops here

You know all about tab stops, right? Those things that you used to set on your Smith-Corona where, when you pressed the Tab key, you moved to the next stop? Nice and simple. Well, tabs are a tad (or a tab) more complex than they were on the old Smith-Corona, but they also do nice, new things.

Using the Tab key

Using the Tab key is a good way to do certain, um . . . tabular stuff, such as creating neatly lined-up columns of text or numbers. Using the Tab key is often not the best way to indent paragraphs, except perhaps for the first line of a paragraph. Tabs are a terrible way to indent every line of a paragraph. If you are pressing the Tab key repeatedly to move text around, you are creating a document that will be very awkward to edit later. To avoid that problem, learn to align paragraphs at the right margin, to indent by formatting paragraphs, or to set tab stops.

For more information on indentation, see the sections "Having it their way: Easy Formats" and "Having it your way: The Format Paragraph dialog box" in this chapter.

Most of the time, the Tab key works much like it did on your typewriter: When you press the Tab key, your text jumps to the next tab stop. In Works, unless you change the Tab stops yourself, stops are at every half-inch from the left margin.

The big difference between tabs in Works and tabs on a typewriter is that the Tab key in Works does its job by inserting a special tab character (normally invisible), whose job could be described as "creating a space between the preceding character and the next tab stop." (If you want to see the Tab character, choose <u>V</u>iew⇨<u>A</u>ll Characters.) Here are four examples of how that tab character behaves:

- ✔ If you begin a line by pressing the Tab key, you insert one tab character, and your text begins at the $1/2$-inch point (assuming standard Works half-inch tab stops).

- ✔ If you begin a line by pressing the Tab key twice, you insert two tab characters, and your text begins at the 1-inch point. (A better solution, however, would be to set your tab stop to one inch and insert one tab character. Setting tab stops often makes editing easier.)

- ✔ If you're typing, and your insertion point is currently at the 2-inch point, pressing the Tab key inserts a tab character, and that character forces subsequent text to begin at the next tab stop: the 2.5-inch point (again assuming standard Works half-inch tab stops).

- ✔ If you add a half-inch worth of text at the beginning of that same line, the text following the tab character jumps to the 3-inch point (which is the next tab stop).

Newfangled tab stops

Your Smith-Corona had only one kind of tab stop. Works (like most word processors) has four kinds of tab stops:

- ✔ **Left tab stop:** The conventional tabs that you're accustomed to are called left tabs in a word processor because, after you press the Tab key, what you type begins after the stop; therefore, the text has its left edge at that point. Works uses left tab stops unless you tell it otherwise, and it presets them every half-inch, starting at the left margin.

- ✔ **Decimal tab stop:** For columns of numbers, you may want to use the decimal tab stop, which aligns every number at the decimal point. You set the tab stop in the position where you want the decimal point to be (or at the end of a number without a decimal point). When you type a number (having first set up the tab stop and then pressed the Tab key to move to this stop), Works types — oddly enough — to the left of this stop. Works continues to type to the left of the stop until you type a decimal point; then it types to the right of the stop.

- **Right tab stop:** Unsurprisingly, the right tab stop is the opposite of the traditional or left tab stop. Instead of the left edge of text aligning with this stop, the right edge does. When you type (having first set up the tab and then pressed the Tab key to move to this stop), Works shifts text over to the left, keeping the right edge of the text aligned with the tab stop.

- **Center tab stop:** After you set up one of these guys, press the Tab key to move to it and then start to type. Works shuffles your characters left and right as you go, in order to keep your text centered on the tab position. Whatever you type ends up centered at the tab stop.

To see the four kinds of tab stops in action, skip way ahead in this chapter and check out the examples in Figure 7-2. How do you set these tab stops? You can set all four types of stops with the help of the Format Tabs dialog box, which is discussed next.

Setting, clearing, and changing tab stops with a dialog box

If you want something other than the conventional tab stops of a left tab every half-inch, the time has come to have a little dialog. A little dialog box, that is — one that helps you set the position and alignment of your tab stops. Check out Figure 7-1. You, too, can get one of these lovely dialog boxes by choosing Format⇨Tabs; but first, read the following discussion about how the Format Tabs dialog box works.

You may find that setting, clearing, and moving conventional left tab stops is easiest by using Works' ruler. See the section "The ruler — a benevolent monarch" later in this chapter. However, to set tab stops very precisely (say, at 1.37 inches), or to set right, center, or decimal tab stops, use the Format Tabs dialog box.

The executive summary of how to use the Format Tabs dialog box goes like this: Work on one tab stop at a time (identified by its position), specify its alignment or leader (the character that fills the space that the tab creates — usually none), and then click the Set button. As you create new stops, they are listed in the larger of the two white boxes under the label Tab Stop Position. You can delete a tab stop or change its alignment by first clicking it in that box and then using the controls in the dialog box.

The blow-by-blow instructions for using the Format Tab dialog box to add, remove, or modify a tab stop are as follows:

1. **Select the paragraphs whose stops you want to set or change.**

    If you don't select anything, Works assumes that you want to format the paragraph where the insertion point is. Select multiple paragraphs to give them all the same tab stops.

Click the type of tab stop that you want.

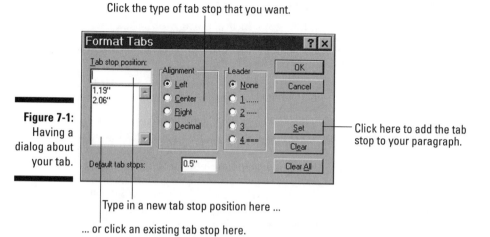

Figure 7-1:
Having a
dialog about
your tab.

Click here to add the tab
stop to your paragraph.

Type in a new tab stop position here ...

... or click an existing tab stop here.

2. Get a Format Tabs dialog box, if you haven't already.

You have two ways to get a Format Tabs dialog box:

- Choose Format⇨Tabs. (Or press Alt+O and then press T.)
- Double-click the top of the ruler bar (where the numbers are).

Any tab positions already set in the selected paragraph are listed in the largest white box at the left side of the dialog box. Works' default tab stops are listed in the box labeled Default Tab Stops.

3. To add a new tab stop, type its position in the box labeled Tab Stop Position.

Click the box immediately under the Tab Stop Position label and type the position you want the tab stop to take (measured from the left margin). Whatever you do in the dialog box — changing alignment and so on — now applies to that Tab stop position.

3a. Or, to modify or clear an existing tab stop, click it in the list box (the largest white area) at the left of the Format Tabs dialog box.

That tab stop position now appears in the box labeled Tab Stop Position. Any settings you make in the dialog box now apply to that tab stop position.

4. Click an alignment for this tab stop in the Alignment area.

See the preceding section, "Newfangled tab stops," for a discussion of the different types of alignment.

5. Click Set to add this tab stop to your paragraph.

When you add your own tab stops, Works removes any default tab stops between the left margin and your new tab stop.

6. **To remove this tab stop, click Clear.**

7. **To clear out all the tab stops in this paragraph, click Clear All.**

8. **Repeat with additional tab stops until you have just the tab stops you want in the Tab Stop Position list box.**

   To review the tabs' alignments, just click them in the list box.

9. **Click the OK button.**

The Format Tabs dialog box also says something about a leader. No, the tabs have not formed a political system. Normally, when you type on a typewriter and press the Tab key, you get a blank area up to the position of the tab stop. That's not necessarily true in Works. A *leader* is what Works puts in this area. For example, in a table of contents, you may want a line of dots or something between the topic and the page number (like the one in this book). To have a leader associated with a tab stop, click 1, 2, 3, or 4 to choose one of the four styles shown in the Leader area; otherwise, click None.

Finally, if you really don't want to set a bunch of individual tab stops but would like to change the spacing of the tab stops that Works provides (the default tab stops), just type a new spacing in the Default Tab Stops text box. These tab stops are important because Works uses them for indenting paragraphs, as discussed in the upcoming sections.

The ruler — a benevolent monarch

Nothing keeps order like a good ruler, so the Works word processor comes equipped with a royal one. Sometimes Works is a *royal* something else, but this ruler is a benevolent monarch.

If your ruler is missing, choose View⇨Ruler. Don't be shy; if a cat can look at a king, you can View your Ruler.

The ruler reigns over indentations, alignments, and tab stops. A modest kingdom, perhaps, but an important one. See how it rules the indentations, alignments, and tab stops in Figure 7-2.

Notice how the left side of the paragraph in Figure 7-2 aligns with the paragraph indent mark. Also, the first line aligns with the first line indent mark. (Pretty reasonable, huh?) The author of the document in Figure 7-2 entered tabs to position things. Dates in the table are aligned along their left edges because this clever author used a particular kind of tab stop, called the left tab stop. For the numbers, he used a decimal tab stop, which caused the numbers to align along their decimal points. And the locations align along their right sides because of (everyone together now — yes, that's right) the right tab stop. Finally, the whole line comes to a stop at the right paragraph indent mark. And now this paragraph comes to a stop, not a minute too soon.

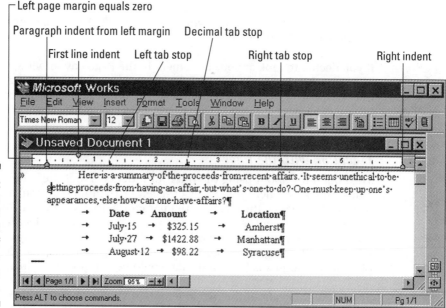

Figure 7-2: The ruler: a kindly and powerful monarch of the word-processing realm.

The ruler shows you what's going on in the paragraph where your insertion point currently resides. Or, if you select a paragraph, the ruler tells about the paragraph you selected. The ruler can apply itself to only one paragraph at a time. If you select a bunch of paragraphs, it shows you the first one.

The totally, utterly cool thing about the ruler is that it not only *shows* you the paragraph stuff, it also lets you *control* the paragraph stuff. I know; this news is pretty exciting, right? Read on.

Reading the ruler

As any good subject knows, it is important to understand your ruler. In particular, with this ruler, understanding what the tick marks and numbers correspond to is vital. Looking at the zero-inch mark, for example, you may well say, "Zero inches to what?"

Well, zero is where the left margin of your page is. All points on the ruler are measured from this left margin.

The tick marks are at ¹/₈-inch intervals if you're using inches. (You can set your indentations and tab stops at even more precisely measured intervals than ¹/₈ inch.) To use units other than inches, choose Tools⇨Options. See the sidebar "Hooked on metrics" in Chapter 4 for details.

The tiny little T leaves — I mean, T-shaped marks — at ¹/₂-inch intervals are the built-in tab settings. You can put in your own tab marks, too, where you want them; but the tab marks you insert look like Ls, not like upside-down Ts. More on tabs in a minute.

If you decide to look at your document in the Page Layout view, your ruler changes a bit. Suddenly, negative numbers appear to the left of zero. The only purpose of the negative numbers is to show how big your page margin is; you can't put anything in the margin. (That would violate its marginosity.) For more on Page Layout, take a look at Chapter 5.

Indenting with the ruler

The cool thing about using the ruler for indents is that the ruler lets you adjust them graphically. Just click the left or right indentation mark and drag it. You change the edges of the paragraph that your insertion point is currently on. To set the edges of a bunch of paragraphs, select the paragraphs before you drag the marks. These edges are technically called the left and right paragraph indentations, not paragraph margins. (Not thinking of them as margins is hard, but that would be marginal thinking.)

The tricky thing about the two indentation marks on the left side is that they are related, like twins. These marks are like a split version of the right indent mark. The top half of this split triangle controls only the first line of the paragraph. The bottom half of the triangle controls the entire paragraph. The weird result of this split triangle is that when you move the bottom half, the top half always moves along with it! The idea is, apparently, that you probably want to keep the first line indent the same when you change the paragraph indent.

So having said all that, here's the blow-by-blow on changing paragraph indentations with the ruler:

1. **Select the paragraphs you want to indent.**

   If you don't select anything, Works assumes that you want to format the paragraph where the insertion point is.

2. **To indent the first line, drag the top triangle of the pair of triangles on the left of the ruler bar.**

3. **To indent the whole paragraph, drag the bottom triangle of the pair.**

4. **To indent the right side of the paragraph, drag the triangle on the right side of the ruler bar.**

You can also change indentations by using a dialog-box approach. The dialog box is not as cool and graphical as the ruler, but the dialog box is easier to use for those of us who are riding in a car across Connecticut at the moment with a mouse that keeps falling off our knees as we try to move those tiny triangles around. See "Having it your way: the Format Paragraph dialog box" earlier in this chapter.

Tab stops on the ruler

For setting nice, normal tab stops of the conventional sort that you would approve marrying into your family (left tab stops, I mean), the ruler is ideal. For anything newfangled and outlandish, such as decimal or right tab stops, see "The tab stops here" earlier in this chapter. The ruler bar shows you these crazy newfangled tabs, but it quite stodgily refuses to have anything else to do with them (other than remove them, that is).

Works already provides a nice set of built-in tab stops, spaced about every $1/2$ inch (if you're using inches). (The built-in tab stops are the little upside-down T marks under the tick marks.) If you want more tab stops, just follow this complicated instruction:

Click in the bottom half of the ruler where you want your tab.

That's all.

Your (left) tab marks look like tiny arrows that go left and then up. (An arrow that goes straight up is a center tab stop; if the arrow has a decimal point next to it, the tab is a decimal tab; and if the arrow goes right and then up, the tab is a right tab.) Here's what to do with the tabs when you've got them:

- To move your tab marks around, drag 'em. The built-in default marks that fall before or between your marks are conveniently removed.

- To remove one of your tab marks, drag it off the ruler and into the document, where it evaporates in the rarefied atmosphere of your prose.

- To go for an exotic right, center, or decimal tab mark, double-click the ruler bar and see the section "The tab stops here," earlier in this chapter.

Having it your way: The Format Paragraph dialog box

For one-stop shopping in the world of paragraph formatting, use the Format Paragraph dialog box shown in Figures 7-3 and 7-4. This two-card dialog box supplies nearly all your paragraph formatting needs. Indentations, alignments, breaks, mufflers — you name it; everything paragraphish except for tab stops.

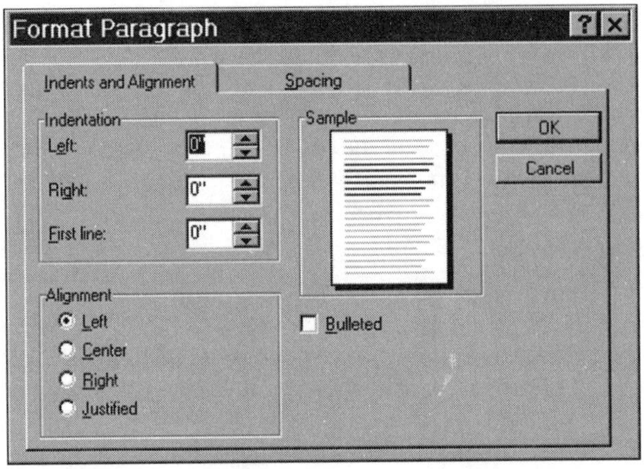

Format Paragraph

| Indents and Alignment | Spacing |

Indentation
Left: [0"]
Right: [0"]
First line: [0"]

Sample

OK
Cancel

Alignment
- Left
- Center
- Right
- Justified

□ Bulleted

Figure 7-3:
The Indents And Alignment card from the Format Paragraph dialog box.

Format Paragraph

| Indents and Alignment | Spacing |

Spacing
Before: [0li]
After: [0li]
Line spacing: [Auto]

Sample

OK
Cancel

□ Don't break paragraph
□ Keep paragraph with next

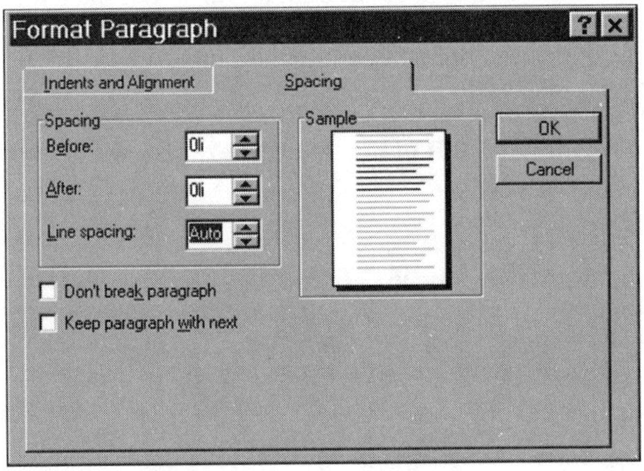

Figure 7-4:
The Spacing card from the Format Paragraph dialog box.

Begin by placing your insertion point in a paragraph to be formatted or selecting several paragraphs. Then get a Format Paragraph dialog box in either of two ways:

- ✔ Choose Format⇨Paragraph. (Or press Alt+O and then press P on the keyboard.)
- ✔ Double-click the left or right indent marks on the ruler bar.

The box looks like two index cards — one named Indents And Alignment, and the other named Spacing (which does breaks). You can switch between them by clicking the top tab of the hidden card. Both cards have a Sample box that shows you what the reformatted paragraph may look like on a page.

You use the Format Paragraph box by making whatever changes you want on the two cards and then clicking the OK button. Nothing is changed in your document until you click OK. If at any time you click the Cancel button, you return to your paragraph unchanged.

Indents, alignments, and bullets

The Indents And Alignment card has an Indentation box, an Alignment box, a Sample box, and a Bulleted check box. The Indentation box contains three boxes that work as follows:

- ✔ **Left:** Sets the distance between the left paragraph margin and the left page margin.

- ✔ **Right indentation:** Sets the distance between the right paragraph margin and the right page margin.

- ✔ **First line:** Sets the distance between the left page margin and the beginning of the first line.

You can type a number into any of the three boxes and get that many inches of indentation. Or you can click the up or down arrows beside the boxes to raise or lower the number inside. By using these controls, you can indent paragraphs without having to type tabs. You can also control indentation with the ruler bar, discussed earlier in this chapter.

In the Alignment box, click the white dot next to your chosen alignment's name. You can get any of the four basic alignments (Left, Center, Right, and Justified). (If you've forgotten what these terms mean, see "Alignments: Making your lines line up" earlier in this chapter.)

- ✔ A *bulleted* paragraph has a black dot next to it and is indented a little, like this paragraph. To bullet a paragraph, click the check box next to Bulleted to put a check mark in it. (Clicking an empty check box puts a check mark in it if it is empty, and clicking a checked box makes it empty.)

Spacing between paragraphs and between lines

The Spacing card of the Format Paragraph dialog box (shown in Figure 7-4) tells Works how this paragraph should get along with its neighbors and how much space to put between its own lines. Here's how to use the Spacing card:

- ✔ To tell Works how many lines to skip before or after the paragraph, type numbers into (or click the up and down arrows next to) the Before and After boxes.

✔ To tell Works how many lines to skip between lines of the paragraph, use the Line spacing box. Setting Line spacing to 2, for example, double-spaces the paragraph. You can use fractional lines greater than 1, such as 2.5, as well.

✔ To prevent Works from putting part of the paragraph on one page and part on the next, click in the Don't Break Paragraph check box to put a check mark there.

✔ To make sure that this paragraph and the next stay on the same page if at all possible, put a check mark in the Keep Paragraph With next check box. (Of course, if the paragraphs are more than a page long, there is no way to keep them on the same page.)

Having it their way: Easy Formats

If your taste in paragraph formatting is at all like the taste of most other humans on the planet, you're in luck. (Actually you're in luck even if your taste is pretty weird, as long as it matches the taste of somebody at Microsoft.) Works has a couple dozen real pretty off-the-shelf formats, called Easy Formats, that you can choose from.

An Easy Format consists of a paragraph format — and in some cases, a character format as well, which applies to all the characters in the paragraph.

To use an Easy Format:

1. **Select the paragraphs you want to format.**

   If you don't select anything, Works assumes that you want to format the paragraph where the insertion point is.

2. **Click the Easy Formats button.**

   It's the button near the right end of the toolbar, and it looks like a document with a gleam or sparkle on its corner. What you get is a menu with Create From Selection at the top, More Easy Formats at the bottom, and five strange-looking names in between.

   Those five names refer to the five most recently used paragraph formatting styles. (Bet you never thought of paragraph formatting styles as having names, but unlike all those poor Unsaved Documents, they do.)

3. **If you recognize one of the five listed formats from its name, click it.**

   Done. Your paragraph is reformatted. Don't like it? Undo it by pressing Ctrl+Z, and go back to Step 1.

4. If none of the listed format names are familiar to you, click More Easy Formats.

Now you see the Easy Formats dialog box, pictured in Figure 7-5. On the left is the complete list of format names. The Sample box in the center gives a hazy rendition of how the selected format looks on a page. The Description box gives you the technical details of the selected format. ("Prestige body" is my favorite. Want one? Just a click is all it takes.)

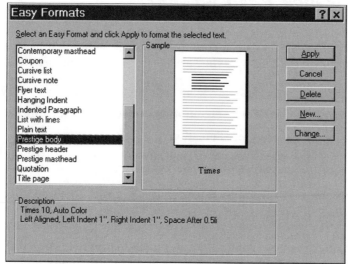

Figure 7-5:
Easy
Formats, the
fast food of
paragraph
formatting.

5. Select a format from the Easy Formats dialog box.

You do this step by clicking the format's name in the list on the left side of the box. Check out the Sample box to see if your selection makes the text look like what you want. If your selection does not suit you, click another format name. After you've chosen one that looks promising, move to Step 6. Or you can decide that reformatting was all a bad idea and click Cancel, which returns you to your pristine, unreformatted paragraphs.

6. Click the Apply button.

The Easy Formats dialog box goes away, and your reformatted paragraphs await you.

If you're hunting for something amusing to do instead of working, cruise through some of the Easy Formats. The Coupon format is a hoot, and so is Cursive note.

Until you have confidence that you know what you're doing, stay away from the Change or New buttons in the Easy Formats dialog box. These buttons transport you to the cleverly named Change Easy Formats or New Easy Formats dialog boxes, which have more power than most of us really ought to wield.

Having it your way all the time: Creating your own Easy Formats

If you find yourself using the same combination of character and paragraph formatting again and again (and the combination is not already an Easy Format), you can put it on the Easy Format list. All you have to do is:

1. **Select a paragraph that is already formatted the way that you want.**

2. **Click the Easy Formats button; a drop-down menu appears.**

3. **Choose _C_reate From Selection.**

   This step invokes the New Easy Format dialog box, with most of its buttons grayed out.

4. **Name your format by typing in the box with the blinking cursor.**

5. **Click the _D_one button.**

Now your newly named format can appear on the Easy Formats menu. (See "Having it their way: Easy Formats," earlier in this chapter.)

Pages, Margins, and Sideways Documents

All this stuff about letters and paragraphs and stuff is just dandy, but what about the document? How big is a page, what's on what page, and what are the margins? Good questions.

Works begins (as usual) by assuming a bunch of stuff about the page — the _page defaults_:

- ✔ You're using $8\frac{1}{2}$-x-11-inch paper, oriented the normal way for a letter.

- ✔ Top and bottom margins are 1". Left and right margins are 1.25". If you're using headers and footers, they are .5" from the top and .75" from the bottom, respectively.

The places where Works puts page breaks follow from these settings and from how big and airy you want to format your characters and paragraphs. You can change these page breaks if you like.

Most of this formatting-of-the-overall-document stuff is tucked away inside the Page Setup dialog box.

Page Setup

To set up your document's overall appearance (which is not to imply that it looks like a pair of old overalls), do the following:

Choose File⇨Page Setup. (Or press Alt+F and then press G.)

This action wins you a Page Setup dialog box. When you first use this Page Setup command, the top card is the Margins card shown in Figure 7-6. These cards all deal with different aspects of page setup and printing. Click a card's tab, sticking out at the top, to choose it. (If you change to another card before quitting the Page Setup dialog box, that card is on top the next time that you use this dialog box.)

Each card in the dialog box also shows you a Sample to give you a rough idea of what your document can look like using the changes you make. One quirk to be aware of is that if you type something into a box, the Sample doesn't show your changes until you click in a different box.

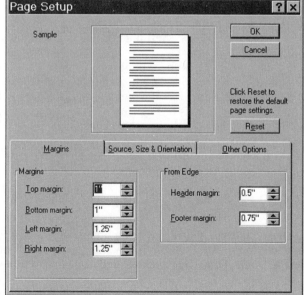

Figure 7-6:
Page Setup stuff looks like Mom's recipe card file, but without the blueberry pie stains. This is the card for Margins.

Margins

Using the Page Setup dialog box in Figure 7-6 (choose File⇨Page Setup if the Page Setup dialog box is not already up), click the tab marked Margins.

To change one of the margins listed on this card, click the box for a margin and edit the margin setting or type in a new number. If you're not sure how to do that, see Chapter 1 for more information.

The default unit is inches, so if you want inches, just type the number. If you want to use another unit, type the number and then one of the following abbreviations for the unit: **cm** for centimeters, **mm** for millimeters, **pi** for picas, and **pt** for points. If you live in a sensible country that uses metric units, you can change the default. Flip over to Chapter 4 for more on metrics.

The Sample doesn't show your changes until you click in a different box from the one you just edited. The Sample box is just weird that way.

To go back to using the default margin values, click the Reset button.

Click OK if you're all done setting up the page.

Sideways documents

If you want to print sideways, most PC printers these days let you do that. Because you can't normally put paper sideways into your printer, your printer has to be able to type sideways — which your printer can probably do, unless it uses type-wheels like some typewriters use. You just have to let Works know that sideways printing is what you have in mind. Use the Page Setup dialog box (choose File⇨Page Setup if the box is not already up).

In the Page Setup dialog box, click the tab marked Source, Size & Orientation. Then click Landscape in the lower-left corner to print sideways. (Portrait is the usual orientation, like the *Mona Lisa*.) The page icon, with the letter A, illustrates how type is to be printed on the page. The Sample also changes to show you how the lines of text run.

Click OK unless you need to set up something else, such as the paper size.

Different-sized documents

If you're using anything other than $8^1/_2$-x-11-inch paper (or if you're using an envelope), you need to tell Works about it. (Works has special features for envelopes: See Chapter 8.) Use the Page Setup dialog box (to pull it up, press Alt+F and then press G).

1. **In the Page Setup dialog box, click the tab marked S̲ource, Size & Orientation.**

2. **On the S̲ource, Size & Orientation card, click the box marked Si̲ze.**

   Use the scroll bar to find more.

3. **Click one of the standard paper or envelope sizes in the box that drops down.**

   If you're using a paper size that's not shown here, click the box marked Width and type in a new value; then do the same for Height. (Width always refers to the direction that a line of text runs.) After your last change, click in a different box from the one that you're in and check the Sample to see if things look roughly correct.

4. **Click the R̲eset button if you want to return to the default paper size.**

5. **Click OK if you're all done setting up the page.**

Page breaks

When you fill one page, Works begins another page automatically as you're typing. If you want the page to break at an earlier location, you can put in a page break yourself. If you want the page to break later, forget it. Works can't squeeze any more on a page unless you change some formatting.

Most of the time, Works' automatic page breaks are just fine because Works counts lines and measures spaces much better than you can (it being a computer program and all). But occasionally you know something that Works doesn't, such as the fact that this particular line is the start of a new chapter and really needs to come at the top of a page. Then you want to be able to put in a page break by hand. (Well, by typing on the keyboard or something.) This is what has happened in Figure 7-7. p̲l̲2̲8̲

You can avoid an inconvenient page break when it breaks up a paragraph or breaks between two consecutive paragraphs that you really want to keep together. Look at "Having it your way: The Format Paragraph dialog box" and Figure 7-4, both in this chapter. p̲l̲2̲0̲

You can also use page breaks to make a blank page (by putting in a pair of them) or to force a page to appear on the left or right side in a bound document (such as this book). Don't try this last trick until you have finished making all the edits. (Otherwise, you may have to repaginate the entire book.)

Here's how to put in your own page break:

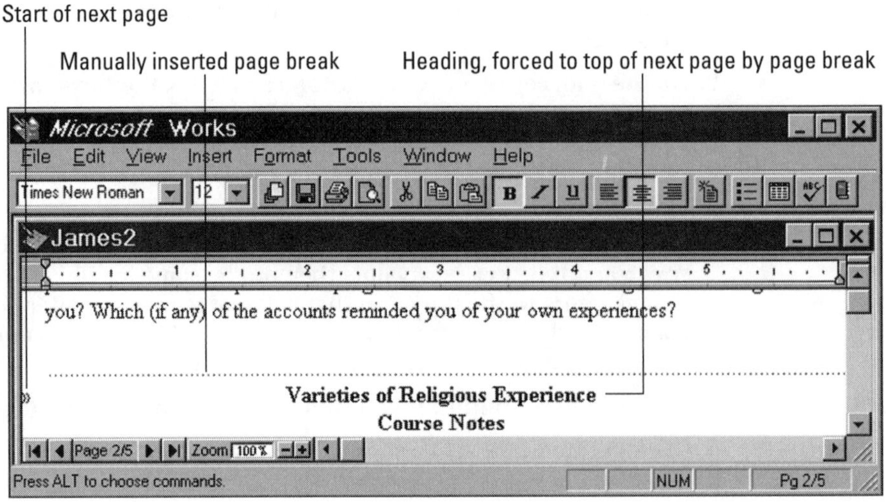

Start of next page

Manually inserted page break   Heading, forced to top of next page by page break

Figure 7-7:
Give
yourself a
break — a
manual
page break.

you? Which (if any) of the accounts reminded you of your own experiences?

Varieties of Religious Experience
Course Notes

1. Click exactly where you want the page break to occur.

If the page break is to occur between paragraphs, click at the beginning of the first line of the paragraph that's going on the next page. Clicking at the beginning of the first line avoids problems with invisible paragraph marks.

2. Press Ctrl+Enter or choose Insert⇨Page Break.

A dotted line appears; this is your page break symbol, as shown in Figure 7-7. You can delete, cut, paste, or drag the page break symbol just like any other symbol on the page. To select the page break by itself, click in the left margin next to the symbol.

Your manual page break appears on the screen as a faint dotted line. After your page break, Works continues to do its own normal, automatic page-breaking thing. In the Normal view, Works' automatic page breaks can be a little hard to find. The only indication is the little >> mark in the left margin at the top of a page. In Page Layout view, page breaks are really obvious. (For more information on what your document really looks like, go to Chapter 5.) p 89

Don't do any more page-breaking than you absolutely must. If you try to do your own break for every page, you can have a mess on your hands if you add or delete text later. If you add or delete text later, you must then reposition every page break!

Chapter 8

Fancier Word-Processing Documents

· ·

In This Chapter

▶ Bulleted lists

▶ Headers and footers

▶ Page numbers

▶ Footnote fundamentals

▶ Tables and charts

▶ Lines and borders

▶ Columns

▶ Envelopes

· ·

*I*t's payoff time! You've paid your dues. You've editorially slashed your way through the jungles of text and stood your ground in the face of pouncing paragraphs, rampaging thesauruses, and terrible tab stops. Now's the time to have a little fun. (*Fun* in the highly abstract, metaphoric sense of the word, that is. If you really find yourself eagerly looking forward to adding footnotes to a document, you may want to consider enlisting the aid of some competent professional.)

One way to make a fancier document is to add graphics of various kinds, such as charts or pictures. This chapter discusses charts, but if you want to add pictures, see Chapter 21.

Bulleted Lists: Shooting from the Toolbar

It's a jungle out there, and a few bullets may come in handy — bulleted lists, that is. Bulleted lists are made up of indented paragraphs, each with a little dot next to its first line. The paragraphs may be single- or multi-line (regular) paragraphs; Works doesn't care.

If you want simple, big-black-dot-style bullets, you can get them easily from the Bullets button on the toolbar. (The icon on the Bullets button looks like a bulleted list.) All you have to do is type your paragraphs in the usual way, select the ones you want to bulletize, and then click the Bullets button.

The Bullets button indents your paragraph to the first default tab stop — the stops marked with little upside-down Ts on the ruler — not tab stops that you have created. To change these tab stops, see Chapter 7. You can also adjust indentation from the keyboard. Each time you press Ctrl+M, the indentation increases by one tab stop. Pressing Ctrl+Shift+M does the opposite — it shrinks the indentation by one tab stop.

You can remove bullets without an anesthetic. Just select the proper paragraphs and hit the Bullets button again.

Bullets are a paragraph-format kind of thing. So you can get a new, prebulleted paragraph by pressing Enter within any bullet-formatted paragraph. This feature lets you type with bulleting *on* and spawn new bulleted paragraphs as you go.

Heavy Ammo: The Format Bullets Dialog Box

Bullets of any make and caliber are available from the Format Bullets dialog box, shown in Figure 8-1. To use this dialog box for your ammo, click in the paragraph to be bulleted (or select several paragraphs by dragging across them); then choose Format⇨Bullets.

Click the bullet of your choice in the Bullet Style box. Adjust the bullet's caliber in the Bullet Size box by either typing a number into the box or clicking the up-/down-arrows next to the box. Click the Hanging Indent check box to set or clear the check mark there, and watch the effect in the Sample window.

Click OK when you have the format you want. Or disarm your paragraph by clicking the Remove button in the Format Bullets dialog box. The box closes and the bullet disappears.

Headers, Footers, and Page Numbers

You probably don't need to be told what page numbers are, but headers and footers may be unfamiliar to you. *Headers* and *footers* are chunks of text that

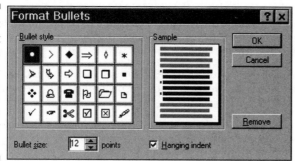

Figure 8-1:
The Format
Bullets
dialog box,
where
Works
stores its
heavy
ammunition.

appear on every page of a document in a special location at the top (for headers) or at the bottom (for footers). Headers and footers are typically used for chapter or section titles or to remind everyone who the author is.

How do page numbers fit into this discussion of headers and footers? Page numbers in Works are a special feature that you add to a footer (or a header).

Inserting headers and footers

In Works, you don't create a header or footer for each page individually. You create a single header or footer that appears on every page of the document. Usually the text of a header or footer is exactly the same on every page, but there are a couple of special cases. One special case is page numbers. (For every page to have the same number would be kind of useless.) Another special case is the first page of a document. You can, if you like, have a header or footer on every page *except* the first one.

To put a header or footer into your document, just follow these instructions:

1. **Choose View⇨Header (or Footer). (Or if you are in Page Layout view, you can just move the insertion point to the header or footer box by clicking it.)**

   This step does a couple of things. First, it puts your document into Page Layout view. Second, it moves the insertion point to the header (or footer) box on the current page.

2. **Type the text that you want to appear on each page.**

   Anything that you can put in ordinary text, you can put in a header or footer. Bold, italic, giant fonts, alignments, Easy Formats — anything goes.

3. **If you want page numbers, the date or time, or the document name to appear in your header or footer, move the insertion point to the place you want your choice to appear, click Insert on the menu bar and make a selection from the drop-down menu.**

   If you then click Page Number or Document Name, a special code appears in the header or footer box. (These special codes look like *page* and *filename*. But oddly enough, just typing *page* or *filename* from the keyboard won't do the trick.)

   If you want your first page to be some number other than 1, you need to use the Page Setup dialog box. Move to Step 4.

   Clicking Date and Time takes you to a list of many, many possible date and time formats. Click the format you like, and it gets inserted into the header or footer. The outcome may look like something you could easily have typed yourself, such as "4:15 Wednesday." But every time you print or print preview your document, the date and time are updated.

4. **If you want to prevent header or footer text from appearing on the first page, choose File⇨Page Setup.** *p125*

   The Page Setup dialog box appears. (You can see it in Figure 7-6 in Chapter 7.) The Page Setup dialog box has three cards on it. Click the tab that says Other Options: This action exposes the Other Options card. On this card's left side are three check boxes: No Header On First Page, No Footer On First Page, and Print Footnotes At End. Click the one(s) that you want.

   The Other Options card of the Page Setup dialog box also allows you to select whatever number you want to appear on your first page. (All right, all right, the number has to be an integer. You can't choose a number like π. Good grief!) Type a number into the Starting Page Number box at the top of the card, or click the up-/down-arrows.

   When you are done with the Page Setup dialog box, click OK.

Inserting single-line headers and footers (with page numbers)

The header and footer boxes come equipped with their own special tab stops: a center tab in the center and a right tab on the right margin. These tabs make life easy if you just want a one-line header (or footer) that has something on the left, something in the center, and something on the right. So the following is what you can do if you want a header that has, for the sake of an example, the document name on the left, a page number in the center, and the date on the right:

1. **Choose View⇨Header.**

   Or click Footer if you want to do a footer. Everything else is exactly the same.

2. **Enter what you want to appear on the left side.**

   To create the example header, you would choose Insert⇨Document Name. This step inserts the code `*filename*` into the left side of the header box. This is just an example; if you don't want the document's filename, simply type what you want.

3. **Press the Tab key.**

   The insertion point is now in the center of the line.

4. **Enter what you want to appear in the center.**

   To create the example header, choose Insert⇨Page Number. This action puts the code `*page*` into the center of the line. If you want, you can get fancy and type the word **Page** right before the code. This means that the fourth page says "Page 4" rather than just "4". (If you do this optional step, remember to leave a space before the code. Otherwise, you get "Page4".)

5. **Press the Tab key.**

   Now the insertion point is on the right edge of the line.

6. **Enter what you want to appear on the right.**

   For our example, you would choose Insert⇨Date and Time. This action opens up a list of date and time formats. Click one.

High-quality books (like this one) have different headers on the left and right pages. Don't even try to do that in Works; you're likely to sprain your head (or foot). If Microsoft had put every possible feature into Works, how would they sell their higher-priced word processor?

Adjusting header and footer margins

Anybody who has ever slept in a short bed is sensitive to having suitable margins for their headers and footers. To change your header or footer margin, choose File⇨Page Setup to get the Page Setup dialog box. Click the tab marked Margins and type in a new margin value for your header or footer.

Headers are supposed to appear within the top and bottom page margins. So in the Page Setup dialog box, you must make sure that the header margin is less than the top page margin and that the footer margin is less than the bottom page margin. Otherwise, you're back to the short-bed situation, and nobody's happy — least of all, Works. (What actually happens is that Works simply ignores you and resets the margins while you're not looking.)

Footnote Fundamentals

When I get old (which should be by next Friday, at the very latest), I won't bore younger people with tales of how I trudged miles to school in the deep snow. Oh, no — I plan to bore younger people by telling them how we used to do footnotes before there were word processors. But if you want to be bored, you don't need me; you can just read the manual. (Besides, how can I tell whether you're younger than I am?)

Here's how to do automatically numbered footnotes:

1. **Put the insertion point just after the text you want to footnote.**

2. **Choose Insert⇨Footnote.**

   The footnote footman (in the form of an Insert Footnote dialog box) comes to your aid.

3. **Click the Insert button in the Insert Footnote dialog box.**

   The Works footman switches you to Page Layout view (if you weren't there already) and transports you to a mysterious region: the footnote area at the bottom of your current page. The insertion point is waiting, right after an automatic reference number that Works provides.

4. **Type in your footnote text, beginning with a space (for appearances).**

5. **Press the Page Up key or scroll up to get back to where you were typing.**

If you don't like numbers and would rather use asterisks or something else, all you need to do is to change Step 3. Click Special Mark in the Insert Footnote dialog box. Then type the mark that you want (usually * or **) in the Mark box and click the Insert button. If you later change your mind and decide to return to numbers, choose Insert⇨Footnote and then choose Numbered instead of Special Mark.

To delete any footnote, just delete its reference mark in the text. The mark *and* the footnote go away, and the remaining footnotes are renumbered.

If you find yourself doing really heavy-duty footnotes, as you would if you were writing a scholarly thesis of some sort, you should check out a few of the TaskWizards. (You find TaskWizards by clicking the Task Launcher button on the toolbar.) Works provides you with a School Reports/Thesis Wizard and a Bibliography Wizard.

Doing It by the Numbers: Tables, Spreadsheets, and Charts

When you want your word-processing document to display a bunch of numbers in an attractive, comprehensible way (or at least in as attractive and comprehensible a way as numbers allow), you need a table, chart, or spreadsheet in your document. Works lets you use any of these three ways of displaying numbers, depending on your needs.

To take full advantage of all the cool features Works provides for tables and charts, you need to know how to use the spreadsheet and charting tools. Check out Parts III and VI, respectively, for more on these tools. On the other hand, you may be saying, "Just let me get this table into my report, and I promise I'll never, ever go near a number again." In that case, this section is for you.

Works provides three ways to create a table:

- ✔ **The unofficial way, using the Tab key, provides simple tables with little formatting.**
- ✔ **The official way, using Insert➪Table, does nice formatting.**
- ✔ **The spreadsheet way, using Insert➪Spreadsheet, does nice formatting and charts, too.**

If you need to chart some data in your document, you must do it the spreadsheet way. Otherwise, the choice is yours.

Typing a table without a license

If you want only a very simple table, with no gridlines and no easy way to chart its numbers, then Works doesn't need to know what you're up to. You can make an "unofficial" table as you would on a typewriter. Each line of the table is just a funny-looking paragraph, as far as Works is concerned. You can see an example of such a table in Figure 7-5 in Chapter 7.

To create an "unofficial" table, start with a new paragraph; you can use it for the first row, including your column headings. Format your paragraph with tab stops where you want your columns. Use left or center tab stops for this header text. (For more information on tab stops, check out Chapter 7.) Type the column headers in this paragraph, separating them by pressing the Tab key; you may want to use bold text for the column headers throughout. Make sure to keep your lines short enough so that Works doesn't wrap them onto the next line. (Remember that Works doesn't know what you're doing, so it can't help you.)

Press the End key to go to the end of this first line; then press the Enter key to make a new paragraph that has exactly the same tab stops as your first paragraph. Use this new paragraph for your first line of data in the table. If some columns have numbers, you may consider changing the tabs for those columns to decimal tabs.

Press the End key to go to the end of this second line; then press the Enter key to make a new paragraph that has exactly the same tab stops as the paragraph that preceded it. (A pattern emerges, no?) This third paragraph is for your second line of data. Continue on like this until your table is done.

To dress up your table with horizontal lines, you can apply a bottom border to each of the row paragraphs (and maybe even a heavier border across the column-headings row). See "Lines, Borders, and Shade" later in this chapter.

Creating a table the official way

A table in Works is a spreadsheet's younger brother — affable and good-looking, but not nearly so hard-working. When you make a table, you're actually using the spreadsheet tool, but Works does its best to hide the ugly details from you. Sounds lovely, but Works' habit of hiding details can lead to problems if you need to do a lot of updating or if you want to make a chart of the data later on.

Here's the shortcut rundown on making tables:

1. **Make a blank line for your table.**

   Click the last line of the paragraph that you want the table to appear *after*, press the End key to move the insertion point to the very end of that paragraph, and then press the Enter key. (You don't have to make a blank line for your table; you can put it in the middle of a sentence, if you like. Tables are inserted wherever the insertion point is.)

2. **Click the Insert Table button in the toolbar.**

   The Insert Table button is the one over on the right that looks like a tiny, illegible calendar. (Or you can choose Insert⇨Table.) The Insert Table dialog box appears on the scene. See Figure 8-2.

3. **Size and format your table.**

   Type the number of rows and columns that you need into the two boxes at the upper left of the Insert Table dialog box (or click the up-arrow or down-arrow alongside the boxes to increase or decrease the number already in a box). Don't forget to add a row for your column heads and a column for your row heads. The Example in the dialog box remains five-by-five — its function is to show off the formats, not the sizes.

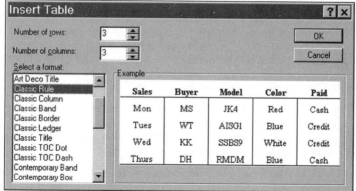

Figure 8-2:
The Insert
Table
dialog box.

On the left side of the dialog box is a list of possible formats. Each time
you click a name, the Example box on the right changes to show you
how that format looks.

4. Click OK.

You now see a window that's cut up into rows and columns like a
spreadsheet. This window is your table-to-be (see Figure 8-3). This
table-to-be looks a little too big for the space, and it has some junk
around the outside that you really don't want. But don't worry — the
junk all goes away by the time that you're done.

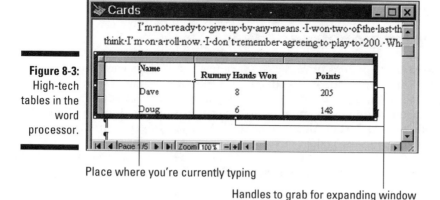

Figure 8-3:
High-tech
tables in the
word
processor.

Place where you're currently typing

Handles to grab for expanding window

5. Type in the contents of your table.

The square *(cell)* that you're currently typing in is the outlined one (the
active cell). To move to another cell, either press any of the arrow keys
on the keyboard or click another cell with your mouse.

The format that you chose in Step 3 takes care of all those nasty details, such as what gets centered and what font and style to use in any given cell. You can change these details with all the usual text-editing commands, but if you've chosen a good format, you probably won't want to do much.

6. **Size the window that contains the table.**

   You can grab the little handles on the sides of the window (refer to Figure 8-3) and push or pull on them to make the window larger or smaller. You keep the same number of rows and columns, but they get bigger or smaller to fit the space you decide upon.

7. **Click anywhere on your document outside of the table window.**

   Wow! After a brief wait, all the spreadsheet-like stuff goes away, and you're left with a table!

To cut, paste, or copy the table, select it by clicking it and then use the usual editing tools, such as Ctrl+X to cut or Ctrl+V to paste.

You can't edit the table just by selecting it and typing, though. To edit the table, you have to put it back into its spreadsheet form. Double-click anywhere on the table to do that.

When you're working on a table in the word processor, you are actually using the spreadsheet tool, so don't be surprised if the menus that drop down from the menu bar are a little different from the word-processor menus.

Creating a spreadsheet

In the earliest versions of Works, spreadsheets and tables were the same things. They're still not all that different. Tables are designed to make getting the right display a little easier, and spreadsheets are designed to make manipulating the numbers a little easier. For more details, read about spreadsheets in Part III. Meanwhile, here's how you insert a spreadsheet into a word-processing document.

1. **Make a blank line for your spreadsheet.**

   Click the last line of the paragraph that you want the table or chart to appear *after,* press the End key to move the insertion point to the very end of that paragraph, and then press the Enter key.

2. **Choose Insert⇨Spreadsheet.**

   The Insert Spreadsheet dialog box appears. If Create a New Spreadsheet isn't already the selected option, click it.

3. Click OK.

Whoa! What's all this?! And why does it have its fat little edges splotted all over my text, you ask. "All this" is a tiny window on a spreadsheet. This tiny window looks sort of like a table if you ignore all the letters and numbers around the outside edges. Naturally, the letters and numbers mean something, but if you're getting that deeply into creating a spreadsheet, you ought to read about spreadsheets in Part III.

4. Expand the spreadsheet window to the size you need.

The spreadsheet window has little handles just like the table window shown in Figure 8-3. With spreadsheets, the handles adjust the number of rows and columns. The spreadsheet's cells stay the same size, but you get more or fewer of them. For more columns, click the tiny black handle in the center of the right edge and drag it to the right. For more rows, click the handle in the center of the bottom edge and drag it down.

5. Type in the contents of your table.

The square that you're currently typing in (the *cell*) is the outlined one (just like the one in the table in Figure 8-3). To move to another cell, either press any of the arrow keys on the keyboard or click another cell with your mouse. In this window, your mouse cursor is a big fat + symbol.

Numbers may change appearance when you change cells. Controlling the appearance of numbers is a bit tricky. The easiest way to pretty up your table is to use the AutoFormat command in the Format menu; you can read about formatting spreadsheets in Chapter 11.

6. Click anywhere on your document outside of the table window.

Check it out. All those letters and numbers around the outside go away, and you're left with something that looks an awful lot like a table, although maybe not quite as pretty. Your creation still has some funny edges with handles, but it looks better. The funny edges are visible because your spreadsheet has been *selected*. To make the edges go away, click once again anywhere on your document outside the spreadsheet.

To cut, paste, or copy the entire spreadsheet, select it by clicking it and then use the usual editing tools, like Ctrl+X to cut or Ctrl+V to paste. While the spreadsheet is selected, you can also use the handles to show more or fewer columns (as you did in Step 3). To edit the spreadsheet, first double-click it to put it into an editable mode.

Inserting a spreadsheet from a file

If the spreadsheet already exists as a Works file, getting all or part of it into a word-processing document is easier than if you have to create the spreadsheet on the fly. (Creating anything on a fly is tough — they're just too small.) First, open the spreadsheet document by choosing File➪Open; now both documents are open. In the spreadsheet window, select the range of cells you want to copy and then press Ctrl+C. Switch to the word-processing document window (choose Window and then the document name from the drop-down menu that appears), click where you want the spreadsheet, and press Ctrl+V.

Creating charts

To do charts in Works, you have to start with a spreadsheet in your document. (If you don't have one, go back to "Creating a spreadsheet" earlier in this chapter.) Creating a basic bar chart from data in a spreadsheet is pretty easy. For anything more than that, though, you really need to read about charting in Chapter 19.

1. **Double-click the spreadsheet in your document.**

2. **Highlight one row of numbers (or several adjoining rows of numbers) in your table.**

   Click the first (leftmost) cell of the first row that you want to chart; hold down the mouse button and drag to the last (rightmost) cell of the last row that you want to chart. Release the mouse button.

   If you include a first row or column of words, they are used as labels for the chart. If you want them to be used differently or you don't like the way they look, go to Chapter 19 for further information.

3. **Click the tiny, squinty bar chart icon in the lower-left corner of the spreadsheet.**

   Wow! A chart appears, and suddenly you are using the Works chart toolbar buttons and menu selections Chapter 19 talks about.

4. **Click anywhere on your document outside of the chart area.**

You should end up with nice bars and a legend. (If not, I know of some nice bars with legends in Key West — drop me a line.)

To change the size of the chart, click one of the handles (little black squares) around the periphery and drag it. (Drag the ones along the sides sideways and the ones along the top and bottom vertically.)

Click somewhere in the text of your document to deselect the chart and see the final effect.

To change the chart data, double-click the chart; then click the tiny icon that looks like an illegible calendar in the lower-left corner of the chart window. This move turns the chart back to a spreadsheet, which you can edit.

Lines, Borders, and Shade

Nothing like a few good lines to liven up the party! Works has got 'em, in the form of *borders* around paragraphs. You want a horizontal line? A horizontal line is a *bottom* or *top* border on a paragraph. A vertical line? A vertical line is a *left* or *right* border alongside your paragraph. If you want to box in your paragraph or box in a set of paragraphs, you use an *outline* border. You can even draw a border around your whole page. Want to give your paragraph some shade? (It can get awfully hot down there by the border.) No problemo.

How far do these border lines go? Horizontal borders run from the left to the right indent of the paragraph (which, for normal paragraphs, is from the left to the right page margin). Vertical borders run the height of the paragraph for as many lines as are in the paragraph.

What about a line by itself? To get a stand-alone horizontal line, like the *rule* across a letterhead, use a blank line (single-line paragraph) with a top or bottom border. This step lets you set the line width independently of the width of your surrounding paragraphs. Unfortunately, there's really no such thing as a stand-alone vertical line like you may want to have for a typing-style table (see "Typing a table without a license" earlier in this chapter). You can get a vertical line between columns, however; see "Columns," coming up soon.

Because these borders are actually a part of paragraph formatting, if you create a new paragraph by pressing the Enter key while working in a bordered paragraph, the new paragraph is bordered, too. (By *working*, I mean where you have your insertion point, but saying "insertion point" all the time sounds so nerdy.)

Marking your borders

Here's how you, too, can create borderline documents, just like the pros:

1. **For a horizontal line by itself, create a new paragraph.**

   Click the last line of your current paragraph, press the End key, and then press the Enter key. If the line is to be shorter than the space between the page margins, drag the left and right indent marks (the inward-pointing triangles) on the ruler to mark the length of the line you want to insert.

   or

   For a border around a group of paragraphs, select the group.

For this technique to work, the selected paragraphs should all have the same left and right indents. Drag the left and right indent marks (the inward-pointing triangles) on the ruler to change indents.

or

For a border on a single paragraph, click anywhere within the paragraph.

2. **Choose Format⇨Borders and Shading.**

   The Border patrol arrives on the scene in its three-card, four-wheel-drive dialog box. Have your passport ready.

3. **Click the tab of the Borders card if it isn't already displayed.**

4. **Click as many borders as you want in the Border dialog box.**

   Click the check boxes of the Border area of the dialog box: Left, Right, Top, Bottom, or all the way around (Outline) — whatever. A check mark indicates which borders are selected. The only choice that needs an explanation here is Outline With Shadow, which not only outlines your paragraph but gives it the illusion of three dimensions by giving the paragraph a shadow on the page. (This effect is either "way cool" or "to gag on," depending on your taste.)

   If you select a bunch of paragraphs and want an outline around the bunch, click Outline. If you want each paragraph to have its own border, as in the rows of a table, select the sides individually; ignore the gray in some check boxes.

5. **Click the line style you want in the Line Style area of the dialog box.**

   If you have a color printer, click the box labeled Color and choose a color from the list that drops down.

6. **Click the OK button in the dialog box.**

To remove a border, do Steps 1 through 3 to get the Borders card back. The check boxes on the lower right describe the current borders of the paragraph. (Any border that is on will have a check mark in its check box.) Click the check mark in the check box of any border that you want to get rid of. Click OK in that dialog box when you're done.

Making shady paragraphs

If you have a really red-hot paragraph, you can draw the reader's attention to it by putting it in the shade. Here's how:

1. **Do the same thing that you did in the preceding section for borders.**

   See "Marking your borders." You should now be looking at the Borders and Shading dialog box.

2. **Click the tab of the <u>S</u>hading card if it isn't already displayed.**

3. **Click a shading pattern in the box on the left side of the card.**

4. **If you have a color printer (or just want to make the document look cool on the screen), click foreground and background colors.**

   Watch the sample box to make sure that you aren't creating something hideous. Hideousity happens — there's a little Dr. Frankenstein in all of us.

5. **Click the OK button in the dialog box.**

Columns

Works lets you put your text in columns, although it doesn't give you a lot of help in formatting a page that uses columns. (How else could Microsoft sell you a higher-priced word processor?)

To make all the text in your document wrap in columns, do the following:

1. **Choose F<u>o</u>rmat⇨<u>C</u>olumns.**

   The very straightforward Format Columns dialog box appears. (If you are not already working in Layout view, Works asks if you want to switch to that view; click Yes.)

2. **Enter how many columns you want in the <u>N</u>umber Of Columns box.**

3. **Enter how much space you want between the columns in the <u>S</u>pace Between Columns box.**

4. **Click the <u>L</u>ine Between Columns check box to add a vertical line between your columns.**

5. **Click the OK button.**

Here are a few tips to deal with Works quirks when using columns:

✔ The vertical line between columns, if you choose it, doesn't appear in Layout view; choose <u>F</u>ile⇨Print Pre<u>v</u>iew to see if the line is present.

✔ If you're using columns to make a newsletter, you probably want a banner at the top of the newsletter, spanning all columns. You can type such a banner into the Header space if you don't mind it appearing on all pages.

✔ Text flows automatically through the columns. To force a particular piece of text to wrap to the top of a column, add blank lines before that text.

The Envelope, Please!

May we have the envelope, please? And the winner is . . . you! You win because printing envelopes is one of the dirty little jobs that Works makes easier than it used to be. In the dark ages of word processing (five or six years ago), printing an envelope was a job that took a squadron of software engineers, five phone calls to the printer and software vendors, four Tylenol tablets and, ultimately, a ballpoint pen. (Another tale I can bore younger people with when I get old.)

Meeting the Works envelope gnome

The Works word processor has an envelope tool that is really designed for doing bulk printing of envelopes. (I like to refer to the envelope tool as the envelope gnome — it works automagically like a wizard, but it's uglier.) If you really want to print a large number of envelopes using a database of addresses, see the Appendix. In this chapter, I talk about printing a single, simple envelope. Here's how the gnome is supposed to work:

This tool, or gnome, lives in the Tools menu; when you call it into existence, it gives you a dialog box with eight cards on it, as shown in Figure 8-4.

The top card (the Instructions card) is a checklist of things that have to be set up before Works can print envelopes for you — but some of the check boxes apply only if you are printing a large number of envelopes by using a database.

The Works envelope gnome is designed to take you through each item on this list. To get through the list, you can click the Next button on the lower right; the gnome moves you to the next item on the checklist, taking you to the next card. (Alternatively, you can click the button next to each step or the card tabs.) The gnome steps you through the process, always returning to the Instructions card and showing you check marks for the steps that are now done.

When the gnome is done with the checklist, it creates a new and special page at the start of your document, all properly formatted to be an envelope. When you go to print your document, you can choose to print either the envelope (this special page) or the rest of the document. Works conveniently remembers the return address and fills it in for you automatically whenever you print an envelope after that. (You can change the return address if you like.)

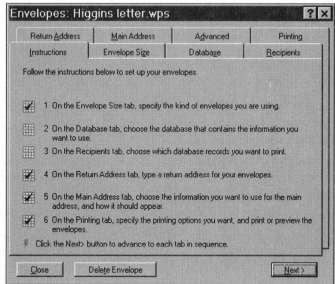

Figure 8-4: The Envelope tool's Instructions card. Only four or fewer steps are really necessary for a single envelope (the steps are shown here with check marks).

Creating and printing a single envelope

If you want to print only a single envelope, going through all eight cards of the Envelope gnome is confusing, boring, and unnecessary. Here's how to bypass all the unnecessary stuff and print a single envelope.

I'm going to assume that you've written a letter or some other document and that you have that document open in Works. If you're just, say, sending a clipping to a friend but want a nicely printed envelope, then start a new word-processing document.

1. **Press Ctrl+S to save your document.**

   If you're working with a letter or other existing document, saving the original document is insurance in case you mess up something. (You can just close the messed-up document without saving it and then reopen the original document.)

2. **If your document is a letter and already has the recipient's name and mailing address in it, select (highlight) the name and address portion.**

   Otherwise, move on to Step 3.

3. **Choose Tools⇨Envelopes.**

   If this is the first time that you have printed an envelope since you started Works, you may get one of Works' First-Time Help dialog boxes, which offer to help you do the following: 1) take a tour of envelopes and labels, 2) create an envelope, or 3) print an envelope. I suggest that you take the tour once, for fun: Click the Quick Tour Of Envelopes And Labels button and follow the directions. When you return to the First-Time Help dialog box, click Don't Display This Message In The Future, and First-Time Help never bothers you again. Then click the To Create Envelopes button.

The envelope gnome pops up the Instructions card of the Envelopes dialog box.

4. **Click the Envelope Si<u>z</u>e tab.**

   Choose a size from the list. If your envelope doesn't match any of the ones listed, click the Custom button and enter your envelope's dimensions.

5. **Click the <u>M</u>ain Address tab.**

   If, in Step 1, you initially highlighted the recipient's name and address in your letter, it appears in the Main Address text box when the Main Address card comes up. You can edit the recipient's address now if you like. If you didn't select an address, this text box is blank, and you can fill it in by clicking the text box and typing. Press the Enter key at the end of each line.

   Ignore all the field choosing and other junk on this card.

6. **Click the Return <u>A</u>ddress card.**

   If you have never printed an envelope before, the Return Address text box is empty. Type in your name and address. If you have printed an envelope before, the return address is the same as the last time you printed an envelope; edit the return address if you need to.

7. **To preview or print your envelope, click the Printing card.**

   Click the Preview button to see your envelope in Print Preview.

   Click the Print button to actually physically commit ink to paper. After a minute or so, your printer is ready to print. Your printer may wait for you to put an envelope in it manually, unless it has a stack of envelopes already in an envelope feed. Every printer handles envelopes differently; insert the blank envelope the way the printer manual tells you. You may also have to press a button to tell the printer that you have inserted an envelope; on most common printers, you won't have to.

8. **Click the <u>C</u>lose button.**

   Ptooey! The envelope gnome spits out a properly formatted envelope page, leaving it sticking to the top of your document. A special envelope/page break (the dotted line) separates the envelope page from your document. (Thank goodness, gnome spit being what it is.)

The envelope page that you just created is now attached to the document. You can edit the envelope page or format it just like any other page of your document. You can also call on the envelope gnome again to edit the text, if you prefer. If at any time you decide you won't need the envelope again, you can delete it. Choose Tools⇨Envelopes from the menu bar; then click the Delete Envelope button at the bottom of the Envelopes dialog box. Works asks you if deleting the envelope is okay; click the Yes button.

After you have attached an envelope to a document, you have a choice of what to print whenever you print your document — the envelope or the rest of the document. Here's how to print an attached envelope:

1. **Choose File⇨Print (or press Ctrl+P).**

   A Print dialog box scurries out of the woodwork. Make sure that your printer is turned on.

2. **Click Envelope in the What To Print area of the Print dialog box; then click the OK button.**

   (As a convenience, if you have been working on the envelope and your insertion point is still on the envelope page, Works has already selected Envelope. If you left your insertion point in the main document, Works has selected Main Document.)

3. **Click the OK button of the Print dialog box.**

If all has worked well, you soon have a nicely printed envelope. If not, well, there's always the ballpoint pen. Here are a few things that can go wrong and information on how to fix 'em:

✔ **Nothing appears to happen when you print:** Your printer may be waiting for you to manually feed an envelope into it. If no way is available to manually feed the printer an envelope, follow these steps: Click the envelope page. Choose File⇨Page Setup from the menu bar. Click the Source, Size & Orientation card and (in the Paper dialog box) in the drop-down menu for Source, choose Default Tray. Try printing again.

✔ **The envelope jams:** After you carefully extract the smushed envelope, try printing again with a new envelope, but this time, sharpen the crease of the edges of the envelope by running a hard object across them (or by running the edge between your thumbnail and middle finger tip). If this fails, try adjusting the paper thickness control of the printer or using a thinner weight of envelope.

✔ **Stuff is printed in *very* wrong places:** In the previous instructions for "Creating and printing a single envelope," Step 4 is to choose the envelope size. Probably the real envelope is not the size you specified. Or you may not be putting your envelopes into the printer properly. Some printers have a special manual-feed guide that you should use.

Finally, check to make sure that Windows 95 is set up for exactly the model of printer that you are using (see Chapter 4).

✔ **Stuff is printed in *somewhat* wrong places:** See the possible reasons given in the preceding paragraph. Another possible remedy is to click the envelope page and adjust margins by choosing File➪Page Setup.

Part III
Setting Sail with Spreadsheets

"Kevin here heads our Works software development team. Right now he's working on a spreadsheet program that's sort of a combination Lotus 1-2-3/FrankenWolf."

In this part . . .

Ever since the invention of the spreadsheet, PC users have been able to circumnavigate the world of calculations with ever-increasing ease. If you've been left standing at the dock, looking wistfully out to sea, Part III is your ticket to adventure on the high seas.

Here are the fundamentals of entering data and doing calculations with Works' spreadsheet tool, with tips for making the job faster and easier. Whether you're planning your finances or just making lists, Works' spreadsheet tool can save you a lot of tedious hours on the calculator.

"Heigh, my hearts; cheerly, cheerly, my hearts; yare, yare: take in the top-sail; 'Tend to the master's whistle. — Blow till thou burst thy wind, if room enough!"

The Tempest, Wm. Shakespeare

Chapter 9

Spreading Your First Sheets

So, you're ready to set sail into the uncharted seas of calculation? Well, batten down the hatches, hoist the anchor, strop the strmf'r'sq's'l, and add a few other such nautical allusions. With the Works spreadsheet hoisted squarely to the wind (hold the book open to this page, which is about as windy as they get), you can reach exotic lands where budgets, business plans, alphabetized lists, expense analyses, profit-and-loss statements, surveys, scientific experiments, and sales forecasts live. After you get the general idea of spreadsheets, you discover all kinds of exciting things to do with them — most of them legal, moral, and non-fattening (but still rather nice).

If you have never used spreadsheets before, however, you need to know a few basics first, which is where this chapter comes in. Here you find out what you can do with a spreadsheet, what's what in the spreadsheet window, how to navigate around in spreadsheets, and how to enter text and numbers. To do calculations and the more exciting stuff, see the next chapter.

If You've Never Used a Spreadsheet Before

If you've never used a spreadsheet before, try to think of it as a table of numbers and calculations where all the calculations are done for you, or as a calculator that shows you all the numbers you're adding up or multiplying. Or you may think of it as gnomes sitting on a chess board with calculators, where the pawns are numbers and the rooks add up rows and columns, and the queen is actually a copy machine, and, um, well . . . hmmm. This isn't helping, is it?

Truth to tell, you can't fully appreciate a spreadsheet until you've used one (sort of like an electric toothbrush, but even more fun — if that can be imagined). The best concept to start with is to imagine something that can automatically add up rows and columns of numbers in a table. Spreadsheets do that familiar task quite easily.

So what's the big deal?

The first big deal with spreadsheets is that they make doing most calculations a great deal easier than doing them on a calculator — especially long or complex calculations, such as mortgages, retirement plans, or statistics. One reason why calculations are easier is that, because spreadsheets are tables, you can see and change all the numbers at any time. Few calculators let you see all the numbers you've entered (unless you have a printing or other fancy sort of calculator).

Even fewer calculators let you back up and change a number and then recalculate. This ability to change a number in a spreadsheet and then immediately see the result lets you do "what-if" analyses. For example, what if inflation goes to 8 percent? When can I afford to retire? Or, what if I switch to no-tillage corn farming? Do the labor savings offset the higher pesticide use? What if I sell this computer? Can I then afford to pay someone else to do all this stuff?

Like calculators, spreadsheets can do all kinds of fancy calculations on the numbers they contain: sums, averages, net present value, sines, cosines — all kinds of stuff. They can even do calculations based on the results of other calculations, or calculations based on time — 30-day running-average annualized yield from an investment, for example. If you know how to do a certain calculation on a calculator, you can make a spreadsheet do the calculation, too.

The second big deal with spreadsheets is that they let you visually organize your data into rows and columns. Try to find a calculator that does that. You can even have several different tables of rows and columns. The Works spreadsheet lets you dress up your tables with borders, colors, lines, and text formatting so that you can easily see what's going on.

Because spreadsheets are laid out on a grid, you can use them to create business forms of various kinds. You can even fill in those forms right in Works, do calculations on the data you've filled in, and print out the results.

The third big deal with spreadsheets is that they can be used for simple lists and collections of data — the names of students in your class and their grades, inventories of equipment and their dollar values, and so on. Spreadsheets kind of overlap with databases in this sense, with spreadsheets being more useful for smaller projects or projects involving more calculation, and databases being more useful when lots of data and summary reports are needed.

The final big deal is that after you have data in a spreadsheet, you can turn that data into a chart in minutes. I look at this in more detail in Chapter 19.

What can you do with a spreadsheet?

People use spreadsheets for all kinds of stuff. Here are some examples:

- Doing budgets
- Recording and plotting your daily weight and calorie count
- Recording lists of people and how much they owe or have paid
- Creating invoices, bills of sale, and other business forms
- Recording, totaling, and forecasting sales
- Tracking and computing expenses
- Planning finances
- Analyzing statistics
- Recording experiments
- Convincing your spouse that you're working when you're really playing Minesweeper

Nearly anything you can do with a calculator works better on a spreadsheet. Some of the things you can do in a Works spreadsheet are the following:

- ✔ Add columns of numbers
- ✔ Add rows of numbers
- ✔ Compute the average, standard deviation, and other statistics on rows or columns of numbers
- ✔ Compute depreciation, net present value, and other financial results
- ✔ Find the minimum or maximum value in a set of values
- ✔ Compute the number of days between two dates
- ✔ Compute the number of dates that you've eaten in two days
- ✔ Sort lists alphabetically or numerically
- ✔ Find specific items in a list

In general, you should use spreadsheets for anything that involves creating tables, making charts, doing calculations, or keeping short lists of things.

What shouldn't you do with a spreadsheet?

You should not plot to overthrow the world or cheat on your taxes; it reflects badly on the software industry. (Like you care, right?) But mostly, you should not do anything that can be done better with another Works tool. For example:

- ✔ If you are writing a report that includes spreadsheets, don't write the report using the spreadsheet tool. That's as bad as using the knife blade in your Swiss Army Knife for a screwdriver. Write the report in the word processor and copy the spreadsheets into the word-processing document.
- ✔ If you're making long lists of things that you may want summarized — say, an inventory — use the database tool of Works.
- ✔ If you're making a list of names and addresses to use for mailings, use the database tool.

Starting Out

Enough woolgathering. Time to collect our crew, spread our spreadsheets to the wind, and set forth into the Sargasso Sea of making calculations. Here's how to get to the spreadsheet tool.

If you're already running Works, choose File⇨Open (to open an existing spreadsheet document file) or choose File⇨New (to start the Task Launcher). If Works isn't already running, fire it up, and you get the Works Task Launcher. From the Task Launcher, you can either start a new spreadsheet document or open (or find) an existing one.

To review how to start Works and the different ways of starting a spreadsheet document, check out Chapter 1. That's also where you can find stuff about using the mouse, keyboard, commands, menus, and dialog boxes.

To get a nice, shiny, untrammeled, new spreadsheet document from the Task Launcher, click the Works Tools card tab (or press Alt+T) to bring up the Works Tools card; then click the Spreadsheet button on the Works Tools card. You are now gazing at the spreadsheet window, its toolbar, and other assorted paraphernalia.

But wait! Maybe you don't want a nice, shiny, untrammeled, new spreadsheet document. Maybe you want a predesigned, pre-trammeled spreadsheet, such as an invoice spreadsheet or a spreadsheet for recording your students' grades. Well, okay. You can get those by starting up with a wizard or a template. (See Chapter 1 for the basics of starting with a wizard, and see the Appendix for more specifics about wizards and templates.) But until you know a bit more about spreadsheets, you may find wizards and templates a bit tricky to use. The folks who designed them did a lot of fancy formatting, locking certain areas so that you don't accidentally change them, and used other tricks, which you will learn about in this part of the book as well as in the Appendix.

What's what in the spreadsheet window

Figure 9-1 shows you what's what in your spreadsheet window. (*Spreadsheet window* is my name for how the Microsoft Works window looks when you're using the spreadsheet tool.) Works has given the spreadsheet document shown the forlorn name of Unsaved Spreadsheet 1 — one of the nerdy sort of startup names Works gives new documents that haven't yet been saved as a file. Near the top of the Works window is the usual Works menu bar with all the commands, and underneath that is the spreadsheet toolbar with all its buttons and icons.

Don't try to memorize all this stuff unless it's 3 a.m. and you really, really need to get back to sleep. Stick a pencil or small inanimate object of your choice here and come back whenever you need to refresh your memory.

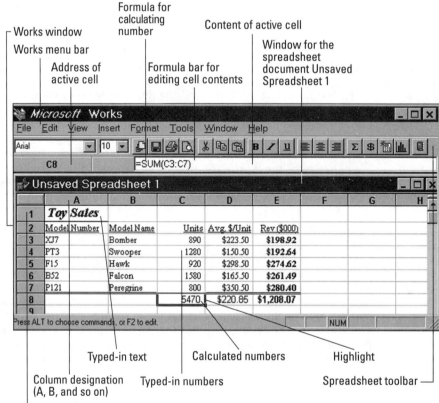

Formula for calculating number

Content of active cell

Works window

Works menu bar

Window for the spreadsheet document Unsaved Spreadsheet 1

Address of active cell

Formula bar for editing cell contents

Figure 9-1:
Your window into the spreadsheet world.

Typed-in text

Calculated numbers

Highlight

Column designation (A, B, and so on)

Typed-in numbers

Spreadsheet toolbar

Row designation (1, 2, and so on)

The spreadsheet menu

As in fine restaurants and programs everywhere, one way you give commands to the Works spreadsheet tool is by using a menu. You click on the item you want. Works menus are like the menus at franchised fast-food joints: They look pretty much the same no matter what joint — or tool, in this case — you are in.

In fact, the first line of the menu bar (the line with File and all the other command words on it) for the spreadsheet tool is identical to the one for the word-processor tool. Of course, you find some interesting differences when you go to use the menu bar: The little menus that drop down when you click on these command words are somewhat different. Rather than cram a bunch of menu descriptions here, this book explains the spreadsheet menu differences as it goes along.

The command menus that drop down when you choose File or Edit are very much the same as for Works' other tools. The File and Edit menus include commands for starting a new document, opening an existing document file, closing a document, saving a document to a file, and making basic edits. Even the spreadsheet's Edit⇨Find command is practically the same as in the word processor.

Works has a broader variety of tools than most other programs, and in order to cover all these tools, this book can't afford to repeat descriptions of identical commands. The tradeoff, unfortunately, is that you'll have to jump around a bit in the book, and I have to use more of those reference icons.

Most of the commands for the File and Edit menus are discussed in detail in Part I. Basic printing is discussed in Chapter 4 (which is cleverly named "Basic Printing").

The spreadsheet toolbar

The other popular way to give commands to Works (other than traditional shouting methods) is with the toolbar — the thing with all the picture-laden buttons under the menu bar (see Figure 9-2). The toolbar is just a faster way than the menu bar to do some of the same things. You click on a button and stuff happens.

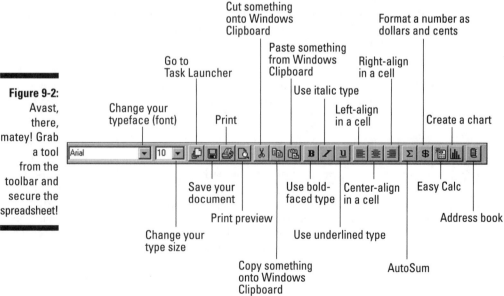

Figure 9-2: Avast, there, matey! Grab a tool from the toolbar and secure the spreadsheet!

That's toolbar, not crowbar. No matter how much you are tempted, do not use a crowbar to give commands to Works.

Most of the spreadsheet toolbar is similar to the toolbar in other Works tools. All buttons but four (the AutoSum, Currency, Easy Calc, and New Chart buttons), for example, are the same as the ones in the word processor. (For more on Works' toolbars, see Chapter 2.)

I don't go into detail about these buttons here, but I bring them up as we go along. Here's where to go to read about the buttons that are particularly interesting for spreadsheets:

- **Left, Center, and Right Align:** See the section on changing alignment in a cell in Chapter 11.

- **Format a number as dollars and cents:** See the section on formatting numbers in Chapter 11.

- **AutoSum:** See the section on creating formulas with point-and-shoot in Chapter 10.

- **Create a chart:** See Chapter 19.

The spreadsheet document

The spreadsheet document (the window with the title bar Unsaved Spreadsheet 1 in Figure 9-1) looks like a big table, which is correct because that's what a spreadsheet is. Each row in this table has a number, which appears at the far left of the table, in tasteful battleship gray. Each column has a letter, at the top, also in gray.

A spreadsheet has no pages; it's one vast table. The size of your spreadsheet — in theory only — can be more than 16,000 rows by more than 250 columns. In reality, you'll run out of memory (and so will your PC) long before you can make a spreadsheet that big.

As is usually the case with Windows programs, you can look at only a small piece of the document at a time. (This is good. Imagine how illegible a long document would be if it were squooshed to fit entirely on your PC screen!) To see more of the document, scroll the document up or down, left or right, using the gray scroll bars along the right and bottom sides (see instructions on how to get around in your document in Chapter 2). Chapter 23 tells you how you can *freeze* your column and row headings in place on your screen so you know what rows or columns you're looking at while you scroll around in the rest of the spreadsheet.

Cells

A *cell* is one of those little boxes on the spreadsheet; it's the intersection of a row and a column. Everything you type goes in a cell.

Each cell has an address so that you can talk to Works about it in your calculations, graphs, and other activities: "Hey, Works! Multiply the number at this address by 18," to paraphrase. A cell address is made up of the column letter and row number, smushed together like this: B12, which would be the cell at column B and row 12.

Cell addresses figure prominently in everything you do in a spreadsheet. For instance, Works displays the address of a cell you click on (the *active cell*) to the left of its formula bar. In Figure 9-1, I have clicked on the cell in column C, row 8, so C8 appears in the space labeled "Address of active cell."

Laying Out Your Spreadsheet

A spreadsheet looks like a table with rows and columns. It usually has a title in the upper-left corner, column headings across the top, row headings down the left side, and numbers and stuff in the middle, just like in Figure 9-1.

Fine. But when you create your own spreadsheet, what are those rows and columns going to represent? In Figure 9-1, the rows correspond to the individual toy models, allowing the company to show how sales vary from model to model and to then sum up to get total sales. The columns correspond to things someone may want to know about those toy models.

You can arrange data into columns and rows in any way you like. Bear in mind, however, that columns take up more space than rows on the screen. Following are a few tips about choosing your layout:

✔ There isn't any easy way to turn rows into columns or columns into rows, so think about your problem a bit before deciding whether to use rows or columns.

✔ Sketch your layout on paper. The best layout is usually the layout you use for the same table on a sheet of paper.

✔ You don't need to worry about exactly how many rows or columns you may need or what order to put them in. You can add or rearrange rows and columns easily later on.

Entering and Editing Data in Cells

If you have a rough idea in your head for your spreadsheet, it's time to start entering data. Working in a spreadsheet is not quite like typing on a typewriter, however, so first read about how you can move around and enter different types of stuff into the spreadsheet.

Moving from cell to cell

The easiest way to move from cell to cell is to move your mouse so that the mouse cursor (a big, fat plus sign: +) hovers over the new cell, and then click. The newly clicked-upon cell is then surrounded by a rectangular halo that Microsoft calls the *highlight*. (In computer heaven, the halos are rectangular.) This highlight indicates which cell you're about to type in, edit, or otherwise muck around with. Microsoft calls this the *active cell*. Notice that the address of the cell you've currently selected appears near the upper-left of the Works window, under the font window of the toolbar. (Of course, you can't click what you can't see. To view various areas of your spreadsheet, use the scroll bars on the right side and bottom of the document window.)

You can also move the highlight with the navigation keys on your keyboard. Those are the arrow keys, the Page Up and Page Down keys, and the Home and End keys. And, as a special added bonus in the spreadsheet tool, you can also use the Tab key. These keys move the highlight in the ways listed in Table 9-1.

Table 9-1	Navigating Spreadsheets with Keys
Navigation Key	*Where It Moves the Highlight*
Left-arrow/right-arrow	One column's worth left or right
Up-arrow/down-arrow	One row's worth up or down
Tab	One cell to the right
Shift+Tab	One cell to the left
Page Up/Page Down	One window's worth up or down
Ctrl+Page Up/Ctrl+Page Down	One window's worth left or right, respectively
Home	To column A of the row you're currently in
End	To the last column you used, in the row you're currently in
Ctrl+Home	To cell A1
Ctrl+End	To the last row and column you used

If you know the cell address you want to go to and it's nowhere nearby, here's a faster way to get there: Press the F5 key. An itsy-bitsy Go To dialog box appears. Type the cell address — **Q200**, for example — and click the OK button.

Typing stuff in cells

How do the cell-dwellers get into their cells? You put them there, of course, either by typing or by copying and pasting. The first cells, naturally, have to get there by typing, because there isn't anything to copy yet. So I'll start there, with the first cells. This chapter explains typing text and numbers into a cell. Chapter 10 covers calculations.

Typing something into a cell involves the following simple procedure:

1. **Click a cell.**

   Or move your highlight to it with the arrow or other navigation keys.

2. **Type.**

   Use the Backspace key to delete any mistakes.

3. **After you have the text, number, or formula the way you want it, press the Enter key or move to another cell with a mouse-click or a navigation key.**

If, while typing, you get a change of heart and decide not to type anything at all into the cell, press the Esc key.

It's okay to type more stuff than will fit into a cell's width. If the cell or cells to the right are empty, Works displays the excess on top of those empty neighboring cells. (It does not actually put the excess in those cells, however.) After those neighboring cells are filled, the excess will no longer be displayed. Everything you typed will still be in the cell where you typed it, but you need to expand the column width to see it all on your screen or on the printed page.

If you type more text than can be displayed in a cell, or if you type a number that turns into a bunch of ##### characters, your column is too skinny. See "Changing column widths and row heights," coming up next in this chapter.

Changing column widths and row heights

One of the big juggling acts with spreadsheets is getting the column widths just right. (While I'm at it, I cover row heights, because you adjust them more or less the same way.)

There you are, traipsing along, making, say, a list of the students in your class: Smith, Jones, Yu, and then . . . Okiniewskiwitz! If there's nothing in the cell to the right of Ms. Okiniewskiwitz's name, the text just slops over into that cell. If there is something in the cell to the right, Ms. O's name will look like it's been chopped off. (The full name is still in the cell — Works hasn't forgotten it or anything — but it just looks truncated.) You need a wider column.

Why would you need to increase the height of a row? The most common reason is to allow two or more lines of text in a single cell. A column heading that reads, for example, "Assumed Rate of Inflation," would be rather wide. By increasing row height, the line can wrap to two lines. You can also accommodate larger type by increasing row height.

The simple way to change the width of a column (or the height of a row) is to do the following:

1. **Position your mouse cursor over the gray area that has the column letter (or row number) in it.**

2. **Slowly move the cursor toward the right-hand edge of the column (or the bottom edge of the row); the cursor changes to a double-headed arrow labeled Adjust.**

3. **Click and drag to the right, and the column gets wider. Drag to the left, and it gets smaller. (For rows, dragging up makes a row shorter and dragging down makes it taller.)**

A more precise way to change the width of a column or the height of a row is with the Format Column Width or Format Row Height dialog boxes:

1. **Click or otherwise highlight the column (or row).**

   To set a group of columns to the same width (or a group of rows to the same height), drag across them to select them.

2. **Choose Format➪Column Width (or Row Height).**

   The Format Column Width (or Format Row Height) dialog box springs into action.

3. **Type a new width number into the box marked Column Width (or Row Height).**

   If you are setting column width, the width number equals roughly how many characters wide the column is, assuming 10-point type.

   If you are setting row height, the height number is in *points* (as in a "12-point font").

4. **Click the OK button.**

To enter multiple lines of text in a row, you must increase the row height and also make sure that line wrapping is enabled. To determine the row height you want, multiply the font size you are using by the number of lines you want. Choose 24, for instance, to allow two lines of 12-point type. To enable line wrapping, choose Format⇨Alignment. On the Alignment card of the Format Cells dialog box that appears, click to put a check mark in the Wrap Text check box. Text will now wrap automatically to a second line when the length exceeds the column width. To force the text to break at a particular place, add extra spaces between the words where you want the break to occur.

To automatically set a column's width, double-click the column letter at the top of the column. The column is sized to fit the largest entry.

Entering different kinds of cell content

There are three kinds of cell content in the spreadsheet world, and Works treats each of them differently. A cell can contain only one kind of content. The three kinds of cell content are:

✔ **Text** (in Figure 9-3, the model names are text)

✔ **A typed-in number** (in Figure 9-3, the revenues)

✔ **A number that results from a calculation** (in Figure 9-3, the totals in the last row)

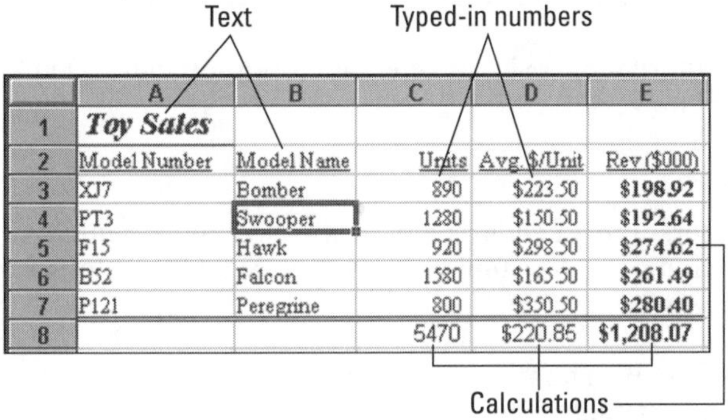

Text   Typed-in numbers

Figure 9-3:
Contents of
a few
example
cells in the
Toy Sales
spreadsheet.

	A	B	C	D	E
1	*Toy Sales*				
2	Model Number	Model Name	Units	Avg $/Unit	Rev ($000)
3	XJ7	Bomber	890	$223.50	**$198.92**
4	PT3	Swooper	1280	$150.50	**$192.64**
5	F15	Hawk	920	$298.50	**$274.62**
6	B52	Falcon	1580	$165.50	**$261.49**
7	P121	Peregrine	800	$350.50	**$280.40**
8			5470	$220.85	**$1,208.07**

Calculations

This section explains how to enter the first two kinds of cell content: text and typed-in numbers. Calculations are explained in Chapter 10.

Typing text

To simply enter some text, such as a column heading or title — something that won't be used in a calculation — just click on the cell and type the text.

Press the Enter key when you're done. Works recognizes any entry containing letters as being a text entry.

After you've typed your text and pressed the Enter key, you may notice that, up in the formula bar, Works sticks a quote character in front of what you typed. The quote mark doesn't appear in the cell, just in the bar. This character is Works' subtle way of saying that it interprets the contents of this cell as text, not as a number or calculation.

Sometimes you have to enter that quotation mark yourself. Keep an eye peeled for the following situations:

✔ You type a numeric entry that you intend to use as text (a serial number or zip code, for example), but it happens to consist of all numerals. The zip code 07920, for instance, will end up as the number 7920 if you don't begin it with a quotation mark.

✔ You type something that you intend to use as text, but it begins with the symbol =, +, or -. Typing +/-10% as, say, a column heading, will cause Works to display an error message because it thinks you tried to type a formula (and did it badly).

✔ You want your text entry to begin with a visible quotation mark ("), such as "Junior's" monthly allowance.

In any of these situations, type a quote (") character before you type anything else. This rule means, for instance, typing **""Junior's"** to make "Junior's" appear in the cell. If you find it hard to keep your eyes peeled for the preceding three situations, you can simply acquire the habit of beginning with a quotation mark every entry that you intend to be text.

Text entries require only a single, opening quotation mark. Don't add one at the end of the entry.

Typing numbers

Entering numbers into a cell is as simple as entering text into a cell. Just click on a cell and type the numbers in. Here are a few options you have for entering numbers:

✔ You can precede a number with a minus sign (-) if it's negative, or you can use a dollar sign ($) if it's money. If the number represents negative money, you can begin the number with -$ or you can enclose the number in parentheses. Works displays negative dollar amounts in parentheses: Negative five dollars is displayed in a cell as ($5). Use as many decimal places as you need, but Works displays the numbers rounded off to two decimal places if you use the dollar sign or parentheses.

- ✔ You can put commas at the thousandth point, but Works throws them out (unless you tell it differently — see the discussion of formatting numbers in Chapter 11).

- ✔ For percentages, follow the number with the percent sign (%). Remember that 100% is the same as 1.00.

- ✔ If you're a scientific type, you can use scientific notation: 1,253,000,000 can be typed 1.253e9, or 1.253E+09, for example. In fact, if you type in a big number, Works automatically shows it in this format. (You can tell Works to use a different format by changing number formatting, as Chapter 11 discusses.)

Don't follow a number with units, as in *36 fathoms.* If you put *fathoms* in the same cell as *36,* Works thinks the entire entry is supposed to be text, not a number, and won't be able to do calculations with the entry at all. If you want to display units in your spreadsheet, you have to type them in as text in another cell, but don't expect Works to recognize them as units. For instance, dividing 12 inches by 3 feet should result in .333, but because Works doesn't see or care about your units, it would divide 12 by 3 and give you an answer of 4. The simplest way to avoid such problems with units is to use the same units throughout your data (meaning don't mix inches and feet, for example).

After you finish typing the number and press the Enter key (or move the highlight), notice that the number is smushed against the right side of the cell (or *right-aligned,* in dweeb-speak). If you've previously typed any text, notice that the text is smushed against the left side of the cell. This is how Works aligns numbers and text unless you tell it differently. I'll get into "telling it differently" in the section on cell alignment in Chapter 11.

$!@($?)&$!!! What's all this ######### ?

If you're typing a number that's too wide for the column, you often get a distressing result. You get a bunch of pound (or "score") symbols, #####, in the cell, which is a message from Works saying, "I can't print this here; make the column wider, will ya?" Sometimes this situation occurs because the cell in question has the wrong number format — some formats are wider than others. If you use Works' default format for numbers, called *General* format, Works simply switches to nice, compact scientific notation when a number gets too large. You may or may not approve of this switch. For details on number formats, see the section on formatting numbers in Chapter 11.

Specifying where to edit

To set up Works to perform editing in the formula bar, the cell itself, or both places, choose Tools⇨Options from Works' menu bar. In the Options dialog box that appears, click the Data Entry tab to view the Data Entry card. Choose one of the three options in the box labeled Cell Data Entry Modes and then click the OK button.

Editing inside a cell

You may have noticed something a bit odd as you typed things into cells. Works is normally set up so that, when you type things into cells, you're actually typing in two places at once: in the cell you've selected and in the formula bar. If you do observe this phenomenon, your copy of Works is set up to allow you to do either of the following whenever you edit:

- ✔ Edit the contents of a cell by working in the formula bar.
- ✔ Edit the contents of a cell by working in the cell itself.

Personally, I like this editing flexibility. If you prefer to always edit in one place, you can change Works' setup. See the sidebar, "Specifying where to edit," for information on how to make the change.

Here's how to edit the contents of a cell, either in the formula bar or in a cell:

1. **Click the cell that you want to edit.**

   The cell shows its little rectangular halo and displays the contents of the cell in the formula bar.

2. **Click in the formula bar to edit in the formula bar, or double-click the cell to edit in the cell. (Or, press F2 and let Works decide where you edit.)**

   Wherever you choose to edit, a vertical line — an insertion point like the one in the Works word processor — appears to help you in your editing task.

3. **Move the insertion point to the place you want to edit.**

   To do this, move your mouse pointer over your data; the mouse pointer changes to an I-beam shape. Position that I-beam where you want to type or delete something, and then click. The insertion point jumps to that position.

4. **Use the Backspace or Delete keys to get rid of the old stuff you don't want.**

   To change or delete a bunch of characters at once, drag the I-beam cursor across those characters to highlight them, and then type replacement characters or press the Delete key. (To select an entire word or formula, double-click it.)

5. **Type in the new stuff.**

   As usual in Works, if you type over text you have highlighted, you replace that text.

6. **Continue clicking and editing until you're done; then press the Enter key.**

If you prefer, you can use the arrow keys instead of the mouse to position the insertion point in the formula bar.

Two interesting buttons are located next to the formula bar: one with an X and the other with a check mark. Here's how to use them:

- ✔ **Click the X to cancel your edit and return the cell to its original condition.** (This works just like pressing the Esc key.)

- ✔ **Click the check mark to enter the contents of the formula bar into the cell.** (This works just like pressing the Enter key. If you're entering a formula, Works also checks for errors.)

Working with Ranges: Groups of Cells

One nice feature of spreadsheets is that you can do calculations and other operations on groups of numbers. For instance, you can sum a column of numbers, or average all the data in your spreadsheet without having to add one number at a time. Any block (rectangular block, that is) of cells is called a *range*. A range can be a large, small, skinny, or wide rectangle of cells anywhere in your spreadsheet. A range can be just two adjacent cells, a column, a row — even the entire spreadsheet. Read on for how to work with ranges.

Selecting a range of cells

The easiest way to point out a range of cells to Works, either because you are about to format them all in some way or because you are referring to them in a calculation, is to select them. (The other way is to refer to them by their range address, described in the following section.) The mouse or keyboard technique for selecting a bunch of cells is pretty much the same as the technique for selecting bunches of stuff in all Works' tools, as the following shows.

For spreadsheets, you have three methods of selecting multiple cells:

- ✔ Click and drag the mouse cursor across the cells you want to select. You can move across or up and down, highlighting any row, column, or rectangular area. Release the mouse button when done.

- ✔ Click on one end or corner of the range of cells that you want to select. Then press the Shift key together with an arrow key or another navigation key to expand the highlight. Release the keys when done.

- ✔ To select an entire row or column, click the column letter or row number (in the gray area of the spreadsheet). To select the entire spreadsheet, click the unmarked button where the row-number and column-letter areas intersect (the upper-left corner).

To select an entire column full of cells, click the top cell and then press Ctrl+Shift+down-arrow. To select an entire row of data, click on the leftmost cell and then press Ctrl+Shift+right-arrow. The selection stops at the first blank cell in the column or row. (Or, if you start with a blank cell, the selection stops at the first cell with data.)

I actually prefer using navigation keys to using the mouse when I select ranges in spreadsheets. Navigation keys simplify expanding the highlight to include exactly the cells you want. When you press an arrow key, the highlight's edge moves by precisely one row or column. With the mouse, I tend to slop around too much. Of course, if I were not riding New Hampshire's Kancamagus Highway with my mouse pad on my knee, I might do better. (Hey, that could be a catchy little tune for the '90s, ". . . for I come from Kancamagus with my mouse pad on my knee. Oh, Susannah! . . .")

Referring to a range by its address

The way Works describes a range in its formulas (calculations) and in various dialog boxes is by using the range's *address*. You will need to understand range addresses in order to use these formulas and dialog boxes. A range's address combines the addresses of the two cells in opposite corners of the range, with a colon (:) in between. Which cell address comes first doesn't matter.

Here are the addresses of a few of the ranges shown previously in Figure 9-3:

All the model names	B3:B7 or B7:B3
All the model names	B3:B7 or B7:B3
Everything concerning the XJ7	A3:E3 or E3:A3
All the column sums	C8:E8 or E8:C8
All cells representing amounts of money	D3:E8 or E8:D3

Trying out an example spreadsheet

Here's an example of a spreadsheet. Figure 9-4 shows the first week of a diet plan for an anonymous, but very earnest, calorie-counting person.

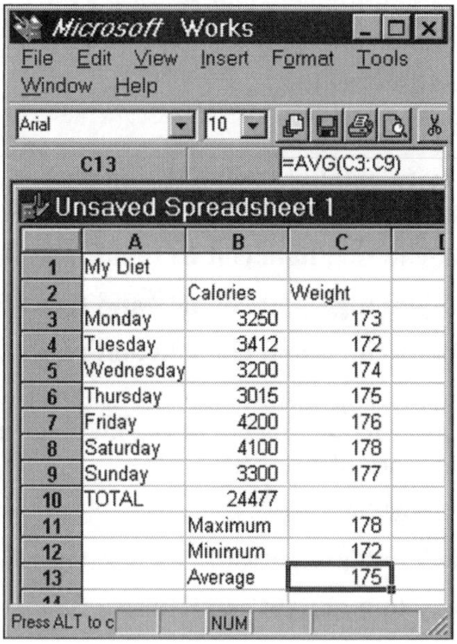

Figure 9-4:
A typical
first-week
diet, with
typical first-
week
results.

Here's how to duplicate this spreadsheet (18 quick steps to weight control!):

1. **To get a fresh spreadsheet, press Ctrl+N. When the Task Launcher screen appears, click the Works Tools tab and then click the Spreadsheet button.**

2. **The current active cell (where the highlight is) is A1. Type** MyDiet **and press the Enter key.**

3. **Click on cell B2 (column B, row 2). Type** Calories **and press the Enter key.**

4. **Press the right-arrow key to highlight cell C2. Type** Weight **and press the Enter key.**

5. **Click on cell A3 and type** Monday.

6. **Press the down-arrow key and type** Tuesday. **Keep pressing the down-arrow key and entering days of the week through Sunday. On the seventh day, rest.**

To avoid manually typing the days of the week, you can try out Autofill here, instead. See the section "Entering Sequential Headings and Data Automatically with Autofill" later in this chapter.

7. **Click on cell B3 and type** 3250.

8. **Press the down-arrow and type** 3412. **Refer to Figure 9-4 for the other calories and keep on like this through Sunday.**

9. **Click on cell C3 and type** 173. **Refer to Figure 9-4 for the other weights and keep on like this through Sunday.**

10. **Wake up, it's about to get interesting.**

11. **Click cell A10 and type** TOTAL.

12. **Press the right-arrow key to highlight cell B10 and type** =SUM(B3:B9). **Press the Enter key. Wow! Magic! The total calories for the week.**

13. **Press the down-arrow key to highlight cell B11 and type** Maximum.

14. **Press the down-arrow key to highlight cell B12 and type** Minimum.

15. **Press the down-arrow key to highlight cell B13 and type** Average.

Now make it interesting by typing in the formulas, as described in the remaining steps. Don't worry if you don't understand them right now; just type them in. I explain formulas in Chapter 10.

16. **Click cell C11 and type** =MAX(C3:C9).

17. **Press the down-arrow key to highlight cell C12 and type** =MIN(C3:C9).

18. **Press the down-arrow key to highlight cell C13 and type** =AVG(C3:C9). **Press the Enter key.**

With any luck, you should be looking at an exact duplicate of Figure 9-4.

Notice that you save some effort by not pressing Enter every time you type something (although you may press Enter, if you like). All you need to do is highlight a new cell to enter whatever you've typed in the previous cell.

Try changing some of the calorie or weight values and see what happens to the calculated values at the bottom.

Copying, Moving, and Deleting

Works provides a variety of features that lets you copy, move, and delete chunks of your spreadsheet. These features work pretty much the same way in every tool in Works. For the general picture, take a look at Chapter 3.

Here's how these things work in your spreadsheet. Note that copying and moving are a little different in spreadsheets than they are in the word processor:

- ✔ To delete a cell or range, select it and then press the Delete or Back-space key.

- ✔ To move a cell or range, select it and then slowly move your mouse cursor across the thickish frame that appears around the selected area until the cursor changes to an arrow labeled *drag*. At that point, click with the mouse button and drag a copy of the frame that appears to the new location. Release the mouse button, and the cells are moved.

- ✔ To copy, do the same thing as for moving, but hold down the Ctrl key while you drag.

- ✔ Another way to copy is to select the cell or range to be copied and then press Ctrl+C to copy to the Windows Clipboard. Click the cell where you want the copy, and press Ctrl+V to paste. If you're pasting a range of cells, click where you want the upper-left corner to go.

- ✔ To make multiple copies of a cell, click the cell to copy and then press Ctrl+C. Then highlight a range and press Ctrl+V. All the cells in the range will be filled with a copy.

- ✔ To cut something out and paste it elsewhere, select the something to be cut and then press Ctrl+X; then click wherever you want a copy and press Ctrl+V. If you're copying a range, select the range and then just click where you want the upper-left corner to go.

You can use the buttons on the toolbar in place of the key combinations:

- ✔ Ctrl+C is Copy, the button with two documents overlapping.
- ✔ Ctrl+V is Paste, the button with the clipboard.
- ✔ Ctrl+X is Cut, the button with the scissors.

Here are a few things to remember when moving and copying things around:

- ✔ When you move or copy something to already-occupied cells, the original contents are replaced by what you moved or copied.

✔ When you move a cell (say you're moving what's in A1 to B5) that is used in a formula (say, =A1/3), the formula changes to use the new address (in this example, B5/3). See Chapter 10 if you're not familiar with formulas.

✔ When you copy a formula, the addresses in it change. See the section on the mysteries of copying formulas in Chapter 10.

Inserting and Deleting Rows and Columns

There you are, a high-priced lifestyle consultant, typing up your monthly invoice for September. You've got a row for each day that you worked. You've made it to September 30, and suddenly you remember that you taught your client country-and-western line dancing on Saturday the 18th. Swell — what do you do now?

Well, you can select everything after the 18th and move it down a row, but how tedious and pedestrian! No, no, — a with-it, '90s kind of person like you should be inserting rows. Or columns, or whatever. Here's how:

1. **To insert a row, click anywhere in the row that you intend to be** *under* **your new row.**

   For example, to insert a row above row 5 and below row 4, click row 5.

2. **To insert a column, click anywhere in the column that you intend to have to the** *right* **of your new column.**

   For example, to insert a column between C and D, click column D.

3. **Choose Insert⇨Insert Row *or* Insert Column.**

Deleting a row or column (as opposed to just deleting its contents and leaving the row or column blank) is a similar procedure: Click anywhere in the row or column you want to delete; choose Insert⇨Delete Row *or* Delete Column. Clicking Insert in order to delete may seem odd, but (as Walter Cronkite used to say on the evening news) that's the way it is.

When you insert a row or a column (say, a new row 5), and one of your formulas includes a range that spans that row or column (say, =SUM(A1:A10)), the new row or column is included in the formula. However, if you insert a new row or column *on the edge* of a range of numbers (say, a new row 1 or a row 11), the new row or column is *not* included in the formula. So if you have an alphabetic list and add an Aaron or Zykowski, you may want to check to see that your totals are defined correctly.

Entering Sequential Headings and Data Automatically with Autofill

Sometimes the entries in a row or column — especially row and column headings — follow some predictable sequence. That sequence may be 1, 2, 3; or January, February, March; or Monday, Tuesday, Wednesday, where there is an equal interval between each entry. Unfortunately, typing in these predictable sequences can be really boring. After awhile, you find yourself thinking, "This sequence is so predictable. This thing I'm typing on is a computer. Couldn't the computer, like, *predict* or something?"

The answer is yes. In general, you need to type in only the first two items from one of these sequences, and Works can take it from there. To try this, follow these instructions:

1. **Type the first two items from the sequence in adjacent cells.**

   In the example in Figure 9-4, for example, you would type **Monday** in A3 and **Tuesday** in A4.

2. **Select the two cells that you just typed in.**

3. **Move your mouse cursor to the lower-right corner of the two-cell block that you just selected, until the word FILL appears under your cursor.**

4. **Click and drag over all the cells that you want to be filled automatically.**

   In the example in Figure 9-4, you would drag until the highlighted area included the two cells that you had typed, plus the next five in the same column.

5. **Release the mouse button.**

Presto! Works extends the sequence to fill the selected cells. Was it worth figuring this out just to avoid typing the names of five days? Maybe, maybe not. But if you ever need to type all the days of a *year* into a row or column, you may come to think very fondly of Autofill.

Autofill will only give you a sequence that is *arithmetic* (that proceeds at equal intervals), like 2, 4, 6, 8. Autofill will not give you a sequence that is *geometric* (that proceeds at equal multiples) like 2, 4, 8, 16.

This Autofill trick is actually a special use of the Fill Series command in the Edit menu. You can read more about the use of Fill Series in the section on filling cells with numbers in Chapter 23.

Saving Your Work

As the banking industry says, "Save regularly, and watch your interest grow," or some such avuncular aphorism. (Bankers are, or used to be, fond of avuncular aphorisms and kept hothouses full of them at their country estates.) Likewise, you should regularly save your spreadsheet document as a file. Doing so won't make your interest grow — unless the electricity fails, in which case your interest will grow immeasurably.

Saving your spreadsheet document is very much like saving any other Works document: Choose File⇨Save, or press Ctrl+S, or click the button with the diskette icon on the toolbar. If you need a refresher on saving files, see Chapter 2. For basic information on files and disks, see Chapter 1. Note that if you're working in some distant corner of the spreadsheet when you save it, you are returned to that distant corner when you reopen the spreadsheet.

Chapter 10
Making Calculations

. . . .

In This Chapter

▶ Using Easy Calc

▶ Creating and understanding formulas

▶ Using and understanding mathematical operators

▶ Understanding functions

▶ Creating formulas by pointing and shooting

▶ Copying formulas

▶ Turning off automatic recalculation for large spreadsheets

. . . .

*W*orks gives you the means to create darn near any calculation you need. You have two fundamental ways to approach doing calculations in Works spreadsheets:

✔ Works' Easy Calc, an automated take-you-by-the-hand approach to doing calculations

✔ The traditional write-it-yourself approach (aided, if you like, by a special point-and-shoot feature)

Easy Calc is a great feature for doing simple calculations, and it is a useful teaching tool for learning how calculations are done. Easy Calc is less helpful for more complex calculations and doesn't help you at all if you have to edit a calculation. To do those jobs, you need to know how formulas are written and what the formula gibberish means. In this chapter, I introduce you to both Easy Calc and the write-it-yourself method, showing you how formulas are written and explaining a few tricks that can make the job easier.

The General Idea of Spreadsheet Calculations

In spreadsheets, which are essentially big tables, you do calculations by putting *formulas* in cells; those formulas refer to various other cells in the spreadsheet. For instance, to sum up a column of numbers, you might put a summing formula in the cell at the bottom of the column. That formula would refer to all the cells containing the numbers you wanted to sum. After you enter a formula in a cell, that cell displays the *result* of the calculation (not the formula itself). The nice thing about the way spreadsheets do calculations is that any time you change the data (one of those numbers being summed, for instance), the formula cell immediately displays the new result.

Spreadsheets can display many different calculations at once, such as calculating the sums of several columns of data or displaying the sum, average, and minimum and maximum values of a single block of data. To help you do multiple calculations, spreadsheets come with another important feature: the ability to copy formulas. After you have written a formula, you can reuse that formula by copying it. For instance, if you had many columns to sum up, and they all had the same number of data cells (say, 20 cells in the column), you could simply copy your summing formula from the bottom of one column to another similar column (or columns). See "The Joys and Mysteries of Copying Formulas", later in this chapter for the tantalizing details of this process.

Using Works' Easy Calc

The Works engineers knew that many people are not fond of writing formulas or anything that looks like math, so they created a special tool called Easy Calc. Easy Calc asks you questions about where your data is and where you want the result of the calculation, and then it builds a formula for you. Of course, you need to know what sort of data the calculation you are doing will require. If you are computing Net Present Value, for instance, Works expects you to be able to give it a value for the Rate of Return.

Figure 10-1 shows an example of a spreadsheet ready and waiting for formulas. In the figure, the spreadsheet is for determining an average cost per night for lodging during a Canadian vacation. The data is entered, including an exchange rate for how many Canadian dollars I get for my American dollars. I'm now ready to enter my calculations.

Here's how to use Easy Calc to perform basic calculations on data you have entered in your spreadsheet:

1. **Choose Tools⇨Easy Calc from the Works menu bar.**

   The Easy Calc dialog box appears, listing buttons for a few of the most popular calculations, such as sums and averages, plus an Other button, which takes you to the vast range of other calculations that Works can do.

I will add my first formula here.

	A	B	C	D	E	F
	easycalc.wks					
1	**Our Canadian Vacation Lodging Expenses**					
2		**No. of**	**$$ Paid**	**$$/night**	**U.S.**	
3	**Hotel**	**Nights**	(Canadian dollars)		**dollars**	
4	Calgary Value Hotel	2	$167.90			
5	Banff Discount Lodging	1	$126.75			
6	Rancho Cheapo Cabins	1	$110.65			
7	Castle Mtn. Campground	2	$24.00			
8	Lake Louise Campground	2	$30.00			
9	Wabasso Campground	5	$75.00			
10	Riverside Cabins	1	$144.85			
11	Kootenay Hootnanny Lodge	1	$155.95			
12	Marble Canyon Campground	3	$36.00			
13	Jasper Honeysuckle Lodge	1	$189.55			
14	**Totals:**					
15	**Exchange Rate: CN$/1 US$**	1.56				
16	**Average Cost Per Night:**					
17						

Figure 10-1:
A spreadsheet ready to add formulas.

2. **Click the button for the kind of calculation you want to do.**

   If you don't see the calculation you want in the buttons displayed, click the Other button. (See the sidebar "Doing 'other' calculations in Easy Calc" later in this chapter.)

   In the example of Figure 10-1, I first want to compute the dollars per night for each lodging place, which means that I click the Divide button to divide the total dollars in column C by the number of nights in column B.

   A different Easy Calc dialog box now appears.

3. **Enter the numbers or the cell addresses that the Easy Calc dialog box prompts you to enter.**

   You can type numbers into the white boxes, if the number doesn't already appear in your spreadsheet. If the number does appear in your spreadsheet, either type its cell address (such as B12 for column B, row 12) or click on that cell. (To click on a cell, you may have to drag the Easy Calc dialog box to one side, or use the vertical or horizontal scroll boxes on the right or bottom side of your spreadsheet window to see the portion of the spreadsheet that you need.)

   If Easy Calc prompts you for a range, you can either type in the range (such as B1:D20) or drag your mouse cursor across the range to highlight it.

   See Chapter 9 if you don't understand cell addresses or ranges.

   If you make a mistake, click in the white box containing the mistake and try again. If you have made a mistake in a previous step, click the Back button.

An example will help make this step clear: If I were adding formulas to the example spreadsheet of Figure 10-1, at this step I would now be looking at the Easy Calc dialog box (see Figure 10-2). I would click first on cell C4 and then cell B4 to enter the numbers that Works requires.

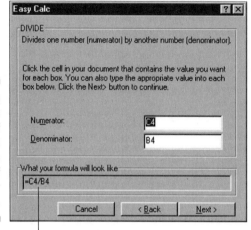

Figure 10-2:
Dividing the
contents of
one cell
by the
contents of
another
cell.

The formula Easy Calc is preparing for you

At the bottom of the Easy Calc dialog box, Works shows you the formula it has constructed for you. This display is a good way to figure out how formulas are written.

4. **Click the Next button, and enter additional numbers, text, ranges, or cell addresses, as prompted by the Easy Calc dialog box.**

   Depending on the sort of calculation you ask for, Easy Calc will need additional information. You may need to go through one or two more dialog boxes, clicking Next each time to proceed.

5. **The final piece of information Easy Calc will ask for is the cell address where you want the result to appear. You may type the cell address or click that cell; then click the Finish button.**

   In the example of Figure 10-1, I would choose cell D4 for my result, and then click the Finish button.

Here are some of the other calculations I can do for the spreadsheet of Figure 10-1:

   ✔ Computing American dollars from Canadian. This calculation would involve dividing the Canadian dollars in column D (beginning with D4) by the currency exchange rate in cell B15 and putting the results in column E (beginning with E4).

✔ Computing the total number of nights, just as a check to make sure that I didn't miss any. This calculation would involve summing the range B4:B13 and putting the result in cell B14.

✔ Computing the total cost by summing C4:C13, with the result in cell C14 (for Canadian dollars) and then doing the same for the American dollars in column D.

✔ Computing the average cost per night for lodging in American dollars. This calculation can be done by averaging the range E4:E13 and putting the result in cell B16. Or it can be done by dividing the total cost in cell D14 by the total number of nights in cell B14.

Some of this calculation work can be made easier by copying formulas. For example, I can copy from cell C14 the formula that summed Canadian dollars, and I can paste it in cell E14, where it sums American dollars.

The same trick would not, however, work well for copying the formula for computing American dollars in cell E4 to the other cells in column E. The copied formulas would fail to refer to the exchange rate in cell B15. As the formula was copied for each of the nine rows, the copies would refer instead to cells B16, B17, and so on, through B24. To understand why this error occurs and how to prevent it, see "The Joys and Mysteries of Copying Formulas" later in this chapter.

Doing "other" calculations in Easy Calc

If basic arithmetic and averaging won't do the job that you have in mind, Works is capable of doing lots of other calculations, called *functions*, which you can access by clicking the Other button in the initial Easy Calc dialog box. (See "You're Invited to a Function" later in this chapter for more details about these mathematical marvels.) Here are the steps for doing "other" calculations in Easy Calc:

When you choose Tools⇨Easy Calc and click the Other button, the Insert Function dialog box swings into action. In this dialog box, a list box labeled Choose A Function shows all the functions that Works offers. Scroll down the list to find the function that you want.

If you don't see what you want on the main list, click a category in the Category area to reduce the display of functions to A specific type. For example, to see only mathematical and trigonometric functions in the Choose A Function box, click Math And Trig. (Oddly, the SUM function is in the Statistical collection.)

Click a function in the Choose A Function area. You can see a brief description of what the selected function does at the bottom of the Insert Function dialog box.

Finally, click the Insert button. Easy Calc resumes its helpful dialog, as in Step 3 of the preceding instructions.

Writing Formulas: Beyond Easy Calc

Writing your own formulas (as opposed to using Easy Calc to write them for you) lets you do more powerful calculations in a single cell. To do a calculation, you type a formula into a cell. You can design a formula to do a lot of work all at once, like the following: `=(SUM(B1:B8))/(SUM(C9:C17))*A17-3.7`

Believe it or not, this formula is not a random collection of symbols. It means something, or at least it does to Works. This section will help you write formulas like that one (or simpler ones).

Works doesn't care whether you write formulas, cell addresses, or ranges in uppercase or lowercase letters. Works may convert some of the lowercase letters to uppercase letters, but that's its business.

Entering a formula

As you type a formula into a cell, the formula appears in both the cell itself and the formula bar. You can do your typing and editing in either location. To use the other location, just click there. See Chapter 9 for more information on typing things into a cell.

There's a disconcerting result of entering a formula, whether you type it yourself or let Easy Calc do the job: After you've entered the formula, the formula itself doesn't appear in the cell; the *result* of that formula (the answer) appears there! Disconcerting, perhaps, but very tidy. After all, you're interested in the answer, not the formula. Your calculator shows you only answers, right? A calculator doesn't show which buttons you pushed to get an answer. Neither does Works. So you pick where on your spreadsheet you want the *result* to appear, and that cell is where you type in the *formula*.

To enter a formula into a cell (whether you type directly into the cell or into the formula bar), do this:

1. **Click the cell where you want the formula.**

   Or use the navigation keys to move the highlight to that cell. Use a blank cell; don't try to put the formula in the same cell that holds the numbers that you're using in the calculation.

2. **Type an equal sign (=) and then a mathematical expression.**

   Spreadsheet formulas are mathematical expressions, which look something like this: `=5.24+3.93`

   Starting Works formulas with an = sign is usually necessary so that Works knows that you're doing a calculation and not entering text or a number. Sometimes Works can figure that out for itself, based on what you type, but why trust to luck?

3. Press the Enter key.

Or click the check mark on the formula bar, or move the highlight by clicking in another cell, or press a navigation key.

These actions enter the formula into the cell, which then displays the result. *The formula remains in the cell,* but only the result is displayed.

If you are doing a calculation, enter only the right side of the equation, (**=5.24+3.93**, for example). Don't enter the left side. Some folks try to assign the value to a cell by typing **A1=5.24+3.93**, for example. If you type such an equation, however, the equation ends up as text, not a calculation.

If you typed **=5.24+3.93** into a cell and pressed the Enter key, the cell would show the answer: 9.17. Isn't that exciting! *This* is why people spend thousands of dollars on computers and software. Well, maybe not; you may have been able to do that more easily on a five-dollar calculator. What you can't do on a five-dollar calculator, though, is type something like this: **=5.24+B1**

Hmmm. Shades of algebra. What this formula really means is, "Show me the sum of 5.24 and whatever is in cell B1." If B1 has the number 3.93 in it, you get 9.17. If B1 has the number 6 in it, you get 11.24. You can keep plugging new numbers into cell B1 and watch the answer change in the cell that has this formula in it.

Okay, this is amusing, but wait! There's more! What if you want a formula to add up a bunch of cells? You can type **=B1+B2+B3+B4+B5+B6+B7+B8**

Pretty boring. You can see where this may drive you back to your calculator. So to avoid losing your business, the software folks came up with a better idea. Rather than type all these cells and + signs, how about saying to Works, in effect, "Sum up the range B1 through B8." You say this by entering **=SUM(B1:B8)**

Because B1 through B8 are all neighboring cells covering a rectangular area — a column, in fact — they can be expressed as a range. (See the section on describing groups of cells in Chapter 9 for information on ranges.) If you want to include cells or additional ranges that aren't within that range, you can add them to the formula individually, like this: `=SUM(B1:B8, F15:B52,X15)`

"Which means *what?*" you may ask. Well (aside from being a way to string together the names of a bunch of great airplanes), *B1:B8* is a column, *F15:B52* is a rectangular block of cells, and *X15* is a single cell. If there were numbers in all those cells, the preceding formula would add them up.

SUM and other built-in calculations are called *functions.* And, used correctly, they do — function, that is. Works has a whole passel of other functions for doing all kinds of things. (More about those in the section "You're Invited to a Function," later in this chapter.) You don't even have to remember the funct-ions, as you see in "Point-and-shoot for functions," also later in this chapter.

All calculations, no matter how complex, are done this way in the spreadsheet: by mixing numbers, mathematical operations (such as addition and subtraction), and functions together to make formulas.

Seeing and editing formulas

The spreadsheet displays only the result of a formula, even though the formula actually remains in the cell. "So," you may well ask, "how can I see my formula?"

You can see an individual formula at any time by clicking its cell (or using the navigation keys to place your highlight on the cell) and looking in the formula bar. Figure 9-4, back in Chapter 9, shows a formula in the formula bar.

You edit a formula the same way that you edit any other contents of a cell: To edit using the formula bar, click the cell, and then click the formula bar. To edit directly in the cell, double-click the cell. (See the section on editing inside a cell in Chapter 9.)

To see all the formulas in your spreadsheet, choose View➪Formulas from the menu bar. This turns on a Formula view that's pretty ugly but does show all your formulas. You can work using this view, if you like. To turn off the Formula view, do the same thing you did to turn it on.

Hello, operator?: Mathematical operations

In a previous section, I employed the + symbol to represent addition in a formula. Table 10-1 shows some of the other common operators (math actions) and other symbols that you can use to create your mathematical formulas. This table also shows the order in which Works performs the operation, if two or more operations are in the cell.

Table 10-1	Math Operators	
Symbol	*Action*	*Order of Evaluation*
^	Raised to the power of	First
*	Times (multiplied by)	After ^
/	Divided by	After ^
−	Minus	After ^, *, and /
+	Plus	After ^, *, and /

The order in which you use operators in your expressions can be important. Following the basic rules of math, Works (just like calculators) calculates the formula in groups, performing exponential (that's the ^ symbol) calculations first and the addition calculations last.

Table 10-2 has some examples of mathematical expressions and what they do. Pretend for the moment that you're typing the function in cell B4.

Table 10-2	How Mathematical Expressions Work
Function in Cell B4	**What It Does**
=A2+A3	Adds the number in A2 to the number in A3 and shows the result in B4.
=10+A3/D8	Divides the number in A3 by the number in D8, adds 10 to the first result, and shows the final result in B4.
=A2*A3+B12	Multiplies the number in A2 by the number in A3, adds to that the number in B12, and shows the final result in B4.
=A2+A3*3.14+B12^3	Cubes the number in B12, multiplies the number in A3 by 3.14, adds those two results together with the number in A2, and shows the result of the whole mess in B4.

By putting an expression in parentheses, ( ), you force Works to evaluate that expression first. Works evaluates the expression (2+3)*4 as 5*4, giving 20 as the result. Without the parentheses, the expression is 2+3*4. In that case, Works does the multiplication first, creating 2+12; then it does the addition, giving 14 as the result. When you use parentheses within parentheses, the expression in the innermost pair is evaluated first. When you use too many parentheses, you may end up being dragged off to be "evaluated" yourself.

You're Invited to a Function

Works has quite a few of those convenient built-in functions, such as SUM, which are very inviting. Functions produce some sort of value as a result, which you can in turn use within a formula, as in SUM(A2:A22)/B4. Here are some functions, in addition to SUM, that people tend to use often:

AVG(cells)   The average of the values in the cells

MAX(cells)   The maximum value among the cells

`MIN(cells)`	The minimum value among the cells
`SQRT(cell)`	The square root of the value in the cell
`ROUND(cell, # of digits)`	The value in the cell rounded off to some number of digits

The word *cell* in the preceding list means that you should type in a single cell address, such as B1, not the word *cell*. And the word *cells* means that you should type in a range, such as B1:B8. For *cells,* you can also type in a bunch of ranges and individual cell addresses, all separated by commas. For example, you can use `=MAX(B1:B8, D5:D13, F256)` to give a result equal to the maximum value among all those cells. (Microsoft uses the term *range reference* instead of *cells*.)

When I say *# of digits,* I mean a number, such as 2 or 3. (Oh, all right. Instead of a number, *# of digits* may also be a cell that contains the number of digits or another function that produces a number of digits, but that's getting complicated.)

In formulas, as in resumés, it's against the rules to be your own reference. If one of the cells that a function *refers to* is the cell that your function is *in,* you're in trouble. You're also in trouble if the formula in your cell makes reference to another cell, which in turn makes reference back to your cell. And so on. In short, if Works needs to know what *is* in C4 in order to calculate what *ought* to be in C4, there's a problem. If you're lucky, Works tells you that you've got a *circular reference* and refuses to go on until you fix the problem. If you're not lucky, Works just merrily calculates something bizarre and does not tell you why.

Getting information about functions

There are so many functions that even a short list would be more than this book could handle. How many functions are there? To be precise, there are very many functions — maybe even a gaggle of them. These functions are described in two places: in the spreadsheet tool itself and in the Works Help feature. I discuss the spreadsheet tool's listing in "Creating Formulas the Point-and-Shoot Way" later in this chapter.

To read about functions by using the Help feature, do this:

1. **Press F1.**

   This step gets you to the Index card of the Help Topics window.

2. **Type the word** functions: **(including the colon) in box number 1.**

   You can see a number of folders having to do with functions. Several of these are the functions arranged by type — date functions, financial functions, mathematical functions, statistical functions, and so forth. If you don't see the folder that you want, scroll down by using the scroll bar on the right side of the window with the folders.

3. Click the folder covering the type of function that you're looking for.

If you want a function that does averages, for example, click the functions: statistical folder, which gives you a list of documents describing all the functions of this type.

4. Click the document (which all begin "To use . . .") describing any likely looking function.

Help appears in a window on the right side of the screen. You may need to move the Help Topics window to see the Help document.

5. In the Help window, click the More Info tab, and then click the button for Overview or Quick Tour.

The Step-By-Step information isn't particularly helpful in understanding how the function works. The Overview talks about functions in general, not the specific function you have chosen to read about. The Quick Tour is specific to the function you have chosen. If the function described doesn't sound like one that you wanted, click another function in the Help Topics window.

6. Click the Close button in the Help Topics window to return to your document.

Using non-mathematical functions

What Works' math, financial, and statistical functions do is usually clear to people who work in jobs that use those sorts of calculations. Like most spreadsheet programs, however, Works also contains functions that do useful things other than math. These functions can be a bit confusing, no matter what your profession is. My suggestion is to use Easy Calc to apply the functions, because it provides a bit of explanation. See the earlier section "Using Works' Easy Calc" and the sidebar "Doing 'other' functions in Easy Calc" near the beginning of this chapter. There are too many non-mathematical functions to cover in this book, so the following are just a few tips about the most popular types.

If you want a function to search for, display, or otherwise use text, you must put the text in quotation marks.

Date and time functions

Date and time functions are math functions that swallowed a perpetual calendar. They know how many days are in February, 2010, for instance, and what day of the week each date falls on. (I barely know what day of the week today is.) To work the way you want them to, these date and time functions require proper formatting, so they are discussed together with formatting numbers in Chapter 11.

Lookup functions

Lookup functions can automate jobs where you would have to look something up in a table. For instance, if you enter your equipment inventory in a table, you can use VLOOKUP to identify the department that owns a piece of equipment. You would program the VLOOKUP function to search down the leftmost column of that table for the serial number you enter in, say, cell A2, and then go across to the Department column, two columns to the right, and display the text that the function finds there.

Lookup functions are also useful for scientific work, where you would look something up in a table based on a number or a calculation — say, the strength of an adhesive based on average curing temperature. You can have the spreadsheet average a group of temperature measurements, and then you can use the average value to look up the adhesive strength in a table.

Each function requires that you enter certain values or addresses of cells that contain those values. Easy Calc prompts you for these values. Type the values or click on the cells containing the values. If you are typing the function yourself, you enter these values in the specified order, separated by commas, in the parentheses following the function name.

Logical functions

Logical functions are useful for situations where, depending on how a calculation comes out, you want the spreadsheet to decide "yes" or "no" (or "blue" or "green" or whatever pair of choices you have in mind). The most useful logical function is the IF function, which is written like this:

IF(*condition*, *value if true*, *value if false*)

Where this function shows value if true, condition, and value if false, you don't actually type those words; you enter values or cell addresses. This function displays (takes on the value of) the value if true if the condition you specify is true; otherwise, it displays the value if false. For instance, the function IF(A3=5, kewl , bogus) displays the word kewl if the value contained in cell A3 is exactly 5; otherwise, it displays bogus. Instead of text, you can enter numbers or the addresses of cells that contain text or numbers.

Conditions are expressed like this: A1<5 (the value in cell A1 is less than 5). Or, more complicated, avg(A1:A30)<=B1 (the average of the values in cells A1 through A30 is less than or equal to the value in cell B1). Operators for comparison are <, >, =, <=, >=, and <> (not equal); look up "operators: comparison" in Works help.

Creating Formulas the Point-and-Shoot Way

Typing formulas is okay until you get to the part where you have to enter a range. In order to type in the range address, you have to leave your formula behind and go find out where your data is. Or, you have to go look up the way the formula is supposed to be written. What a pain. Fortunately, Works provides a far more convenient way to enter ranges and other things in your formulas. I call it the *point-and-shoot* approach, and you use it while you are creating formulas in the formula bar.

You can point-and-shoot cell addresses and ranges, and you can point-and-shoot functions. You can do a whole summation just by pointing and shooting. The details are in the sections following this list, but here's the big picture:

- **Cell addresses and ranges:** As you're typing a formula, if you need to enter a cell address (such as A1 — you know, the steak sauce) or a range (such as B4:A1, which is what people used B4 steak sauce), just go click on the cell or highlight the range while you're typing.

- **Functions (**SUM **and so on):** Whenever you're typing in a formula and you need a function, you can insert one by just choosing it from a nice list. Pause in your typing of the formula, and choose Insert⇨Function in the menu bar to get a dialog box with the nice list in it.

- **Autosum:** Whenever you have a column (or row) of numbers that you want to add up, just select the empty cell at the bottom of the column (or at the end of the row) and click the Autosum button on the toolbar. The sum formula then appears in the empty cell, with the column or row automatically entered.

Point-and-shoot for cell addresses and ranges

Here's the blow-by-blow for entering cell addresses in a formula that you're creating:

1. **Click a cell and start creating your formula.**

   Type an = sign, for example. Or you can click in the white area of the formula bar and type an equal sign there. Type your formula right up to the point where you need a cell address or range. If you're using the SUM function, for example, type the following (including the left parenthesis): **=SUM(**

2. **When your formula needs a cell or range address, select (highlight) whatever cell or range you want to use.**

   Click a cell or drag the mouse pointer to select an area. (Or use the navigation keys.) The cell address or range you select is automatically entered in your formula in the formula bar. How about that?! The address or range is highlighted to show off the fact that you didn't actually type it in but are pointing at it. If you selected the wrong address or range by mistake, just select a different one.

Do not press the Enter key at this point! If you press Enter prematurely, Works thinks that you're done typing the formula.

3. Complete your formula.

Type the closing parenthesis, if it's not already there, or enter whatever the next math symbol is. The next character you type appears right after the cell or range address in the formula. For example, if you started with =SUM(and selected the range B5:B15, the formula reads =SUM(B5:B15, so type the final parenthesis: **)**.

If you have additional addresses to enter, do them the same way. To multiply the sum in the example by the contents of cell D5, continue by typing the multiplication symbol (*) and then pointing to cell D5.

4. Press Enter when you're done.

Point-and-shoot for functions

Here are the details on how to pick a function from a list instead of typing it in:

1. Click a cell and start creating your formula.

Type an = sign or click the formula bar. Type your formula right up to the point where you need a function.

2. Choose Insert⇨Function.

The Insert Function dialog box swings into action. At this point, the big list box labeled Choose A Function shows all the functions that Works offers. Scroll down the list to find the function that you want.

3. If you don't see what you want on the main list, click a category in the Category area to reduce the display of functions to a specific type.

For example, to see only mathematical and trigonometric functions in the Choose A Function box, click Math And Trig. (Oddly, the SUM function is in the Statistical collection.)

4. Click a function in the Choose A Function area.

You can see a brief description of what the selected function does at the bottom of the Insert Function dialog box.

5. Click the Insert button.

The dialog box goes away, leaving you with your chosen function typed into the formula bar. However, Works doesn't know yet what cell or cells you want the function to apply to, so it leaves text as a place-holder in the places where cell addresses go.

6. **Edit the formula to put in cell addresses.**

   You have two ways to go. If you like, you can type in the cell addresses you need and delete any extraneous text. Or you can highlight some of the placeholder text, and then use the point-and-shoot method for addresses and ranges (described previously) to replace it.

7. **Press Enter when you're done.**

Point-and-shoot for summing columns or rows

Thanks to Works' Autosum feature, summing a row or column of numbers is a piece of cake. Here's exactly how to do it:

1. **To sum up a column of numbers, place your highlight on the cell beneath the last number, or**

   To sum up a row of numbers, place your highlight on the cell to the right of the last number.

2. **Click the Autosum button on the toolbar — the button with the Greek letter sigma on it (Σ).**

3. **Press the Enter key.**

If you use Autosum on a cell that is *both* at the bottom of a column *and* at the end of a row, Autosum sums the column, not the row.

The Joys and Mysteries of Copying Formulas

Copying is not what most folks think of as an exciting activity, unless they are confused by the sign over their employer's copy department, which often reads "Reproduction." But rest assured that copying can be a far more interesting activity than you suppose when it comes to spreadsheet formulas.

Where copying formulas works well

In a spreadsheet, you often have a column or row in which essentially the same formula is used over and over again — when you're summing a set of columns, for example. If the only difference from column to column is the range being summed, you can save a great deal of effort by copying the formula rather than retyping it. Works automatically takes care of giving the formula the correct, new range.

For formula copying to work easily, one condition must be true: The location of a formula relative to its data must be the same for all copies as for the original. For instance, if the original formula is immediately under a column of 20 data cells, each copy must also be immediately under its own column of 20 data cells. In Figure 10-1, for instance, I can easily copy the formula that will appear in cell C14 to cell C15. If the original formula uses a cell that is three columns over and one row down from its address, each copy must be provided with a number three columns over and one row down from *its* address.

Here's how to copy a formula across a row or down a column. The procedure for copying is really just the same as copying a number or text or anything else (although the result is unique):

1. **Enter (or click) the formula you want to copy.**

   If you intend to copy the formula down a column, entering the formula in the top cell is traditional. If you intend to copy your formula across a row, the traditional place to enter the initial formula is the leftmost cell of the row. But any old place will do.

2. **With the formula selected, press Ctrl+C or click the Copy button on the toolbar.**

   This copies the formula to the Windows Clipboard.

3. **Select the rest of the row or column where you want the copies to appear.**

   You may include the original formula cell in your selection, if you feel it makes life easier. It doesn't matter.

4. **Press Ctrl+V or the Paste button on the toolbar.**

   Bingo, you're done.

The best way to explain what happens when you copy a formula is with an example: Figure 10-3 shows part of a spreadsheet. Three columns of numbers are shown: C, D, and E. The top five numbers in C and E are typed in; the last number in each column is the sum. The D column is calculated from the C and E columns. So the figure contains ten typed-in numbers and eight formulas.

Rather than write eight formulas, I had to write only one. Here's how I did it:

1. **I summed column C by selecting C8 and clicking the Autosum button on the toolbar.**

2. **I summed column E by selecting E8 and clicking the Autosum button on the toolbar.**

	A	B	C	D	E
1	_**Toy Sales**_				
2	Model Number	Model Name	Units	Avg. $/Unit	Rev ($000)
3	XJ7	Bomber	890	$223.51	$198.92
4	PT3	Swooper	1280	$150.50	$192.64
5	F15	Hawk	920	$298.50	$274.62
6	B52	Falcon	1580	$165.50	$261.49
7	P121	Peregrine	800	$350.50	$280.40
8			5470	$220.85	$1,208.07

Figure 10-3:
Copying formulas can save you a lot of typing time.

3. I entered the formula =1000*E8/C8 **into cell D8 and pressed Enter.**

In case you're curious, the 1000 is there because the revenues in column E are expressed in terms of thousands of dollars. (Multiplying by 1000 expresses them in terms of dollars.)

4. I clicked the Copy button on the toolbar to copy the formula in D8.

5. I selected the range D3:D7.

6. I clicked the Paste button on the toolbar to paste in copies of the formula.

Each copy of the formula uses cells on a different row, which you see in the formula bar when you click those cells. The formula in cell D5, for example, is =1000*E5/C5; in cell D6, it's =1000*E6/C6; and so on. Pretty neat, huh?

Here's what happens to cell addresses when you copy formulas:

✔ **When you copy a formula to a new column, the letters change.**

That is, the column portions of any cell addresses in your formula change. They change by exactly the number of columns that you move: If you copy something three columns to the right and you have an address of A1 in your formula, it changes to D1, Q17 changes to T17, and so on.

✔ **When you copy a formula to a new row, the numbers change.**

That is, the row portions of any cell addresses in that formula change. They change by exactly the number of rows that you move: If you copy something three rows down and you have an address of A1 in your formula, A1 changes to A4, Q17 changes to Q20, and so on.

If you copy a formula to a new row and column, both the row and column change in any cell addresses in that formula.

When you _move_ a formula (by dragging it), or cut and paste the formula, the addresses in the formula do not change. Addresses change only when you _copy_ something — either by dragging or by using the Copy and Paste commands (Ctrl+C and Ctrl+V).

When formulas don't copy right

Sometimes copying doesn't work the way you want it to. Commonly, this situation occurs when you've got a single value somewhere that you want to use in a row or column of calculations. Back in Figure 10-1, the formula in cell E4 (American dollars) depends on the exchange rate in cell B15. If you copy that formula to the other rows (E5, E6, and so on), the reference to B15 changes rows — to B16, B17, and so on — and is wrong.

To avoid this problem, you can enter each formula separately instead of copying. But if you would prefer to copy, there is a trick that lets you copy properly. To keep a cell reference from changing when you copy, put a dollar sign in front of the column letter and/or row number in the formula. For example, in cell E4 of Figure 10-1, you would type **=D4/B15** instead of **=D4/B15**. When that formula is copied to the next row, the E4 changes to E5, but B15 remains the same. This copying trick is called *absolute addressing*.

If you use the point-and-shoot method of entering addresses, when you "point," press the F4 key to create an absolute address like B15. Press it again to get B$15, and again to get $B15. This trick also works when you enter cell addresses in Easy Calc.

What this all boils down to is: *Put a dollar sign in front of any portion of a cell address that you want to keep from changing when the formula is copied.* For example, a formula using A$8, copied down one row, still reads A$8. If A$8 is copied one column to the right instead, A$8 changes to B$8. The part with the dollar sign does not change; the rest does.

The dollar sign, here, has *absolutely nothing* to do with dollars (U.S. or Canadian) *or* currency formatting; use of the dollar sign is just an ancient convention in spreadsheets, probably started by Dan Bricklin when he did VisiCalc, or by one of the other spreadsheet pioneers.

Recalculating Large Spreadsheets

Works recalculates all its formulas whenever you change any cell's contents. As a result, a really big spreadsheet can slow you down; you have to wait for Works to recalculate every time you enter something.

If your spreadsheet seems to take a long time to recalculate, you can switch to manual calculation, which makes Works put off recalculating formulas until you press the F9 key. To switch from automatic to manual calculation (and vice versa), choose Tools⇨Options from the menu bar. The Options window is a collection of cards, one of which is named Data Entry. Click the tab of that card. Now click the Use Manual Calculation check box.

Chapter 11

Tidying Up and Printing Your Spreadsheets

. . . .

. . . .

Making a spreadsheet is one thing. Getting the spreadsheet ready for prime time — formatting its numbers and dates properly, giving it a face lift, and finally, printing it out — is another.

Are your spreadsheets looking kind of clunky, industrial, and bland? In this chapter, I examine how to use AutoFormat and borders to add beauty and grace and also how to use alignment and other formatting to add style and deep, philosophical significance. (Didn't know it was that easy, did you?)

Are your dates always late? Or do your dates seem to last forever? This chapter helps with those date dilemmas by describing how to deal with dates, time, and basic date-and-time arithmetic. (The chapter helps because you can read it while you're waiting for your date to begin or end. Reading this chapter also gives you that air of elevated intellectual capacity that always attends someone seen reading a ...For Dummies book, thereby impressing the heck out of your date.)

Are your lists feeling out of sorts? This chapter shows you how to bring alphabetical or numerical order to your lists of people, places, or things, and how to safely include calculations in your sordid — oops, I mean *sorted* — lists.

Finally, this chapter delves into the unique opportunities that spreadsheets present for really messing things up when you print. Why, this chapter even provides some solutions.

Formatting in One Swell Foop!

Back when disco ruled and quiche was the trendy food of the day, spreadsheets were dull, boring grids. No more! Today's spreadsheet sports designer colors, shadings, lines, borders, 3-D shading, and fancy fonts in different sizes and styles.

Works is no slouch when it comes to formatting; you can apply all of these fancy formats as you like, where you like. But Works has also combined a bunch of formatting into various stylish ensembles, which Works refers to as *automatic formatting*. Automatic formatting (*autoformatting*) is truly a great idea.

Autoformatting your entire spreadsheet

Figure 11-1 shows what happens to the toy sales spreadsheet when it's decked out in an automatic format called 3-D Effects 2. All kinds of stuff has changed here, even the formats of some of the numbers. Zowie! All these changes resulted from a few mouse clicks.

The AutoFormat feature presumes that you have a fairly classic table structure: rows, columns, and maybe (though not necessarily) totals. If you meet these standards, AutoFormat away:

1. **Make sure that you have column and row headings.**

   Or, if you don't have 'em, at least have a blank row above and a blank column to the left of your table. (Use these for your title row and column in Step 2.)

2. **Select all the rows and columns, including title row and column and total row and/or column.**

   If you have a title for the whole spreadsheet, you can include or exclude it, as you like. I excluded the "Toy Sales" line in Figure 11-1.

Figure 11-1:
Auto-
formatting:
Just a few
clicks can
get you a
whole new
look.

	A	B	C	D	E
1	*Toy Sales*				
2	Model Number	**Model Name**	**Units**	**Avg. $/Unit**	**Rev ($000)**
3	XJ7	Bomber	890	223.505618	198.92
4	PT3	Swooper	1280	150.5	192.64
5	F15	Hawk	920	298.5	274.62
6	B52	Falcon	1580	165.5	261.49
7	P121	Peregrine	800	350.5	280.4
8			5470	220.8537477	1208.07

3. Choose Format⇨AutoFormat.

The AutoFormat dialog box of Figure 11-2 leaps into action.

Click a format here.

What the selected format looks like.

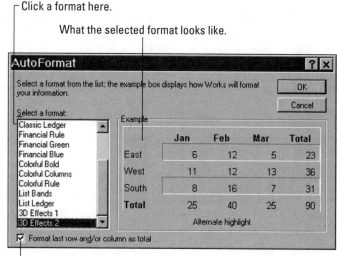

Figure 11-2:
The
AutoFormat
dialog box.
If only
reformatting
my car was
this easy.

Click here to turn on/off the special formatting on the last row and column.

4. Click any interesting-sounding format in the Select A Format list box.

The Sample area shows you what the format looks like. If you don't like this format, click another format. If you don't like any of 'em, press the Esc key.

5. Look at the Format Last Row And/Or Column As Total check box.

If you haven't used a total row or column, or if you have your total somewhere other than at the end of the range, make sure that this box is blank. If you do have a total row or column, check the box, but look at the example to see whether this particular format puts the total in the same place you did.

In the toy sales example, I chose to leave the box blank because cell D8 is an average, not a total.

6. **Click the OK button.**

Foop! There's a brief flurry of activity, and suddenly your spreadsheet looks like the inside pages of a quarterly report. If you don't like the results, press Ctrl+Z immediately to undo the formatting — before you make any other changes to the spreadsheet — and try again.

7. **Throw in some finishing touches if you want.**

In Figure 11-1, I would probably do something to get rid of the long decimal expansions in D3 and D8, either by using the ROUND function (see the section on point-and-shoot for functions in Chapter 10) or by selecting column D and changing to currency format. (See "Formatting numbers" later in this chapter.)

Formatting the appearance of characters

One of the ways that you can fool with the appearance of the text, numbers, and formulas in your spreadsheet is to change the font, size, style, or color. Appearance formatting is one of those things that works the same way for all the tools of Works.

For the full details on formatting characters, refer to Chapter 3. The executive summary goes like this:

You have three ways to change how your type looks as you enter it:

- ✔ **Alternative 1.** Choose the font, size, and style from the toolbar.

- ✔ **Alternative 2.** Choose font, size, style, or color from the Font card of the Format Cells dialog box. To get this dialog box, choose Format⇨Font And Style.

- ✔ **Alternative 3.** (To change style only) Press Ctrl+B for bold, Ctrl+I for italic, and Ctrl+U for underline.

To change the appearance of characters that are already typed, just select them first and then use one of these three alternatives.

Formatting numbers

Numbers? You want numbers? Works has got your number. In fact, you've probably never realized how many ways there are to write numbers.

Formatting numbers is not quite like formatting text. After all, when you change the formatting of text, the characters themselves don't change — just their font and style change. But when you format numbers, the actual characters and punctuation change to different characters and punctuation, adding dollar signs or parentheses, for example. The number itself doesn't change, but it puts on a radically different face. Sometimes it doesn't even look like a number any more.

For example, if you put the number 3284.2515 in a cell and use your formatting options (which Table 11-1 lists), you can make that number look like any of the stuff in the How It Looks column of Table 11-1.

Table 11-1	Different Formatting for the Number 3284.2515	
How It Looks	*Format Name*	*About That Format & Options You Can Specify*
3284.25	General	As precise as possible for the column width; this is how Works formats numbers unless you tell it otherwise.
3284.251	Fixed	Specifies decimal places (in this example, *three*).
$3,284.25	Currency	Dollar sign, comma, specifies decimal places; negative numbers appear in parentheses. Optional: negative numbers also in red.
3,284.25	Comma	Like Currency, but no dollar sign.
328425.15 %	Percent	Displays number multiplied by 100, adds percent symbol; specify your decimal places.
3.28 E+03	Exponential	Single digit number with power of ten; specify your decimal places (in this example, *two*).
03284	Leading Zeros	No fraction, displays as many digits as you specify (in this example, *five*); adds zeros or trims leading digits to do so. Good for zip (postal) codes.
3248 3/10	Fraction	Expresses fractional part as fraction: Choose halves, thirds, quarters, eighths, tenths, and so on (in this example, *tenths*).
TRUE	True/False	If zero, displays FALSE; if not zero, TRUE.

(continued)

Table 11-1 *(continued)*

How It Looks	Format Name	About That Format & Options You Can Specify
November 21, 1908	Date	Interprets number as number of days since 12/31/1899; Works uses this format when you enter a date.
6:02 AM	Time	Interprets fractional part of number (only) as fraction of one day; displays fraction as hour of that day. Works uses this format when you enter a time.
3284.2515	Text	If format applied *before* number is entered, turns number into text. Useful for serial numbers or other numeric codes.

Date and time formats are among the weirder ones in this list because they make numbers look like text. For more on using them, see "Formatting dates and times" later in this chapter.

Currency format is the easiest to apply: Select the cell or cells to format and click the toolbar button with the $ icon on it.

You don't actually format numbers in the spreadsheet tool; you format *cells*. The cell can be empty when you format it, and when you type a number in that cell, the number takes on that format. If you type text in that cell, the text is not affected. If you delete an entry from a cell, the number format remains.

Works starts with every cell having the General format. The way to change the format of specific cells is as follows:

1. **Select a cell or bunch of cells.**

   Click the cell or highlight the bunch of cells.

2. **Choose Format⇨Number.**

   The Number card of the Format Cells dialog box presents itself for duty.

3. **Click any format in the Format area of the dialog box.**

   A sample appears in the Sample area near the bottom of the dialog box. If a number is already in the cell, that number is used in the sample. If you don't like what you see, click another format. See Table 11-1 for notes about these formats.

Some formats allow you to specify how many digits are to the right (or left, in the case of Leading Zeros format) of the decimal point. Normally, Works uses two digits here. To change this situation, just type a number to go into the Decimal Places box.

The Currency and Comma formats let you optionally put negative numbers in red; just click the check box marked Negative Numbers In Red.

The Fractions format normally reduces fractions: If you choose $^1/_{32}$, and your number ends in .125, it shows $^1/_8$. If you really want $^1/_{32}$ or whatever fraction you've chosen, click the check box marked Do Not Reduce.

4. Click the OK button.

Changing Alignment in a Cell

Another way to change the appearance of something in a cell is to change its alignment: smushed left, smushed right, or smack dab in the center of a cell are the basic choices. Normally, Works aligns text to the left and numbers to the right, but you don't have to live with that.

Alignment is another one of those things that works pretty much the same (at least for the basics) in all the Works tools:

- ✔ Select a cell or cells and then click the Left, Center, or Right Align button in the toolbar. (These buttons are the ones with the lines on them.)

  When you specify an alignment, the alignment sticks to the *cell,* not to what's in the cell. If you specify alignment for a blank cell, whatever you type later gets aligned accordingly. If you delete what's in a cell, the alignment remains in the cell.

- ✔ You can tell how any cell is aligned by clicking it and observing the alignment buttons on the toolbar. If one of them is depressed, the cell is aligned in that way.

- ✔ To remove an alignment, click the alignment button that is depressed. (The Alignment reverts to left alignment.)

These basic alignments, plus some other fancier alignments, can also be found on the Alignment card of the Format Cells dialog box. I don't get into those things here, but if you want to experiment with that box, choose Format⇨Alignment.

The clockwork behind dates and times

Here's what's behind the scenes: Works computes dates by giving every day a number; Works starts the sequence at January 1, 1900, which is represented as 1. Days are whole numbers. Hours and minutes in that day are represented by a fractional portion. So the number that represents 8:00 AM on January 1, 1900 is 1.333333333. Works runs out of dates on June 3, 2079, so don't make any hundred-year plans.

If you type in a date or a time, Works shows it to you as a date or a time, which is nice. But Works secretly changes the entry to a number. If you type **8 AM**, for example, Works enters 0.333333333 and chooses a *time format* for the number. If you type in a date, Works enters the number for that date and applies a *date format* that resembles the format in which you typed the number.

Making Dates

You've probably made your share of bad dates; now try good dates. Works provides date arithmetic, formatting, and functions so that you can calculate things based on time without having to recite to yourself, "Thirty days hath September, April, June, and December . . . or was it November?"

Entering dates

If you're North American, you can enter a date into a cell in most of the ways you would consider normal (like August 28, 1945). If you're European, you have to use the weird, backward American way. Table 11-2 shows good and bad ways to enter the date of August 28, 1945. The bad dates aren't really bad; Works just takes them as text because they are in the wrong format, so you won't be able to do any calculations with them. If you want them simply for labels, though, feel free to type them the "bad" way.

Table 11-2	Good and Bad Dates
Good	*Bad*
August 28, 1945	August 28 1945
8/28/45	28/8/45
8/28/1945	Aug. 28,1945
8 / 28 / 1945	8-28-1945

To enter a date in the current year, just enter the day and month part (8/28, for example). To enter today's date, press Ctrl+; (that's Ctrl and the semicolon key). Amazing!

To enter a date that's current all the time, like on a day/date watch, type in the formula =**NOW()** and format the cell with a *date format* (see "Formatting dates and times" later in this chapter). The date is updated every time you change a cell or press the F9 (recalculate) key.

Entering times

As with entering dates, there are "good" ways to enter times that Works understands as time; any other ("bad") way causes Works to interpret the entry as text. But, as they say, you gotta (everyone together now . . .) "take the good times with the bad." Sorry. Had to do that. See Table 11-3 for good and bad ways to enter times.

Table 11-3	Good and Bad Times
Good	*Bad*
2:30PM	230PM
14:30	1430
8:00	0800
8 AM	8 AM EST
8am	eight o'clock

To enter the current time, press Ctrl+Shift+; (that's Ctrl+Shift+semicolon).

To enter a time that's always current, like the time on a clock, type in the formula =**NOW()** and format the cell with a *time format* (see "Formatting dates and times" later in this chapter). The time is updated every time you change a cell or press the F9 (recalculate) key. (Again, if you're using *manual* recalculation rather than the normal *automatic* recalculation, you have to press the F9 key.)

Doing basic date and time arithmetic

Works' spreadsheet tool lets you do calculations based on time, but you have to be a little careful. Works secretly uses numbers to represent dates and makes them look date-ish by using a *date format*. If you do calculations, the results may come out as funny numbers instead of the date, number of days, or number of hours that you were hoping for. The following instructions can generally keep things working well.

Subtracting dates; adding days to dates

If you have two dates, by subtracting you can easily calculate exactly how much time elapses between them.

Calculating intervals between dates can be depressing if you're single and your social life is less than satisfactory.

You subtract dates just as you subtract regular numbers, except that each date either has to be in its own cell or, if you're using the dates in a formula, in single quote marks (apostrophes) and in the slash-date format, as in '9/15/94'. Here are the rules of date subtraction:

- ✔ To use dates in a formula, type the dates in single quote marks and in the slash format: ='9/15/95' - '4/14/95'.

- ✔ To write a formula using dates that are in separate cells, type something like =B4-B8, where cell B4 has one date and B8 has the other. Dates can be entered in cells B4 and B8 in any acceptable format.

- ✔ The first date in a subtraction should be the later of the two if you want a positive number.

- ✔ The result that you get is the number of days between the dates.

After you read "Formatting dates and times" later in this chapter, you may be tempted to format the result of date subtraction with a date format, just on general principles. Do *not* do it! Such an action has confusing results. For example, the answer to '9/15/95' - '4/14/95' is 154 days. If you now put that into date format, Works gives you June 2, 1900 — day 154 for Works. (See the sidebar "The clockwork behind dates and times" earlier in this chapter.) Unless the space-time continuum is more complicated than we think, this information is useless. Leave the result as a number of days, with a regular old number format.

Adding dates sounds like the logical complement to subtracting them but, in fact, is complete nonsense. (Christmas plus the Fourth of July equals . . . what?) You can, however, add *days* to dates by using a formula. Just as in subtraction, to put the date right into the formula, use single quotes around the date and use the date-slash format. For example, ='9/15/94' + 35 adds 35 days to September 15.

If you're adding days to a date to compute another date, such as adding 35 days to September 15, 1994, *do* use a date format; otherwise, you just see a weird number. See "Formatting dates and times" later in this chapter.

Subtracting and adding times

You subtract time in much the same way as you subtract dates. You can use times either in cells by themselves or as parts of a formula:

✔ If you're going to enter a time directly in a formula, put single quotes around it (`10:00 PM` or `22:00` , for example). For minutes, the hour is zero, as in `0:30` for thirty minutes.

✔ If the times are in cells of their own, you can omit the single quotes.

The only trouble with subtracting times is that the result may need a little fixing up because Works uses units of days for time, not hours or minutes. Here's a quick example.

If you're a hotshot lawyer making, oh, $450 an hour, you, of course, want to bill your clients precisely for your time. So perhaps you keep three columns for each client: one (say, column B) for starting time, another (column C) for ending time, and the third (column D) for the difference between the two. You make the following entries in, say, row 3:

Cell B3	Cell C3	Cell D3
10 AM	10:15 AM	=C3-B3

The only problem is that the result in column D will be 0.010416667. That number represents the fraction of a day that equals 15 minutes. There are two problems with this result:

✔ The number doesn't look like minutes or hours.

To fix this appearance problem, use a time format (see "Formatting dates and times" and "Formatting numbers" in this chapter); the best time format to use is one of the 24-hour formats — the ones without AM or PM after them.

✔ Even if you fix the format, if you use this number to calculate your fee, you'll go broke!

If you multiply your time in column D (0.0104) by your rate of $450, you will earn only $4.65 — a pittance to a high-priced person such as yourself. You spend more than that for a cup of cappuccino in the lobby coffee shop.

Your problem is that Works keeps track of hours as fractions of a day. One hour is $1/24$ of a day. So to fix the problem in this example, you would multiply by 24. The "fix" rules go like this:

✔ To convert the result of time subtraction to hours, multiply by 24. The formula in column D of the example would be (`C3-B3`)`*24`.

✔ To convert the result of time subtraction to minutes, multiply by 24*60. The formula in column D of the example would be (`C3-B3`) `*24*60`.

Now for time addition. Adding *hours of the day* together is just as nonsensical as adding dates together. (What is 2 p.m. plus 3 p.m.?) But you can certainly add *times* together or sum up a bunch of times. (Two hours plus three hours is five hours. No problem.) If you bill by the hour, adding up time is useful — it allows you to eat, for one thing.

To add or sum times, enter your times by using time format as you type (for example, 1:36 for one hour and 36 minutes); time format is easier on your brain. Also, format the formula cell that sums the times up with a 24-hour time format (without the AM or PM). If you're going to enter the times right into the formula, make sure that you put the times in single quotes: 1:36 .

Formatting dates and times

Every now and then, while you're doing some date arithmetic, instead of seeing a nice, date-looking result, you get a weird number, such as 16679. No problem. What you've got there is the date serial number that Works actually uses when it handles dates. (Quick, how many puns can you make out of "date serial"?) Most of the time, Works manages to hide from you how it really handles dates. When Works fails, you need to format the number as a date. (Unless, of course, you don't care what the date looks like.)

Also every once in a while, you may want dates to be formatted a little differently than Works normally does them. Instead of August 28, 1945, you may want 8/28/45, or maybe even 8/45, ignoring the day; heck, you may just want the month: August. No problem again. Works can do all of these tasks.

When you enter a date or time in a format that Works recognizes, Works actually stores a secret serial number and then formats the cell with a date or time format pretty close to the one you typed.

Here's how to format numbers as dates (or reformat dates):

1. Select the cell or cells to format.

2. Choose Format➪Number.

The Number card of the Format Cells dialog box appears on the screen.

3. Click Date in the Format area of the dialog box.

Date will already be selected if the cell is currently date-formatted; if this is the case, you can skip this step.

4. Click one of the date formats in the Date area of the dialog box.

5. Click the OK button.

You can also change formatting for time. If you don't like 2:30 PM and prefer 24-hour time, you can change the time to read 14:30. Use the same step-by-step procedure as for dates, except make these changes: In Step 3, click Time in the Format area of the dialog box, and in Step 4, choose a time format in the Time area of the dialog box. Among the formats are also choices for displaying seconds, as in 9:56:48 PM, if seconds are important to you.

Changing formatting does not change what's really in the cell — it only changes the appearance. If you reformat August 28, 1945, to appear on-screen as just August, the number in the cell remains 16677. If you aren't convinced, press Alt+V and then F to turn on the Formula view. The Formula view shows the true contents of every cell. Press Alt+V and then F again to go back to the Regular view.

Adding Borders and Gridlines

There's no excuse for ugly spreadsheets anymore. Pity. Now folks have to spend a lot of time duding up stuff in order for it to be appreciated by anyone else. Fortunately, Works takes much of the pain and strain out of prettying up spreadsheets with its AutoFormat feature (see "Formatting in One Swell Foop!" earlier in this chapter).

Alas, sometimes you still need a few lines to dress things up further: a line along a column, or across a row, or outlining a table. For this effect you need borders.

Borders are lines along the top, bottom, or sides of a cell. Combined properly, these lines can create the appearance of a border on or around a single cell, a range, or any given area of your spreadsheet. Used individually, borders are useful for such things as the summation line at the bottom of a column.

If you use borders, notice that some of them are so thin that they're masked by the gridlines that normally cover a spreadsheet. To turn off the gridlines, choose View⇔Gridlines. (Or press Alt+V and then G.) The same action turns the gridlines back on.

Here's the step-by-step procedure for putting a border on cells:

1. Select (highlight) the cell or cells that you want to apply a border to.

You can apply a border to either a single cell or a range of cells at one time.

2. Choose Format➪Border.

The Border card of the Format Cells dialog box materializes.

3. Choose what line style you want for your border(s).

Click any of the Line Style examples shown in the dialog box. The top style signifies no line at all; choose it for turning off borders.

4. Choose what type of border or borders you want in that line style.

Click one or more of the boxes in the Border area of the dialog box.

Outline applies your chosen line style to all sides of the cell. If you've highlighted a range, you get a border around that range.

Top, Bottom, Left, or Right can apply your chosen line style to that particular side. If you've highlighted a range, the border is applied to every individual cell in that range, *not* to the range itself.

To select a border and turn it on, click its box. The chosen box gets outlined, and your chosen line style appears there. To turn off the border, click its box again once or twice until no line remains in the box. (If the box becomes shaded, that signifies to Works that a cell in your selected range already has a border, and that Works should not change that border.) Repeated clicking cycles the border through the states of being on, off, and (if a border already exists) no change.

To choose a color for whatever border is currently outlined, click the down-arrow button to the right of the box marked Color, and choose a color from the list that drops down.

5. If you want different line styles on other borders, repeat Steps 3 and 4.

6. Click the OK button.

A typical thing to do with borders is to put a line over a row of column sums. To do that task, highlight the row of sums and apply a Top border to the range.

Making and Sorting Lists

One of the things that you can do with a spreadsheet — that you can also do with a database — is keep a list. Now, keeping a list may not seem particularly exciting; and if you were just "keeping" a list, you'd be silly to lay out the bucks for a spreadsheet program.

TIP

But given a sufficiently long list, you may have several things you want to do with your list: sort it alphabetically or numerically, find particular entries in that list, or do calculations based on things in that list. Works' spreadsheet tool can help you do these things. If, however, your list is going to be more than a couple of hundred entries long, or if you will want some sort of summary report (such as the total weight of items shipped to each zip code in a shipping list), you may want to consider using the database tool instead.

The nice thing about using spreadsheets for lists is that spreadsheets have lots of rows — one row for each item on your list. You can treat these rows the way that you treat file cards, by using one row per "card" and putting the different things that you put on a file card in different columns. In geek-speak (computer gibberish), each row is a *record,* and each column is a *field.*

Figure 11-3 shows a simple list that you can keep in spreadsheet form: a list of pledges and a note of whether they've been paid.

	PLEDGES.WKS						
	A	B	C	D	E	F	G
1	**Pledge List**						
2	Pledge #	Last Name	First Name	Phone	Pledge Date	Amount	Paid?
3	1	Snodgrass	Mortimer	555-8750	September 15	50	TRUE
4	2	Horstwhipple	Gertrude	555-9165	September 15	40	TRUE
5	3	Meulhueser-Eck	Henrietta	555-1826	September 15	50	TRUE
6	4	Cheeseworthy	Stilton	555-9190	September 16	20	TRUE
7	5	Phoghorne	Legolas	555-1725	September 16	15	TRUE
8	6	Towcester	Bill	555-2462	September 16	80	
9	7	Eelgrass	Steve	555-9152	September 16	50	
10	8	Dibblesby	Horst	555-6152	September 19	40	
11	9	Wikketton	Florence	555-4625	September 19	35	
12	10	Smith	Alan	555-4628	September 19	45	
13	11	Smith	Alan, Jr.	555-2451	September 19	25	
14							

Figure 11-3:
Keeping a list of donors in a spreadsheet.

Here are some tricks that you can use to create this list. One of the basic tricks is *preformatting* entire columns, which means applying a number format before any data is entered. (Or "data *are* entered," if you're an unreconstructed classicist.)

✔ Give each pledge (row) a number so that if you later rearrange the rows, you can get them back in the original order. This setup also helps keep the Alan Smiths separate, giving you a unique tracking number for the pledge so that you can, say, put the right person's name on dunning letters and not harass the wrong guy. (Now if you can just tell their checks apart.)

✔ As each pledge is contacted by phone, the date of the call and the amount pledged are entered. The easy way to enter today's date is to press Ctrl+; (Ctrl + the semicolon key) in the date column. To preformat the entire column with the kind of date format you want, select the whole column by clicking the column letter (E, in this example) and then applying date formatting.

✔ I chose not to format the Amount column because what else would it be but currency? I don't accept barter pledges in chickens or corn. If you do want to preformat the column in currency, preformat it by clicking the column letter (F, in this example) and then clicking the $ button in the toolbar.

✔ When the pledge is received, you can just make any sort of mark in the Paid? column. I chose to get fancy, preformatting the column with the True/False number format. Typing **1** into that column when someone pays results in a TRUE appearing there.

Sorting lists

One of the nice things that Works can do for you is sort lists. (I'm still working on getting it to sort laundry; I'm starting with laundry lists.) You may, in the example in Figure 11-3, want to alphabetize the list by last name so that you can more easily compare it to, say, a purchased list of prospects. (You don't want to call someone twice.) Or you may want to order the list by amount pledged so that you can single out the generous for special attention next year.

Works can sort your list in alphabetical or numerical order. Before you go running off to sort your list, however, decide on the following sorting options:

✔ Which column to sort by primarily (for example, last name)

✔ Which column to sort by secondarily, for those instances when the primary column has duplicates (for example, first name)

✔ Which column to sort by if duplicates exist in the secondary column (if you care about sorting those duplicates)

✔ What order you want the list in: A – Z and 1, 2, 3, . . . (ascending) or Z – A and . . . 3, 2, 1 (descending)

(The order can be different for the primary and secondary sorts, such as having last names in ascending order and dollar amounts pledged in descending order.)

In the pledge example, where you want to compare the list to an alphabetical list of prospects, you probably want to sort on column B (last name) primarily, and in ascending order. In case of redundant last names, use column C (first name) as the secondary sort column, also in ascending order. You probably don't care about any tertiary sort.

If you have any calculations or spreadsheet work of any kind (other lists, other tables) off to one side of your list (in the rows you are going to sort), highlight the area you want to sort before using the Tools⇨Sort command. Then choose Tools⇨Sort, and in the Sort query box that appears, choose Sort Only The Highlighted Information. Otherwise, when you sort the rows of your list, the entire width of each row is reshuffled (all columns), which mangles anything typed off to one side.

The procedure for sorting goes like this:

1. **Save your spreadsheet as a file, in case anything goes wrong.**

   If anything *does* go terribly wrong and Ctrl+Z doesn't undo it, close the messed-up spreadsheet without saving it and then reopen the original file.

2. **Select (highlight) all the rows in the list.**

   You can use any column or columns in this selection; your choice doesn't matter. Make sure that you don't include any column sum row, or that row is sorted along with your records. You may include or not include the header row; do as you like. (I deal with header rows in Step 9.)

3. **Choose Tools⇨Sort.**

   The Sort dialog box appears with its first question: Do you want to sort only the columns you selected, or all columns? (It asks this question even if you have selected all the columns already.)

4. **Click OK.**

   This action produces the second Sort dialog box, displayed in Figure 11-4, which asks which column to sort on and whether to sort in ascending or descending order. The Sort dialog box also asks whether one of the rows you've selected is the header row, so it will know to leave the header row alone.

5. **Choose, from the Sort By list box, the column that you want to sort by.**

6. **Click either Ascending or Descending.**

   Ascending means that rows containing low numbers (or letters) in your chosen column go at the top of the list; rows with high numbers (or letters) go at the bottom. Descending means the opposite.

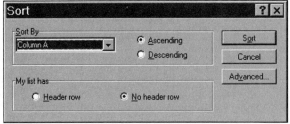

Figure 11-4:
Sorting on
one column.
Clicking
Advanced
gets you a
triple-
decker
version.

7. **Click either** <u>H</u>**eader Row or** <u>N</u>**o Header Row.**

   If the cells you highlighted in Step 2 include a header row, click Header Row. Otherwise, click No Header Row.

8. **If you're concerned about sorting when your chosen column has duplicates (say, sorting the multiple Smiths by their first name), click the Advanced button.**

   You are presented with a sort of triple-decker version of the Sort dialog box, with the top deck containing the column and sort order you just specified. In the second "deck" from the top (the Then By box) select a second column and sort order (click either Ascending or Descending). If there may be duplicate entries in this second column, go to the bottom deck, choose a third column, and sort order in the same way.

9. **Click the Sort button.**

   Works sorts your list (that is, your rows are shuffled around in the order that you specified). To return to the original order, you can press Ctrl+Z as long as you haven't made any other changes. If you're clever and created a column in which you give each record (row) a unique number, you can always sort by using that column for Sort By and restore the original order.

You can dress up your list with the AutoFormat feature, just as you can with any other spreadsheet. A couple of formats are even made especially for lists: List Bands and List Ledger. See "Autoformatting your entire spreadsheet" earlier in this chapter.

Calculating in lists

Putting your formulas in the right place is important if you are using your spreadsheet to keep a list. If you're going to do a calculation based exclusively on data in a single row, put the formula in that row. If you're going to do calculations on multiple rows in a list, doing them in the area above the

list is best. If you put them at the bottom, you're going to have to continually insert new rows for data as the list expands. If you put them off to the
side, they are likely to be mangled by the sorting process.

In general, don't write formulas that refer to specific cell addresses within
your list. (Formulas that refer to ranges are okay.) When you sort the rows,
those specific cell addresses will all have new data. Unless you're very
clever and that's what you had in mind, the result will be nonsense.

Also be very careful about using formulas with ranges that include a group
of rows, such as =SUM(F3:F13). If you sort the rows, the range in the
formula remains unchanged — (F3:F13) — but it refers to different data.

It *is* safe to write a formula that refers to all the rows: for example, one that
sums up the Amount column. But you must be careful to make sure that the
range in the SUM formula expands to include any new rows that you add.
When you add new rows, do it by inserting a row (choosing Insert⇨Row)
above the bottom row. The range in the summing formula expands to
include the new row.

Dealing with Printing Peculiarities

Printing spreadsheets is pretty much like printing anything else in Works, so
for the general, gory details, see Chapter 4. However, following are a few
peculiarities about printing spreadsheets:

- ✔ To print only a range of the spreadsheet, not the entire spreadsheet,
  select a range and use the Set Print Area command: choose Format⇨Set
  Print Area. To go back to printing the entire spreadsheet, select the
  entire spreadsheet (Ctrl+A) and repeat the Set Print Area command.

- ✔ Works splits up your spreadsheet to get it to fit on a printed page. If the
  spreadsheet is bigger than the page, you literally have to cut and paste
  pages together to re-create the original layout. Use the Print Preview
  feature (choose File⇨Print Preview) to see how your spreadsheet is
  going to print.

To control page breaks yourself, you can split up the document horizontally
and/or vertically and create page-sized pieces. Here's how:

- ✔ To split the document along a vertical line, begin by selecting a column.
  Click the letter of the column (in gray at the top of the spreadsheet) to
  the *right* of where you want the break. Now choose Insert⇨Page Break.
  A dashed line appears along the left edge of the selected column,
  indicating the break. The break runs the entire length of the spreadsheet, although it may not show up on your screen in places where you
  have fancy formatting.

✔ To split the document along a horizontal line, select the row *below* where you want the page break (click its row number in gray at the left side of the spreadsheet) and choose Insert⇨Page Break again. The break runs the entire width of the spreadsheet.

✔ If you forget to select a row or column before choosing Insert⇨Page Break , a tiny Insert Page Break dialog box appears. In this dialog box, click Column for a vertical break or Row for a horizontal one, and then click the OK button.

✔ If you click on a cell adjacent to an existing vertical page break and insert a new page break, Works assumes that you want a horizontal one now and gives you the horizontal page break you want with no pre-amble or discussion. Conversely, if you click below a horizontal break and insert a new page break, Works assumes that you want a vertical page break.

✔ To get rid of a page break, put your cursor to the right of the page break (for vertical), or under the page break (for horizontal); choose Insert⇨Delete Page Break.

Part IV
Doing Active Duty at the Database

The 5th Wave   By Rich Tennant

"DO YOU WANT ME TO CALL THE COMPANY AND HAVE THEM SEND ANOTHER REVIEW COPY OF THEIR DATABASE SOFTWARE SYSTEM, OR DO YOU KNOW WHAT YOU'RE GOING TO WRITE?"

In this part . . .

When you need to get your data to follow orders, march in neat rows and columns, or report on developments in the field, you need a database. When you have large squadrons of names, numbers, or other data, the Works database can help you marshall your facts into usable form.

The database tool helps you sort, list, find, and report on anything from membership lists to inventories. In this part, you'll discover how to create a database, interrogate it, and make reports back to headquarters based on the data contained within.

> "Therefore my lords, omit no happy hour; that we may give furtherance to our expedition."

King Henry V, Wm. Shakespeare

Chapter 12

Reporting for Duty at the Database

● ●

In This Chapter

▶ Understanding databases

▶ Getting started with databases

▶ Designing databases

▶ Working in different views

▶ Entering fields and data

▶ Navigating your views

▶ Creating a database example

▶ Using printing options

▶ Saving your work

● ●

*T*he time has come to give your data a little discipline. Have your scraggly collections of names and addresses, inventory lists, and what-have-you report for duty at the database and give them the Works. Here's where your data learns to get organized, march in rows and columns, and respond promptly to your orders and questions.

Using a Database

If you've never used a database before . . . well, actually, you probably have used a database before, but it was probably on paper, a more sensible (able to be sensed) medium than a computer. If you've ever used a library card index, a Rolodex, a dictionary, or a phone book, you've used a database. A *database* is just a collection of information that has some organization to it. (For example, every card in a Rolodex has the same structure: a line for a name, usually last name first; a couple of lines for an address; a line for the phone number; and so on.)

The thing that you may never have used before is a database manager or (as in Works) a database tool. When you put a database on a computer, a *database manager* or *tool* is the thing that you use to read the database and to put information into the database. Because databases are always accompanied by database tools, people get lazy and lump the terms together, calling the whole ball of wax a database.

What's the big deal?

The big deal with computer databases and database tools is that not only does the tool let you read the database, it also helps you find things quickly. (Not your car keys, though. Sorry.) Making a list of everyone in your Rolodex who has the same zip code (postal code) will take you awhile. But use a computer database, and the whole task takes hardly any time at all. (Of course, you've got to figure out how to use the database in less than six months in order to make it worthwhile. That's where this book comes in.) Looking for something (or things) in a database is called *querying*.

A database helps you do other things that would be a pain in the wrist to do by hand. Take organization, for example. To organize a meeting of people who live in the same general area, you may want to find everyone who works for the Acme Corporation and whose zip code is one of, say, three possible codes. Or you may want to sort things. You may want to sort your organization's membership list by street so that you can organize neighborhood meetings. A database makes these kinds of tasks a breeze.

Computer databases are also great for storing numerical information because the database tool lets you make statistical reports. If you store your business inventory in a computer database and record each item's value and department, you can easily find out the total inventory value for each department. If you record the item number and salesperson for every sale, you can quickly figure out sales commissions and the remaining inventory levels. Analyses such as these are generally called *reports,* and Works has a special ReportCreator tool in the Tools menu to help you get them just right.

Fields and records: How information is stored

Works talks a lot about fields and records, so you need to understand what they are. The Rolodex metaphor is great for understanding fields and records, which are part of every database program.

Each card in your Rolodex is like a *record* in a database. (If you don't have a Rolodex, think of a recipe card file; each recipe card is a record.)

Each card has the same blank areas to fill out: name, telephone number, and address, at the very least. These blank areas are called *fields* in computer databases. Each field has a name, like the *Address* field in a Rolodex (or *Cooking Time* if you're thinking of recipe cards). Each record has different entries in those fields, which typically describe a person (as in the Rolodex), a transaction (such as a sale or a phone call), an object, or a location.

Sorting, filtering, and reporting: Finding only the information you want

Although having a lot of information well-organized into fields and records is very nice, that benefit alone wouldn't convince *me* to use a database instead of a Rolodex or card file. No, what sells me on databases is that they can help you find the information you want — and only that information. If a database is very small, of course, you can just rummage through it. But the reason that you have a database is that you have a lot of data, and rummaging through it to find the information is just not practical. Three ways in which the Works database helps you find and display data are:

✔ **Sorting** lets you organize records alphabetically (by last name, for example) or numerically. Sorting your database records also groups similar records together. For example, when you sort based on zip code, all the records sharing a common zip code will be grouped together.

For the full scoop on sorting, see Chapter 15.

✔ **Filtering** shows you only certain records in your database. For example, to find all 12-year-olds in your school database, you can create a filter that, using the Age field of your database, screens out every child but the ones you want. You can also filter based on multiple fields. If you want all the 12-year-olds who are, say, not in your charming town of Mudville, that can be accommodated, too.

For information on filtering, see Chapter 14.

✔ **Reporting** filters, sorts, and organizes records into a report or summary form for printing. For example, you can create a report of your customers in the state of California, grouped by zip code, with subtotals of, say, sales for each group for the month of December.

For more on creating reports, see Chapter 15.

Doing Database Duty

You can start a new document in the database tool as you do with any other Works tool. (Choose the tool you want — the Database, in this case — from the Works Tools card of the Task Launcher.) To review the method for

---

The spreadsheet connection

Works' database tool and its spreadsheet tool have a great deal in common, except that the database tool does calculations differently. (See Chapter 15 for more about calculations.) The List view of a Works database looks (and can be controlled) very much like a spreadsheet. You can easily cut and paste data between the List view of a database and a spreadsheet without too much confusion. You may want to learn about spreadsheets at some point in order to pick up some tricks for working with databases in the List view. Take a look at Part III for more information on spreadsheets.

---

starting Works, the Task Launcher, and the various ways of starting a new document or opening an existing document, check out Chapter 1. If you're a little vague on using commands, menus, and dialog boxes, see Chapter 2.

Before you start a new database document, however, you should spend a little time thinking about your database design. See the section, "Designing Your Database" in this chapter; then see "Creating Your Database" for details on starting a new database document.

Designing your own database can be time-consuming. If you prefer someone else to do the groundwork, Works has many predesigned databases for things like address lists or membership lists for your soccer team. You can get a predesigned database by starting with a TaskWizard or template (choose either of these off the TaskWizard card in the Task Launcher). For more on templates, certain specific TaskWizards, and the fancy tricks that TaskWizards do, see the Appendix.

The database window

Figure 12-1 shows you what I call the *database window,* which is simply what the Microsoft Works window looks like when you're using the database tool. Your window will look like this after you have created or opened a database.

A slightly modified version of the usual Works menu bar appears near the top of the Works window, and the database toolbar is underneath the menu bar.

Don't try to memorize all the stuff in these figures. Stick a pencil here or an unused stick of gum or turn back the corner of the page and come back whenever you need to refresh your memory.

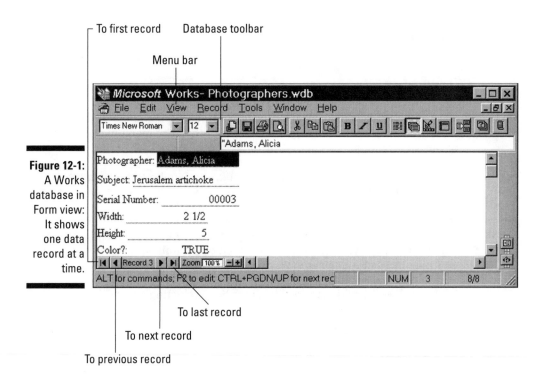

To first record   Database toolbar

Menu bar

Figure 12-1:
A Works
database in
Form view:
It shows
one data
record at a
time.

To last record

To next record

To previous record

Make a mental note that Figure 12-1 is showing you one of two main *views* of a database. The view shown here is called *Form* view, and the other, which looks like a spreadsheet, is called *List* view. (A third view, *Form Design* view, looks like Form view but is designed as an editing feature to let you change how Form view looks.)

The database menu

In the database tool, the menu bar (the line with File and all the other command words on it) looks almost exactly as it does for the word-processor and spreadsheet tools. The menus display some differences when you go to use them, and they differ slightly between the three views: Form view, List view, and Form Design view.

Many of the basic commands are the same, however, especially the ones in the menus that drop down when you click File or Edit. The File and Edit menus include commands for starting a new document, opening an existing document file, closing a document, saving a document to a file, and making basic edits. Even the Find command is practically the same as in the word processor or spreadsheet. Most of these commands are discussed in detail in Part I, the basic skills chapters.

I cover the other commands — the commands that are specific to databases — one at a time, as I go along in this chapter.

The database toolbar

The thing with all the decorative buttons under the menu bar is the database toolbar. The toolbar is just a faster way than the menu bar to do some of the same things. You click a button and stuff happens.

Many of the buttons on the database toolbar are similar to those in other Works toolbars (see Figure 12-2). For more on Works toolbars, see Chapter 2.

Most of the buttons on the toolbar are the usual suspects mentioned in Part I for starting, saving, printing, doing basic cut-and-paste edits, changing fonts, and getting help. The remainder are specific to databases. Here's where to go for a discussion of what each of these buttons refers to:

- ✔ **List, Form, and Form Design view:** See "Selecting a view" in this chapter.
- ✔ **Insert a record:** See Chapter 13.
- ✔ **Insert a field:** See Chapter 13.
- ✔ **Create or apply a filter:** See Chapter 15.

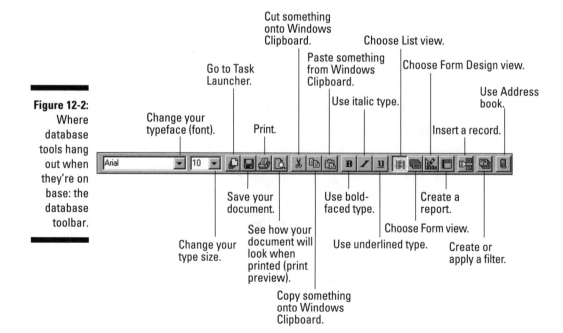

Figure 12-2: Where database tools hang out when they're on base: the database toolbar.

Cut something onto Windows Clipboard.

Choose List view.

Paste something from Windows Clipboard.

Go to Task Launcher.

Choose Form Design view.

Use Address book.

Use italic type.

Change your typeface (font).

Print.

Insert a record.

Save your document.

Use bold-faced type.

Create a report.

See how your document will look when printed (print preview).

Choose Form view.

Change your type size.

Use underlined type.

Create or apply a filter.

Copy something onto Windows Clipboard.

> ✔ **Create a report:** See Chapter 15.
>
> ✔ **Use the Address book:** See the Appendix.

To quickly see what a button on the toolbar does, place your mouse cursor over the button (don't click) and wait half a second. A tiny yellow sign appears and gives you a tiny description.

Designing Your Database

Unless you're using a TaskWizard, you do have to design your own database. Well, no, that's not quite right; you *can* slap it together in a devil-may-care fashion, but you will pay a price later as you add or rearrange things and must reenter data. So it's best to use the following procedure as a guideline for designing your database:

1. **Make a list of the things that you want your database to group and describe, and give the list a title.**

   Ask yourself, "What is this list about?" It might be a list of your friends, your clients, your photographs, the houses your real estate business is selling, or your collection of antique popsicle sticks.

2. **Ask yourself, "What do all of these things have in common that is important to include in a description?"**

   Imagine that your database is actually a list on paper, and that you are now creating columns. What information would each column contain? What do you want to be able to recall about each thing? If it were a paper list of photographs, you may imagine having columns for Subject, Date, Type (print or slide), and Where Filed. And while you're at it — if you're going to be so nice and organized — you may even consider giving each photograph a serial number in a Serial Number column.

3. **Take a piece of paper (remember paper?) and a pencil (a digital printing instrument) and write down a list of field names, based on the imaginary column headings that you just created.**

   Guidelines for choosing fields appear after this list.

4. **Consider setting up some standards for the way you will enter information in these fields.**

   Standards make finding things and generating reports easier. If you decide to have a field for Color, for instance, standardize on *purple,* and shun *violet.* Write down a list of the names you will use for colors in the Color field. If you refer to the same thing by two different names, you have to work twice as hard to find all the data again. If you can't think of any standards to begin with, wait until you begin entering data and some standards will occur to you.

Here are some guidelines for choosing your fields:

- ✔ Provide a field for anything that you may want to search for or report on: date, manufacturer, color, price, vendor, nickname, neck size, and so on.

- ✔ Use a separate field for things that may not exist in every record. For example, will you always enter the area code for phone numbers, or will you leave it off for local numbers? If you may occasionally leave the area code off, it's a good idea to create a separate field for the area code.

- ✔ If you're not sure whether to separate things, like a person's first name and last name, the safest solution is to use a separate field for anything that is separable. For example, the names of many people in your database may begin with Mr., Ms., or Mrs.; when you use your database, life is easier if this type of title is in a separate field.

- ✔ Provide a serial number field. This ensures that each record has something unique to identify it, in case the descriptions are otherwise identical. A serial number field also ensures that you can reconstruct the original order in which you entered the data.

Now you're ready to take the next step, which is to actually create your database document. Read on.

Creating Your Database

Works bends over backward to help you create your database. First of all, Works has a variety of TaskWizards for such functions as address books, inventories, personnel files, and the like. (There is even a "start from scratch" TaskWizard, although, frankly, I think you can do as well or better without it.) Second, even when you start without benefit of a TaskWizard, Works guides you step by step through the initial tasks.

For more on starting a database with some of the more popular TaskWizards, see the Appendix. In this chapter, I take you through the more flexible process of creating a database yourself. To start a fresh, untrammeled database document (or perhaps *untrampled*), do the following:

1. **If the Task Launcher is not on your screen, choose File⇨New from the menu bar, or press Ctrl+N.**

2. **From the Task Launcher, choose the Works Tools card, and then click the Database button.**

The first time that you start a new database document after starting Works, Works guides you through the creation of fields by popping up the First-Time Help dialog box, shown in Figure 12-3.

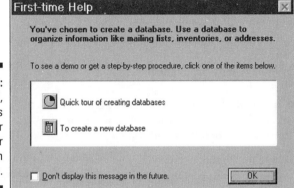

Figure 12-3:
Ever helpful,
Works lets
you either
take a tour
or get down
to business.

3. **If the First-Time Help dialog box appears, take the tour once, just for fun.**

   Works returns to the First-Time Help dialog box when you're done. Click the box labeled Don't Display This Message In The Future, and Works won't bother you with this dialog box again; from now on, it will go straight to the Create Database dialog box of Figure 12-4.

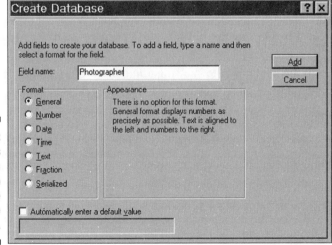

Figure 12-4:
Enter fields
one at a
time with
the Create
Database
dialog box.

4. **Click the button marked To Create A New Database in the First-Time Help dialog box.**

   The Create Database dialog box of Figure 12-4 leaps into view. (So does the Help panel, most likely. You don't need it, so minimize it by clicking the button labeled Shrink Help on that panel.)

Works is now ready for you to begin creating your database fields. Read on!

New fields of endeavor

When you create a new database (without using a TaskWizard), your principal job is entering fields. Here in New England, we wear our rubber boots and watch where we step when we enter fields. No such precautions are necessary for your database.

Here's the procedure for creating new fields by using the Create Database dialog box shown in Figure 12-4. Repeat this procedure for each field that you think that you need. If you discover that you need to change an earlier field, it's easier to wait until you have all the fields done and then go back and make changes.

1. **Enter a name for a field in the <u>F</u>ield Name box; the field name must be shorter than 15 characters.**

   For example, in Figure 12-4, I'm starting to create a database of photographs that I use in my business. The first field I want is one for the photographer's name. (Don't bother to dress up your field name by adding a colon at the end of the name; Works will add one for you in Form view.)

2. **Choose a format for the field (in the Format area of the dialog box):**

   (These formats are very much like the number formats for spreadsheets. Refer to the section on formatting numbers in Chapter 11 of this book.)

   • **<u>G</u>eneral:** You can use the General format for most fields, but there are a few special circumstances, such as fields containing dates, dollars, or fractions, where you may want to choose something other than General. Formats can also be changed later, after you have the database built. You can change the format even after data has been entered, but it's best to decide on the format before you enter your data.

   • **<u>N</u>umber:** Use this if you want dollar signs, commas, percentages, or scientific notation to appear without having to type them in. A list of examples appears when you choose Number; choose a format from the list. Number format also includes TRUE/FALSE for fields like the Color? field in Figures 12-1, 12-5, and 12-6, where you can enter a 1 for TRUE or a 0 for FALSE.

- **Date or Time:** Use these if you want the flexibility to be able to change the way dates or times appear in your database. Use this, too, if you will need to take advantage of Works' capability to subtract dates, such as calculating elapsed time.

- **Text:** Use this if you will be entering data with a mix of letters, numbers and symbols, or codes (like some zip code) that begins with zero. Otherwise, the zip code 01776 will turn into 1776.

- **Fraction:** Use this, and Works automatically rounds off data entered in decimal form, like 2.125, into mixed-number fractional form, like $2^1/_8$. Choose what fraction you want the number rounded off to in the list that appears. This is useful for listing things in nonmetric dimensions, such as inches. Works will "reduce" a fraction like $^4/_8$ to $^1/_2$ unless you click the check box marked Do Not Reduce.

- **Serialized:** This is a very useful format when you want to create a serial number field (and most databases do need some unique number for each record, which a serial number provides). Choose this, and you won't even have to enter a number in this field; Works will do it for you automatically each time that you enter a new record. In the Next Value box, enter the number that you want the next record to start with. If you want the number to increment by something other than 1, enter that increment in the Increment box.

3. **Specify a default value for the field, if this field will often contain the same value.**

   At the bottom of the Create Database dialog box, you can optionally specify a default value by clicking in the check box and typing the value in the box at the very bottom. A *default value* is data that appears automatically whenever you create a new record, and it saves you time. For example, if most of the photographs in my photography database are done by the same person, say Johnson, I could make *Johnson* my default value. Then whenever I record a new photograph in my database, Johnson would automatically be typed in. (I could replace it with another name if the photographer were not Johnson.)

   Fields that use default values behave oddly when you go to enter data into a record: *The default value will not appear until you enter data in at least one other field.*

4. **Choose the Add button (in the Create Database dialog box).**

   This action adds the field you just specified to the database, and it lets you move on to the next field. If you are done creating fields, choose the Done button.

When you're done, your database is ready for you to add some data. But wait! How come it looks like a spreadsheet? Shouldn't it look more, um, database-y? Well, the odd thing about databases is that they can look like darned near anything. Read the following section for the details on viewing your database.

Selecting a view

One reason why people sometimes get a bit confused when using a database tool is that the tool can show your data in different ways, called *views*. Unlike your Rolodex, which has real pages that you can touch, feel, and scribble notes on, computer databases are pretty ethereal. The computer can display the data in various ways, depending on what you tell it to do.

Works has a total of four views. Two of the four are views you will use most often for casually browsing through your records: the *Form view* and the *List view,* which are shown in Figures 12-5 and 12-6. Works also has a special *Form Design view,* which lets you design the page you see in Form view, specifying where each field appears. The fourth view is the *Report view,* which sounds useful but is a bit too weird for most people to use easily. *p 255* Chapter 15 will guide you in the basics of using the Report view. Some tasks can be done only in one view or another, so if you find that you can't do a particular task, consider changing views. For example, you can add fields only while in List view or Form Design view. This book will tell you if something can be done only in certain views.

Here's what the different views do for you:

  ✔ **Form view** lets you enter and look at data as if it were entered on a paper form. This view shows data the way you see it on your Rolodex: one record at a time. Figure 12-5 shows a database in Form view. The

Figure 12-5: My database for cataloging photographs in Form view, showing record 6.

field names (Photographer, Subject, Serial Number, Width, Height, and Color? in Figure 12-5) are followed by blank lines where data is entered. By using Form Design view, you can position your fields anywhere on the Form view page by simply dragging them.

✔ **List view** looks like a pad of lined paper on which you copied all the information from your Rolodex, using columns for the fields of, say, Name, Address, and Phone Number. You can see several records at once. Figure 12-6 shows the same database as Figure 12-5, but in List view. In this view, your database is a big spreadsheet-like table with rows and columns. The rows, which are numbered along the left side, are individual records. (Blank rows are records in which you haven't entered data yet.) The columns are your fields.

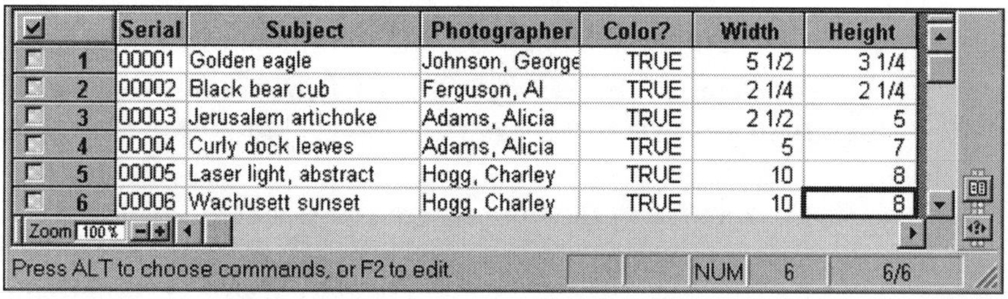

Figure 12-6:
Same database as Figure 12-5, in List view, showing records 1-6.

✓		Serial	Subject	Photographer	Color?	Width	Height	
☐	1	00001	Golden eagle	Johnson, George	TRUE	5 1/2	3 1/4	
☐	2	00002	Black bear cub	Ferguson, Al	TRUE	2 1/4	2 1/4	
☐	3	00003	Jerusalem artichoke	Adams, Alicia	TRUE	2 1/2	5	
☐	4	00004	Curly dock leaves	Adams, Alicia	TRUE	5	7	
☐	5	00005	Laser light, abstract	Hogg, Charley	TRUE	10	8	
☐	6	00006	Wachusett sunset	Hogg, Charley	TRUE	10	8	

Zoom 100% – + ◄

Press ALT to choose commands, or F2 to edit. NUM 6 6/6

✔ **Form Design view** lets you edit the Form view. The Form Design view provides features that let you move, resize, reformat, or otherwise change how the fields will look in Form view. You can also add text, such as headings or explanations, or even add illustrations to your forms by using Form Design view.

To switch between views, you can do any of the following:

✔ Click the List view, Form view, or Form Design button on the toolbar. (They are the buttons just right of the **B/U** (Bold/Italic/Underline) buttons. If you don't know which button is which, pause your mouse cursor over one and read the tiny yellow tag that appears.)

✔ Press the F9 key to go to Form view.

✔ Press Shift+F9 to go to List view.

✔ Press Ctrl+F9 to go to Form Design view.

✔ Choose View➪List, Form (or Form Design) from the menu bar.

Moving and resizing fields

If you don't like the position or size of your fields in either Form view or List view, changes are a simple matter. Just remember the following:

- ✔ To change the size or position of your fields in Form view, you must use Form Design view.

- ✔ In List view, you can make changes right there; you don't need to change views.

Moving fields in Form Design view

To move the position of a field as it appears in Form and Form Design view, do the following:

1. **Switch to Form Design view, if you're not there already.**

   To switch to Form Design view, click the Form Design button on the toolbar, or choose View⇨Form Design from the menu bar, or press Ctrl+F9.

2. **Click and drag the field where you want it.**

   To move a bunch of fields at once, select them first. One easy way to select a group of fields is to hold down the Ctrl button and click each field that you want to move. Let up on the Ctrl key, and then click and drag the whole lot of them.

Moving fields in List view

To move a field (column) in List view, do this:

1. **Click the top cell of the column — the one with the field name in it. This action selects the field/column.**

2. **Click the top cell of the column and drag the column to the left or the right. The dark vertical line that appears between columns indicates where the column will be placed when you release the mouse button.**

Resizing fields in Form Design view

If a field is too small to display your data in Form or Form Design view, you can resize the field. (You may have to move adjoining fields to allow for the change in size.)

1. **Switch to Form Design view, if you're not there already.**

   To switch to Form Design view, click the Form Design button on the toolbar, or choose View⇨Form Design from the menu bar, or press Ctrl+F9.

2. Click the underlined area to the right of the field name.

The field is highlighted, and three tiny, gray squares, called *handles,* appear in the highlight. Figure 12-7 shows a blown-up view of the highlighted area.

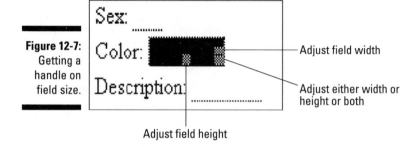

Figure 12-7:
Getting a
handle on
field size.

Adjust field width

Adjust either width or
height or both

Adjust field height

3. Adjust the field size by dragging the handles.

To make a field wider, drag the handle at the center of the right edge to the right. To make the field higher (to add lines), drag the handle at the center of the bottom edge down. The handle at the corner lets you drag both width and height at the same time.

To adjust field size more precisely, click the underlined area next to the field name; then choose Format⇨Field Size to get the Field Size dialog box. Enter a width (how many characters) and a height (how many rows) for the data entry.

Resizing fields in List view

To resize a field (change column width) in List view, you can either drag a column edge or use the Field Width dialog box:

✔ To change the width of the column by dragging, move your cursor to the gray row at the top of the columns, where the field names are. In this row, slowly move your mouse pointer across the right-hand edge of the column that you want to change. When the pointer changes to a double-headed-arrow-sort-of-deal with the word *Adjust* attached, click and drag the column edge left or right.

✔ To set the width of a column more precisely, use the Field Width dialog box. First click any cell in that column to select the column. Then choose Format⇨Field Width from the menu bar. When the Field Width dialog box appears, type a number slightly larger than the maximum number of characters you expect for data in this field and press the Enter key.

To make your field size just large enough to hold the longest entry in your database, double-click on the field name (in the top cell of the column).

Navigating in Different Views

An important part of your basic training at the database is navigation. You don't want your metaphoric half-tracks wandering all over your metaphoric field. Here's how to get around with minimal casualties and good gas mileage.

If you've applied a filter, some records will be hidden as you navigate your database. To see them all, choose Record⇨Show⇨1 All Records from the menu bar. See Chapter 14 for more information on using filters.

Navigating in Form view or Form Design view

In Form or Form Design view, you're looking at a representation of a page that is 8 ½ x 11 inches, unless you've fooled with the Page Setup commands. You can look at any part of the page or type anywhere on the page.

To scroll around vertically or horizontally, use the scroll bars on the right side and bottom of the document window (see Chapter 2 if you don't recall how to use scroll bars).

To move around vertically on the page, you can also use the navigation keys (arrows, Home, End, Page Up, and Page Down).

The dashed lines indicate page boundaries, so you need to keep your fields above and to the left of them.

To advance from one field to the next, press the Tab key. Press Shift+Tab to move in the opposite direction.

To move between records, use one of these methods:

- ✔ To advance to the next record, press the Tab key after the last entry on the page (record).
- ✔ Another way to advance one record is to press Ctrl+Page Down. To go backward, press Ctrl+Page Up.

✔ Yet another way to advance or go back one record is to click the inner left- or right-arrow in the following gadget in the bottom-left border of your document window:

✔ To go to the first or last record in your database, click the outer left- or right-arrow in that gadget.

✔ Or, to go to the first record, press Ctrl+Home; to go to the last record, press Ctrl+End.

Navigating in List view

Navigating a database in List view is almost exactly like navigating a spreadsheet, so if you know how to do that, you're in fat city. If not, here's the scoop.

To look around your database in List view, use the scroll bars on the right side and bottom of the document window (see Chapter 2 if you don't recall how to use scroll bars). To see more fields, use the horizontal scroll bar at the bottom of the window; to see more records, use the vertical scroll bar along the right side of the window.

To do anything to a cell (the intersection of a row and column), simply click that cell. (Notice that your mouse cursor is a big, fat plus sign in the database tool, as it is in the spreadsheet tool.) Around the cell appears a rectangle that Microsoft calls the *highlight*. This highlight indicates the "active" cell: the one you're about to type in, edit, format, or otherwise muck around with.

The Tab, Shift+Tab, and the navigation keys on your keyboard will also move the active cell, just as they do in Works' spreadsheet tool. See the discussion of moving from cell to cell in Chapter 9.

Entering Data

To enter data into your database, you generally fill out one record at a time, starting with the first record. In a nutshell, the procedure is just to click on a cell (List view) or in a field (Form view) and type.

Use any of the techniques mentioned in the section "Navigating in Different Views," earlier in this chapter, to move from one field or record to the next. A popular method is to use the Tab key to advance from one field to the next (Shift+Tab to go backward). If you press Tab at the end of one record, you'll automatically move to the first field of the next record.

Following are a few tips for entering data:

✔ To put a new record into your database, just add it at the end: Press Ctrl+End in Form view; press Ctrl+End and then press Tab in List view.

✔ When you use other-than-General formatting for a field, the appearance of the data you enter may change after you enter it. This procedure can be a convenience for data entry. For example, if you choose a Date format of the form "January 5, 1996," you can enter the date as 1/5/96, but Works will display it as January 5, 1996.

✔ For fields formatted as TRUE/FALSE fields, you can enter the number 1 for True or 0 for False, or you can type the words TRUE or FALSE.

✔ If the symbol ######## appears after you have entered some data, the field is not wide enough to display the data. Make it wider! (A quick fix is to double-click the field name in the top cell of the column, if you're in List view. See "Moving and resizing fields" earlier in this chapter.)

Creating an Example Database

It's show time! Here's an example of how to create a database. (The example is a very simple, five-field database for cataloging photographs.)

The Rule of This Design, as dictated by its omnipotent creator (me), is that there shall be five fields: Photographer, Subject, Width, Height, and Color?.

The standards for the data are as follows: The Photographer field contains the last name first, a comma, and then the first name; the Subject field contains a short description of what's in the photo; the Width and Height fields give the dimension in inches and $1/8$ fractions of an inch; and the Color? field is a TRUE/FALSE field indicating whether the photo is in color (TRUE) or black and white (FALSE). If I wanted to be on the safe side, I would use a separate field for the first and last name of the photographer, but I'm feeling reckless.

1. **To start a new database document, press Alt+F and then N. When the Task Launcher appears, choose the Works Tools card and then click the Database button.**

2. **A First-Time Help dialog box may appear. If it does, click the button marked To Create a New Database.**

3. **The Create Database dialog box arises. Type** Photographer **into the Field Name box and click the Add button. (Do *not* press the Enter key.) You use the General format for this example, so there's no need to change the format. A new, blank field form appears in the Create Database dialog box.**

4. **Type** Subject **into the Field Name box and click the Add button.**

5. **Type** Serial **into the Field Name box. In the Format area, choose Serialized. Click the Add button.**

6. **Type** Width **into the Field name box. In the Format area, choose Fraction. In the Appearance box, choose** ¹/₈**. Click the Add button.**

7. **Type** Height **into the Field name box. In the Format area, choose Fraction. In the Appearance box, choose** ¹/₈**. Click the Add button.**

8. **Type** Color? **into the Field name box. In the Format area, choose Number. In the Appearance box, scroll to the bottom and choose True/False. Click the Add button and then the Done button.**

Your database is created! Well, the structure of it, at least. But your database still needs some data.

Now start entering data. You can do this in either List view (which is what you are looking at) or Form view. Simply click a cell (in List view) or a field (in Form view) and type. Or you can use the Tab key to advance to the next field.

Printing Your Database

Printing databases is pretty much like printing anything else in Works, so for the general details, see Chapter 4. Here are a couple of peculiarities about printing databases, however:

- ✔ When you print in Form view, you normally print one record on a page. If your records are small, you may prefer to combine them on a page. To do so, choose File⇨Page Setup to get a Page Setup dialog box. Click the Other Options card in this box, and then click the check box marked Page Breaks Between Records to clear the check mark from it. Adjust the spacing between records by clicking the up-/down-arrows in the Space Between Records box.

- ✔ When you print in List view, you normally see just data, no headings. You can have the field and record headings print out if you choose. You can also have gridlines printed. Choose File⇨Page Setup to get a Page Setup dialog box. Click the Other Options card in this box. Click the appropriate check box: the one marked Print Gridlines and/or the one marked Print Record And Field Labels.

- ✔ To force a page break at a particular point in a List view of records, first select the row you want at the top of the next page. (Click the numbered gray button at the leftmost end of that row.) Then choose Format⇨Insert Page Break.

✔ To force a page break between columns in a List view, first select the column you want on the next page. (Click the gray button with the field name at the top of the column.) Then choose Format⇨Insert Page Break.

✔ To print only certain records, you first have to mark them: Switch to List view and click the check box in the leftmost column of each row that you want to print. Choose Record⇨Show⇨2 Marked Records from the menu bar and then print. See the section on marking and hiding in Chapter 14.

Saving Your Work

Databases are in dire need of salvation — and yours is no exception. I urge you to save your work promptly because I don't want to be accused of making a "salvator" dally. What I mean to say (having perhaps exercised a little too much artistic license) is that you need to save your database document as a file, regularly, so that you don't lose data.

Saving your database document is very much like saving any other Works document: Choose File⇨Save, or press Ctrl+S, or click the toolbar button with the diskette icon. (See Chapter 2 if you need more information.) For basic information on files and disks, see Chapter 1. For more on Salvador Dali, see your local library.

Chapter 13

Making Changes in Your Database

*A*ll is flux, and before you can say *tempus fugit,* you may need to make some changes to your database: Your friends move, so you have to change your address database; your customers grow successful (thanks to you) and sprout new divisions, so you have to create a Division field in your customer database; or maybe you just decide to make your database a bit more readable. Here's how to keep your database up to date and looking snazzy!

Editing Data and Field Names

When you need to change some data or a field name in your database, the tool you can rely on to be present in all views is the *formula bar.* (See Chapter 12 if you're unfamiliar with database views.) The formula bar works just the same as the formula bar in the Works spreadsheet tool, if you're familiar with that tool. You can see the formula bar located just under the toolbar in Figure 13-1.

Here are the details of editing data or field names using various views. (Remember, to switch to a view, choose View and then List, Form, or Form Design from the drop-down menu.)

> ✔ To edit data (someone's last name, for example, in an address database), you can use either the List or the Form view. Click the data; then click the formula bar.

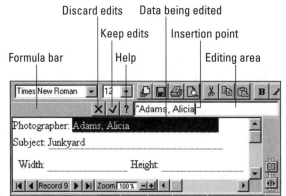

Discard edits Data being edited

Keep edits Insertion point

Formula bar Help Editing area

Figure 13-1:
Using the
formula bar.

✔ To edit a field name you can use either the Form Design or List view. In Form Design view, click the field name; then click the formula bar. To edit a field name in List view, click anywhere in the field's column. Then choose Format⇨Field from the menu bar. Edit the field name in the Format dialog box that appears and then click the OK button.

The formula bar works like this:

1. **When you click on a cell, Works copies the data value or field name into the white text box of the formula bar.**

2. **When you click in the formula bar, you begin editing the data value or field name in the formula bar's text box.**

   (Details of editing follow this numbered list.)

3. **When you're done, you either click the check mark button on the formula bar or just press the Enter key.**

   The new, edited stuff replaces the old stuff in the database.

The editing process works like this: Use the insertion point — the vertical line that you also see in the Works word processor — to edit text and data. The insertion point is where characters appear when you type and where they vanish when you backspace or delete.

To move the insertion point, move your mouse pointer over the formula bar, which causes the pointer to change to an I-beam shape. Position that I-beam where you want to type or delete something and then click. The insertion point jumps there. When you type, the characters are inserted at the insertion point. When you press the Backspace key, the character before the insertion point gets deleted. Press the Delete key, and the character after the insertion point gets vaporized.

If the data you're editing is very long, you may not be able to click near the end. In that case, click where you can and use the navigation keys (left/right arrow keys, Home, or End) to move the insertion point.

The X next to the formula is the "whoops" button. Clicking this X has the same result as pressing the Esc key. Either one abandons your edits and leaves whatever you were editing in its original state.

Clicking the check mark has the same result as pressing the Enter key. Either one enters the contents of the formula bar into the cell.

In List view, just as in spreadsheets, you don't need the formula bar to edit data. You can edit data right in its cell: Just double-click the cell, and the insertion point you need for editing appears in the cell.

Surviving (Or Using) the Protection Racket

If you find that Works complains when you try to edit data, the complaint probably arises because the field that you're working in is protected against data changes. This situation happens when you use certain TaskWizards. Here's what to do to defeat this protection scheme:

1. **Switch to either List view or Form Design view.**

2. **Click the protected field.**

3. **Choose Format➪Protection from the menu bar to get a Format Protection dialog box.**

4. **If you find a check mark in the Protect Field check box, click that check mark to clear it. Then click the OK button in that dialog box.**

On the other hand, you may want to use this protection racket yourself. By protecting a field, you can help avoid accidental changes to important data. This protection is especially valuable if you are working with another person who may not realize how important some data value is. To protect a field, you follow the same four steps just listed, only you turn the check mark on in Step 4 by clicking the Protect Field check box.

Conducting Field Exercises

Strategically speaking, there is a time to advance upon a field and a time to retreat from a field. This stratagem is general knowledge (known by generals). Likewise, in database work, there's a time to add fields and a time to remove them. Well, no problem (as certain teenagers and hotel personnel are tiresomely fond of saying instead of "You're welcome"). Here's how to add or remove a field.

Adding new fields

You can add new fields in either the List view or the Form Design view. The advantage of using List view is that the process is very simple. The advantage of using Form Design view is that, after you add a field, you are then conveniently in the correct view for positioning or sizing the field. The choice is yours!

Adding new fields in List view

In List view, the fields are columns. Follow these steps to create new fields in List view:

1. **New fields are columns that go to the right or left of existing columns. Click in the column next to which you want to add a new column.**

2. **Choose Record⇨Insert Field from the menu bar; then choose 1 Before (to put a new field to the left of your chosen column) or choose 2 After (to put a new field to the right of your chosen column).**

   An Insert Field dialog box graces your screen, bearing a familiar face: It looks and works just like the Create Database dialog box you used in the beginning (when you created your database). See Chapter 12 if you need instructions on how to use the Insert Field dialog box.

3. **Type in a name for the field (and a special format if you need it) and choose the Add button.**

4. **For additional fields, repeat Step 3.**

5. **When you're done adding fields, click the Done button in the Insert Field dialog box.**

Adding new fields in Form Design view

Here's how to add fields in Form Design view:

1. **Click where you want the field to appear. Don't click to the right or below any dashed line you see at edges of the window: That dashed line is the page margin area, which is visible when your Works window is sufficiently large.**

   A set of coordinates tells you where you are on the page, if you care. Look in the upper-left corner of the Works window, just under the font box in the text bar. The number after X gives the horizontal position from the left edge of the page; the number after Y gives the vertical position from the bottom edge.

2. **Type a field name of fewer than 15 characters, followed by a colon (:) — as in Last Name: — and press Enter.**

   A dialog box appears, asking for a field name and format, just as the dialog box appeared when you first created your database. Click the OK button when you're done.

When you enter a field name in Form Design view, don't forget to end the field name with a colon. If you don't, Works assumes that you are just putting an annotation on the form, not adding a new field.

Removing fields

Removing a field is so easy it's a little scary. When you remove a field, you also remove all the data that's in it — data that represents a lot of work on somebody's part. But if removing a field, along with all its data, is what you really intend to do, go for it. If you think that you may want to access the field and its data again sometime, do this: Before you delete the field, save your unmodified database with a new name, using the File➪Save As command.

Removing a field in List view is a little safer than removing a field in Form Design view because you can undo the deletion if you accidentally delete the wrong field. For no particularly good reason that I can think of, Works allows you to undo (with Ctrl+Z) in List view, but not in Form Design view.

Here is how to remove a field in both views:

- ✔ **Form Design view:** Just click the field name and press the Delete key. A warning box appears on the scene to ask whether you want to Delete this field and all of its contents? and warns that you won't be able to undo this delete. If you really do want to delete the field, click the OK button.

- ✔ **List view:** First, click anywhere in that field's column; then choose Record➪Delete Field in the menu bar. A warning box appears, asking whether you in fact want to Permanently delete this information? If you really do want to delete the field, click the OK button.

Zap! It's dead, Jim.

Adding, Inserting, and Deleting Records

Many unprincipled people have wished, over the years, that they had the ability to add or delete certain records in their files. If only they knew how easily you can add or delete records when you've got a Works database.

Adding a record

When you've acquired yet another antique popsicle stick for your collection, you will want to add another record to your popsicle stick database. The easiest way to add a record is to add it to the end of your database. To get to the end:

- ✔ In Form view, press Ctrl+End.
- ✔ In List view, press Ctrl+down arrow and then press the down arrow (without the Ctrl key).

A record is an entire page or row of related data, not just datum. (If you are of the pre-compact disc, or *vinyl*, generation, think of these records as albums, not singles.)

Inserting or deleting a record

To add a record at a particular point in your database, you insert it. First, indicate to Works where you want to insert the new record. In Form view, just move to that record. In List view, click that row. Then do the following:

- ✔ **To insert a record:** Choose Record⇨Insert Record from the menu bar. Or click the Insert Record button. (If you're uncertain which button that is, slowly move your mouse pointer across the buttons and read the labels that pop up.) A blank record appears for you to fill in.
- ✔ **To delete a record:** Choose Record⇨Delete Record from the menu bar. The record is then deleted and you are left gazing upon the next higher record in the database.

All the records following the one you inserted or deleted are renumbered.

You can alternatively delete just the contents of a record rather than the record itself. This trick is useful if you are replacing an item listed in your database (say, a deceased computer in your inventory). In List view, click the row number (in the gray area on the left) to highlight the entire row — or highlight just as much as you want to delete — and then press the Delete key. The record is now blank (except for serialized fields), and you can enter new data into it.

Copying and Moving Data

Years ago, in school exams, the consequences of copying data were severe. That's too bad because today copying is an essential skill for entering data into databases. (So there, Mr. Schweinkopf!) Copying is a great time-saver and helps enforce your rules for consistent data, such as always using the word *purple* and not *violet* in your Color field.

In any database, many records may have exactly the same data. In a pediatrician's medical database, the term *otitis media* (middle ear infection) would sum up the better part of a week's work. Kids get ear infections like lawns get dandelions. It's surprising that there aren't fast-food-style drive-through kids' ear exam and dispensary outlets. ("Stick your head in the clown's mouth, Junior; we'll get a toy at the window with our antibiotics.")

Anyway, what a boon to the bored pediatrician-in-a-box to be able to just copy the Diagnosis field data from one patient-encounter record to another, rather than retype it. Copying prevents typos, too. Nine out of ten doctors recommend copying.

Copying with the Clipboard

To copy data from one record to another, switch to List view and use the Windows copy and paste functions described in Chapter 3. (Choose View⇨List or press Shift+F9 to switch.) To copy a single piece of data, click the cell that you want to copy and press Ctrl+C. Then click the cell where you want a copy and press Ctrl+V.

You can also make multiple copies of that single cell (as you may need if you get a busload of kids at your Doc-in-the-Box, all with *otitis media*). Copy the cell with Ctrl+C; then drag down across the rows (records) where you want copies to highlight those cells. Then press Ctrl+V. Each cell gets a copy of the original cell.

You can also copy data from multiple fields (such as the date and the diagnosis fields) at once, as long as the two fields are in adjoining columns. Highlight any group of cells in the row that you want to copy and press Ctrl+C. Then click the leftmost cell where you want to paste a copy and press Ctrl+V. To paste copies in multiple rows, highlight the leftmost cells in several rows before pressing Ctrl+V.

Copying and moving by dragging

Another way to move or copy data is by dragging — preferably in List view. To copy data by dragging it, hold down the Ctrl key; then click and drag a copy of that data to any other record or field. To move data, simply click it and drag it to the new location (without holding down the Ctrl key).

List view is best for dragging copies because you can drag between records (rows). In Form view, you can't drag between records.

Applying and Changing Formats

Just as your mother said, appearances are important. You can do a number of things to change the way your field names and data appear in a Works database. The formats you can change are as follows:

- ✔ **Field:** How Works interprets and displays your data: as a number, time, or text.

- ✔ **Alignment:** Whether data or a field name is left- or right-justified, or centered, for example.

- ✔ **Font:** What typeface and style the data or field name appears in.

- ✔ **Border:** For borders around data or field names.

- ✔ **Shading:** To apply a background color or shade to data or field names.

You set fonts, borders, and shading independently for List view and Form view. Formats you apply in one view do not apply to the other view. For instance, a tasteful magenta shading of a field in List view does not create a magenta background in Form (or Form Design) view. But field and alignment formats do apply to all views, regardless of which view you use to choose them.

To change any of the previously listed formats, do the following:

1. **Choose either List view or Form Design view.**

   To format the appearance of a field name (as opposed to data in a field), choose Form Design view.

2. **Click in a field to select that field (or select several fields by highlighting them).**

   In Form Design view, you can format either the data area (the underlined part of a field) or the field name area. Click either area to format it. To change the Field formatting (formatting of data as text, numbers, or time), click the data area.

3. **Choose Format from the menu bar; then choose either Field, Alignment, Font, Border, or Shading.**

   If the Field option is grayed-out (not available), it is because you are using Report Design view, and in Step 2 you clicked on the field name. Works is being uncooperative because Field formats apply only to data, not field names. Picky, picky. Click the underlined data area of the field to make Works happy.

The Format dialog box (shown in Figure 13-2) appears, displaying the card that matches your choice in Step 3 in the preceding numbered list of steps.

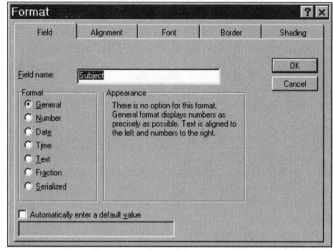

Figure 13-2:
The Format
dialog box,
where
appear-
ance is
everything.

Here is the executive summary of what you can accomplish in each card of the Format dialog box:

✔ **The Field card** lets you specify the same kind of formatting that you specified when you first created the field, telling Works to display the value as a date, a fraction, or a dollar amount, for example. Changes to Field formats affect all views.

If you change a field from General or Text to a Date or Time format, you may have to reenter the data in that field.

✔ **The Alignment card** allows you to click Left, Right, or Center respectively to left-justify, right-justify, or center text in its field. Choosing General aligns text to the left, numbers to the right. If you are using List view, you can choose to make text wrap around within a cell in List view by clicking the Wrap Text checkbox. If, in List view, your rows are higher than a single character height, you can also align text vertically: Click Top, Center or Bottom.

✔ **The Font card** works just as it does elsewhere in Works. See Chapter 3 for more information.

✔ **The Border card** lets you put an outline around a field or data for emphasis, if you like. Click a line style from the list presented. Click the top line-style box (with no line in it) to turn off a border.

✔ **The Shading card** lets you apply a background color or pattern. Choose a pattern from the Pattern box; patterns are made up of two colors, given by your selection of foreground and background colors. Unless you have a color printer or don't intend to print at all, sticking to Auto for both colors is best.

When you print in Form view, having a lot of space between fields on the same line can be annoying. For instance, when you print address labels, you probably don't want a big gap between the city and the state. When you design the form, however, you have to use a City field wide enough for, say, "Lake Memphremagog," which pushes your State field way over to the right. When you print, if the city in a given record is short, like Big Sky, Montana, a lot of open space appears before Montana. (As it does in real life, come to think of it.) Works provides a trick to get rid of this excess space during printing. Using Form Design view, click either the field name or data area of the field that is on the right (the State field, for instance). Choose Format⇨ Alignment. Choose the Alignment card, and then click the Slide to Left check box. Use print preview to check the result.

Chapter 14

Finding and Filtering in Your Database

. . . .

In This Chapter

▶ Finding data

▶ Hiding and showing records

▶ Creating a filter

▶ Applying a filter

▶ Deleting a filter

▶ Using multiple criteria

▶ Using math in filtering

. . . .

*W*hen interrogating an enemy prisoner, you expect him to be reluctant to impart information. When interrogating a database, you have the opposite problem: The database offers too much information — volunteering, as it were, name, rank, serial number, birth date, sock size, and mother's middle name, a thousand times over. Finding out just one piece of data becomes tremendously difficult.

You have three ways to solve this problem and find the data that you're looking for with Works' database tool:

⮑ **Find:** The simplest solution, if you're looking for those records that contain one particular piece of data (such as the word *tubular*), is to have the database tool *find* records containing that specific word, number, or phrase.

⮑ **Filter:** If you're looking for the records that contain some combination of information in specific fields (such as *tubular* in the Description field and the number 90210 in the zip code field), you apply a *filter*.

⮑ **Sort:** If you just need an ordered list — ordered alphabetically or numerically by the contents of a particular field — you perform a *sort*. For information on sorting, see Chapter 15.

If you apply a filter or a find, Works shows you the records that you requested and *hides* the rest. To see all the records again, click Record⇨Show⇨1 All Records.

Finding Specific Data

To locate records that contain a specific word, phrase, or number, the simplest thing you can do is to perform a find. (The Find command is very much like the Find commands in the word processor or spreadsheet, if you're familiar with those.)

You can tell Works to find either the *first* instance of that word, phrase, or number, or to show you *all* instances. Here's how to do it:

1. **Press Ctrl+Home (which takes you to the top of the document) so that Works begins its search with the first record of the database.**

2. **Choose Edit⇨Find from the menu bar (or press Ctrl+F).**

   A small but helpful Find dialog box appears.

3. **Type the word, number, or phrase that you're searching for in the box marked Find What.**

   You must specify lowercase or uppercase. Searching for *Copy Paper* won't find records containing *copy paper.*

   Type only as much as you remember or need. To find copy paper, printer paper, or any kind of paper, type **paper**. (On the other hand, don't type too little: *pa* will also find padding and packing material if those words are hanging out in your database.)

   The symbol **?** can substitute for a single character and help you find a broad range of records. When searching for zip codes, for example, the number 0792? will find all the zip codes beginning with 0792.

   The symbol ***** can substitute for one or more characters as long as the * is preceded by at least one other character. For example, M*. will find Mr., Mrs., and Ms. (but not Miss — because this particular search specifies that a period must come at the end).

4. **To find all records that contain your word, phrase, or number, click All Records in the Match area of the Find dialog box. To find just the next record, click Next Record.**

5. **Click the OK button.**

If you choose to find All Records in Step 4, Works shows you only those records that meet your search text criterion and hides the others. When you're done reviewing or printing the result of your Find, choose Record⇨Show⇨1 All Records to reveal all the records in your database again.

Using Selected Records: Marking and Hiding

Do you have certain records that you just don't want to appear on your printout, on your screen, or in your database report? Well, do as millions do when the auditor comes to call: Hide those records! (Not that I recommend hiding any particular records; auditors know about databases, too!) Works uses three concepts to help you hide or display only the records that you want:

- ✔ **Hiding** is a way to make records invisible in List or Form view, in printouts, or in reports.
- ✔ **Showing** is the opposite of hiding.
- ✔ **Marking** is a convenient way to identify a group of records for hiding or showing.

To hide an individual record, first either click the record in List view or move to it in Form view; then choose Record⇨Hide Record from the menu bar. To show hidden records, choose Record⇨Show⇨4 Hidden Records.

To hide several records, mark them first: In List view, click the check box in the leftmost column (*marking column*) of each row that you want to hide. (To mark a group that's all together, click the top record's check box; then drag down the marking column.) In Form view, choose Record⇨Mark Record for each record. Then choose Record⇨Show⇨3 Unmarked Records from the menu bar.

To hide most of the records and only show a few, mark the records that you want to *show* by using the method described in the preceding paragraph. Then choose Record⇨Show⇨2 Marked Records from the menu bar.

To show all records — hidden, marked, or otherwise — choose Record⇨ Show⇨1 All Records from the menu bar.

To clear all marks, go to List view and click the check mark at the very top of the marking column.

Filtering Your Data

The Find command is a nice, simple way to find records containing a particular word or number. Sometimes, however, you need to find records with certain combinations of data in various fields, such as all the members of your organization who have more than two kids and who live out of town. Or maybe you want to find members who have contributed $100 or more, in the hope of pressing them for another contribution.

To find these big givers, you need to filter your data — strain out all the poor of purse or soul. When Works filters your data, Works goes through your database, record by record, comparing what's in those records to certain criteria that you've given it and hiding from view those records that don't meet the criteria. Did Widow Jones give only $50 from her pension? If you are filtering for an amount of $100 or more in your Contributions field, Works hides Mrs. Jones' proud record. (Sorry, there is no filtering for moral character.)

The gadget that you use for applying a filter is the Filter dialog box, shown in Figure 14-1. To get one of these little gems, do the following:

✔ Choose Tools➪Filters from the menu bar, or

✔ Click the Filters button on the toolbar.

The first time that you create a filter, Works displays a First-Time Help dialog box and lets you choose to either take a tour of filtering or get down to work. Take the tour once (click the Quick Tour Of Filters button); then, when you are returned to the dialog box, click the Don't Display This Message In The Future check box if you want to keep this dialog box from showing up again. Finally, click the To Create And Apply a New Filter button.

You can have many criteria at once.

Filters are stored by name.   Each criterion has three parts.

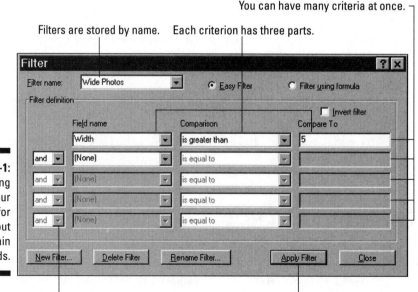

Figure 14-1: Telling Works your criteria for picking out certain records.

How to combine criteria.   View your database through the filter.

If you have not previously created any filters for your database, a Filter Name dialog box springs up; enter a descriptive name that's no more than 15 characters long for your filter. For example, if you are filtering to display big contributors and hide the rest of the data, you can type **Big Contributor**.

The trick to applying a filter is figuring out how to describe the data that you're looking for. Having the capability to write regular sentences, such as "Show me all the records for families with more than two kids and who live out of town" would be nice. It would be nice if we could all go to Barbados for the winter, too, but that's not going to happen any time soon, either. Filters in Works are a little bit like sentences, but not like sentences that your sixth-grade English teacher would approve of. (Excuse me: ". . .of which your sixth-grade English teacher would approve.")

To construct the description of what records you want, you need three pieces of information:

- ✔ **The field name:** This is where you want Works to look. For example, the No. Of Children field if you had such a field and wanted to find families based on the number of children they have.

- ✔ **The "comparison":** The way to test the data in the field. For example, to test that the data in the No. Of Children field is greater than some value.

- ✔ **The "compare to" value:** What you want Works to compare the data to — such as *2* for two kids.

For a single criterion, you enter these three pieces of information in the top, three-part line of the Filter dialog box. The Field Name and Comparison boxes allow you to choose from drop-down lists that are available when you click the down arrow adjoining those text boxes.

Some other examples of single-criterion filters are:

- ✔ The entry in a No. Of Children field *is equal to* 2.

- ✔ The entry in a Description field *contains the word* Mikado.

- ✔ The entry in a Town field *is not* Mudville.

- ✔ The entry in an Age field *is greater than or equal to* 21.

Here's how to perform a single-criterion filter, step by step. Performing a single-criterion filter is like building a sentence out of three parts; when you're all done, you can read the three parts in sequence, and the parts read like a sentence.

1. **Choose Tools⇨Filters from the menu bar.**

   If you have not previously created any filters for this database, the tiny New Filter dialog box pops up and asks you to enter a name for your new filter. Do so.

   The Filter dialog box now takes up residence on your screen.

   If you have previously created filters, the name of your most recent creation appears in the Filter Name box, and the filter criteria are displayed. You can click the down arrow adjoining the filter name to choose from previous filters. To create a new filter, click the New Filter button in the dialog box and enter a filter name in the New Filter dialog box that pops up.

2. **Choose a field: Click the down-arrow button next to the box marked Field Name; then click any field name in the list that drops down.**

   Works has tentatively chosen the first field name in your database, and that field name is initially displayed here. Pick whatever field you need Works to search through.

3. **Choose how to compare: Click the down-arrow button next to the box marked Comparison; then click any comparison in the list that drops down.**

   Works has tentatively chosen *equal to* only because equal to is the first comparison in the list. Choose any comparison that you like.

   For purposes of comparison:

   > Later dates are greater than earlier dates.

   > Later times are greater than earlier times.

   > Letters that fall later in the alphabet are greater than earlier ones.

4. **Choose a value for the comparison: Click the box marked Compare To and type in a word, phrase, or number.**

   In filters (unlike in finds), Works doesn't take note of capitalization. The words *Potato* and *potato* are identical as far as Works is concerned.

   You can use the ? and * characters just as you do in a Find command, if you like. See "Finding Specific Data" earlier in this chapter.

   When you're done, read across the line that you just entered in the Filter dialog box and combine the three parts of the criterion into a crude sentence, such as "Width . . . is greater than . . . 5." This is your criterion; Works can then find those records in which the Width field contains a number greater than 5.

5. **Press the Enter key or click the Apply Filter button to execute the filtering.**

If you're not in List view at this point, switch to it (press Shift+F9 if you're in Form view). Seeing what's going on is just easier if you're in List view.

You're done! In List view, you see only those records that meet your criterion. The other records are hidden to get them out of your way. When you're done looking over your success, choose Record➪Sh<u>o</u>w➪<u>1</u> All Records to make the other records reappear.

Managing Filters

Creating a filter takes a bit of work; so, for your future convenience, Works saves your filters, storing all that criterion stuff you did in the Filter dialog box. Works saves each filter under the name that you gave it.

The reason that Works saves filters is (A) so that you can fool around with them until they're correct, and (B) so that you can easily switch from one to the other, applying them to your database when you need them (see "Applying filters," coming up). The idea is that you're likely to want to have a few standard filters that you make on your database regularly.

One quirk is that you can't have more than eight saved filters — any more than eight, and you have to delete one in order to create a new one.

Editing filters

To change a filter, simply return to the Filter dialog box, call up a filter by name, and adjust the criteria. Here's the blow-by-blow description:

1. **Choose <u>T</u>ools➪<u>F</u>ilters in the menu bar (or click the Filters button on the toolbar).**

   The Filter dialog box springs to life.

2. **Click the down arrow adjoining the <u>F</u>ilter name box and choose the filter that you want to edit from the list.**

3. **Change your filter criteria (the other stuff in the Filter dialog box).**

4. **Click the <u>A</u>pply Filter button to see how the filter works.**

To change the name of a filter, click the Rename Filter button. Enter a new name in the Filter Name dialog box that appears.

Applying filters

To apply the filter that you've used most recently, just press F3.

To apply any other filter to your database:

1. **Choose Record⇨Apply Filter.**

2. **Choose any filter in the Filter list that drops down.**

Zap. You're looking at all the records that match your filter criteria. To restore all the hidden records, choose Record⇨Sh_ow⇨1 All Records.

Deleting filters

If a filter isn't quite right or you don't need it anymore, deleting the filter is easy:

1. **Choose Tools⇨Filters (or click the Filters button on the toolbar).**

   The Filter dialog box forces its attentions upon you.

2. **Click the down arrow adjoining the Filter name box and choose the filter that you want to delete from the list.**

3. **Click the Delete Filter button.**

   Works puts up a warning box to make sure that you want to do this. Choose the Yes button.

4. **Click the Close button of the Filter dialog box when you're done deleting.**

Using More than One Criterion

You can have Works use up to five criteria at one time in a filter, which is why the Filter dialog box has five rows. This five-criteria feature lets you narrow down or expand your search.

For example, if you want only the families in your database that have more than two kids and also live out of town, you create a second row for the Town field, specifying that the town selected should not equal your town of Mudville. Figure 14-2 shows such a two-part filter.

To do more than one criterion, just fill out the first one as usual. Choose either and or or in the box that begins the next line; then fill out the second criterion in a similar fashion. Do the same for any other criteria that you need.

For the example in Figure 14-2, you need to tell Works that both criteria must be met on each record that it finds:

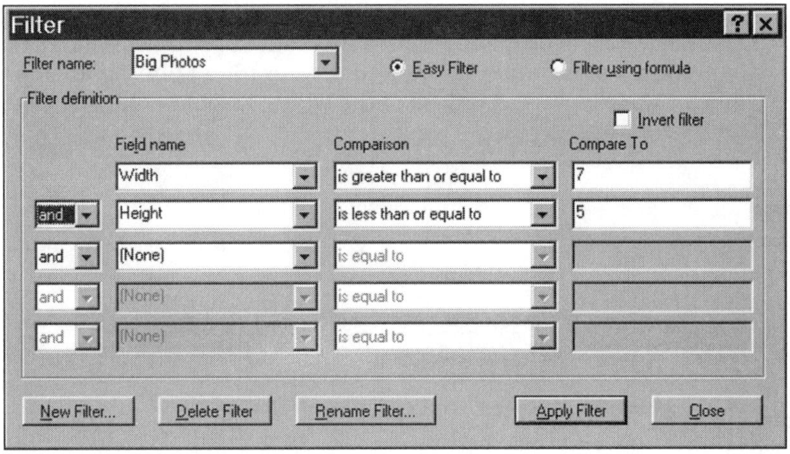

Figure 14-2:
Using two
criteria for a
query.

The photograph width `is greater than or equal to` **7** inches.

AND

The photograph height `is less than or equal to` **5** inches.

So you click the `and` selection.

You use the `or` selection to specify that a record can meet either criterion. If `and` is changed to `or` in Figure 14-2, the search results in photographs that are less than or equal to 5 inches high (but can be any width) as well as photographs that are at least 7 inches wide (but can be any height).

You can also have multiple criteria lines using the same field, one on each line: for example, `width is greater than or equal to 7` on the first line *and* `width is less than or equal to 14` on the second line. This search would find all photos with a width between 7 and 14 inches.

If you set your logic up incorrectly and end up filtering *out* things that you wanted to filter *in,* click the Invert Filter check box in the Filter dialog box. This method is also a good way to look at the filtered-out crowd and make sure that the filter is working correctly.

Trickier Filtering Using Formulas

Sometimes you need to filter on something that just isn't in your database. For example, in my Photographs database, there's a *width* and a *height,* and I can create a filter for a certain range of those dimensions. But if I wanted a photograph that fits a certain ratio of height to width, I couldn't make a filter using straightforward criteria. No field for *ratio* is available.

One solution to this sort of problem is to use formulas, using field names, mathematical expressions, and Works functions to describe the filter that you want. For example, if I wanted to filter for all photographs where the height was 80 percent or less of the width, I would enter the criterion shown in Figure 14-3.

Figure 14-3:
By using a
field name
and some
math, I can
filter for
height-to-
width ratio.

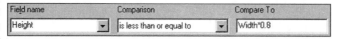

The Works *functions* I refer to are the same as for the spreadsheet. For a complete listing of functions by type, choose Help⇨Index from the menu bar, and type **functions:** (note the colon). Click any folder that begins with Functions:.

You can use formulas in the Compare To box, for example. In Figure 14-3, I am comparing the value in the Height field to 80 percent of the value in the Width field. The formula in the Compare To box, Width*0.8, does the trick.

Formulas and functions can get pretty powerful and complex. For this sort of work, if you are familiar with computer programming or complex logical and mathematical expressions, you can switch to a Formula view of your filter. In the Filter dialog box, click the Filter Using Formula option.

This stuff is not for the faint of heart or the mathematically challenged!

To get the idea of how this view works, click Easy Filter and set up a few criteria. Then click Filter Using Formula. You can see how field names and operators combine to create a logical expression that evaluates as *true* when the right criterion is met. Some of the operators you can use besides > are =, <, #NOT#, #AND#, #OR#, and the ever-popular <>, which means not equal. If the purpose of these operators is not obvious to you, don't use them.

Chapter 15
Sorting, Reporting, and Calculating

● ●

In This Chapter

▶ Sorting data

▶ Creating standard reports

▶ Viewing your report

▶ Improving the appearance of your report

▶ Reporting on selected records

▶ Doing calculations on your database

● ●

*T*he real value in a database is not that it lets you amass an army of data on your computer; the real value is that a database helps you find, display, and compute meaningful answers from that army of data. Sorting, reporting, and calculating are Works' key features for extracting order from your chaos.

Sorting lets you see records in a convenient order, such as alphabetical order. In addition, just as the alphabetical sorting in a telephone book inherently groups all the Smiths together, sorting in a database inherently groups things together, such as all the members of your softball league who have similar batting averages. In the Works database tool, you can sort on any field; in fact, you can sort on several fields at once. You can sort on all sorts of things (sort of). You'll never be "out of sorts" with Works . . . (*Whack! Ouch! Okay, okay, I'll stop with the sordid puns. For now.*)

Reports are also an important feature of any database tool. Reports let you list records, summarize data statistically (providing sums, averages, counts, and the like), and organize this information in a nice, readable form to print out and give to other people. Sorts and reports can be also combined with filters (as Chapter 14 discusses) so that you can focus on a subset of your database — say, only your sales in Sasketoon — and not have to peruse the whole database at once.

In addition to the statistical summaries that Works can provide in a report, like summing up all your sales for the month in a given country, Works can provide other useful forms of automatic calculation. For instance, as you enter a sales order as a record in your sales database, Works can add up the cost of each item to compute your customer's total due. You can also add calculations to Works reports, such as dividing the total sales revenues by the total number of orders to compute the average sale per order.

Sorting

Give your data its marching orders. But first, tell the data what order to march in: alphabetical or numerical. Do you want to sort your inventory alphabetically by location or numerically by value? No problem; it's your choice. Do you want to sort your mailing list numerically by ZIP Code and then alphabetically by street name within each ZIP Code? Again, no problem. Works does it all.

If you already know how to sort in Works' spreadsheet tool, the database sorting process may seem very, very familiar to you.

Before you go running off to sort your database, decide how you want it to be sorted. Works lets you sort by up to three fields, which, in turn, lets you have a list in which your records are sorted by:

Categories (say, by ZIP Code),

Subcategories (by street name within each ZIP Code), and

Sub-subcategories (last names of people living on the street)

You can also choose what order you want the various groups in: A–Z and 1, 2, 3 . . . (ascending) or Z–A and . . . 3, 2, 1 (descending).

Using List view to see the results of sorting is generally easier, so if you're currently in Form view, I suggest that you switch to List view (press Shift+F9). Now, here's how to sort:

1. Choose Record⇨Sort Records from the menu bar.

The first time you sort, Works displays a First-Time Help dialog box and lets you choose to either take a tour of sorting or get down to work. Take the tour once (click the Quick Tour Of Sorting button) then, when you are returned to the dialog box, click the Don't Display This Message In The Future check box if you want to keep this dialog box from showing up again. Finally, click the To Sort A Database In Alphabetic Or Numeric Order button.

The Sort Records dialog box, shown in Figure 15-1, jumps gaily into your lap (so to speak). In Figure 15-1, you can see how Works makes selecting a field for sorting easy by providing a drop-down list of all your field names.

2. Choose the principal field to sort on.

Click the down-arrow button next to the box labeled Sort By and then click a field in that list. In a mailing list database, you may choose ZIP Code for this field. In Figure 15-1, I chose the Photographer field in my catalog of photographs.

Figure 15-1:
Choosing what fields to sort on in the Sort Records dialog box.

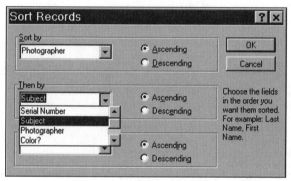

3. Choose a sorting direction for that field.

Click Ascending to go from A–Z or in the order 1, 2, 3. . . .

Click Descending to go from Z–A or in the order . . .3, 2, 1.

4. Optionally, do the same for second field and third field.

If you fill out the information in the Then By list (for example, choosing the Street Name field in a mailing list), Works sorts based on that field when two or more records have identical data in the first, or primary, field. (Plenty of folks have the same ZIP Code, for example. If your principal field is ZIP Code, the Then By field lets you put the identically zipped records in, say, alphabetical order by street name. If you don't fill out this information, the records won't be in any particular order within each ZIP Code.) The final Then By field does the same thing for duplicate entries in the second field.

5. Click the OK button.

If you're in List view, you see your database with its records shuffled around in the order you specified. Keep the following points in mind when viewing your database in List view:

✔ Note that records don't keep their original record numbers (the number at the far left of each row in List view) when they're sorted. This is one reason why having a serial number field is important: The serial number field lets you reconstruct the original order by sorting on that field.

✔ You can combine a sort with a filter if you just want to sort a portion of your database. Do the filtering first, which hides all records you don't want. (See the section on filtering your data in Chapter 14.) Then sort on the remaining records. When you're done, you can bring all the records back into view by choosing Record⇨Show⇨1 All Records.

Figure 15-2 shows the result of sorting a database by photographer's name and then subject.

Figure 15-2:
Sorting
groups of
records
with
identical
data
together.

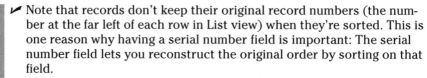

✓		Serial	Subject	Photographer	Color?	Width	Height
☐	1	00004	Curly dock leaves	Adams, Alicia	TRUE	5	7
☐	2	00003	Jerusalem artichoke	Adams, Alicia	TRUE	2 1/2	5
☐	3	00007	Red sails in the sunset	Adams, Alicia	TRUE	10	8
☐	4	00008	Earthworms	Allworthy, Fred	FALSE	7	5
☐	5	00002	Black bear cub	Ferguson, Al	TRUE	2 1/4	2 1/4
☐	6	00005	Laser light, abstract	Hogg, Charley	TRUE	10	8
☐	7	00006	Wachusett sunset	Hogg, Charley	TRUE	10	8
☐	8	00001	Golden eagle	Johnson, George	TRUE	5 1/2	3 1/4

Works sorted on this field . . .

. . . then on this field

Reporting

Reports seem to make the world go 'round in some organizations. If that's true for you, Works is ready to help you make a report "heard 'round the world." But first, let me make sure that you know what I'm talking about when I say *report.*

A Works report is intended to be printed, not viewed on your PC screen.

A Works report is made up of two kinds of information:

✔ A list of records very much like the List view

✔ A summary based on your records

For example, a mail room may have a database consisting of the packages that have shipped, the date of shipping, the destination ZIP Codes, the package weights, the shipper, and the cost of shipping. (The mail room may also have a database with the football pool bets, but if the employees are smart, they won't keep their football pool database on the hard disk where the boss can see it.)

From the shipping database, management may want reports on how cost-effective various shippers are, how much product is being shipped by weight every month, how much is shipped to each ZIP Code, the average weight shipped, and other typical, nosy management requests. All these reports require either a summary of some sort or a list or both.

What's a standard report?

To make creating a report easier for you, Microsoft took some of the basics of report creating and made dialog boxes that help step you through the creation process. The result of using these dialog boxes is what I call a *standard report*. You can then make a more elaborate report by modifying this standard report.

A standard report from the shipping department's database may show all the packages sent, together with a summary of total weight and total cost of all the records. Such a standard report would look something like the one shown in Figure 15-3.

The report in Figure 15-3 contains lists of shipments grouped by shipper, with total weight and average weight shipped for each group, and total and average weight at the bottom. Not bad for a little database program!

What a standard report doesn't give you

Keep in mind that a standard report doesn't give you a couple of things that you may want:

- First, a standard report doesn't give you a report that gives answers calculated from two or more fields. For example, you may want a report that computes average shipping cost per package by summing all the costs, counting all the records, and dividing the total cost by the total number of packages. You can do this task in Works by modifying a standard report, but a standard report alone will not do the trick.

- Second, a standard report doesn't give you labels and special report formatting to make the report easier to read. But you can use Works' database tool to modify a standard report, adding a lot of the same formatting features that the spreadsheet and word-processor tools have, such as different fonts and styles, alignments, and borders.

```
                                          shipping.wdb - Wt. by Shipper

      Shipper    Weight


      CityZIP        0.73
      CityZIP        0.94
      CityZIP        0.21
      CityZIP        0.67
      CityZIP        0.75
      CityZIP        0.95
      CityZIP        0.18
      CityZIP        0.82
      GROUP TOTAL Weight:              5.26
      AVERAGE Weight:                  0.66


      DinEx          0.80
      DinEx          0.44
      DinEx          0.63
      GROUP TOTAL Weight:              1.86
      AVERAGE Weight:                  0.62


      Hercules       0.05
      Hercules       0.03
      Hercules       0.37

      ---- ( I cut out some stuff here )----


      PSU            0.04
      PSU            0.76
      PSU            0.60
      GROUP TOTAL Weight:              1.40
      AVERAGE Weight:                  0.47
```

Figure 15-3:
One of the
standard
reports
Works can
make. (I
chopped
out the
middle so
the report
would fit on
this page.)

```
      Rural Xpres    0.87
      Rural Xpres    0.58
      Rural Xpres    0.08
      GROUP TOTAL Weight:              1.53
      AVERAGE Weight:                  0.51

      Zowiefast      0.98
      Zowiefast      0.80
      Zowiefast      0.96
      Zowiefast      0.76
      Zowiefast      0.86
      GROUP TOTAL Weight:              4.36
      AVERAGE Weight:                  0.87


      TOTAL Weight:              14.98
      AVERAGE Weight:             0.58
```

In this chapter, I look at how to create a standard report and then show you how to do these few useful modifications.

Creating a standard report

Works makes it fairly simple to create a standard report, but you have to play your cards right! The ReportCreator dialog box deals you six different *cards* that you have to fill out.

To begin your quest for a standard report, awaken the mighty ReportCreator from its slumber: Choose Tools➪ReportCreator from the menu bar.

A tiny Report Name dialog box requests that you name your report. Use 15 characters or fewer. This name doesn't appear on your report; it just identifies your report so that you can use this report again.

Then the ReportCreator dialog box, shown in Figure 15-4, swings into action and deals you its six cards.

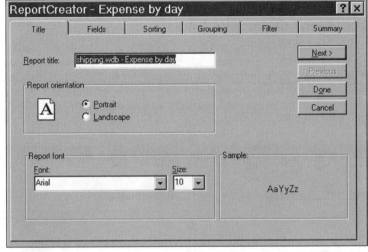

Figure 15-4:
The Report-
Creator's
Title card.
Fill out all
six cards
and you win
a report!

You don't have to take the six cards in strict left-to-right order, but Works presents them to you in that order when you use the Next button on the ReportCreator dialog box. To work on a different card at any time, just click that card's tab.

First card: Title, orientation, and font

The top card of the hand that the ReportCreator deals you is the Title card. The title is what appears on the top of your report. Works suggests a title for you, made up of the database filename and the name that you gave the report, but you can come up with a better one. Works also suggests that the report be created in the portrait orientation (taller than it is wide) and the 10-point Arial font, but Works also allows you to change these selections.

1. **Click the Report title text box and enter a title if you don't like Works' suggestion.**

   How about a title like *Commander of North American Operations*. No, just kidding; type in something boring and industrial, such as Shipping Costs.

2. **Choose Landscape orientation, if you are making a w – i – d – e report (that is, a report with a lot of fields on it; the number of fields depends on how wide your fields are). Choose Portrait orientation if your report is tall.**

3. **Choose a Font and Size in the Report font area.**

When you're done, click the Next button or the tab for the Fields card.

Second card: Choose your fields

The second card the ReportCreator deals you is the Fields card, shown in Figure 15-5. Here, you choose which of the fields in your database you want to appear in your report and in what order. (In the report, fields appear in columns, going left-to-right in the order you specify here.) Also, you can specify whether you want field names as headings for those field columns.

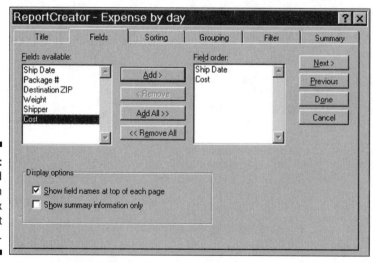

Figure 15-5:
Copy field
names from
the left box
to the right
box.

Follow these steps to choose the fields that you want to appear in your report:

1. Click a field name in the left-hand box (Fields Available).

The list in the Fields Available box is a list of the fields you have in your database. The basic procedure in this dialog box is to copy field names from the left box to the right box.

Click a field that you want to appear in your report.

2. Click Add to copy that field to the right-hand box (Field Order).

The right-hand box is where you accumulate a list of the fields that are to appear in the report.

(Every time you add a field, the highlight in the left-hand box moves down, for your pleasure and convenience. So to copy a series of field names, you can just keep clicking the Add button.)

3. Repeat Steps 1 and 2 for each field that you want in the report.

If you want them all, click the Add All button.

If you change your mind about a field, click that field in the right-hand box and then click the Remove button. To remove all the fields from the right-hand box and start again, click the Remove All button.

4. If you don't want the field names at the top of your page, click the Show Summary Information Only check box.

Normally, you want them. Figure 15-3 has 'em.

When you're done, click the Next button or the tab for the Sorting card.

Third card: All sorts of stuff!

This card may look familiar to you if you have already done sorting in the Works database tool. *Sorting* is the ordering of records alphabetically, numerically, or by date or time. (In Figure 15-3, for example, I sorted by the Shipper field — which is a text field — so Works sorted it alphabetically: The report starts with CityZIP and ends with Zowiefast.) In Figure 15-6, I've decided to sort by date.

Here's the procedure — bear in mind that you don't have to sort at all. Your report can just display stuff in the order in which it was entered (or previously sorted). You do have to specify sorting if you want groups in your report (see the Grouping card). But if you don't want to sort (you're feeling "out of sorts"), just click the Next button.

1. Choose the principal field to sort on.

Click the down-arrow button next to the box labeled Sort By and then click a field in that list. In Figure 15-6, I want to see things in order of shipment date; I don't care about ordering shipments within a date, so I don't sort on any other field.

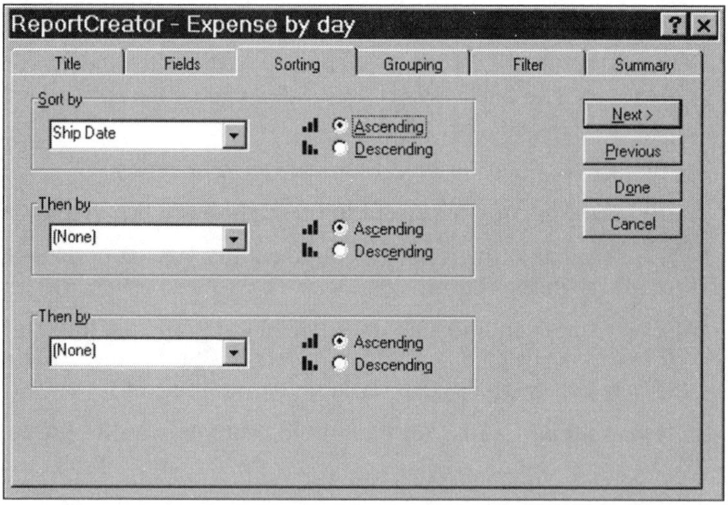

Figure 15-6:
What order
do you want
your data
listed in?

2. Choose a sorting direction for that field.

Click Ascending to go from A–Z or in the order 1, 2, 3. . . .

Click Descending to go from Z–A or in the order . . . 3, 2, 1.

3. Optionally, do the same for a second and third field.

If you want additional sorting, use these fields. (For example, if for each date I wanted shipments listed in order of increasing cost, I would choose Cost as my second field.)

When you're done, click the Next button or the tab for the Grouping card.

Fourth card: Groupings

Works can group records together that have identical values in some field. For example, if I have a bunch of shipments all on the same date, Works can group those together in my report. (See Figure 15-7.)

Here's the scoop on grouping:

✔ You don't have to group at all. Not feeling groupish? Just click the Next button.

✔ To create a group, click the When Contents Change check box. The other check boxes then come alive because they all control things that you can do to a group. The When Contents Change check box is so called because Works puts a space between groups when the contents of the specified field change. (For example, when the date changes in the Ship Date field.)

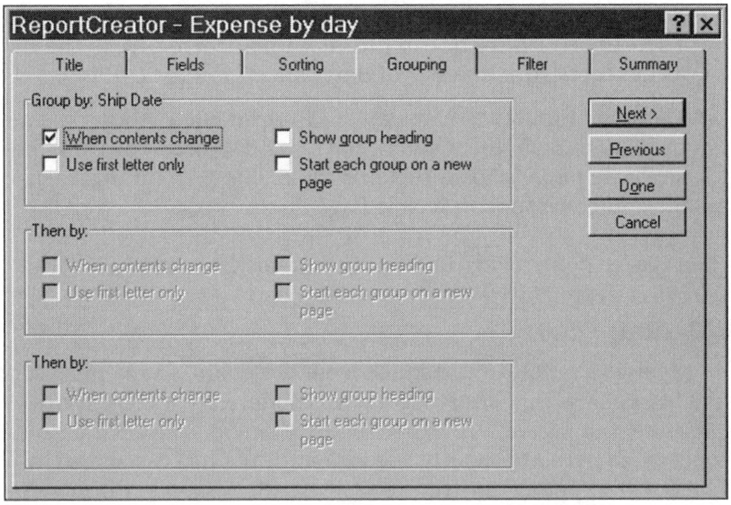

Figure 15-7:
Choosing to group by one field only.

✔ You can group only on fields that you have selected to appear on this report (on the Fields card) and have chosen for sorting (on the Sorting card). If I wanted to group on, say, the Cost field, I would have to go back to the Sorting card and add that field. Each field you have selected for sorting appears on the Grouping card.

✔ You can have groups, subgroups, and sub-subgroups — that's why three identical areas are on this card. For example, I can group ship- ments by date, "then by" shipper, "then by" ZIP Code. The order in which you chose your fields on the Grouping card determines the order in which your fields appear on this card; that order, in turn, determines whether you can use a field as a group (top area), subgroup (middle area), or sub-subgroup (bottom area).

✔ You can create groupings based strictly on the first character of a data entry. For example, if you had a list of last names, you probably wouldn't want to group by each name (many groups would be only one name long), but by initial letter: all the A's together, the B's together, and so on. To do this type of grouping, click the Use First Letter Only check box.

✔ You can use a heading to identify each group. For example, if you are grouping by ZIP Code, you can head each group with its ZIP Code. Heading each group with its ZIP Code is somewhat redundant, however, because the ZIP Code appears in every line of that group anyway, making it rather obvious what group it is. Nonetheless, if you like this sort of thing, click the Show Group Heading check box.

Works' ReportCreator doesn't properly handle dates as group headings. The ReportCreator doesn't format them correctly, so the dates appear as numbers (the number of days since January 1, 1900)!

✔ For some reports, you may want to print each group on a separate page. For example, in a national sales database, you may need to send a separate page to each region's sales office. To do this task, click the Start Each Group On A New Page check box.

When you're done, click the Next button or the tab for the Filter card.

Fifth card: Filters

Filters let you separate the sheep from the goats, so to speak (or the wheat from the chaff, if you are a vegetarian). Filters are a bit lengthy to discuss right here, but I go into more detail on filters in Chapter 14. The filters that you can use here are exactly the same as the ones discussed in Chapter 14. In fact, if you created any of those filters discussed in Chapter 14, they appear in the Select A Filter box here.

The executive summary on filters is that filters allow you to selectively hide certain records from your report. For example, packages shipped by the regular postal service may not belong in this report, so you would create a filter that says (in filter-ese) *Shipper . . . is not equal to . . . U.S. Postal Service.*

To create a filter, click the Create New Filter button and see Chapter 14 for further instruction. After you have created a filter, the filter appears in the Select A Filter text box. You can modify that filter with the Modify Filter button, if you need to.

If you have not created any filters, the ReportCreator gives you two options anyway, in the Select A Filter text box. Choose one:

✔ **(Current Records)** means that you want to display any records that are not hidden in your database. If you apply a filter, certain records are hidden and do not appear in the report.

✔ **(All Records)** means just that: Display all the records in the database.

Be brave; you are almost done. Click the Next button, or click the Summary tab of the ReportCreator, to wrap up your report with a few summaries.

Sixth card: Statistical summaries

At this point, you are gazing (glassy-eyed) at the Summary dialog box of Figure 15-8.

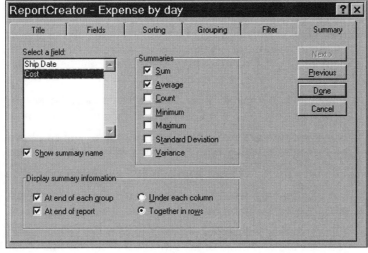

Statistical summaries are useful things. Statistical summaries are how you get the answers to such questions as, "What are the total sales for January in the Eastern region?" or "What is the batting average for each team?" or "Why are my eyes glazing over?" (Just kidding about the last one. The answer is, your eyes are going buggy from staring at your computer screen or reading this book too long.)

Summaries are optional. If you don't specify any summaries and you just click the Done button in the ReportCreator, you get a report that simply lists all the records in your database, displaying the fields that you chose on the Fields card — sorted and grouped, if you chose those features.

If you want statistics (including sums) on a certain field or fields, here's what to do:

1. **Click the field in the Select A Field box.**

2. **Choose the kind of statistical summary (or summaries) that you want for that field.**

   Click a check box in the Summaries area to select a particular kind of summary. Heck, click a batch of 'em if you want several different kinds of summaries.

   Average computes the average of all the numbers in the field, *Minimum* shows you the smallest (or most negative) value, and so on.

3. **Repeat Steps 1 and 2 for each field that you want summarized.**

   Each field can have its own set of summaries.

It's important to do this card carefully because summaries can't easily be changed after you've clicked the Done button. Be careful that you don't sum when you want to count. Sum adds up the numerical value of all the records in the selected field. Count just counts the records in a field. Also, don't accidentally sum up the wrong field (such as the date field)!

4. **Click Show Summary Name. This option makes Works label the summary as a sum, or an average, or whatever you choose.**

5. **If you created groups on the Grouping card, you can have a summary appear under each group by clicking At End Of Each Group.**

6. **Choose where you want your summaries to appear in the report.**

   Click Under Each Column to put your field summaries at the bottom of their respective columns.

   Click Together In Rows to put each of your field summaries in a separate row at the bottom of the report (or at the bottom of each group, if you chose that option).

7. **Click the Done button.**

   Things whiz around on your screen, ultimately delivering . . .

   . . . a big, confusing mess, and then one of those little boxes with the exclamation point in it! What the heck?!? This isn't what you had in mind! Where's that nice report??

Hang in there. Read the little dialog box, which is assuring you that The report definition has been created and asking whether you want to preview the report or modify it. I suggest that you choose Preview. Choosing Modify doesn't gain you much — it just leaves you gazing at the big confusing mess (called the Report view).

Click the Preview button, and Works shows you your report in Print Preview mode. Remember that the main purpose of a report is to make a nice report to print out — not to view on your screen. Read on to figure out exactly what's going on here.

Laying your cards on the table: Viewing your report

If you've been following along, you are now viewing your report in Print Preview. (For details on how Print Preview works, check out Chapter 4.) Click the Cancel button when you're done viewing.

After you leave Print Preview, what's on your screen at this point is not your actual report. Instead, what is on your screen is the Report view — a view most people don't find very comprehensible, and a view that's not necessary for most work. This view displays the rather intimidating report definition that tells Works how to construct your report. Don't be too upset — if it weren't for that nice ReportCreator dialog box, you would have had to enter all that intimidating stuff by hand.

You probably want to get out of the Report view and go back to a List or Form view. To go back, just click View and then click either List or Form in the menu that drops down.

Now that you're done defining a report, your named report exists as part of your Works database document. As with filters, you can call up this report at any time, and the report takes into account any new or changed data in your database. Also, as with filters, you can have only eight reports; any more, and you have to delete one by choosing Tools➪Delete Report and double-clicking the report name in the dialog box that appears.

You can reuse this report over and over as you add data. Just click View➪Report. Double-click the report name in the dialog box that appears.

Modifying your report — the easy way

Works makes it easy to modify your report — within limits. You can easily modify the sorting, grouping, and filtering. You can't as easily change fields or summaries. Here's the scoop on how to modify report settings:

- ✔ **Sorting:** Choose Tools➪Report Sorting
- ✔ **Grouping:** Choose Tools➪Report Grouping
- ✔ **Filtering:** Choose Tools➪Report Filtering

All of these steps take you to a Report Settings dialog box, where the cards look exactly like the cards in the ReportCreator, except that only these three functions (instead of six) are available. Refer back to the preceding discussions of sorting, grouping, and filtering for instructions.

Modifying and enhancing your report — the hard way

If you can't make the changes that you want from the Report Settings dialog box (the easy way), or if you want to get a better-looking report than the standard one, you need to go the hard way by using the Report view.

Using Report view is not for the easily confused! Explaining how to use the Report view in detail would take too long in this book, so I only give you the executive summary and a few instructions on how to change things. Fortunately, you may rarely need to resort to editing this report definition to create the reports you need.

You can use Report view to create the report you need in one of two ways:

- ✔ Create a report from scratch by writing one of those scary-looking report definitions you see in the so-called Report view.
- ✔ Modify the standard report definition.

My money's on the second option.

To modify an existing report definition, switch to the Report view: Choose View➪Report, click the report name in the View Report dialog box that appears, and then choose the Modify button. You are confronted with a strange-looking spreadsheet-kind-of-thing.

Each row in the Report view has a special function. Down the leftmost side are special labels that identify what part of the report is being controlled by that row. For example, report titles are entered in a row labeled Title; blank rows of any type just provide extra space.

The vertical position of the row corresponds to the position of that row in the final report. Title rows, for example, are at the top; summary rows are at the bottom.

Anything in bold text is text that literally appears on the report. Anything else is a special term referring to fields, calculations, and other parts of the database and its report.

The following are several types of rows you will find:

- ✔ **Intr Name** rows print the name of a field (if =Name appears) or some other text ("Next day") at the beginning of a group if the report is divided into groups.
- ✔ **Record** rows print the field contents of each individual record in the report.
- ✔ **Summ** rows print summaries that appear for groups.
- ✔ **Summary** rows print summaries for all the data in the report.

You can add these sorts of special rows if you think that you understand their functions from these very brief descriptions and the descriptions that follow in this chapter. (Or, if you want to try to understand them by playing around with them.) Click the row above which you want to add a row and then choose Insert➪Insert Row from the menu bar. Choose a row type from the list in the Insert Row dialog box that appears and click the Insert button.

Adding or deleting fields

A typical standard report displays only a few of the many fields in your database. To add a new field to your report in Report view (which is the only view in which you can do this task), see Figure 15-9 for an example, and do the following:

1. **Locate the row labeled Record in the leftmost column.**

2. **Find the first blank cell available in that row and click it.**

   A black border appears around that cell, as shown in Figure 15-9.

3. **Choose Insert⇨Field Entry from the menu bar, and the Insert Field Entry dialog box shown in Figure 15-9 appears.**

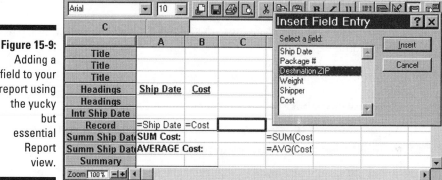

Figure 15-9:
Adding a field to your report using the yucky but essential Report view.

4. **Choose the field that you want to add to your report from the list in the Insert Field Entry dialog box.**

   In Figure 15-9, I'm adding the Destination ZIP field.

5. **Click the Insert button.**

6. **Add a heading, if you want.**

   Find a row above the current cell labeled Headings (which probably has other headings in it), and simply type in a heading. (If no row is labeled Headings, choose Insert⇨Insert Row from the menu bar and choose Headings from the Insert Row dialog box that appears.) Format the text that you type with bold, underline, or any other font, style, or alignment formatting that you like. If a Summ something-or-other field appears under the cell that you have just typed, you want an underline. (See "Adding or deleting summaries" later in this chapter for more information about adding summaries.)

7. Add an underline by choosing Format⇨Border, choosing Bottom in the Format dialog box, and then clicking OK.

To delete a field from the report, look in the row labeled Record for a cell containing an equal sign (=) followed by the field name. Click that cell and then press the Delete key.

To see whether these mysterious actions really gave you what you wanted, go to Print Preview. (Click the document-with-a-monocle icon button or choose File⇨Print Preview.)

Adding or deleting summaries

A report may have two kinds of summaries: group summaries and overall summaries. In Report view, group summaries are controlled by rows labeled Summ (and then the field name). Overall summaries are controlled by rows labeled Summary.

You can put your new summary on a row by itself, or add your summary to an existing summary row.

To put your new summary on a row by itself:

1. Click any row above which you want to add a summary.

A good choice is the row below an existing Summ or Summary row.

2. Choose Insert⇨Insert Row from the menu bar.

3. Select Summary or Summ [some field name] from the list of row types in the Insert Row dialog box, and click the Insert button.

For example, if you are adding a new summary to a group grouped by ZIP Code, you can choose Summ ZIP Code.

4. In the A column of your new row, type a label for this summary, such as TOTAL: Weight.

5. Click in the column where you want the summary to appear in this row.

You can choose any column of this row (column D, for example) that is not overlapped by the label that you typed.

6. Choose Insert⇨Field Summary from the menu bar.

The Field Insert dialog box appears.

7. Choose a field from the list and click the kind of summary you want in the Statistic area of the dialog box; click the Insert button when you're done.

To see whether you really created the summary you wanted, go to Print Preview. (Click the document-with-a-monocle icon button or choose File⇨Print Preview.)

To add a summary to an existing Summary row, start with Step 5 in the preceding list, in which you select an unused cell in that row. That cell is where your new summary appears.

To delete an entire Summary row, click the row to be deleted, and then choose Insert⇨Delete Row from the menu bar. To delete a single summary from a row with several summaries, first use Print Preview to see which column the summary is in. Then click Cancel in Print Preview to return to the Report view. Click in that column of the Summary row (you will find a formula beginning with the equal sign there) and press the Delete key.

Fixing up appearances

When most reports first appear, they don't look any better than I do when I first appear in the morning. Here are a few things you can do in Report view to improve your report's appearance.

To switch to Report view, choose View⇨Report, click the report name in the View Report dialog box that appears, and then choose the Modify button.

Much of the report's appearance can be set the same way that spreadsheet appearances are set. The commands and procedures are similar, if not identical. If you're already familiar with Works' spreadsheets, you probably know how to do many of the formatting tasks in the following list. If you are not familiar with Works' spreadsheets, here is a quick summary:

- **Adjust report column widths:** Click and drag the crack between the column letters (the gray cells with the letters A, B, C, and so forth, across the top of the columns).

- **Align data within the report columns:** Click the column's letter to select the column. (Click and drag across the column letters to choose multiple columns.) Either choose one of the alignment buttons on the button bar, or choose Format⇨Alignment to get to the alignment page of the Format dialog box. Double-click the Alignment you need. (Typically, Left, Right, Center, or Center Across Selection does the job.)

- **Edit the column headings:** Click a report heading (in a row labeled Headings) and make edits to the heading text by using the formula bar.

- **Change font, font size, or style:** Select either a report heading (click it in a row labeled Headings), an entire column (click its column letter), or the entire report (press Ctrl+A). Then choose a new font, type size, or style (bold, italic, or underlined) by using either the toolbar or the Format⇨Font and Style command.

✔ **Change number formats:** To make your numbers look right — with dollar signs preceding monetary figures and zeros leading ZIP Codes — you need a number format. Select the column that needs fixing (click its column letter) and choose Format⇨Number from the menu bar. The Number card of the Format dialog box appears. Click a Format, choose any Options, and then click OK. See the section on fields in Chapter 12 for more information on number formats.

✔ **Borders:** To put lines and borders around rows and columns, first select the row (click its label, such as Headings, in the gray column at the left of the row) or column (click its column letter) and choose Format⇨Border. Click a Line Style, click a Border, and then click the OK button. See the section on applying and changing formats in Chapter 13 for more information.

Calculating

The Works database tool can perform calculations that you may find useful, but also somewhat confusing to perform without some study. Works' database tool can perform calculations for you in two locations:

✔ **You can make a calculating field.** For instance, while entering a shipping record, you may enter an item's weight in pounds, and in the calculating field Works would compute the item's weight in kilograms.

✔ **You can add calculations to a report (in addition to the calculations already provided by summaries).** For instance, a report in a manufacturing and sales database could compute profit margin by adding up the total cost from several cost fields (parts, labor, and so forth) and subtracting the total from the total sales.

Calculations in fields provide results based on a single record. Calculations in reports provide results based on all records or a group of records in your database.

In Works' database tool, calculations are similar to calculations done in the spreadsheet tool. You may find the discussions of formulas and functions in Chapter 10 useful if you haven't performed calculations in Works before.

You write formulas for Works databases by using the same sort of terms you use in spreadsheets, but with some important differences:

✔ As in spreadsheet formulas, you use various *operators* such as + (add), - (subtract), * (multiply), and / (divide) together with *constants* such as the number 2.04.

✔ Use field names to represent values instead of using cell addresses or ranges as you do in a spreadsheet — for instance, you may write the formula =Price-Cost to calculate an item's profit margin in a database, whereas you would write =B2-B1 in a spreadsheet.

If your field names are the same as Works function names, like Date, enclose the field name in quotation marks (Date) in your formula. Otherwise, Works may think you intend to use a function.

✔ Use Works functions, such as if(), sum(), or avg(). In reports, because they summarize the results of many records, you can use only statistical functions, like sum() or avg(). In fields, you can use a much larger variety of functions.

Following are a few examples of calculations for a database in which Cost and Weight are the names of two fields:

✔ =Cost/Weight, if used in a field, would provide each record with a computed field that displays the cost per pound *of that item* (that record).

✔ =sum(Cost)/sum(Weight), used in a report, would divide the total of all entries in the Cost field by the total of all entries in the Weight field, giving average cost per pound *for all items* (records) in the database.

✔ =if(Weight>10, Overweight! ,), used in a field, would provide each record with a field that displayed the warning "Overweight!" if the item weighed over ten pounds. You cannot use the if() function in a report, because it is not a statistical function.

To better understand what is going on in Works calculations, read on.

Adding a calculating field to your database

To add a field to your database that does calculations, follow these steps:

1. **Switch to List view, if you're not already using that view: Choose View➪List.**

2. **Add a field using Record➪Insert field.**

   For a review of inserting fields, see the section on adding new fields in Chapter 13.

3. **Click the name of the new field at the top of the column to select that field.**

4. **Type the equal (=) sign to begin entering a formula.**

5. **Type the remainder of the formula, using field names, constants, functions, and operators.**

For instance, to compute an item's cost per pound, you divide that item's cost by its weight: Assuming your field names are Cost and Weight, you would type =Cost/Weight. As you type your formula, instead of actually typing field names, you may "point and shoot": Click on the columns corresponding to the fields.

If you need help remembering how to write a function, choose Help⇨Show Help; as you type the function's name (such as =date) into your field, Help displays an Overview window. (If Show Help doesn't appear on the Help menu, click the tiny button with a question-mark symbol on the lower-right side of the Works window to reinflate the Help window.)

If you are using statistical functions such as sum(Cost) in field calculations, you probably misunderstand how field calculations work. Field calculations work on only one record at a time, so sum(Cost) is the same as Cost. To sum the values in the Cost field, you must put your calculation in a report, not a field.

6. **Press the Enter key when you're done, or click the Checkmark button on the formula bar.**

To see the result of your new field, choose File⇨Print Preview.

Adding or modifying calculations in reports

Why add or modify a calculation? The standard report you get from the ReportCreator doesn't provide any calculations other than a statistical summary of a single field. So, although your shipping department report may contain total weight shipped and total shipping charges, the report won't be able to print the average cost per pound of shipping (total shipping charges divided by total weight shipped) unless you create your own formula to perform the division.

To add or modify calculations in your reports, you must use Works' rather confusing Report view. Choose View⇨Report; click the report name in the View Report dialog box that appears, and then choose the Modify button.

Your standard report probably already performs calculations, which are a good place to start to understand report calculations. If, for instance, you included any summaries when you used the ReportCreator, those summaries are the result of the ReportCreator writing formulas that use Works' statistical functions. If you summed up the numbers in a field, for instance, the ReportCreator wrote a formula that used the sum() function.

To see these existing calculations, click a cell in any Summ or Summary row. As you click these cells, the formula bar displays the cell's contents. Any cell where the contents begin with an equal sign (=) contains a formula. The formula contains one of Works statistical functions: sum( ), avg( ), max( ), min( ), max( ), count( ), std( ), or var( ), depending on the type of Summary you chose in the Summary card (shown in Figure 15-8).

You can write similar formulas to perform more complex operations. For instance, to compute the range of values in the Cost field of your database, you would use the formula =max(Cost)-min(Cost). When writing report formulas, you do not use field names alone, such as =Cost; instead, use the field names within Works statistical functions.

Where do you write these formulas in Report View? You can write them in a Record, Summ, or Summary row. Enter the formulas in any blank (empty) cell in that row; whatever column you write the formula in is the column in which the result will appear on your report. You can also edit an existing formula: Start by simply clicking the formula, and edit it as you would a spreadsheet formula. (See Chapter 10 for details.) Here's how to choose which row to use:

- ✔ To perform a calculation on all the records in the report, enter the formula in the Summary row. For instance, to compute the shipping cost per pound for all the shipments in your report, enter your formula in any available (blank) column of the Summary row. You can also add a new Summary row by choosing Insert⇨Insert Row and selecting Summary from the list that appears.

- ✔ To perform a calculation on each group (or subgroup) of your report, enter the formula in a Summ row for some field name. For instance, if you group by Shipper as in Figure 15-3, to create a calculation of shipping cost per pound for each shipper, enter your formula in the Summ Shipper row. (If your report uses subgroups, such as ZIP Code groups within each shipper, you have additional Summ rows. If you wanted to compute cost per pound separately for each ZIP Code handled by the shipper, you would enter your formula in the Summ Destination ZIP row.)

- ✔ To perform a calculation on each record of your report, enter the formula in a Record row. Because this calculation is performed on each record, it appears on every line of the report and looks like a calculating field. For instance, if you wanted to display weight in kilograms for each shipment, but your data was in pounds, you would enter the formula =Weight*2.204 in a blank cell of the Record row.

Feel free to add text in any blank cell that you want to appear on the printed report. Figure 15-10 shows an example Report view with additional calculations for cost per pound, and Figure 15-11 shows the resulting report. The text and summaries that I added are in italics.

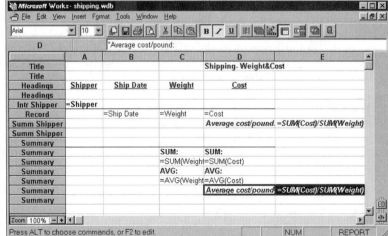

Figure 15-10: Adding Cost per Pound labels and formulas in Report view.

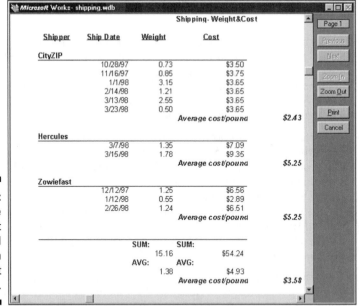

Figure 15-11: Viewing the new Cost per Pound results in print preview.

Part V

Exploring the Internet Wilderness

The 5th Wave   By Rich Tennant

"You know, I liked you a whole lot more on the Internet."

In this part . . .

*I*f, to you, *online* is where the laundry goes when the clothes dryer breaks, take heart! No, Works can't fix your dryer. But it can take your PC online — connect it to the Internet, to the computer at work, or to a PC in Poughkeepsie. Microsoft's Internet Explorer, a separate program from Works 4.5, is your vehicle for a surfin' safari on the Internet's World Wide Web — the ultimate online wilderness. A special Internet Connection Wizard makes sure that you can get online without being hung out to dry. Chapters 16 and 17 give you the big picture, get you online, and show you how to surf the Internet on the World Wide Web.

If, on the other hand, your idea of online excitement is telecommuting from your bedroom to your company computer, Works' built-in communications tool may be just the ticket. Chapter 18 tells you how to get on board, whether you're telecommuting or sending files to your accountant in Aruba. With Works survival tools and the chapters of Part V, you may find exploring the online wilderness as easy as a walk in the park.

> "I pr'ythee, let me bring thee where crabs grow; And I with my long nails will dig thee pig-nuts; Show thee a jay's nest, and instruct thee how to snare the nimble marmozet; I'll bring thee to clust'ring filberts, and sometimes I'll get thee young sea-mells from the rock: Wilt thou go with me?"

The Tempest, Wm. Shakespeare

Chapter 16

Gearing Up for Internet Adventure

. . . .

In This Chapter

▶ Going online

▶ Understanding the Internet

▶ Gathering what you need

▶ Getting online quickly

▶ Installing and launching Internet Explorer

▶ Using the Internet Connection Wizard

▶ Finding an Internet Service Provider and setting up Windows yourself

. . . .

*O*kay, just what is all the noise about, anyway? What is "being online," and why has the whole world gone wild over the Internet? Good questions, pilgrim — questions best answered by plugging in and going online yourself. This chapter explains how and why to get yourself online to the Internet by installing Microsoft's Internet Explorer.

Preparing to "Go Online"

Being (or going) *online* means different things to different people, but the broadest definition of being online is that your PC is communicating in some way with another computer. But why on earth would you want your PC to talk to any other computer? Doesn't it get into enough mischief by itself? Well, here are a few reasons why:

✔ **To exchange typed messages with another person (electronic mail, or e-mail).** Often you can exchange pictures or other files (such as Works files) with other people, too, by electronic mail.

✔ **To use programs that run on other computers.** For instance, if you are a salesperson, you may be able to run a sales-order entry program on your company's big computer from your home office.

✔ **To send Works files or other files to another person who has a PC.** For example, you may want to send your Works financial spreadsheet to your accountant.

✔ **To look up something in the vast heaps of information publicly available on the Internet on nearly any topic you can name.** The World Wide Web (or *Web*) is the Internet service that is best known for this information.

✔ **To obtain software — often for free — from the Internet (again, usually from the Web).**

You can do some of these things by using Works' built-in communications tool (described in Chapter 18) and connecting to a larger computer or another PC. Works' communications tool simply turns your PC into a computer terminal that lets you run old-fashioned text-only (like MS-DOS) programs on distant computers. For instance, if your company or university computer normally uses terminals for sending e-mail with a DOS-like text-only program, you may be able to send e-mail from your home PC with the help of Works' communications tool. But going online is a lot easier and more fun when using a Windows-style program like Internet Explorer rather than using text-based programs.

Another way to join in these online activities with a Windows-style program is by subscribing to a *value-added* online service, such as America Online or CompuServe. These services are private commercial networks that also offer links to the Internet. They provide you with their own software and with special services (the "added value") that are not available to non-members.

Fortunately, with the advent of Windows 95 (and future versions of Windows), and with Internet Explorer now included with Works, you can connect directly to the Internet and use cool graphical software. "But," you ask, "what's the big deal about the Internet?" Read on.

Understanding the Big Deal about the Internet

One big deal about the Internet is that it runs on existing computers and networks all over the world, which makes it inexpensive and accessible. The other big deal is that because no single company or government owns it, programmers have been free to create all kinds of Internet services. The following are just a few of the most popular services:

✔ **Electronic mail (or *e-mail*):** Private messages or files sent from person to person. These messages can include attachments of pictures or other files.

✔ **The World Wide Web (or *Web*):** Public document files (including text, pictures, sound, or video) transmitted to you on request and displayed on your screen.

✔ **File transfer (or *ftp*):** Public files (containing practically anything at all, including programs) transmitted to or from your PC's disk at your request.

✔ **Newsgroups (or *news*):** An ongoing exchange of messages on a particular subject where anyone can read or add messages (sort of like graffiti).

✔ **Chat (or *a stupefying way to spend large sums of money and time*):** A live public dialog on a subject, where everyone types lines of text to each other, and the lines appear, one after the other, all in a single window.

Each service you want to use requires you to have software for that service. For e-mail, you need e-mail software; for the Web, you need Web software like Internet Explorer. Some software can handle several services: Internet Explorer, for example, can provide Web and limited ftp service.

The biggest deal of all for the Internet is undoubtedly the World Wide Web. The Web is a collection of public electronic documents that you can read with a Web browser, like Microsoft's Internet Explorer or Netscape's Navigator or Communicator programs. Web documents are created by individuals or organizations who want to sell something, persuade you, or simply inform you for reasons of their own. Web document files are placed on a computer that runs a *Web server* program at a particular address on the Internet. If you, by using your Web browser, tell that Web server what document you want, it delivers the document for your viewing pleasure.

You can find information — including text, pictures, sounds, or even video — on pets, medicine, money, sex, artichokes, science, history, coffee beans, politics, solar energy, mathematics, child raising, wild animals, music, genealogy, or construction of atlatls. You can buy stuff or do your banking. You can also download software for free from the Web, including software for other services like e-mail. "Sounds great! How do I sign up?" you ask. Read on.

Gathering Everything You Need

Whether you use Works' communications tool or use Internet software to go online, one thing is essential: a modem. A *modem* is a PC hardware accessory that connects your PC to another computer (and its modem) via a phone line. The modem does the dialing and turns your data into screeching noises that the other computer's modem can understand. See the "Getting a Modem" section, coming up in this chapter.

If you're only going to connect to another PC or to a remote computer that runs text-based software, you don't need anything else but the modem. You can use Microsoft Works' communications tool. See Chapter 18 for more on using this tool.

If you want to connect to the Internet, however, you also need the following stuff (but don't panic as you read the list — a wizard exists that can help you get what you need):

✔ **An Internet Service Provider (ISP):** An ISP has a big computer permanently connected to the Internet that your PC can connect to by calling on the phone line. The big computer "speaks Internet speak" (called *TCP/IP*) to your PC.

✔ **Dial-up TCP/IP software on your PC:** This is software that works with your modem to call your ISP's computer by phone and "speak Internet speak" to that computer. Windows comes with dial-up networking software that you may or may not have already installed.

✔ **Software on your PC for each Internet service:** You already have Internet Explorer for Web browsing and ftp service. For e-mail or news, you need other software that you can download from the Web or buy. (Such Internet software for your PC is called *client* software in geekspeak.)

Besides collecting all this stuff, you also need to install it and set it up properly. You need to tell your ISP who you are (and send them money every month). You need to tell Windows' dial-up software how to connect to your ISP. (Your ISP provides the information.) Finally, you need to set up your PC software, such as your Web browser or e-mail software.

Whew! Sounds like a lot of effort, right? It can, indeed, be a lot of effort, but Microsoft really, really wants you to go online, so they have given you a shortcut. If you install and launch Internet Explorer, an Internet Connection Wizard does all the rest for you (helps you get an ISP and sets up your PC to go online). See the "Meeting the Internet Connection Wizard" section later in this chapter.

You may need the Windows installation diskettes or CD if your PC has never been set up for networking before. If you don't have the Windows diskettes or CD, you need to have a very forceful conversation with the company that sold you your PC.

Getting a Modem

If your PC is fairly new, it probably has a modem installed in it already. If not, you need to buy a modem. (Check the invoice or brochure for your computer if you're not sure that it has a modem installed.)

Modems are available as *internal modems,* which live inside your PC, or *external modems,* which are separate boxes with cables that plug into the back of your PC. Internal modems are cheaper and tidier, but external modems have a switch that lets you turn them on and off manually in case something goes wrong in the software that normally turns the modem on or off.

Modems differ in the speed at which they can send and receive data. Faster is generally better because of the Web's graphics, audio, and other non-text media. Go for a speed of 33,600 bits per second (bps).

Follow the instructions in the package to connect your modem to your PC. Those instructions will probably also tell you how to install your modem in Windows. If no instructions for installing the modem in Windows are provided, use Windows Help. Click the Windows Start button and choose Help. In the Help dialog box that appears, click the Index card tab, and then type the following: **modems, setting up**. Click the Display button. Follow the instructions in the Windows Help box that appears.

Going Online the Fast Way

The absolute fastest way to get online is Microsoft's Internet Connection Wizard. Interested? Well, because you're in a rush, I'll cut to the chase. With a modem installed (and turned on, if it's an external modem), do the following:

1. **Install Internet Explorer by double-clicking the icon on your Windows screen labeled Setup for Microsoft Internet Explorer 3.02.**

2. **Launch Internet Explorer by double-clicking its globe-with-magnifying-glass icon labeled The Internet.**

    The Internet Connection Wizard appears.

3. **Follow the wizard's instructions.**

The wizard lets you choose an Internet Service Provider from a list and also sets up your PC for you. This wizard does many complex and amazing things, some of which are mentioned in the upcoming section, "Meeting the Internet Connection Wizard." The following sections provide additional details about installing and launching Internet Explorer and about using the wizard.

Installing Internet Explorer

When your modem is connected to your PC and your phone line, the time has come to install the Web browsing program that comes with Works 4.5: Internet Explorer. Works 4.5 comes with Internet Explorer 3.02. Later distributions of Works may come with Internet Explorer 4, which works a bit differently, and may install a bit differently, too. But most likely, you'll still be able to use most of the instructions in this chapter and Chapter 17.

When you install Works 4.5, a setup icon labeled Setup for Microsoft Internet Explorer 3.02 takes its place on your Windows screen (desktop). Double-click that icon and follow the instructions that appear, clicking Yes or OK as necessary as the dialog boxes fly by. If the setup icon isn't present, put your Works 4.5 CD in your CD drive. Double-click the My Computer icon, click with your *right* mouse button on the CD-ROM disk (usually D:) and choose Open from the drop-down menu. Double-click the MSWorks folder now visible, and then double-click the file msie302.exe.

After a few minutes of activity on your screen, the Setup program tells you that you must restart your PC before the installation process is complete. The program asks if it should restart your PC now, and if you click Yes, it will do so. If you click No, you won't be able to use Internet Explorer until you next restart your PC.

You can now get rid of the setup icon labeled Setup for Microsoft Internet Explorer 3.02. Click on the icon and then either drag it to the recycle bin or press the Delete key on your keyboard.

Launching Internet Explorer

Windows provides two main ways to launch, or *run,* Internet Explorer:

- ✔ Click the Start button on the Windows start bar; then choose Pro-grams⇨Internet Explorer.
- ✔ Double-click the Internet Explorer icon on your Windows screen (the icon is a globe-with-magnifying-glass symbol labeled The Internet).

From time to time you will also find files listed on your disk drive that display the Internet Explorer globe icon. If you double-click such a file, Windows launches Internet Explorer and opens that file in the Internet Explorer window.

When you launch Internet Explorer, a dialog box may pop up, whining that `Internet Explorer 3.0 is not currently your default browser` and asking if you would like to rectify this situation. If you choose Yes, any time a Web browser is required (such as when you double-click on a Web file on your PC), Internet Explorer will be launched. If you have a different browser that you would like to use most of the time, click the check box marked Always Perform This Check When Starting Internet Explorer, and then click the No button.

Meeting the Internet Connection Wizard

The very first time you launch Internet Explorer, an Internet Connection Wizard appears on the scene to make sure you can connect to the Internet. (If you need the wizard again later, you can find it by clicking the Windows Start button and then choosing Programs⇨Accessories⇨Internet Tools⇨Get On The Internet.)

Click the Next button in the wizard dialog box to proceed from one step to the next. The second wizard screen you see is the Setup Options screen, shown in Figure 16-1. Your choices are:

- ✔ **Automatic:** Choose this if you don't currently have an ISP and you want the wizard to help you get one. You will need your credit card and, possibly, your Windows setup CD or diskettes.

- ✔ **Manual:** Choose this if you already have an account with an ISP but haven't yet set up Windows to connect to it. You may need your Windows setup CD or diskettes.

- ✔ **Current:** Choose this if you already have an ISP and have set up Windows' Dial-Up Networking to connect to it.

As you proceed through the wizard process by clicking Next, the wizard takes a variety of actions, all of which depend on your choice in the Setup Options screen.

Figure 16-1:
Choosing Automatic setup does all the technical stuff for you.

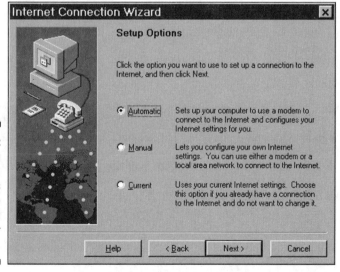

If you have previously set up Windows for an ISP, the wizard may periodically ask whether you want to remove the DNS servers. If you are using the wizard to switch to a new ISP, choose Yes. If you are adding a second ISP and you will use the new ISP more often, choose Yes; otherwise, choose No.

If you choose Automatic setup, the wizard dials into a Microsoft "referral center" and downloads a list of ISPs Microsoft has made special arrangements with in your area. Choose an ISP by clicking the check mark icon next to it, or you can ask for more information by clicking the document icon. Choosing an ISP connects you to a special signup page. If this process fails for any reason, click Cancel way at the bottom of the list of ISPs, and try launching Internet Explorer again.

After many screens of signing up, plus additional wizard screens directing you to do various things, you're all set to go online to the Internet. Launch Internet Explorer again. If you don't succeed in getting online, take a look at the instructions in the "Finding an Internet Service Provider Yourself" and "Setting Up Windows Yourself" sections later in this chapter.

Going Online: The Dialing Process

When you launch Internet Explorer, Windows begins a process of automatic dialing. No, it's not surreptitiously dialing Bill Gates with your credit card number. The automatic dialing is dialing your Internet Service Provider (ISP) so that you can go online to the Internet.

In Windows 95, a Connect To window appears soon after you launch Internet Explorer. If that window does not appear, double-click the My Computer icon on your screen, double-click the Dial-Up Networking folder in the window that appears, and then double-click the icon for your ISP in the next window that appears.

When the Connect To window appears, you enter the account name (unless it's already filled in) and the password assigned to you by your ISP. As you type the password, asterisks (****) appear in place of the characters you type, to thwart anyone who may be looking over your shoulder. To avoid having to type the password in the future, if the Save Password check box is not grayed-out, click to place a check mark there. (For strange and complicated security reasons, you can't save a dial-up password unless Windows is set up to request a Windows password when you start your computer.)

Enjoying the Online Experience

When your PC is online, Internet Explorer appears on your screen and immediately goes to a particular address on the Web that it has been told to use as its *start page*. Internet Explorer is initially set up to go to a Microsoft page where you can register and download all kinds of accessories for Internet Explorer.

You can either wait for Internet Explorer to finish loading the start page, or click the Stop button on the Internet Explorer toolbar. If you want to explore someplace else besides Microsoft's home page, click the Stop button and avoid the wait.

Now you're ready to explore (or *browse*) the Web! Web browsing is a big topic, so it gets an entire chapter: Chapter 17.

Finding an Internet Service Provider Yourself

To get on the Internet, you need to do business with a company that lets you connect your PC to its computers to access the Internet. Such companies are called Internet Service Providers *(ISPs)* or Internet access providers. If you install and launch Internet Explorer, an Internet Connection Wizard can help you set up an account with one of the larger ISPs available in your area, in addition to setting up your PC for Internet use. (The wizard may not, however, list local ISPs in your area, some of which may be excellent choices.) See "Meeting the Internet Connection Wizard" earlier in this chapter for more about this option.

You can find local ISPs by looking in the yellow or commercial pages of phone books or in the business pages of your newspaper. National ISPs also exist, including Internet divisions of long-distance access companies like AT&T. Local colleges and universities sometimes offer access, as well.

What sort of ISP should you look for? Local ISPs sometimes offer more bang for your buck, like better help services, lower rates, or more local phone numbers for your PC to call. National ISPs are good if you travel, because your chances are high of getting a local number to call wherever you are. Some smaller ISPs compete by offering reciprocal arrangements with other ISPs when you need remote access.

ISP attributes to look for include local phone numbers, a good reputation for patient and accessible customer service, reliable dial-up access (few busy signals or other connection problems), and low cost. You are better off if you ask other users before you buy. Charges typically range from about $6 to $25 per month. If you discover that you don't like your ISP, switching to another is easy — until you start using e-mail. After you have e-mail, you'll have to notify all your friends about your e-mail address change if you change your ISP.

No matter how you get your PC on the Internet, you need at least the following information from your ISP: your user name (or login ID) and your password.

You may need additional technical information if you need to set up your PC yourself. See the following section, "Setting Up Windows Yourself," for more about setup.

Setting Up Windows Yourself

After you get an ISP, you need to set up your PC to use the ISP's service. If you choose your ISP by using Microsoft's Internet Connection Wizard that starts when you first launch Internet Explorer, the wizard does the setup for you. (See "Meeting the Internet Connection Wizard" in this chapter for more information.)

If you choose your ISP without the wizard's help, use the installation kit most ISPs provide, consisting of a diskette and instructions.

Ask your ISP sales representative if the installation kit you get from the ISP takes care of the entire Windows setup, including the TCP/IP adapter, automatically. If the answer is "no," you are going to need some help from Windows:

1. **Click the Windows Start button and choose Help.**

   The Help dialog box appears.

2. **Click the Index card tab, and then type the following:** Dial-Up Net-working, connecting to the Internet.

3. **Click the Display button.**

   The Windows Help box appears.

4. **Click the button marked How To Connect To The Internet Using Dial-Up Networking.**

From this point on, Windows Help leads you in a pretty long step-by-step process and tells you what additional information you need from your ISP. Follow the instructions, and you'll do fine. If you don't do fine, contact the help desk at your ISP and ask them to step you through the process. If they won't do that, change your ISP!

Chapter 17

Exploring with Internet Explorer

. . . .

In This Chapter

▶ Browsing

▶ Searching

▶ Printing

▶ Downloading

▶ E-mailing and other Internet activities

▶ Minimizing warning messages

▶ Disconnecting

. . . .

*I*nternet Explorer is your Microsoft-built, Microsoft-tough sport utility vehicle for a safari on the World Wide Web (or just the *Web*). But — more importantly — Internet Explorer is free! If you have followed the instructions in Chapter 16, Internet Explorer is now gassed up and ready to roll. Internet Explorer isn't hard to drive, and this chapter gives you basic instructions and tips for navigating the Web.

Double-click the globe icon labeled The Internet on your Windows screen to start your Web-surfing safari. But remember that the World Wide Web, which is what Internet Explorer lets you access, is only one service of the Internet — although it's undoubtedly the most famous service. Web access can also be your foot in the door to the whole Internet, giving you the power to download Internet software for electronic mail and newsgroups. (This chapter includes a few suggestions for getting electronic mail software from the Web.)

Browsing the Web

Browsing is the trendy activity of the late '90s, whether you're into computers, shopping, or eating. Applied to the Web, *browsing* means viewing the documents (together with their graphics and sounds) located at various Web addresses (also known as *URLs*) around the world.

TIP

Browsing versus snoozing

Using the World Wide Web is sometimes so slow that the experience is called the World Wide Wait. To speed up your browsing, turn off the graphics: Choose View⇨Options, and then click the General card in the Options dialog box that appears. Click to clear the check mark labeled Show Pictures. On most Web sites, you will now find text where the graphics were.

Viewing a distant Web document is not quite like viewing a distant mountain through a telescope; it's more like having a copy of the distant mountain shipped to your doorstep piece by piece. The entire document is transmitted to your Web browser, and this transmission can take awhile.

Browsing by typing an address

One way to browse the Web is to specify the address of a document, which is called an URL (and pronounced "earl"). Addresses on the Web are a bit cryptic; you've undoubtedly seen them on TV and elsewhere. They can look like the following addresses:

- ✔ `http://www.snoggle.com`
- ✔ `www.snoggle.com`
- ✔ `www.snoggle.net/users/barney.html`

Technically speaking, all Web addresses should begin with `http://`, but typing that code is boring and tedious, so new Web browsers like Internet Explorer don't require it. You may omit it and just type the rest of the address: `www.brightleaf.com/tracking`, for instance.

If you know the URL of the Web site you want to see (for instance, `www.dummies.com`), you can enter that address in one of two places:

- ✔ **Click in the white area (text box) of the Address bar, normally visible near the top of the Internet Explorer window, and type in the address.** If an address is currently present, you will replace that address with whatever you type. Press the Enter key when you're done.

- ✔ **Choose File⇨Open (or press Ctrl+O), and in the Open dialog box that appears, type the address.** Press the Enter key when you're done or click the OK button.

You can see both of these locations in Figure 17-1; you can use whichever one you please. After the Web page is loaded, its title appears in the title bar of the Internet Explorer window, and its full address (URL) appears in the Address text box.

Type an address

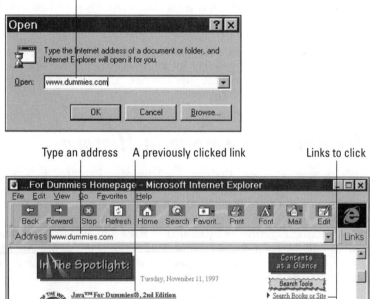

Type an address   A previously clicked link   Links to click

Figure 17-1:
Telling
Internet
Explorer
where
to go.

A graphic that is also a link   Status bar shows a link's address

Browsing by clicking links on Web pages

If you're currently viewing a Web document, you can click on buttons, specially marked text, or certain graphics on the page to view a different document. That other document may be at the same general address (say, dummies.com, run by IDG Books Worldwide, Inc.) or may take you somewhere else altogether (net.gurus.net, run by IECC). The item you click on to view a different document is called a *link* by most people, and a *shortcut* by Microsoft.

The best way to tell whether a word, a graphic, a button, or some other element on the page is a link is to move your mouse cursor over that element without clicking. If the element is a link, some text will appear in the gray area at the bottom of the Internet Explorer window (the status bar), as shown in Figure 17-1. This text describes the Web page to which the link will take you. Sometimes, that text is an instruction to the computer at the other end, so it looks like the technical gibberish in the status bar of Figure 17-1.

Text links are easy to spot. They are usually underlined and often appear in a distinctive color (typically, bright blue). If you have already visited a page that a text link connects to, the color of the text usually changes to a darker or fainter color so that you know you have already explored that link. In Figure 17-1, *Java For Dummies,* 2nd Edition has already been explored.

Some links will start to download a file instead of taking you to another Web page. If that happens unexpectedly, simply press the Esc key to exit from the File Download dialog box that appears. See "Downloading Files from the Web" later on for more information.

Returning to a page in History

Don't know much about History? Well, Internet Explorer does. Each time you use Internet Explorer, it keeps a record of the Web pages you have visited so that you can return to them. You can return to the Web pages you have visited most recently — the ones you have visited since the current launching of Internet Explorer — by using the Back and Forward buttons on the toolbar and the Go menu selection. A list of the Web pages you have visited in the past 20 days is kept in a special History folder. You can access this folder through the Go menu, too.

To move backward in this recent history of visits, click the Back button. To move forward, click the Forward button.

To go to a specific Web page you have visited, click Go on the Internet Explorer menu bar. The menu that drops down, shown in Figure 17-2, displays a portion of your recent history by listing the titles of the Web pages you viewed (or the technical gibberish that told the remote computer how to generate those pages). The titles appear in a numbered list, with higher-numbered pages being the more recently visited ones. The page you are currently viewing is marked with a check mark. Click any page listed to return to that page.

To return to a page you have visited in the past 20 days, choose Go⇨Open History Folder to view a list of shortcuts to pages. To view a page, drag its shortcut to the Internet Explorer window and release the mouse button. (The History folder retains a copy of the shortcut for your future use.)

Figure 17-2:
Going back
to the future
(or the past)
with the Go
menu.

Returning to your favorite pages

Now, just where was that recipe for tripe soufflé? The Web is so vast that
you may never find it again, much to the dismay (or joy) of your dinner
guests. When you are viewing a Web page that you think you may want to
revisit, tell Internet Explorer to add it to your list of favorites.

Choose Favorites on the menu bar (or click the Favorites button on the tool
bar) and choose Add to Favorites from the drop-down menu. The Add to
Favorites dialog box appears. The first thing you need to do is make sure
that the text in the Name box (which is the title of the Web page) is descriptive enough that you will be able to recognize the page by that text. If not,
type new text. Then click OK or press the Enter key.

To return to a favorite page, click the Favorites button or choose Favorites
on the menu bar again, and the title of your favorite page appears in a list in
the drop-down menu. Click on the title to return to that page. If the list
displays a folder, you can click on that folder to see a menu of additional
favorites.

After you have a dozen or so favorites in this list, you may want to add
folders so that you can organize your favorites, or change the names of your
existing favorites. Choose Favorites⇨Organize Favorites to get into the
Organize Favorites dialog box. The instructions there are pretty good, so I'll
simply add that to use the Move, Rename, or Delete button, click the favorite
or folder you want to move, rename, or delete first, and then click the
appropriate button. Also, to move a favorite to a folder, you can drag the
favorite instead of using the Move button.

Searching the Web for Information

Don't know something? Check the Web. The Web is turning into a vast library of information. But unlike your town library (or so I hope), the librarians of the Web are robots, and the quality of information ranges from timeless and irrefutable truths to complete and utter Biscuit Sauce (BS). Only you can determine which is which.

What I call robot librarians are called *search engines* by most people. These robots all live at different addresses (URLs), and they all have different strengths and weaknesses. Although they all differ in the details, in general they let you choose a subject, and then they present you with a page of links to various pages on the subject. Each link is accompanied by a brief excerpt from the page so that you can tell if the page may be of interest to you.

These Web librarians can't really tell whether or not a page contains the information you want; they can only tell if the words you used to describe your subject appear on a given Web page. If you choose a very common word to describe your subject, such as *web,* you will get thousands of listings. Be as specific as you can, such as looking for a *recipe* containing the words *web* and *duck.*

Microsoft has combined the most popular librarians (search engines) into a single page on the Microsoft Web site. Choose Go⇨Search the Web in Internet Explorer to view the page `home.microsoft.com/access/allinone.asp`. Enter a search term, and then choose your librarian.

One of my favorite librarians is AltaVista (which means, I believe, "high view"), at `www.altavista.digital.com`. AltaVista is truly a search engine, which means that you type one or more terms for which you want the engine to search and then click the Search button on that page.

Searching successfully requires some care. Simply entering `web duck recipe` may get you a list of a million or so pages mentioning the World Wide Web, ten thousand pages mentioning recipes, and a thousand pages discussing spider webs, ducks, or duck feet. Most search engines have help pages that you need to read to be successful in your search. Click the Help button on the AltaVista page for some very readable instructions on how to make a search.

The most famous of the Web librarians is Yahoo!, which lives at `www.yahoo.com`. Yahoo! is, technically speaking, not a search engine but a Web guide. A *search engine* searches for a subject you name; a *Web guide* presents you with subjects to choose from, although it may also offer search capabilities. Yahoo! presents you with a list of broad topics and subtopics.

Click on topics or subtopics to see additional subtopics. Keep on drilling deeper into your subject in this way until, at the bottom of the page, you see individual Web pages that may be of interest to you. You can also search for terms as you do at the AltaVista site.

AltaVista and Yahoo! typify the two main types of robots, search engines and Web guides. Here are just a few of the others, in no particular order:

Lycos	www.lycos.com
Infoseek	www.infoseek.com
HOTBOT	www.hotbot.com
WebCrawler	webcrawler.com
Electric Library	www.elibrary.com
Excite	www.excite.com

Saving Items from the Web

When you view a Web page, the page is actually in your browser, so why not save it? Unlike your Works documents, you don't need to save Web documents, but if you'd like to view the text of that page later without going online, saving is an option.

To save a page, choose File⇨Save As File. The dialog box that appears works exactly like the one you use in Works, except that it saves a different type of file.

Internet Explorer normally saves files in a form that, logically enough, can be viewed in Internet Explorer (or any other Web browser); that form is called HTML. (*HTML* stands for HyperText Markup Language, but who cares?) To save the file as an HTML file, simply type a name for the file, choose a folder for it, and then click the Save button as you would a Works document. (Internet Explorer will add the three letter extension .htm to the file.)

You can also save the text of the Web document in a form you can open in a different program, such as Works; this form is called plain text. To save a document as plain text, click the Save As Type box and choose Plain Text (*.txt). (Internet Explorer will add the three letter extension .txt to the file.)

To open a file in Internet Explorer, double-click the file (which launches Internet Explorer) or drag the file to the Internet Explorer window. You can alternatively choose File⇨Open and then click the Browse button to use a familiar Open dialog box. To open a Plain Text file in Works, choose File⇨Open. Use the Open dialog box as you would for a Works document, but first click the Files Of Type box and choose Text (*.txt) from the list that appears.

Internet Explorer doesn't save the graphics (or other media, like sound) that go with a document. In place of the graphics, you will sometimes find boxes with explanatory text. You can, however, save graphics as separate files. Right-click the graphic, and choose Save Picture As from the menu that appears. As you do when you save a file in Works, type a filename (no extension), choose a file folder, and click the Save button. You can view the graphic file in Internet Explorer in the same way you open an HTML file in Internet Explorer (by choosing File⇨Open).

Printing Web Documents

You can print most Web documents just as easily as you print Works documents. In fact, the print command (File⇨Print) is the same as in Works, and the associated Print dialog box is essentially identical to the Works Print dialog box. The printed page will include graphics and, if you have a color printer, color. (Colored backgrounds will, however, not be printed. Thank goodness, or your ink cartridge would be depleted in about a minute.)

Page setup works the same for Internet Explorer as it does for Works, too, except that page size, orientation, and margins are all together on a single card in the Page Setup dialog box. I suggest you use the paper size of Letter $8^{1}/_{2}$ x 11 inches.

There are a few differences, however, between printing a Works document and printing a Web document. The following paragraph describes the differences.

Some pages on the Web use frames, which complicate the printing process. *Frames* are like separate window panes that divide up your browser window. You can usually tell if a Web page uses frames because part of the page stays still while the other part changes when you click on a link. Other indications of frames are that one portion of the window can be scrolled independently of the other parts or borders appear between the frames. Internet Explorer 3 prints only a single frame at a time. To print a frame, first click in that frame and then choose File⇨Print.

Downloading Files from the Web

A Web browser like Internet Explorer gets your foot in the door to the rest of the Internet. Web browsers let you acquire (download) additional Internet software — like mail and news programs — that many companies make available on the Web. You can also download enhancements to your Web browser, known as *plugins, viewers,* or *add-ons.* These enhancements can add special gee-whiz features such as video, enhanced audio, and virtual reality. They can also add more practical features like the ability to view documents in special formats, such as Adobe Acrobat format, that are widely used on the Web.

If you look around carefully, you can find one or more download areas on the Web sites of most PC software vendors. Follow the links and instructions, and eventually you will click on a link that causes Internet Explorer to begin downloading the software.

To avoid computer viruses, be careful to download files only from reputable sources. If you have a virus-scanning program, scan any file that you intend to double-click or otherwise open.

After you click a link that starts a download, a File Download dialog box briefly appears and then an Internet Explorer dialog box asks what you want to do with the file: Open it or Save it to disk. Choose to save the file to disk, and a Save As dialog box appears to allow you to choose where you want to save the file. (Saving to the Desktop is fine.)

The File Download box reappears, usually giving you an estimate of how long the downloading process will take. To stop the download, click the Cancel button. You can browse to other locations while a file is downloading; you can also use Works or do other Internet tasks like checking for e-mail — but your PC's response will be slower.

The software you download is typically in the form of a compressed file, which saves downloading time but adds a step to the normal Windows installation process. If you have virus scan software, use it now on the file you downloaded. Then, to begin installing the software, double-click the file you downloaded. Sometimes, double-clicking the downloaded file only uncompresses the installation files. In that case, one of the files you obtain will be named install.exe, which you need to virus scan, and then double-click to actually install the software.

Using Electronic Mail and News

In this case, no news is bad news, and the bad news is that Internet Explorer doesn't include electronic mail software or an Internet newsgroup reader.

The good news is that with Internet Explorer, you can easily download mail and newsreader programs.

The following are a few of the more popular e-mail programs that you can download from the Web:

- **Eudora:** Visit www.eudora.com and follow the links to Eudora Lite, the free evaluation version of Eudora's very popular software.

- **Pegasus:** Visit www.pegasus.usa.com to download the free e-mail program. (Pegasus makes its money by selling you the manuals.)

- **Microsoft Internet Mail and News:** This software does not work with Internet Explorer 3.02, the version that this book discusses. The software is available as part of, or as an add-on to, version 4.0 of Internet Explorer. You can download Internet Explorer 4.0 for free. Visit www.microsoft.com and follow the links to download (or try www.microsoft.com/msdownload/).

- **Netscape Navigator:** Netscape is the arch-rival of Microsoft in the war to dominate your PC desktop. Netscape's Web browser, Navigator, provides e-mail *and* newsgroup news reading in addition to Web browsing. You can download a copy of Navigator by visiting Netscape at home.netscape.com.

The preceding programs will work with any ISP. Juno, another popular e-mail program, works only with the Juno ISP.

The best way to get online with electronic mail is, of course, to pick up the latest edition of the excellent book *E-Mail For Dummies,* published by IDG Books Worldwide, Inc. This book includes a CD with e-mail and other useful programs.

No matter what e-mail or news program you ultimately use, you need information from your ISP to help you set up that program. E-mail and news programs must interact with *servers* that live on your ISP's computers, so you must tell the program the mail or news server's name in addition to other information.

Coping with Messages

As you browse, Internet Explorer regularly delivers some sort of cryptic message about servers, cookies, security, or certificates, and expects you to respond in some way. Just what is all this excitement about, and how are you supposed to know what to do?

Most of these cryptic messages have something to do with the security and privacy of your personal information, so they can make a person rather nervous. Security and privacy is a topic too big to go into here. To learn more, you can search the Web for information on Web privacy and security. You can also click Help in Internet Explorer, click the Index card, and type *security* to see a list of help files on the subject. The rest of this section deals with some of the other messages you may receive.

Can't find the address

If Internet Explorer can't find a Web page at the address you specify, it eventually gives up and displays a dialog box telling you so. Simply click OK.

If the dialog box says A connection to the server cannot be established, then you probably are using a valid address, but something has happened to the Web site or your Internet Service Provider. If repeated tries don't work any better, you may be trying to reach an invalid address, or the Web site may no longer exist.

"You are about to send information over the Internet . . ."

Whenever you fill out a form to submit on the Web, use a search engine, or do anything else that transmits information, Internet Explorer may present a Security Information dialog box that warns You are about to send information over the Internet . . ., etc., etc. The warning appears because there is a small risk of someone intercepting your information as it gets passed along to the intended address, and possibly even changing it. That event is probably no more likely than someone intercepting your mail in a roadside mailbox. The problem, of course, is that if someone *were* doing this, you may never know.

If you feel you can live with the risk of someone intercepting whatever you are transmitting, click the Yes button on the Security Information dialog box; otherwise, press the Esc key or click No. To read Microsoft's help files on security, click the About Security button.

What about doing business on the Internet? Increasingly, businesses that accept orders and credit card numbers over the Web use secure sites. *Secure* sites work with Internet Explorer to encrypt the data between your PC and their site in a very secure way. If you are browsing a secure site, Internet Explorer displays a lock icon on the status bar at the bottom of its window. When you move from a secure site to an insecure site, Internet Explorer warns you.

Wanna cookie?

I never thought I would be annoyed by cookies (other than fake chocolate chip cookies, that is), but cookies are now one of the most annoying features of the Web. All too often you get a message from Internet Explorer saying that so and so would like to give you a cookie, and would you like to accept it? You can answer Yes or No.

Well, heck, isn't that thoughtful? But what is a cookie? A *cookie* is a chunk of information that a Web site stores on your PC: usually, just an identification (ID) number the site has assigned you. The computer on that site stores information about your visit and tags it with your ID. When you return to that Web site, it will read your ID from the cookie and presumably use the information to make your next visit a more satisfying experience. The site may, for instance, configure its contents to match preferences you selected earlier.

So why wouldn't you want a cookie? Sometimes a few companies join together and use a common cookie so that they can piece together a profile of your interests from your Web site visits — the name and address you entered at site A with the products you inquired about at site B — and use or sell this information.

You have to decide if a cookie is worth the risk. Often, if you decline a cookie, you cannot view a particular page or use some of its features. Most cookies are harmless (except the fake chocolate chip ones, in my opinion).

Certificates

When you browse certain Web pages or choose certain Web links, Internet Explorer presents you with a dialog box (with an official-looking certificate printed in it) that poses a question about accepting a certificate and asks you to choose Yes or No. If you say Yes, you probably have no idea what you're agreeing to, and if you say No, you probably won't be able to do whatever you intended.

Certificates are yet another security measure and another topic too lengthy to go into here. For more information on what certificates are, check the Internet Explorer Help files on certificates or search the Web on that topic.

By choosing Yes on a certificate dialog box, you are in effect saying, "Yes, I trust that whoever issued this certificate knew what they were doing, and that I am *actually* in contact with the organization that I *think* I am in contact with, and that I can rely on their downloadable software to not be an impostor for the real thing." To always "just say Yes" to certificates, see the following section "Minimizing message madness."

If you choose No on a certificate dialog box, not only will you probably be unable to do whatever you intended to do, but you may also receive an `Internet Explorer Script Error` warning box. Just click the OK button on that dialog box if it appears. (As if you had a choice!)

Minimizing message madness

If a message dialog box contains a check box at the bottom that begins In The Future, Do Not Show . . ., you can avoid ever seeing that dialog box again by clicking that check box.

Another way to minimize the message madness is by changing the way Internet Explorer is set up. To change the setup, choose View⊅Options; then click the Advanced tab in the Options dialog box that appears. Then do any or all of the following:

✔ To eliminate the `You are about to send information over the Internet` message, click to clear the check mark labeled Warn Before Sending Information Over An Open Connection.

✔ Click to clear the check mark labeled Warn If Changing Between Secure And Unsecure Mode if that message annoys you.

✔ To always accept cookies, click to clear the check mark labeled Warn Before Accepting 'Cookies'.

✔ To minimize recurring dialog boxes about certificates, click the Security tab on the Options dialog box, and then click the Publishers button there. In the Authenticode Security Technology dialog box that appears, click to place a check mark in the check box labeled Consider All Commercial Software Publishers Trustworthy.

Disconnecting and Quitting

If you are done Web browsing — or if you are simply reading a document and not planning to click on any of its links — go offline (disconnect). You will save connect-time fees by disconnecting yourself from your ISP when you're not actively browsing the Web or downloading software.

To disconnect, find the Connected To . . . dialog box on your Windows screen or restore the dialog box from the Start bar by clicking on the button that displays the name of your ISP. Click the Disconnect button on the Connected To . . . dialog box. After you have disconnected, you can still read, save, or print the document that is in the Internet Explorer window.

To reconnect, double-click the My Computer icon on your Windows screen; in the My Computer window that appears, double-click Dial-Up Networking. In the Dial-Up Networking window that appears, double-click your ISP connection.

To quit Internet Explorer, choose File⇨Close or click the button with the X in the upper right-hand corner of the Internet Explorer window.

Chapter 18

Using Works' Communications Tool

● ●

In This Chapter

▶ Getting ready to use the communications tool

▶ Starting communications

▶ Communicating with the other computer

▶ Disconnecting and reconnecting communications

▶ Saving your communications settings as a document

▶ Exiting the communications document

▶ Reconnecting at a later time

▶ Preserving and capturing screen text for future use

▶ Sending and receiving files between computers

▶ Troubleshooting when you don't get connected

▶ Making text more readable

● ●

*T*he communications tool of Works 4.5 is the very thing you need for computer communications in the '90s. Unfortunately, the '90s are just about over, and so is the usefulness of this tool. Communications are mostly done by networking now (such as Internet communications), and this tool does not handle networking. You may, however, still find the communications tool useful in one of the following situations:

> ✔ **You want your PC to act as a *terminal* to a distant mainframe computer — that is, to act as a keyboard and screen, allowing you to interact with the mainframe computer by reading and typing text.** For instance, if your business has its own special mainframe software for entering sales orders, you may want to use your PC to interact with that software from afar.

✔ **You connect to the Internet by running text-based Internet software on a remote computer.** For example, you may have what is called a shell account on that distant computer, and you may run an electronic mail program on that distant computer to send and receive messages on the Internet.

✔ **You need to connect your PC directly to someone else's PC, not over any sort of network, but over a direct telephone connection in order to exchange files.**

If you face any of these situations, this chapter can help you set up and use Works' communications tool — but you will also need instructions from the folks who operate the distant computer. The first sections of this chapter cover the ideal situations, ones where your phone line and the other computer work in a fairly conventional way, and communications happen as nicely as you would hope. The latter sections deal with the pitfalls of real life, such as when the other computer speaks a less common digital dialect.

Before You Start

Before you can use Works' communications tool, you need to have a few basic items:

✔ **An installed modem**

Follow the installation instructions that come with every new modem.

✔ **The telephone number your PC is going to call in order to talk to the other computer**

✔ **The communications parameters of the computer your PC is going to call**

Most computers use a conventional set of communications parameters that Works also uses, so you may not need this information unless you run into problems.

✔ **Instructions on how to operate the remote computer's software from a terminal (which is what your PC will look like to that terminal)**

Your instructions must include how to log in (say hello), log out (say goodbye), and run programs on that other computer.

Starting the Communications Tool

If you aren't currently looking at Works' Task Launcher, please do so: Press Ctrl+N or choose File⇨New. Then do the following:

1. **Turn on your modem if it's an external modem (which is connected to your PC by a cable).**

   If your modem is an internal modem, it's already on.

2. **Choose the Works Tools card on the Task Launcher. Click the Communications button there.**

   This step launches you directly into a dialog box called Easy Connect, shown in Figure 18-1. If you don't see the Easy Connect dialog box, you will see a dialog box saying that There are no valid telephony devices available. By this statement, Works means that it doesn't think you have a modem. Works then asks Do you want to run the modem setup Wizard? Click the Yes button, and a Wizard can help you tell Windows all about your modem.

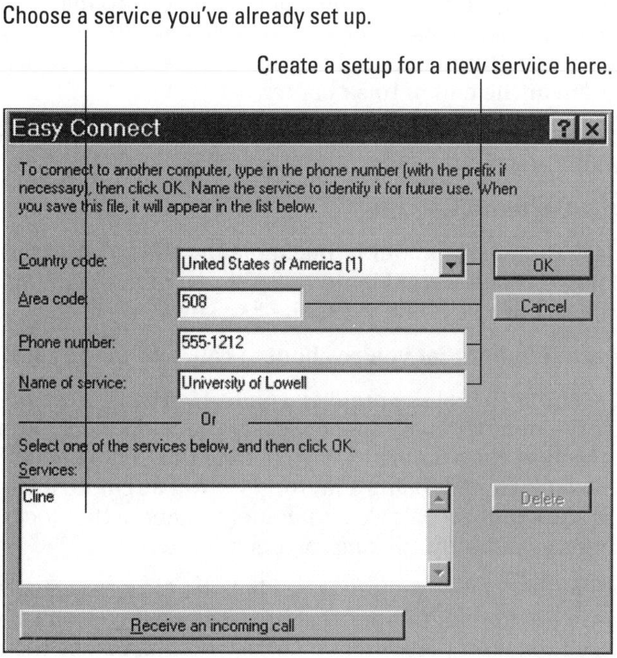

Choose a service you've already set up.

Create a setup for a new service here.

Figure 18-1:
Easy
Connect:
a hopeful
name.

If you are already using Works' communications tool, you can enter Easy Connect by choosing Phone⇨Easy Connect.

3. **If you have previously set up Works for the computer you want to call, click on that setup's name in the Services text box (in the Easy Connect dialog box) and skip to Step 6.**

If you haven't previously set up Works for the computer you want to call, move on to Step 4.

4. **Enter information on the person or online service you want to call.**

Easy Connect is a feature that tries to set up communications by requiring only two pieces of information from you: a name and a phone number for the other computer you are dialing. (Works tries to make a lucky guess on all the other stuff by using conventional communications settings. Such settings work about half the time.)

Choose the country that you want to call by clicking the Country Code box, unless Works has already guessed at the correct country. In the Area Code box, enter the area code of the number you want to call. (If the call is within your area code, leave the box blank.) You can use dashes or spaces within the phone number, if you like.

If you are calling from a location where you need to dial a credit card number or an outside-number access code (like 9), you may need to change a few settings. See "Solving special dialing problems: Modem settings" near the end of this chapter.

Enter a name in the Name Of Service text box. This name identifies the person or service.

5. **Click the OK button.**

Now, Easy Connect is about to begin dialing the number and pops up its Dial dialog box, shown in Figure 18-2. (If you're not ready to actually make the call at this point, press the Esc key.)

6. **Check the number that you're about to call, and modify it if necessary.**

Works is about to dial the number you see in the Dial dialog box. If you see that the number is missing necessary long-distance or other prefix codes (such as the number 1), try clicking the Dial As Long Distance check box. (If you are using a laptop PC from a remote location and you have set up Windows 95's Control Panel to handle that location, choose the proper location by clicking the Location box.)

To modify the number temporarily, click the Modify button and edit the number in the Phone Number text box. The change won't be saved, however. To make a permanent change, you must make the change in the Easy Connect dialog box in Step 4.

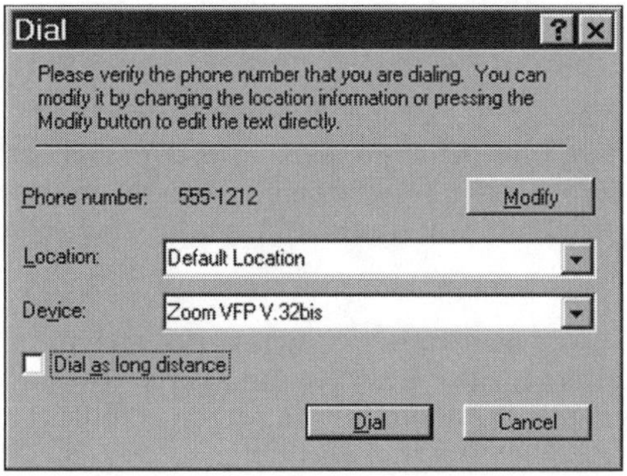

Figure 18-2:
The Dial
dialog box
tells you
that Works
is ready to
dial your
number.

7. Click the Dial button.

This action starts the call. You can hear the dial tone and the modem dialing out (assuming that your modem has a speaker; most do). A Dial Status dialog box appears, displaying the name of the party that you're calling and the number that the modem is dialing. If the number is wrong, click the Cancel button in that dialog box to cancel the call. The Dial Status dialog box also shows the seconds that remain in a 60-second countdown period, after which Works gives up and cancels the call.

If all goes well, the phone now rings at the other computer until the other computer answers or until Works gets tired of listening to the phone ring (which it does in about 60 seconds). If the line is busy or you didn't enter the dialing information properly, Works gives up in a few seconds and you will see the word Busy on your screen.

When the other computer's modem answers, some horrendous noises ensue, distressing dogs and arousing infants. If you're lucky, they soon stop (the modem noises, anyway), and the Dial Status dialog box disappears. Most likely, the word Connect will appear on your screen, followed by some number, such as 2400 or 14400. This message actually comes from your modem and means that the two modems have successfully negotiated the terms and speed (which is what the number signifies) which they will use to communicate with each other.

After your computer's modem and the other computer's modem have connected and the Dial Status dialog box has disappeared, the time has come for the computers to see whether they can speak the same language. If the computers can communicate properly, some text appears on your screen, and you are expected to type something in return. Exactly what appears and what you are expected to type depends on the other computer, as the next section discusses. If the computers don't appear to communicate properly, see "If You Don't Get Connected," later in this chapter.

Communicating

If the computers can communicate properly, you're ready to have a conversation with the other computer. What happens next depends entirely on what the other computer has been programmed to do. At this point, you need to refer to the instructions you received from the other computer's owner or operator.

Your document window acts like paper in a typewriter on which the two communicating parties take turns typing. As each party types and presses the Enter key, the screen fills up, and after the screen is full, it begins to scroll. If you need to see something that was typed earlier, click the arrow at the top of the scroll bar (at the right of the document window) to scroll back. If you can't see the scroll bar, choose Window➪Tile to fit that window (and all open documents) into your Works screen.

Disconnecting and Reconnecting

The proper way to disconnect from another computer depends on that computer, so you must obtain instructions from the computer's owner on how to disconnect. Usually, you need to give a command such as Exit, Quit, or Logout before you hang up; in fact, you may have to exit or quit from several different programs before disconnecting. Some computers, however, don't mind too much if you just hang up on them.

After performing whatever good-bye ritual you have been instructed to do to disconnect from (hang up on) the other computer, you have several alternatives:

✔ Choose Phone➪Hang Up.

✔ Click the Dial/Hangup button on the button bar. (This Dial/Hangup button is supposed to look like two connectors joining. I think that it looks like two snakes facing each other, one with teeth. To make sure that you're on the right button, position your mouse cursor over the button without clicking, and a yellow tag gives the button's name.)

✔ Close the communications document by choosing File➪Close.

Any of these options causes Works to display a query box asking whether it's okay to disconnect. Click the OK button in that box.

Actually, if you have an external modem, you have a final option: Switch off the modem. Works may be a little confused afterward, however, and still think that you're connected. Check the Dial/Hang Up button on the toolbar; if the connectors are connected, click the button to tell Works that you're disconnected.

Do not disconnect by just turning off your computer. Besides the fact that turning off your computer without exiting Works and Windows will leave your computer in a confused state, your modem may remain connected for quite awhile, running up your phone bill!

To reconnect with another computer or a service after hanging up — or if the first attempt to connect failed — try one of the following methods:

- ✔ Choose Phone➪Dial Again.
- ✔ Click the Dial/Hangup button in the toolbar.

If you are reconnecting after being disconnected or intentionally hanging up, the other computer probably will have noticed your absence. If so, you will have to log in again.

Saving Your Settings as a Document

If you plan to call this same computer again later, save the phone number and any other settings that you have made as a document file. Saving a communications document works the same as saving any other Works document. See Chapter 2 to review those details, but here's a quick refresher: Press Ctrl+S or choose File➪Save. The Save As dialog box appears. Type a filename and press the Enter key. When you next see the file (for instance, on the Existing Documents tab of the Task Launcher), the filename will have an extension of .WCM appended to it and a cute but illegible icon of a telephone next to it. Both of these additions identify the document as a Works communications document.

A reasonable person may assume that because Microsoft refers to the file you save as a document, saving would save all the text displayed on your screen — text that resulted from your communications session. After all, that text is in the document window. Well, a reasonable person would be wrong. All that gets saved are the settings that you provided to tell Works how to connect to the other computer. To save the text on your screen, see the section "Preserving what's in your document window" later in this chapter.

Closing the Communications Document

When you're done communicating, you can close the communications document (shut the tool down) or leave the communications tool running and just switch to another Works tool. If you close the document, Works insists on hanging up on any communication currently in progress.

To close the communications document:

1. **Choose File⇨Close.**

   (As Works does in other tools, if you haven't saved your communications settings as a document yet, Works will prompt you to do so.)

2. **If you are still connected to the other computer, Works puts up a query box asking whether it should disconnect; click the OK button in this box.**

   The document is now closed.

Reconnecting after Closing

After you have created and saved a communications document for a remote computer, you can always dial that computer again (or dial a different computer) by doing one of two things:

✔ Open the communications document for that computer. You open a communications document as you would any other Works document (from the Existing Document tab of the Task Launcher, for instance, or by choosing File⇨Open). Works then skips the Easy Connect dialog box and takes you directly to the Dial dialog box.

✔ Start the communications tool as described in the earlier section "Starting the Communications Tool." As Step 3 in that section describes, click the name of the computer that you want to dial in the Easy Connect dialog box that appears.

If you are still in the communications tool (that is, you have a communications document open), you can dial a different computer (open a second communications document) by using Easy Connect. Launch Easy Connect by choosing Phone⇨Easy Connect. See "Starting the Communications Tool" to review the steps for using Easy Connect.

Preserving and Capturing Screen Text

Hungry for a little more substance than the fleeting messages drifting across your screen? Set your snare and capture or preserve some wild text. Reading things on your screen is great, but sometimes keeping them in a file is nice, too. If you're getting e-mail, for example, you can keep your correspondence in files. Or, if you're getting stock market reports, you may want to analyze the data at a later time.

Preserving what's in your document window

The simplest way to save text as a file is to save whatever has so far appeared in your communications window. To do this task at any time:

1. **Choose File⇨Save As.**

2. **Click the Save As Type list box and choose Session Data from the list that drops down.**

3. **Give the file a name and specify a folder (as you usually would in Save As); then click the Save button.**

This action saves as a text file everything that passed by on your screen during your communications session.

Capturing text

If you would rather save just a portion of what is being transmitted to you, you can *capture* the text. Capturing is like turning on a tape recorder for awhile, so you must turn on the capture feature just before the text you want to save is transmitted. Here's how to capture text:

1. **Click the Capture Text button on the toolbar (the camera icon).**

   Or you can choose Tools⇨Capture Text. Same thing.

2. **Give the capture file a name and folder.**

   The Capture Text dialog box arrives on the scene, looking for all the world like the familiar, old Save As dialog box. The Capture Text dialog box works the same way as the Save As dialog box does.

3. **Roll 'em.**

   Do whatever you need to do to have text transmitted to you (perhaps give a command to the remote computer — it all depends on the other computer).

4. **Click the Capture Text button again.**

   Or choose Tools⇨End Capture Text.

That's it. You've captured the elusive communications transmission as a text file. Now you can open that file and read it, edit it, or dress it up.

Cooking with captured files

You've captured some text, so now what do you do with it? To open the file, choose File⇨Open. In the Open dialog box that appears, specify that text file by selecting its directory in the Look In list box, and then type its file name (with the .TXT extension) in the File Name box. If you can't remember the filename, type ***.TXT** instead, press Enter, and then double-click the name when it appears in the File Name list box.

The Open File As dialog box appears on the scene and wants to know what kind of document it should make from this text file: word processor, spreadsheet, or database. The choice is yours, but unless the text is in table form, I suggest that you click Word Processor. Phwzap! In a few seconds, you've got your file in the word processor. Now you can edit or dress up the file.

Sending and Receiving Files

One use for Works' communications tool that is still valid even in these days of networking is to send or receive files directly between your PC and some other computer. You can connect to your company's mainframe computer to send or receive files, or you can directly dial up someone else who has a PC with Works or a similar communications tool (like the Windows' accessory program, HyperTerminal).

If your PC is going to be the computer that is called by someone else (and it doesn't matter which computer calls which), you need to tell Works to answer the phone when it rings. Choose Settings⇨Phone to access the Phone page of the Settings dialog box; then click the Auto Answer Selection there. While you're using the Settings dialog box, click the Terminal card of that box, and then click the Local Echo checkbox. Click the OK button when you're done. Local echo is necessary so that you can see the characters you type. The other person may also need to enable local echo in his or her software. (When you type back and forth to each other, if you see two characters for every one you type, choose Settings⇨Terminal and clear the Local Echo check mark.)

When you call up another computer to exchange files, begin by making sure you can have a dialogue. See if you can receive text on your screen from the other computer, and make sure the other computer is receiving what you type. You can either chat with the other person, if the other computer is attended, or else issue commands to the other computer and see if you receive a response.

When you are ready to transmit or receive a file, decide first whether you truly want to send an entire file or just send the text contained in a file. "Huh?" you say (and not without reason). Works offers two ways you can send or receive files: the Send Binary File command and the Send Text command.

Send or receive a file: The Send Binary File command or button

To send or receive a file using this method, do the following:

1. **Find out what file transmission protocol the other computer uses.**

   Don't let the technobabble panic you. A *file transmission protocol* is just a name describing how a file is sent; you don't have to understand the protocol, just find out its name. The other computer may have several file transmission protocols available to use. The protocol you choose must be a protocol that Works can use, too. Zmodem is usually the best protocol to use with Works; if Zmodem is not available, try Ymodem, Xmodem/CRC, and Kermit, in order of preference.

2. **Choose Settings➪Transfer.**

   The Settings dialog box appears, displaying the Transfer card as shown in Figure 18-3. Click the chosen protocol in the list box marked Transfer Protocol.

Figure 18-3:
Observing
protocol
with the
Transfer
settings.

If you are going to be receiving files, you need to tell Works where to put them. Click the Directory button in the lower-right corner of the Transfer card in the Settings dialog box. Choose a directory in the aptly named Choose A Directory dialog box that appears. The Choose A Directory dialog box works like a simple version of the Save dialog box. Click the OK button when done.

3. **Click the OK button in the Settings dialog box.**

4. **Command the other computer to send you a file or prepare to receive a file yourself.**

   How you command the other computer depends on the other computer. You may have to type several commands, one of which involves telling the other computer what protocol to use. (Sometimes a computer mentions being able to send or receive only binary files. Don't worry. If you have a text file, send it along in the same way as I describe here.)

   If you are directly connected to a user who is sitting at a PC screen as you are, that person must give the command for his or her own computer to send or receive a file, using the same protocol that you are using.

5. **To send, click the Send Binary File button in the toolbar (a file folder with an arrow pointing out of it). To receive, click the Receive Binary File button (same thing, but the arrow points in).**

   A Send File or Receive File dialog box appears, describing your progress in terms of, among other things, percent complete. When the percent complete reaches 100 percent, you're done, and the dialog box goes away. If the transmission process appears to get stuck for a long time (like minutes) at some percentage, click Cancel and then try to send the file again.

Sometimes Works decides to send a Pause signal to the other computer when Works finishes transmitting. If everything appears to come to a halt during or immediately after a transmission, see if the hourglass-icon button on the toolbar is depressed. If the button is depressed, click the button (or take it out to lunch and sing to it to cheer it up).

Send content: The Send Text command or button

Works' Send Text command (or toolbar button) is good for sending text that you would otherwise type on the screen, but the text just happens to be in a file. The Send Text command sends the contents of a text file without sending the file itself. (The other computer just figures that you're a speedy typist; it has no idea that you're sending contents from a file.)

For example, if you use an electronic mail program that runs on a remote computer, you can compose a text file first on your PC. Then you can connect to the other computer, tell it that you are about to type text for a message, and send the contents of your text file instead of typing. This approach to electronic mail gives you the opportunity to reread and edit text before you actually send it.

Sending content works only with *text* files — files that typically have an extension of .TXT on their filename. Sending content does not work with Works' word-processing, spreadsheet, or database files. Here are the steps to sending content:

1. **Connect to the other computer, as described earlier in this chapter.**

2. **Give that computer whatever command it may need to prepare to receive text.**

   For example, the command may be to start creating the body of an electronic mail message. Whatever you transmit afterward would then be the message text.

3. **Click the Send Text button in the toolbar (to the right of the camera icon in the normal toolbar setup) or choose Tools⇨Send Text.**

4. **Carry on as if you had just typed a bunch of text to the other computer. (Tell the other computer to send the e-mail, or whatever, and log out.)**

It's possible that the other computer may think that you are too speedy a typist and get confused. If this situation happens, choose Settings⇨Transfer, find the box marked Line Delay, and enter the number **1** into that box. If the other computer still gets confused, increase this number until the other computer is no longer confused.

If You Don't Get Connected

Failing to connect can happen for lots of reasons. The other line may simply be busy, in which case you may want to wait a bit and try again. Or, something may be wrong with the way Works is set up.

Solving pickup problems: Phone settings

If you have trouble getting the remote computer to pick up the phone, the first place to turn is Phone Settings:

1. **Choose Settings⇨Phone.**

   The Phone card of the Settings dialog box appears.

   - **To have Works redial the phone when it encounters a busy line:** Click Redial. Works makes as many attempts as are dictated in the Redial Attempts box. Between attempts, Works waits the number of seconds shown in the Redial Delay box. To change the number of seconds in either of these boxes, double-click the box and type in a new number.

   - **If you are trying to receive a call from another computer:** Click Auto Answer. The modem picks up after one ring. Alternatively, choose Phone⇨Easy Connect⇨Receive An Incoming Call.

2. **Click the OK button when you're done.**

Solving Bad Connection Problems: Communications Settings

The communications wilderness has lots of biodiversity. Each different computer that you connect to has its own preferred communications settings or parameters. Sometimes, the other computer adjusts to your settings. But if the other computer doesn't adjust to your settings, you will usually see a lot of gibberish (random characters) on your screen, and sometimes you will see nothing at all after the word Connect appears.

Usually, though, you have to adjust to the other computer's settings. Works stores your communications settings as part of the communications document, along with the phone number and name of the other computer.

A lot of computers use two popular settings: *8,n,1* or *7,e,1*. You don't need to know what they mean, but you can switch between these settings at any time without using the Settings dialog box. Just click the toolbar button marked *8,n,1* or *7,e,1*. The three terms in these labels refer to the Data bits, Parity, and Stop bits settings, respectively: 8 means 8 data bits, e means even parity, and 1 means 1 stop bit. Using these buttons affects only these particular settings.

If you discover that the computer you want to call uses other settings, here's how to adjust your settings:

1. Choose Settings⇨Communication.

This action puts you on the Communication page of the Settings dialog box.

2. Click the Properties button.

This step puts you in a Properties dialog box for your modem, as shown in Figure 18-4.

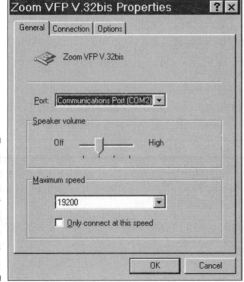

Figure 18-4:
Setting
modem
speaker
volume and
speed in the
Properties
dialog box.

Here's how to modify the individual communications settings. (Click the OK button in the Properties dialog box when you're done.)

 ✓ **Changing the speed of transmission:** Click the General tab of the Properties dialog box. (See the preceding steps to get to the Properties dialog box.) You may want to lower the speed if you have trouble staying connected to the other computer or if intermittent gibberish appears on your screen. The speed is generally set by Works to a number that is higher than or equal to the maximum speed that your modem can deliver. Many of the other computers you call adjust their speed to match yours, but not all of them do that. Find out what maximum speed the other computer can accept. Then, to set your speed to match, click the Maximum Speed box and choose the correct number in the drop-down list.

✔ **Changing data bits:** Click the Connection tab of the Properties dialog box. Different computers use either 7 or 8 data bits. Click the Data Bits text box and choose a number to match the other computer's setting.

For text communication (typing and being typed back at) and transmission of text files (also called ASCII files), 7 data bits is usually fine. For computers that you want to use to transmit or receive binary files (pictures and programs), you may have to change this setting to 8 bits.

✔ **Changing Parity:** Click the Connection tab of the Properties dialog box. Click the Parity text box and choose a parity. The parity you use doesn't make a whole lot of difference, as long as you and the other computer match. Don't worry about what parity means.

✔ **Changing Stop bits:** Click the Stop Bits text box and choose a number to match the other computer's number. Don't worry about what Stop bits are.

Here are a couple of other valuable settings tucked away with the modem Properties dialog box:

✔ **If your modem gives up too soon when making a call:** Click the Connection tab and change the value in the line that reads `Cancel the call if not connected within __ seconds`.

✔ **If you tend to forget that you are connected, running up phone bills:** Click the Connection tab. On the Connection card, click the check box marked `Disconnect a call if idle more than __ minutes`; then set the idle time to a convenient value.

✔ **If you find the modem noise objectionable:** Click the General tab and drag the Speaker volume pointer to the left to minimize the volume.

Making Text More Readable: Terminal Settings

If the text that the other computer sends you is more or less readable but doesn't seem to be printing properly on your screen or has a small quantity of gibberish in it, you need to fool with the terminal settings.

To change the terminal settings, choose Settings➪Terminal. This action puts you on the Terminal page of the Settings dialog box.

PCs in disguise — terminal emulation

When your PC is connected to another computer, your PC is not really acting much like a computer; it's acting more like a type-writer or a teletype. You type stuff, and stuff appears on the screen. In geek-speak, your computer is acting like a terminal. Before PCs existed, large, hulking computers lurked in a back room somewhere. These huge computers had wires running off to terminals (keyboards with screens) in peoples' offices. Under Works, your PC can pretend to be *(emu-late)* certain terminals. If you emulate the wrong terminal, you see gibberish called *escape sequences* every so often on your screen. To make them go away, you must emulate the correct terminal.

Here's how to change the individual settings on the Terminal page. Click the OK button when you're done:

- ✔ **To change terminal emulation:** Find out from the person operating the other computer what terminal you are supposed to be emulating and click that terminal's name in the list box marked Terminal.

- ✔ **If lines don't wrap properly:** Choose a new selection in the End Of Lines area. Click either Add CR or Add LF and see how things work out. Use Add CR if lines appear in a staircase pattern. Use Add LF if lines overwrite each other. Changing the End Of Line setting is sometimes necessary when communicating with Macintosh computers or online services that expect you to be using a Macintosh.

- ✔ **If lines are too long:** Some computers use a very wide screen and type too many characters to appear on your screen in a single line. To make these lines wrap at the end of the screen, click Wrap Around.

- ✔ **If you're communicating with a foreign country:** Special symbols of that country's language may not come out right. Click the country name in the list marked ISO Translation.

- ✔ **If you can't see what you're typing:** Click Local Echo.

The general idea behind the terminal settings is that the other computer is sending special characters called *escape sequences* that are not supposed to be displayed, but are intended to control how the text appears on your screen. If your terminal settings don't match those of the other computer, these special characters are not interpreted properly. The result is that the text appears weird and the special characters are displayed on your screen.

Part VI

Creating Great Works of Art: Graphics

The 5th Wave   By Rich Tennant

"NO, THAT'S NOT A PIE CHART, IT'S JUST A CORN CHIP THAT GOT SCANNED INTO THE DOCUMENT."

In this part . . .

*I*f you can't even draw a straight line, you've come to the right place. Works is good at drawing straight lines; curved lines, too. In fact, Works can give you great works of art — or great works of "chart" — with little more than a few sweeps of your mouse. In this part, you discover Works tools for graphics of all kinds.

Works can turn your spreadsheet data into a bar chart, pie chart, or even a "radar" chart, with only a few hints from you about how you want the chart to look. Need some basic diagrams? Works drawing features let you draw perfect, clean rectangles, circles, and other "blobs" without ever needing an eraser. The WordArt tool lets you create eye-catching headlines with swirling text in funky shapes, patterns, and colors. Works provides a gallery of pictures to liven up your documents, or you can insert your own scanned-in photos for that holiday letter to your friends and relations. Whether you are creating great works of Art, or great works of Tom, Dick, or Sally, Works has something for you.

"Art for art's sake."

— Arthur Anonymous

Chapter 19

Creating a Work of Chart

· ·

In This Chapter

▶ Strolling the gallery of charts

▶ Getting from spreadsheet to chart

▶ Preparing your spreadsheet for charting

▶ Understanding series and categories

▶ Creating any chart

▶ Using the chart window, menu, and toolbar

▶ Changing to a different type of chart

▶ Saving your work of chart

▶ Printing charts

▶ Including charts in documents

▶ Leaving the chart window

· ·

*B*e done with the tyranny of words and numbers. Stroll Works' gallery of charts and find one that expresses the pent-up yearnings of your soul. (Assuming a soul with comparatively modest yearnings, of course. 3-D area charts always do the job for me.)

For a multitool package with plenty of other things on its mind, Works offers a rather nice selection of chart types and variations and makes the job of charting a breeze. Or is it a snap? Whatever. A snapping breeze, perhaps. Very easy, in any event. In this chapter, explore the mysterious link between spreadsheets and charts, learn how to exploit this connection to your advantage, and turn mere rows and columns into graphical eye candy to delight the soul and satisfy the intellect.

A Gallery of Chart Types and Variations

Works offers a veritable optical smorgasbord of charts. Works displays the array of possibilities, as shown in Figure 19-1, when you create a chart in Works. Here are the basic types:

- **Bar:** In a bar chart, each number in a row or column results in a bar. The value of that number determines the height of the bar. For multiple rows or columns of data, bars are differently colored and can be side by side or stacked to show the sum.

- **Pie:** In a pie chart, each number in a row or column determines the size of a slice of a pie. By using Works *variations,* you can display your pie charts whole, with one slice partially removed (a common pie condition in our house), or exploded into its separate slices (which is what happens if you microwave the pie).

- **Line:** Each number you chart in a row or column determines the height of a point along a line. Line charts can appear with dots (the data points), dots alone, or high/low/close (for stock values).

- **Stacked Line:** Stacked line charts are for multiple sets (*series*) of data that you want to display summed together in a way that reveals what portion of the total comes from each set of data. For instance, a stacked line chart could show how sales from your Eastern, Western, Northern, and Southern sales divisions contribute to your total sales. The divisional sales "stack" on top of each other to show the total. In the chart, the bottom line is for data in the first column (or row), the second line is for the sum of data in the first and second column (or row), and so forth.

- **Area:** An area chart is like a stacked line chart, but filled-in with color underneath the lines.

- **Scatter:** A scatter plot puts lotsa dots on an X/Y plot. For instance, if your data is in columns, the first column is for X (horizontal) values, and the second for Y (vertical) values. Therefore, each row in this pair of columns specifies a dot's location in X and Y. Scatter plots are used for showing correlation between two types of measured phenomena, like degree of baldness and IQ in men (strongly correlated; the dots form a nice, straight line).

- **Radar:** Radar plots show data in a connect-the-dots picture of Radar O'Reilly from the TV series *M*A*S*H.* No, just kidding (but it's not a bad idea, is it?). A radar chart is kind of like a line chart going around in a circle: Instead of the line's height varying, its distance from the center varies. Radar plots are useful for showing variations in cyclical events — for example, popularity over several months of different flavors of ice cream by phase of the moon. Which, come to think of it, might sort of resemble Radar O'Reilly. . .

- **Combination:** Lets you mix lines and bars in a single chart.

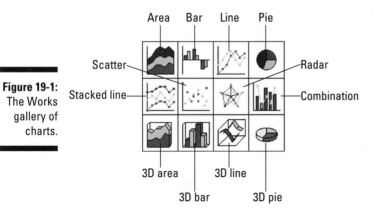

Figure 19-1:
The Works gallery of charts.

I'm not going to get into all of these chart types here. After you learn the basics, you can pick up the others pretty easily.

You can get the basic types of charts in several variations and with various features:

- ✔ **3-D bar, line, and pie charts:** No, you don't have to wear special glasses to see 3-D charts. Works doesn't really mean 3-D; it means that the chart appears to have thickness and shading so that it looks as if it's made of chunks of plastic. Very trendy.

- ✔ **Titles:** You can have two lines in a title that identifies the chart.

- ✔ **Labels:** You can put numbers on the data points (data labels) along bars or lines, or add text that identifies what data is represented by your bars or lines. You can also label *categories* (names for each data value, such as the stuff along the horizontal axis that identifies each bar in a bar chart).

- ✔ **Legends:** A legend is a box that identifies what sets of data the various colors or shades represent. Sales figures, for instance, might be shown in blue, and costs in green.

- ✔ **Axes:** You can have two Y axes if you plot two different kinds of data, such as temperature and weight, on the same chart. You may also use logarithmic scales for things that increase rapidly, such as credit card interest over time.

You can also size the charts to any size you need; put a border around them; and change the fonts, the colors, the shading, the gridlines, and even the shapes of the data points. There. Is that enough? I don't discuss all of these variations here, but you should be aware of what's possible.

Don't worry that everything on-screen is shown in color. If you have a black-and-white printer, the chart comes out with shading to substitute for the various colors. To see how things will look on your printer, use the command <u>V</u>iew⇨Display As <u>P</u>rinted in the menu bar.

From Spreadsheet to Chart:
The General Procedure

Charts and spreadsheets go together like itch and scratch (or Ben and Jerry, or Pinky and The Brain, or whatever your favorite combination is). In fact, the only way you can chart something in Works is by first creating a spreadsheet.

Here's the general procedure for making a chart:

1. **Make a spreadsheet, planning and laying it out carefully for the best charting results.**

2. **Select (highlight) a portion of that spreadsheet, making sure to include row and column headings.**

3. **Choose <u>T</u>ools⇨Create <u>N</u>ew Chart from the menu bar.**

4. **A New Chart dialog box lets you select a bar, line, pie, or other type of chart based on the data and headings in your spreadsheet. It even shows you a sample to help you choose.**

5. **A chart window opens up, displaying your basic chart in color.**

   You are now in the Works charting tool. The menu bar and toolbar now contain charting commands, not spreadsheet commands.

6. **Embellish the chart with titles, labels, and other chartish features.**

7. **Print the chart or put it into another document by copying and pasting it.**

   (You could also *link* it, although I don't recommend this for beginners — see "Using Charts in Documents" later in this chapter.)

Laying Out Your Spreadsheet for Charting

Like an artist preparing a canvas, you should lay out your spreadsheet to simplify your chartwork. Works is pretty good at dealing with various kinds of spreadsheet layouts, but a little care can make your life easier and give you better results.

Here is a checklist for preparing your spreadsheet:

- Put headings on rows and columns.

- Don't use blank rows or columns to separate data from headings.

- Keep sets of numbers together if you want to chart them together. For instance, to chart a column of costs and a column of revenues by month in the same chart, make those columns adjacent to each other. If practical, put your column or row of data adjacent to the column or row headings.

- If you want to plot a row or column of data that is not adjacent to the heading row or column, select the row or column of data and drag to put the data next to the headings.

- Format your data the way you want it to appear on the chart. For currency, for example, use currency formatting.

What the Heck Are Series and Categories?

It sounds like a TV quiz show: As you will discover, Works keeps yammering about series and categories. (As in, "I'll take the charting category for ten points, Pat!") What the heck are these, anyway?

A *series* is the group of numbers you are plotting — a single row or column of data. For instance, in a line chart, a series corresponds to a single line. A series always appears in a single color. A chart can have several series, each series with its own color. In a bar chart, a series would be a set of bars in a single color.

A *category* is a name for each of the numbers in the series. (January, February, and March would each be a category in a series of 12 monthly sales figures, for instance.) If your series are in columns, your categories are the rows. If the series is a column of numbers, for instance, the categories are typically taken from the row headings that run down the column to the left of the data. You include these categories in your chart by including the column headings in your initial selection of cells.

A series label is a description of what the numbers represent, such as Sales or Rainfall. If your series is contained in a column, you may already have a suitable series label in the top cell of the column. If you include that top cell in your initial selection of cells, the label appears automatically in the legend. The legend identifies what series a particular color represents.

How to Create Any Chart

To create a new chart, start with a spreadsheet — preferably one laid out with row and column headings, but any spreadsheet can be charted.

1. Select a range with the data you want to chart.

If you can select a range of cells that includes both row and column headings, so much the better. See Figure 19-2. If blank rows or columns are between your data and its headings (or rows or columns of data you don't want to chart), select only the data you want to plot. You can add the headings later.

Figure 19-2: Include both headings and data in your selection, if possible.

	A	B	C	D	E	F
1	Seedling density	6/89	6/90	6/91	6/92	6/93
2	Red oak	453	437	470	497	452
3	Hickory	27	32	36	43	52
4	Birch	240	260	277	297	319
5	White pine	181	164	149	135	128
6	Hemlock	140	145	148	151	145
7	Sassafras	32	30	27	24	22
8	Sycamore	88	75	67	63	58
9	White birch	23	21	20	17	16
10	White oak	54	49	42	40	37
11						

seedlings.wks — Zoom 100%

For a pie chart, select just the one column (or row) containing the numbers to be charted. If the adjoining column immediately to the left or the row immediately above the data has headings, include that column or row. If the headings aren't adjacent to your data, don't worry.

2. Click Tools in the menu bar and then click Create New Chart in the menu that drops down. Or click the New Chart button (which looks like a tiny bar chart) on the toolbar.

The Create New Chart dialog box shown in Figure 19-3 swings into action. It shows you a sample of a bar chart based on the data you selected. It also tries to figure out if you have included line and column headings; if so, it uses them as labels in the chart.

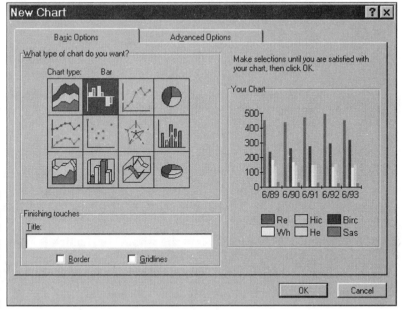

Figure 19-3:
The New
Chart dialog
box initially
suggests a
bar chart.

3. Choose a chart type from the graphical picture gallery.

The sample area on the right shows you what your chart will look like. Works always starts out by showing you a bar chart. To review your other choices, see the first section of this chapter, "A Gallery of Chart Types and Variations." If you're not quite sure what type of chart is being depicted, read the text description that appears in the Chart type line, atop the gallery.

4. If the chart in the sample area looks like the wrong things are being plotted, use Advanced Options.

It's possible that Works has misinterpreted your spreadsheet data and is reading your data series across instead of down, or vice versa. If your chart is displaying the wrong data along the X axis, click the Advanced Options tab on the New Chart dialog box:

a. If necessary, change item 1, Which Way Do Your Series Go?

Remember that a series is a column or row of data that you want to chart in a single color. If your data is in columns, choose Down. Frankly, though, I often find thinking about this too confusing. If the chart looks wrong, I just choose the alternative: either Across or Down. If you want to think about it, though, see the sidebar "How does Works decide what to do?"

b. If necessary, change the settings for First Column Contains and First Row Contains.

If you have numbers in the first row or column and you actually intend them to be category labels for your data, not the data to be charted, click Legend text.

If you have dates or times in the first row or column and you actually intend them to be data and not labels, click A value (Y) series.

c. All better now? Click the Basic Options tab.

5. Enter a title for the chart.

Click the text box marked Title, and type in something descriptive, like **Sales by Quarter**. The sample chart in the dialog box reflects your choice.

6. If you want a border around the whole chart, click Border; if you want gridlines, click Gridlines.

The sample chart shows you what you'll get. You can improve on these features later, too (more gridlines, for example).

7. Click the OK button.

A chart window appears with your lovely work of numeric art in spunky primary colors. To see how it will really look on your (probably black-and-white) printer, choose View➪Display As Printed in the menu bar. (Repeat to go back to color viewing.) Then run out and buy a color printer!

How does Works decide what to do?

Works guesses how you want your data to be organized by looking at the rows and columns in the area you selected in the spreadsheet. If you have more rows than columns selected (the most common situation), Works decides that your data series run down the columns. Accordingly, on the Advanced Options page of the New Chart dialog box, Works displays Down for the direction of the data series. If your data series actually run the other way, click Across.

Works also tries to figure out whether or not you have included labels. Works looks at both the first row and the first column that you selected. If they contain numbers, Works charts them. If they contain text (or dates or times), Works uses the text as legend or category labels.

The Chart Window, Menu, and Toolbar

When you finish creating a new chart, things look a bit like Figure 19-4. (The chart window usually covers up the spreadsheet window a bit more than Figure 19-4 shows.) The chart window has the same name as the spreadsheet, but with Chart 1 appended.

Figure 19-4: The chart window and its brother, the spreadsheet.

Notice that the menu bar has changed a little, and the toolbar has changed a lot. That's because as long as the chart window is active, you're in the chart tool. If you switch to the spreadsheet (by, say, clicking its title bar), you're in the spreadsheet tool. And if you click your heels together three times, you're in Kansas, where the bars don't have menus and you leave your tools in the truck.

You can always switch between windows by clicking Window in the menu bar, and then clicking the window of your choice in the drop-down list. With charts and spreadsheets, you can also switch from one to the other by pressing F3. You can choose from several charts, so a dialog box comes forth with the list of charts available. Double-click the one you want.

If the chart looks rather squished and crowded and the words are chopped off, don't panic. It's just how Works deals with a too-small chart window. Click and drag a side or corner of the chart window to make it bigger.

The chart menu

The chart menu looks and works like menus everywhere, but some parts of it are actually pretty different:

✔ **The File selection** on the menu bar is very much the same everywhere in Works. See Chapter 2. When you save from the chart menu, you save the whole spreadsheet file because charts are part of their associated spreadsheet.

✔ **The Edit selection** gives you not only the usual cut-and-paste stuff described in Chapter 3, but also everything you need for changing what range in the spreadsheet is being charted, or editing the text in the chart.

✔ **The View command** lets you switch between the spreadsheet and any of the charts that are attached to it. (Yes, you can have several different charts attached to a spreadsheet.) The chart windows don't have to be open; this command opens them.

✔ **Choosing Format⇨Chart Type** lets you change the type and variation of the chart. See "Changing Chart Types and Variations," later in this chapter. The toolbar buttons are another place to do the same thing.

✔ **The Format menu** also gives you commands that control appearances: fonts, patterns, colors, axes, borders, legends, and 3-D-osity. (Try formatting your text in Wingdings font for that trendy, Museum-of-Fine-Arts Egyptian hieroglyphic look!)

✔ **Clicking Tools** gives you commands to create, name, and delete charts attached to the spreadsheet.

✔ **Window and Help** are selections that work the same everywhere. See Chapter 2 for more information on Windows and Help.

I cover the most important menu choices in more detail in the remainder of this chapter.

The chart toolbar

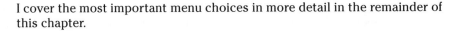

The toolbar, as always, is just another way to give commands to Works (instead of the traditional semaphore flags). About half the buttons (the ones on the left side) are identical to the buttons on the spreadsheet toolbar, covering options such as font, size, saving, printing, and copying.

You can always find out the purpose of a button by placing your mouse cursor over it (don't click). A tiny tag appears with actual English words on it.

The buttons on the right half of the toolbar are, for the most part, WYSIWYG (What You See Is What You Get). That is, they have pictures of charts on 'em. (Really! Just get out your magnifying glass.) Click 'em, and your chart can look something like the icon, only bigger and prettier. See "Changing Chart Types and Variations," the next section of this chapter.

The second-to-last button (with the white arrow and the number 1) is a secret passage to the spreadsheet — specifically, to the first data series in the spreadsheet. If you have a big spreadsheet and are charting just a portion of it, this is a quick way to get to the right place.

Changing Chart Types and Variations

You can change the chart's *type* or *variation* on that type either by choosing Format⇨Chart Type or by clicking a toolbar button. Either way, you get a lovely graphical display of various ways to display your data. For example, if you click the button that looks like downtown Chicago (the 3-D Bar Chart button), you get the dialog box shown in Figure 19-5. (To review the available chart types and variations, see the section " A Gallery of Chart Types and Variations" at the beginning of this chapter.)

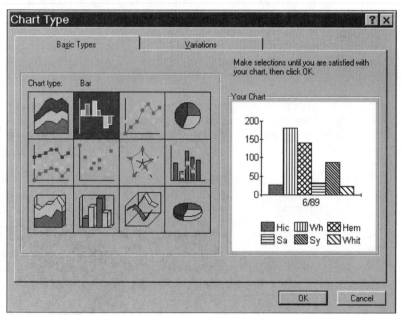

Figure 19-5: A graphical selection of basic chart types; for variations on that type, click the Variations tab.

The top card in the Chart Type dialog box shows you the basic types of charts available, such as bar, line, or 3-D bar. (If you clicked a toolbar button to get here, your chosen type is already selected.) Choose a different type by clicking one of the pictures.

Click the Variations tab, the second card in this dialog box, for different versions of the basic type. Click the chart variation of your choice in this dialog box and then click OK. Some look a lot alike; to see the differences, watch the example chart closely as you switch between the variations.

If you change your chart type or variation, do so before you apply finishing touches, such as data labels (discussed in the next chapter). Changing the chart type or variation may remove these niceties if they aren't used in the new type of chart. If you change back to the old type, your finishing touches will be gone.

Saving (Or Not Saving) Your Work of Chart

Lest your work of chart suffers the depredations of time and crumbles, like the fabled facades of Venice, into the sea, you should take pains to preserve it. In other words, save that sucker.

To save your chart, you save the entire spreadsheet. Do this in the ordinary way: choose File⇨Save. If the spreadsheet is a new document, the Save As dialog box appears, and you give the file a name and a directory to live in.

If your chart is utterly wrong and you don't want to bother trying to rehabilitate it (see instructions in Chapter 21), just get rid of it. If you don't, it hangs around in your spreadsheet file, always getting underfoot when you try to use other charts.

To delete a chart, choose Tools⇨Delete Chart in the menu bar. A modest Delete Chart dialog box comes forth. Click the chart's name. (If the chart's window is still on-screen, you can compare the name in the dialog box against the title bar in the chart's window to ensure that you pick the right one.) Then click the Delete button.

You must click the OK button in the Delete Chart dialog box for the deletion to take effect. Even though the name disappears when you click the Delete key, it's not gone until you click OK.

Printing a Chart

A great piece of industrial art like your chart deserves to be proudly displayed on canvas. Because your printer probably doesn't do canvas very well, you'll have to settle for printing your chart on paper (and proudly displaying it on the refrigerator door, perhaps).

If your chart is going to become part of a document, you'll print that document. See "Using Charts in Documents," the next section of this chapter.

If your chart, like the cheese in the nursery rhyme, is to stand alone, use the same printing commands that you use in any other tool: the Page Setup and Print commands in the File menu.

Here are a few tips for printing charts, mostly having to do with the Page Setup dialog box:

✔ Preview the printout (choose File➪Print Preview). You may be a bit surprised at what your chart is going to look like. It will probably be taller than you had in mind and will have patterns instead of colors if you have a black-and-white printer. Click the image in Print Preview to enlarge your preview on your screen.

✔ Many, if not most, charts fit better if printed sideways (in *landscape* mode). Call up the Page Setup dialog box (File➪Page Setup); click the Source, Size and Orientation tab; and choose Landscape to change to sideways printing. Click the OK button.

✔ To proportion the chart just as it is in the chart window, call up the Page Setup dialog box (File➪Page Setup), click the Other Options tab, and choose Screen size. Click the OK button. The graphics keep the same proportion; the text is whatever point size you have selected.

✔ Other options are (not surprisingly) also on the Other Options page of the Page Setup dialog box. The Full Page, Keep Proportions option keeps the same proportions as the chart window, but fills the page either to the side margins or to the top and bottom margins. Full page expands height and width to the margins and doesn't worry about proportions.

✔ To set the dimensions more precisely by using the Page Setup dialog box, choose either of the two Full page options on the Other Options page and then set the page margins on the Margins tab.

Using Charts in Documents

No doubt about it. Charts liven up a document. But putting charts in a document can be a little mysterious at times. You have two basic ways to put a chart in a document:

- Paste a copy.
- Insert it *(link* it).

The pasting method is straightforward and can be easily done in either a word-processor document or a database document. You just paste a copy of the chart — a snapshot of the chart at the time you copied it. If the data changes, the chart is not updated by Works; you have to paste a new copy. The process, in a nutshell, is to press Ctrl+C while in the chart window and then switch to another document window and press Ctrl+V. To resize the chart, drag the handles around the image.

For more detailed instructions on how to copy and paste a chart into a word-processor document, see Chapter 8. To copy and paste a chart in a database document, use the same instructions. Copying and pasting a chart won't work in a communications document or another spreadsheet, although it will often work in programs outside Works.

The inserting (or linking) method is nice, but a bit fragile and tricky, and in Works this method is limited to word-processor documents. Its advantage is that if the data in the spreadsheet changes, the chart in the word-processor document changes. Its main disadvantage is that if you move or rename the spreadsheet document or rename the chart, the link between the two documents can be broken. Also, controlling the size of the chart in the final document can sometimes be a frustrating experience.

If you decide it's worth the trouble, the inserting procedure goes like this:

1. **Both documents (the spreadsheet with the chart and the word-processor document) must be open. Set up the chart window so that it looks exactly the way you want it to appear. Save your spreadsheet (press Ctrl+S).**

2. **Switch to the word-processor document window and choose Insert⇨Chart.**

3. **In the Insert Chart dialog box that appears, your spreadsheet will be listed in the Select A Spreadsheet box. Click it, and then click the name of your chart (for example, Chart1) in the Select A Chart box. Click the OK button.**

Leaving and Reentering the Chart Window

To leave the chart window, simply close the window: Click the X symbol at the right end of the chart window's title bar (not the worksheet title bar or the Works title bar). This action puts you back in the spreadsheet window. Your chart remains part of the spreadsheet.

To return to the chart window from the spreadsheet, choose View⊅Chart. Double-click the chart's name in the dialog box that appears.

If you close by using the Close command in the File menu, you close the entire spreadsheet. If you exit by using the Exit command in the File menu, you are actually shutting down Works. With either of these actions, Works may ask whether you want to save changes to your spreadsheet — probably a reference to the charts you just added. If you click No, those charts will be lost.

Chapter 20

Polishing Your Work of Chart

• •

In This Chapter

▶ Adding horizontal and vertical lines

▶ Formatting X and Y axes

▶ Using fonts and styles

▶ Formatting numbers

▶ Making chart and axis titles

▶ Changing the legend text

▶ Changing X- and Y-axis labels

▶ Adding data labels

▶ Adding new data series and labels quickly

▶ Using multiple charts with your spreadsheet

• •

*W*hen Leonardo da Vinci painted *The Last Supper,* did he finish one apostle and move on to the next? Or did he go back, add a little wrinkle here, a little twinkle in the eye there, fixing and refining and polishing until the apostles' mothers themselves would not have recognized their kids? Well, we'll never know, and neither will the apostles' mothers, but I thought I should ask. Not out of idle curiosity, either, but to illustrate the point that, like da Vinci, you will want to fool around with your charts until their own mothers wouldn't recognize them (if they had mothers).

So, "Leonardo," here are your tools. In this chapter are most of the things that you are likely to want to fool around with in a chart: adding lines and labels, adjusting fonts and style, adding more data, and even using multiple charts. Go forth and finish your masterpiece.

Adding Lines and Formatting Axes

All those spiffy types and styles of charts, like 3-D area charts, are artistic as all heck, but without lines on them, the charts may occasionally leave your viewers wondering exactly what values they're looking at: "Is that bar 10, 12, or 15 units high?" If you're an economist or corporate PR honcho, you may actually like this vagueness — no, no, I mean moderation of precision — in your presentation. But folks with jobs requiring somewhat more precision will probably want gridlines, more precision on the intervals along the axes, and other axis-related refinements.

The simplest way to get horizontal or vertical lines across your chart is to choose a style that gives the lines to you. That is, when you choose a chart type by choosing Format⇨Chart Type (or by using the buttons on the toolbar that depict various chart types), among the several styles that are presented to you are a couple with vertical and/or horizontal lines: Choose one of these styles. You may have to reenter data labels or other fine points of your chart, however. Choosing a style is best done before getting fancy with labels and lines.

Otherwise, you can get lines and other axis options by formatting the axes. Figure 20-1 shows some options for a 3-D bar chart. Lines that run across the chart horizontally (at intervals along the vertical, or Y, axis) are perhaps most in demand. To get these, see "Formatting the Y axis," coming up next. For lines that run up the chart vertically (at intervals along the horizontal, or X, axis) see "Formatting the X axis" later in this chapter.

Figure 20-1:
Horizontal
lines at
intervals of
25 along the
Y axis
improve this
chart.

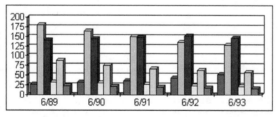

Do you have trouble remembering which axis is Y and which is X? (You're in good company.) Try this trick: Imagine yourself plaintively beseeching the universe, "Why? WHY?!" (Or in this instance, "y? Y?!") Which way do you naturally turn your face? Up, of course. The Y axis goes up. (And if you find yourself spreading your arms to the side as you do this, you can consider your arms to be on the X axis.)

Formatting the Y axis

The Y axis is the axis that goes up towards the heavens. An axis with such lofty ambitions deserves a bit of dressing up. To extend horizontal lines out from the Y axis, or otherwise fool around with the Y axis, choose Format⇨Vertical (Y) Axis. The Format Vertical Axis dialog box appears, looking like the example in Figure 20-2.

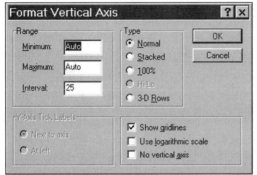

Figure 20-2:
The place
to go for
a more
refined axis.

Here is a rundown of what you can accomplish in the Format Vertical Axis dialog box:

- ✔ For gridlines at each interval along the axis, click Show Gridlines.

- ✔ For more or fewer intervals along the axis, click Interval and type a new value. For example, for a numbered tick-mark along the axis every $50 (or 50 ducks, or 50 inches of rain, or whatever), enter **50**.

- ✔ To start or end the axis at a different value, edit the values in the Minimum or Maximum text boxes, respectively. This option is good when you have a couple of extreme values you're embarrassed about and don't care to present.

- ✔ If you have values over a very wide range (like over several powers of 10; say, from 1 to 1,000), click Use Logarithmic Scale (not available in area charts).

- ✔ To eliminate the vertical axis altogether (economists and PR folks, take note), click No Vertical Axis. Hey, if you let folks see actual numbers, you'll just get a lot of picky debate.

- ✔ You can fool around with what I call the chart's variation by clicking one of the (non-grayed out) entries in the Type area. Sometimes you find variations here that aren't available when you use the Format⇨ Chart Type command or the toolbar buttons (such as line charts expressed as percent fractions).

Formatting the X axis

The X axis is the one that goes across the bottom of the chart. To extend vertical lines up from the X axis or otherwise fool around with the X axis, choose Format⇨Horizontal (X) Axis. The Horizontal Axis dialog box does a jolly buck-and-wing onto your screen. (No, just kidding about the dance part, but it would be fun if it did. I get tired of these dialog boxes just "appearing.")

In scatter charts (also called *X-Y* or *X-Y scatter* charts), the X axis behaves very much as the Y axis does. Accordingly, for scatter charts, the Horizontal Axis dialog box works like the Vertical Axis dialog box, described in the preceding section, "Formatting the Y axis," and does not work as described in this section.

Here are some of the things you can accomplish in the Horizontal Axis dialog box:

- ✔ Click Show Gridlines to, well, show gridlines — the vertical line thingies at every interval.

- ✔ In an area-type chart, where gridlines disappear behind the curve, you can also click Show Droplines: These lines are superimposed on the area curve.

- ✔ To eliminate the horizontal axis altogether, click No Horizontal Axis.

- ✔ To trim out some of the category labels along a crowded X axis, type a larger value in the text box marked Label Frequency. A 3, for example, shows every third label.

Changing Chart Text and Numbers

It's enough to give a sensitive artist fits. We go to all the trouble of making pictures of data, and then we have to put text and numbers all over it to make any sense out of it! Works lets you put text — including titles, series labels, and data labels (the very numbers that you are charting) — in several places in your chart.

Fonts and styles

As far as fonts go, one size fits all in charts. All text and numbers are in exactly the same type (Arial 10-point bold, for example). You can change fonts in the charting tool in any of the following ways, just as you do in any other tool:

- ✔ Click the down-arrow button next to the font or size box in the toolbar and then click a new selection in the drop-down menu.

- ✔ Press Ctrl+B for bold, Ctrl+I for italic, or Ctrl+U for underline.

- ✔ Choose Format⇨Font And Style in the drop-down menu. Select font, size, and style in the Font dialog box.

You can also change fonts by double-clicking any text in the chart. The Font And Style dialog box appears.

If your problem is that the text doesn't seem to fit, it's probably because you're looking at the chart in a rather small window. Works compresses the graphics to fit the window but leaves the type whatever size you make it. Check your chart with Print Preview before you assume that the type is too large.

Number formats

If your numbers need dollar signs, a different number of decimal places, or any of the other formatting that you're familiar with from spreadsheets, this is not your chart's problem! No, it's your spreadsheet's problem.

Return to your spreadsheet window and change the number formatting of your data. See Chapter 11 for more on this.

Chart and axis titles

Titles are important. I once had a cartooning teacher who said that if you can't draw a rabbit, make sure the title says rabbit somewhere. So, if you create an incomprehensible chart, at least give it a good title.

Remember the following points about titles:

- *Chart titles* are the one or two lines at the top of the chart.
- *Axis titles* go along an axis and tell you what the axis represents: months, furlongs, doughnuts, and so on.

To create chart or axis titles, choose Edit➪Titles. The Titles dialog box moves regally into view. Just click the appropriate text box and type.

- You can enter two lines of title for the chart: Chart title and Subtitle.
- To type an identifier to be printed alongside the X or Y axis, click Horizontal (X) Axis or Vertical (Y) Axis.
- Right Vertical Axis is for a second Y axis if you have one.

Click the OK button when you're done.

If your titles don't look very good in the chart window, remember this: They won't really look like that when they are printed. To see how the chart really looks, use Print Preview (choose File➪Print Preview).

Writing your own legends

Now you can make your work legendary by writing your own legend text (called *series labels*). *Legends* are those boxes that identify the contents of a graph by color or pattern. *Series labels* are the text that appears in the legend next to the color or pattern sample. Series labels identify the color or pattern with a particular data series in your chart. Works supplies these series labels for you initially, but you can change them to any text you like.

Where does Works get the text for the series labels it initially creates for you? If you include row and column headings when you select the cells for your chart, Works automatically takes its series labels from those headings. If you don't include the headings (or cannot because of the spreadsheet layout), you get boring automatic labels, such as *Series 1*.

To change the series labels, perform the following steps:

1. **Choose Edit⇨Legend/Series.**

   Works displays the Edit Legend/Series dialog box, shown in Figure 20-3.

   Continue with the remaining steps after the Edit Legend/Series Labels dialog box that appears.

2. **If you have boring labels of the "Series 1, 2, 3 . . ." variety, click the check box labeled Auto Series Labels to remove the check mark that is there.**

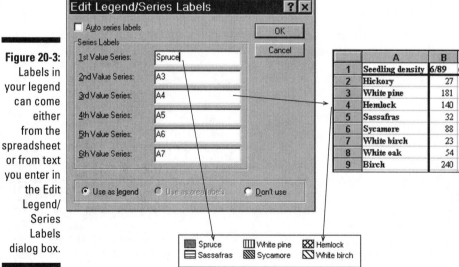

Figure 20-3:
Labels in your legend can come either from the spreadsheet or from text you enter in the Edit Legend/ Series Labels dialog box.

3. **To type in the labels, just click the appropriate box and type, as I do with the label "Spruce" in Figure 20-3.**

The dialog box displays one text box for each series (each color or pattern), labeled 1st Value Series, 2nd Value Series, and so on.

4. **To obtain label text from a cell in the spreadsheet, click the appropriate text box and type the label's cell address.**

In Figure 20-3, I use cell addresses for all Value Series text boxes except the first one. The 3rd Value Series, for instance, refers to cell A4, which contains the text *Hemlock. Hemlock* then appears as the series label in the legend.

Remembering cell addresses is sometimes difficult. To make the job easier, you may want to arrange your windows so that you can see both the chart and the place in the spreadsheet where the labels are. (One way to do this is to choose Window⇨Tile to see all your current windows at once.) Or else just make a note of the cell addresses.

The bottom of the Edit Legend/Series Labels dialog box offers certain mutually exclusive options. The option Use As Legend, already selected, means "display a legend box;" if you don't want to display a legend box, click Don't Use. If your chart is of the Area type, you can choose Use As Area Labels, which places your labels in the body of the chart rather than in a separate legend box.

Click the OK button in the dialog box when you're done.

Data labels

Data labels display actual data values (such as the number 181) in the chart. (The values may be along the line, atop the bars, or alongside the pie slices, depending on what kind of chart you've chosen.) Take a look at Figure 20-4, which has data labels in it.

Data labels for all

To simply print the numbers corresponding to all the points on the chart for every data series, do this:

1. **Choose Edit⇨Data Labels.**

The Data Labels dialog box puts in an appearance.

2. **Click the Use Series Data check box.**

3. **Click the OK button.**

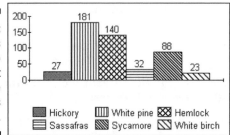

Data labels are great but can be confusing if you have several data series on the chart at once. In Figure 20-4, there's only one data series, so it's pretty easy to read. The trouble with the procedure I just gave you is that it puts numbers on every point of the chart, and if you have many points or several data series, the numbers may overlap or crowd each other. If that problem arises, see the following section "Data labels for the select few."

Text may look crowded in the Works chart window, but it may be okay when printed. Use Print Preview (choose File➪Print Preview) to see how your chart will look when it's printed. If your text does look crowded, another alternative is to use a smaller font.

Data labels for the select few

To put data labels on a particular data series (one line of a line chart, or one set of bars in a bar chart, for example), I suggest you use the following copy-and-paste approach:

1. **Choose Window➪Tile so that you can see both spreadsheet and chart.**

2. **In the spreadsheet window, select (highlight) the range of cells to be used as data labels; then press Ctrl+C to copy the range of cells to the Windows Clipboard.**

   (You will usually want to choose the same range that is used for the series, but it can be a completely different range, as long as it contains the same number of cells.)

3. **Click anywhere on the chart window, and then choose Edit➪ Data Labels.**

   The Data Labels dialog box appears.

4. **If a check mark is present in the Use Series Data check box, clear the check mark by clicking the check box.**

5. **Click in the box for the series you want to label (Series 1 or Series 2, and so on), and click the Paste button to paste the range address.**

   Do not press Ctrl+V, the usual way to paste.

6. **Click the OK button.**

7. **Repeat Steps 2 through 6 for each series that you want to label.**

   Leave a series box blank if you want no data labels on that series.

You can type range addresses, such as B2:B7, into the Series boxes of the Data Labels dialog box instead of copying and pasting from the spreadsheet, but I usually find copying and pasting less error-prone. If you don't mind typing, you can just perform Steps 3 through 6.

Data labels using custom text or numbers

If you want to mark a series with something other than the actual data values — text, perhaps — first create a column of those labels in an out-of-the-way portion of your spreadsheet, say H1:H10. Then follow the steps listed in the previous section, "Data labels for the select few." In Step 2 of that section, select the column of custom labels (H1:H10, in this example).

Adding New Data Series and Labels the Fast Way

If you miss using scissors and paste to create charts, Works has a treat for you. (No, you can't eat the paste.) You can paste new data series, data labels, or category labels from any range in your spreadsheet into your chart. Pasting is the fastest way to add another series of data, add data from some remote part of your spreadsheet, or specify a new range containing a new set of labels.

Category labels are those labels that appear at intervals along the horizontal axis of your chart. Data labels are labels that appear on top of each point in your chart.

Follow these steps to paste a series or label into your chart:

1. **In your spreadsheet, highlight a range of cells — data, labels, or whatever, in a row or column — and press Ctrl+C (the more-or-less universal Copy command).**

2. **Switch to the chart window (choose View⇨Chart and select the chart you want); then press Ctrl+V.**

   (You can also choose Edit⇨Paste Series from the menu bar, but Ctrl+V is the conventional Paste command, so I prefer it. Fewer things to remember.)

3. **In the Paste Series dialog box that appears, click the series that you want to paste data or labels for.**

   If you are pasting new category labels, click Category.

4. **Specify data or labels.**

   If you are pasting data for a series, click Data. (Use this for category labels, too, oddly enough.)

   If you are pasting data labels for a series, click Labels.

5. **Click OK.**

Using Multiple Charts

Creative artist that you are, you're probably not going to be content with a single chart of your spreadsheet. No, you'll want two charts — maybe a line chart to compare annual sales by region and then a bar chart to show total sales by product.

Works lets you create many new charts and keeps them as part of the spreadsheet file. Your good buddies for handling multiple charts are the Tools menu and the View menu. Click Tools and then choose one of the following selections in the drop-down menu:

- **Create New Chart:** This does the customary routine with the New Chart dialog box, described in Chapter 19.

- **Rename Chart:** To keep your charts straight and to buttress their self-esteem, give your charts names. Choosing this command invokes the Rename Chart dialog box. Click the chart you want to rename in the Select A Chart list. Click the Type A Name Below text box at the bottom of the dialog box and then type a name for the current chart. Click the Rename button. The chart name now appears in the chart title bar. Click the OK button.

- **Delete Chart:** This command gives you the Delete Chart dialog box (surprise). Click the chart you want to delete in the list of charts and then click the Delete button. Click the OK button.

- **Duplicate Chart:** This command is handy to create a slightly different version of an existing chart. In the Duplicate Chart dialog box that appears, click the chart to duplicate and then click the Name text box. Type a new name, click the Duplicate button, and then click OK.

To switch between charts, just choose View⇨Chart from the menu bar. A humble View Chart dialog box appears, displaying a list of charts by name. Double-click a name to open that chart window.

Chapter 21

Producing Works of Art

● ●

In This Chapter

▶ Adding images, photographs, or other objects

▶ Drawing with Microsoft Draw

▶ Making and modifying shapes and text

▶ Exiting and restarting Draw

▶ Using ClipArt

▶ Using WordArt

▶ Adjusting graphics in your document

● ●

As my friend Art says, "Expose yourself to Art." Or, in this case, expose your art to your readers. Scary thought? Don't fret. Works' art tools can help you make quick work of artsy stuff, whether the artwork is functional, decorative, or just to show off.

Inserting Images, Photographs, and Other Objects

To insert images, photographs, or other forms of art, Works uses a general-purpose Windows technique known as *embedding objects*. By *objects* Works means any file created by any Windows program. The benefit of using this approach is that you can embed nearly any file. The drawback is that the process can be rather confusing when you perform it. What's confusing is that when you go to embed an object, like a photograph file, Works will probably launch whatever program is used to create that object. (See Chapter 22 to use an alternative method called "Drag and Drop.")

For this discussion, I assume you already have whatever file it is that you want to embed. For instance, if you want to embed a photograph, I assume that you've already used some graphics program and a scanner to create an image file. Now use the following procedure:

1. **Click in your document wherever you want the object to appear.**

2. **Choose Insert⇨Object.**

   The Insert Object dialog box appears.

3. **Click Create From File.**

   The dialog box changes its appearance a bit.

4. **Click the Browse button, and using the Browse dialog box that appears, choose the file that you want to embed just as you choose files when opening a file in Works or any other Windows program.**

   Image files typically end in BMP, GIF, or JPG, so look for those. I suggest, however, that no matter what the file ends in, you don't choose any file that has an icon sporting a tiny Windows flag (like the one on the Start button). This icon means that Windows has no idea what program created the file, and you won't be able to embed it without first *associating* the file type with a program.

5. **If you want any subsequent changes to the image to appear in your document, click the Link checkbox.**

   If you do click the Link checkbox, you must thereafter keep the file in exactly the same folder where you found it, and not change its name.

6. **Click the OK button.**

   Now things get weird. Works will most likely launch a program on your PC. The program Works launches is the one that it thinks created your file. In Windows geek-speak, the program is "associated" with that file type. For some file types, Works will not launch anything, but will simply embed the file into your Works document.

7. **If Works has launched a different program, exit from that program.**

   The standard way to exit any Windows program is to click the X in the upper right-hand corner, or choose File⇨Exit.

Works displays your object in the document, and you can now mess around with the object. To edit the object contents, double-click the object, and Works will again launch the associated program. After you make changes, exit the program. To move, resize, or otherwise fool around with the object as a whole, see the final section in this chapter, "Messing Around with Art in the Document."

Using Draw to Do Basic Blob Art

Few things strike more dread into the heart of the average adult than being asked to draw something. Otherwise brave souls who daily undertake such daunting ventures as business trips, advanced courses in physics, or even (shudder) a field trip with their child's class shiver in their berets at the thought of drawing.

Fortunately, the most artistic endeavor most of us are ever called upon to do is what I call "blob art." *Blob art* is the art of putting together a bunch of simple shapes with lines and text. Microsoft's Draw tool is great for blob art, which is why Microsoft stuffs Draw into various programs that it makes.

Starting up Draw (Inserting a drawing)

The drawing tool is not one of the Big Four tools; it's a sort of helper tool. You can start up Draw only while you're in a word-processing or database document, and the drawing you make can be stored only as part of that document. Works doesn't give you any way to start up Draw by itself or to save drawings as separate files.

To start up Draw (that is, to create and insert a drawing into your word-processing or database document), do the following:

1. Click at the point in the document where you want the drawing.

   In the database tool, you must be in Form Design view.

2. Choose Insert⇨Drawing.

The Microsoft Draw tool springs into action. This Draw tool springs so enthusiastically that, unlike any other tool, it even escapes the boundaries of the regular Works window and has a window of its own. The Draw tool window looks sort of like the window in Figure 21-1 (except that it's initially blank in the middle where Figure 21-1 has some blob art and says, "This is your canvas area!")

Peering through the Draw window

Just as a tidy artist may arrange a workbench, Works arranges your drawing tools and materials neatly around the edge of the drawing area, as shown in Figure 21-1. Here's what you have to work with in creating your work of art:

- ✔ **Drawing tools:** Draw gives you a set of drawing tools along the left edge of the window. Except for the top two (the arrow and the magnifying glass), these tools help you create a shape or type text in your drawing.
- ✔ **Colors:** Along the bottom of the window are two palettes that let you choose colors as you draw. The color marked with a check mark is the "current" color — the one Works will use when you next make a shape.

The Line palette specifies the color of a line or outline. The Fill palette determines what color fills the shape (if you're using a filled or solid shape). Just click a color to make it "current" for the next objects you create.

✔ **Menu bar:** The main job of the Draw menu bar is to let you change or improve the way the tools and palettes work. For example, you may want to use a different line width, change the text font, or get help aligning your shapes. The menu also lets you copy and arrange shapes easily. The Edit and Help selections, for the most part, work pretty much as they do in other Works tools. The other menu selections are unique to Draw, and this chapter discusses the most important ones as it goes along.

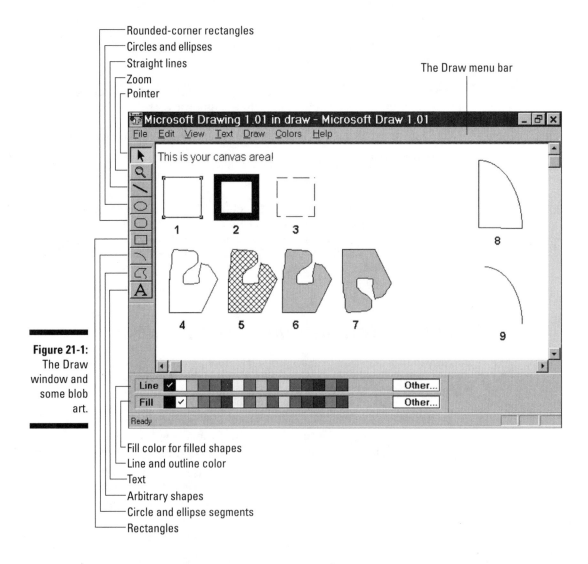

Rounded-corner rectangles
Circles and ellipses
Straight lines
Zoom
Pointer

The Draw menu bar

This is your canvas area!

Figure 21-1:
The Draw window and some blob art.

Fill color for filled shapes
Line and outline color
Text
Arbitrary shapes
Circle and ellipse segments
Rectangles

Making shapes and text

The shapes and text you create in Draw are separate, movable objects, like cutouts lying on a piece of paper. Unless you tell Draw to do otherwise, these objects have fills, or solid centers. Having a solid center means that if you draw over an existing object, you cover it up. After you have created objects, you can delete them, copy them, move them to the foreground or background, shift them around, stretch or shrink them, change their color or line style, fill them or not fill them, rotate them, and flip them end-to-end or side-to-side.

To use a tool, click the tool and then move your mouse cursor into the canvas area. After you do that, using the tool is generally a matter of clicking at various points in the drawing, or clicking and dragging. Pressing the Shift key while you click (which this book refers to as Shift+click) allows you to get certain specialized objects, such as circles and squares, from the more general ellipse and rectangle tools.

- ✔ **Line:** Click where you want one endpoint and drag to where you want the other endpoint. Shift+click forces a line to be horizontal, vertical, or at a 45-degree angle.

- ✔ **Ellipse or circle:** Click and then drag in any direction to create an ellipse. Dragging diagonally makes the shape more circular. To force it to be a circle, use Shift+click.

- ✔ **Rectangle or rounded-corner rectangle:** Click where you want one corner and drag to the opposite corner. For a square or rounded-corner square, use Shift+click.

- ✔ **Ellipse or circle segment:** This tool draws quarter-ellipse segments. (That is, it goes a quarter of the way around an ellipse; see shape 8 in Figure 21-1.) If the Fill is on, the quarter-ellipse gets connected to its center to make a sort of pie-wedge shape. Click where you want the top or bottom of the curve and drag up or down or to the right or left. Drag in a diagonal direction for a more circular shape, or force a quarter circle by starting with Shift+click. Practice a few times to see what's going on. To make a curved line rather than a pie segment, turn off the fill: Choose Draw⇨Filled. For a different curve or segment shape, see "Modifying objects" later in this chapter.

To draw a curved line between two locations, turn off the fill, click at one location, and drag to the other location (see shape 9 in Figure 21-1). The curve always bends up if the second endpoint is higher and down if it is lower, so if the curve bends the wrong way, press the Delete key and then try again starting at the other end of the curve.

✔ **Arbitrary shapes:** The arbitrary shape tool combines straight line segments with arbitrary pencil-like drawings. First, click at a starting point. Then, for a straight line segment, click somewhere else; continue clicking around and you'll get a bunch of line segments. To draw a segment as you would with a pencil, just click and drag. To end the line and make a closed shape, click on the original starting point. (See shape number 4 in Figure 21-1.) To end the line without closing the shape, double-click when you make the last point.

✔ **Text:** To specify a font and style to work in throughout the drawing, click Text and then click the font style (such as Bold) or text alignment (such as Left) in the drop-down menu. A check mark or black diamond indicates the current text settings. To use the text tool, just click anywhere in your drawing and type. Press Enter when you're done.

✔ **Zooming in or out:** Click View in the menu bar and then click any of the percentage selections in the drop-down menu. Smaller percentages make the drawing smaller. You can also use the magnifying glass tool in the toolbar. Click that tool and then click any part of the drawing you want to see close up. Hold down the Shift key while clicking to reverse the action.

Drawing shapes starting from their centers

When you draw an object (line, ellipse, rounded rectangle, and so on), you generally click where you want one side of the object, and drag to the opposite side. Often, however, you want to draw a circle or rectangle around another existing object, and centering your shape on that object is hard to do when you draw from side to side. You want your first click to represent the center of the circle or rectangle, not the edge.

That's what Draw uses the Ctrl key for. In most of the drawing tools, Ctrl+click means that your click is intended to be the center of the object, and as you drag, the object will expand in all directions around that center. (The Ctrl key has no effect on the arbitrary shape, text, or zoom tools.)

There's a simple way to remember what the Ctrl and Shift keys do in combination with a click. Remember your Cs and Ss: Ctrl means Centered; Shift means Specialized. Or press them both at once to get a centered, specialized object.

Modifying objects

To select an object (shape or text) for modification, click first on the selection tool, which is the arrow at the top of the toolbar. Then click on the object. A frame of four square dots appears around the object to tell you that it is selected, as in shape number 1 of Figure 21-1.

To select a whole bunch of objects so that you can modify them all at once, click first on the selection tool (the arrow) and then click and drag diagonally across the shapes to be selected. A dashed rectangle appears (temporarily) as you do so, indicating that whatever objects you've corralled entirely within the rectangle will be selected. If you want to select a bunch of objects scattered all over the drawing, hold down both Ctrl and Shift, and click on each of them individually.

Here are some things you can do to an object (or bunch of objects) that you have selected. (You have to select the objects before you can do any of these.)

- **Move:** Click anywhere within the object and drag. To move straight horizontally or vertically, hold down the Shift key and drag. (Don't forget: You can select a bunch of objects and move them all together.)

- **Copy:** Press Ctrl+C and then Ctrl+V. A copy appears somewhere nearby; click and drag it to the place you want it.

- **Stretch or shrink:** (For shapes, not text.) Click any of the four squares around the shape and drag. Shift+drag makes the stretch either straight horizontal, vertical, or 45 degrees. To avoid distorting the shape's proportions, drag at a 45-degree angle while holding down the Shift key.

- **Line thickness and style:** Click Draw on the menu bar and then move the mouse cursor down to Line Style in the menu that drops down. A list appears; click any line style, such as dashed, or click any line width (shown in points or $1/72$ of an inch). Shape 2 in Figure 21-1 has a thicker line; shape 3 has a dashed line.

- **Color:** To change the line or outline color, click a color in the Line palette at the bottom of the window. To change the fill color, use the Fill palette instead. See the shapes numbered 6 and 7 in Figure 21-1, which have a fill color other than white.

- **Text:** To change font, size, style, or alignment, click Text and then click commands in the drop-down menu. The common keyboard shortcuts, such as Ctrl+B for bold, also work for text in Draw.

- **Fill:** To switch between filled and unfilled, click Draw in the menu bar and then click Filled in the drop-down menu. Unfilled shapes are transparent, showing objects underneath them. An unfilled circle or ellipse segment turns into an arc, as with shape 9 of Figure 21-1.

- **Fill pattern:** To use a fill pattern instead of, or in addition to, a color, click Draw in the menu bar and then move the mouse cursor down to Pattern in the drop-down menu. Click a pattern in the box that appears. (The Line and Fill colors must be different for the pattern to show up.) See shape number 5 in Figure 21-1.

- **Outlining:** To remove an outline from a filled shape, click Draw in the menu bar and then click Framed. (To restore the outline, repeat the command.)

✔ **On-top/underneath:** Objects cover up each other in Draw; to change an object's position in the pile, click Edit in the menu bar and then click either Bring To Front or Send To Back.

✔ **Rotate or flip:** Click Draw in the menu bar and then click Rotate/Flip in the drop-down menu. Click Rotate Left or Rotate Right to turn the object 90 degrees. Click Flip Horizontal for a mirror image or Flip Vertical for upside down. In Figure 21-1, see shape number 7, which is a copy of number 6 flipped vertically.

If you realize immediately that you've made a mistake (maybe you moved something that took you a long time to get in exactly the right place), you can undo it. Ctrl+Z works here just like it does everywhere else.

If you get a few objects positioned just perfectly relative to each other, you can freeze them in their relative positions by selecting them all and choosing Draw⊏>Group. Now Works considers the collection to be one single object, and anything that is done to one is done to all. If you decide later that you want to modify the objects individually, select the grouped object (by clicking any of its pieces) and choose Draw⊏>Ungroup.

Leaving and restarting Draw

When you exit the Draw program, you can either save your work in the document if the drawing is a keeper, or throw away whatever you have done in this drawing session. To exit Draw, choose File⊏>Exit And Return. A query box appears, asking whether Draw should update your document. Click Yes to keep your drawing, or click No to throw away everything you've done since you started Draw.

When you return to your document, the drawing appears in a box with squares around it. See the section "Messing Around with Art in the Document" at the end of this chapter for information on adjusting the drawing's size and position. You can always do further work on your drawing later. Just double-click the drawing in your word-processing or database document to restart Draw.

Clip Art

When your document needs a little pizzazz — not functional, industrial art like blob art or charts — use some clip art. Clip art is nothing more than a bunch of illustrations that you can use in your documents. Works comes with a batch of drawings; you can add more by connecting to the Internet with Microsoft's Internet Explorer.

The clip art feature that comes with Works is called the Clip Gallery, designed to let you find, choose, and organize not only the artwork prepackaged with Works, but also any images, sounds, or video files you add from Microsoft's Web site. The Clip Gallery, which you can summon by choosing Insert➪ClipArt, appears in Figure 21-2.

Clip Art often looks much better in your document than it does in the Clip Gallery, where certain types of art appear rather grainy and blotchy.

Inserting a clip into your document

Here's how to insert a clip in your word-processing or database document:

1. Click in your document where you want the art to appear.

If you're inserting a clip into a database, you must be in Form Design view.

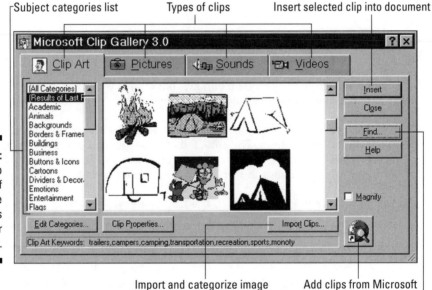

Subject categories list   Types of clips   Insert selected clip into document

Figure 21-2: The Clip Gallery of fine drawings and other artwork.

Import and categorize image   Add clips from Microsoft

Find clips by keyword, filename, or file type

2. Choose Insert➪ClipArt.

You may have to wait, staring at a cursor-turned-hourglass, while Works quietly builds its museum of masterpieces or reads the clips from the Works CD.

3. **Click a subject category in the Categories list. Or click other tabs, such as the Pictures tab, to check for clips there.**

   The Clip Art clips are divided by subject category for your artistic critique and selection. Scroll the gallery window to see more clips in any category. (Works provides nothing in the Pictures, Sounds, or Videos cards of the gallery.)

4. **Click the picture you want.**

5. **Click the Insert button.**

6. **Click the Close button.**

After the art is inserted into your document, you can size it the same way you do for your own drawings. See the final section of this chapter, "Messing Around with Art in the Document" for more information.

You can also copy clip art into Draw to add it to a drawing of your own: Click the art in your document, press Ctrl+X, fire up Draw as described in the earlier section, "Starting up Draw (Inserting a drawing)," and press Ctrl+V to paste the artwork into Draw.

Finding clips

One of the Gallery's best features is that it provides several ways to help you find the clip you need. The clip art that comes with the Gallery is associated with certain subject categories and keywords.

The several keywords that a clip is associated with are displayed at the bottom of the Gallery. The selected clip in Figure 21-2, for instance, has keywords of *trailers, campers, camping,* and more. To find a clip by its keywords, file name, and/or file type do the following:

1. **Click the Find button in the Clip Gallery.**

   The Find Clip dialog box appears.

2a. **To find a clip by keyword, type a single word or phrase in the Keywords box.**

   Enter a word or phrase that describes the subject you are looking for, like *guitar* or *musical instruments.*

2b. **To find a clip by its filename, enter some or all of the letters in its title in the File Name Containing box.**

2c. **To find a clip by its file type, click the Clip Type box and choose a type from the list that drops down.**

3. **Click the Find Now button.**

   If you don't see the clip you want, click other tabs in the Clip Gallery, such as Pictures.

When you use the Find feature again, the settings in the Find Clip dialog box will remain the same as your last search until you click the Reset button.

WordArt

Oh, those madcap Microsoft engineers! First blob art, then clip art, and now word art. What's next, punctuation art? Well, WordArt is definitely fun, and it's also great for getting someone's attention (see Figure 21-3). The Works WordArt feature lets you create special effects for text, like you see in advertisements and brochures.

Here's the basic procedure for getting swoopy, loopy text in your word-processing or database document:

1. **Click at the place you want your text art. (You must be in Form Design view in a database document.)**

2. **Choose Insert➪WordArt.**

   The menu and toolbar now say WordArt, and an Enter Your Text Here dialog box appears. `Your Text Here` appears in the dialog box and in your document, where it has a shaded frame around it. The phrase `Your Text Here` probably doesn't quite get your point across, so move on to Step 3.

3. **Type one or more lines of text in the Enter Your Text Here dialog box.**

4. **Click the list box in the toolbar where it currently says Plain Text to see a gallery of weird shapes for your text.**

5. **Click any shape in the gallery. (Shapes with multiple lines are intended for multiple lines of text in the Enter Your Text Here dialog box.)**

   When you choose a shape, your text becomes an illegible blur in the document, as Works tries to fit the artwork in a standard-height line. I tell you how to fix that, coming up.

6. **Click the down-arrow button next to where it currently says Best Fit in the toolbar and click a larger type size in the drop-down list.**

   Works may display a Size Change dialog box babbling about enlarging a frame and asking the question `Resize WordArt object?` Click Yes.

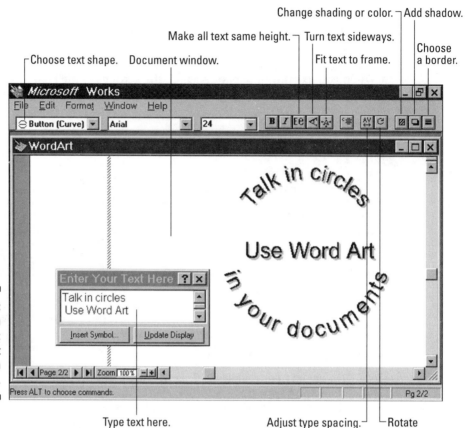

Change shading or color. ┐ Add shadow.

Make all text same height. ┐ Turn text sideways.

┌ Choose text shape. Document window.   Fit text to frame.

Choose a border.

Figure 21-3:
Playing with
WordArt:
Curved text
can turn
heads.

Type text here.   Adjust type spacing. ┘ └ Rotate and skew.

7. **Choose special effects, such as adding a shadow, by clicking buttons on the toolbar. Figure 21-3 shows you what special effect each button creates.**

The special effects are pretty cool, actually. A lot of stuff in Works is fun in a this-beats-working sort of way, but a few of the special effects are fun in a finger-painting, hey-look-at-this sort of way. I give a short description of what they do, but you can't really appreciate the fun ones until you've played with them for yourself.

Three of the buttons do the same thing they do in other Works tools. The buttons marked **B** and *I* change your text to bold or italic. And the text alignment button (which has lines on it and a C) gives you a menu with all the usual text alignment choices (centered, left, right, and so on).

Here's what the rest of the buttons do. I refer to them by their descriptions in Figure 21-3:

The *Make all text same height* button (displaying *Ee*) makes capital and lowercase letters the same height.

The *Turn text sideways* button (displaying a *sideways A*) doesn't actually turn your letters sideways as the sideways A icon suggests. Your letters will remain oriented normally but the line of text will run vertically rather than horizontally.

The *Adjust type spacing* button (displaying *AV*) allows you to adjust the amount of space between letters of your text.

The *Rotate and skew* button (displaying an arrow going in a circle) allows you to turn your text at any angle. (Unlike the *Turn text sideways* button, this button really can turn your letters sideways.)

The *Change shading or color* button (displaying diagonal lines) allows you to control what your letters are made of. (This result won't show up very well unless you make really big letters, though.) Want your letters to be made of little silver bricks with blue mortar between them? Why not?

The *Add shadow* button (displaying a box with a shadow) makes your text cast a shadow on the page. You get to choose the direction of the light source, so the shadows can be long, short, forward, backward, and so on.

The *Choose a border* button (displaying three lines of different thickness) lets you put a border around your letters. Of course, unless you've used the Shading button to fill those letters with something other than solid black, you won't see the border.

8. **Click the Enter Your Text Here box to type your text. Click the** U**pdate Display button to see the results.**

   Works tries to put the box in a convenient place on the screen, but it doesn't always succeed. If the box blocks your text, you can always click the box's title bar and drag it somewhere else. You can't resize the box, though, so if you have more than two lines of text, you can't see all of the text at once.

   If you need a symbol in the text you are entering, click the I**nsert** Symbol button. This button produces a box full of special symbols, such as accented vowels, copyright marks, and so forth. Click whatever one you'd like to insert into your text.

9. **When you're done, click in the document anywhere outside of the gray-shaded frame.**

To edit your WordArt, double-click it. Double-clicking is how you edit any graphical object in a Works document, such as clip art, drawings, or charts.

Messing Around with Art in the Document

When you return to your document from Draw, the Clip Gallery, or WordArt, the illustration you have created appears in a nominal size that Works thought was best, with no frame or text wrapping around it — nothing. What a way to treat a great work of art!

To resize, redimension, move, or make text wrap around the illustration, first click the illustration. The illustration then appears in a box with squares around it.

- **To resize the illustration,** click and drag any of the squares around the illustration.

- **To modify the illustration,** double-click the illustration, and you return to the original tool.

- **To put a frame around your illustration,** choose Format⇨Borders and Shading from the menu bar. Click a line width and, if you like, a color.

- **To change the illustration's dimensions,** choose Format⇨Picture from the menu bar (or click the illustration with your right mouse button and choose Format⇨Picture from the menu that appears). In the Format Picture dialog box that appears, enter new values for the width and height of the picture.

- **To make text wrap around the illustration in the word-processor tool,** choose Format⇨Picture as you did earlier, and click the Text Wrap tab. Then click the Absolute button.

- **To position an illustration in the database tool,** in Form Design view, just drag the illustration.

- **To position an illustration in the word-processor tool,** Choose Format⇨Picture and then click the Text Wrap tab. Click the Absolute button and then adjust the horizontal, vertical, and page number settings in the Picture Position area. Click the down-arrows next to those settings to choose standard left/right/center or top/center/ bottom positioning. Even easier: After Absolute text wrap has been chosen, click the OK button, and you can just drag the picture anywhere.

Part VII
The Part of Tens

The 5th Wave   By Rich Tennant

A word to the wise, kid— put that mouse down and learn to hotkey from app. to app. if you expect to gain any respect around here.

PRISON LIBRARY

In this part . . .

As on *Sesame Street,* this part is brought to you by the number 10: ten nifty tricks, ten things NOT to do, and other digital decalogues. If you didn't find what you wanted in the rest of this book, you might just find it here.

Tenth Night — Early play by Wm. Shakespeare.

Chapter 22
Ten Nifty Tricks

*R*emember those great ads for magic tricks in the back of comic books? Well, continuing in that tradition, here at the back of this book is a bunch of nifty, almost-magic tricks. You probably won't amaze your friends with these tricks, but you may actually begin to enjoy your PC, which is magic enough.

Drag and Drop Graphics into Documents

In this book, I usually try to use techniques that don't require going outside of Works. The following trick is so nice, however, that it's worth a little excursion into Windows.

When you want to put an image into a Works word-processing document (or a database form in Form Design view), the easiest approach is to drag the image file from another window and drop it into your document. Here's how to do it:

1. **If the Works window is filling your screen, reduce its size.**

   If you see a button with two overlapping rectangles in the upper right-hand corner of the Works window, click that button. If you don't see such a button, move your mouse over any corner of the Works window until the mouse cursor turns into a double-headed arrow; click and drag toward the center of the Works window.

2. **Open a Windows window that lists your graphics file.**

   Using a My Computer window is probably the easiest approach. Find the My Computer icon on your screen (usually in the upper left-hand corner) and double-click it. In the window that opens, double-click the disk drive where your graphics file is located. Additional windows will open; double-click file folders in those windows until you see your graphics file listed.

3. **Drag the graphics file into your Works document.**

   After a brief pause (during which another Windows program may make a brief appearance), your graphic image should now appear in your document. See the discussion about messing around with art in Chapter 21 for instructions on moving, sizing, or controlling text flow around your image.

Drag and Drop Documents into Works

This is a trick that nearly every Windows program can do. Open a My Computer window (or Windows Explorer window) on your screen. (For instructions, see the section, "Drag and Drop Graphics into Documents.") When you want to work on a document file, just drag it from the My Computer window over to the Works title bar. Release the mouse button, and Works opens the file. Even if the file is not a Works file, Works tries to import it.

Fill 'er Up: Filling Cells with Numbers

For sheer boredom, you just can't beat typing a series of numbers or dates into a spreadsheet or database. So don't do it. First, type a starting number into the top cell of the column you want to fill or into the leftmost cell of the row. (Use List view in the database tool.) Then, highlight that cell and the rest of the range to be filled. To fill the range with an increasing or decreasing series, click Edit in the menu bar and then click Fill Series in the drop-down menu. In the Fill Series dialog box that sprouts up, click the kind of units you want (plain numbers or dates). Click the Step By box and type the increment or decrement you want between each cell, such as -1. Click OK and you're done.

Freeze Your Head (ings)

When spreadsheets become larger than one screen's worth, you have a hard time seeing your column and row headings anymore. So lock them in place, or freeze them. Click the cell that's just under your column headings and just to the right of your row headings. Choose Format➪Freeze Titles from the menu bar. Now you can scroll all over the place and those headings will stay in place. To undo your freeze, repeat the action. To freeze just horizontally, select a row; to freeze just vertically, select a column.

Freeze-Dry or Customize Your Workspace

If you work on pretty much the same documents all the time, you can preserve your workspace; that is, tell Works to remember what documents you're using and reopen those document windows automatically when you start the program again. First, set up your workspace the way you want it. Then choose Tools➪Options and click the View tab in the Options dialog box. Click Use Saved Workspace At Startup; then click the Save Workspace button. Next time you start Works, it reloads those documents.

The Options dialog box that you see here holds all kinds of possibilities for customizing Works behavior. One of my favorite changes is getting rid of that Help screen that appears at startup: On the View card, click Show Help At Startup to clear the check mark. Another change is to get rid of the jerky word-at-a-time highlighting in the word processor: Click the Editing tab and clear the check mark labeled Automatic Word Selection.

Import and Export Documents

Works can read files from other programs or create files that other programs can read. When you go to open a file, the Open dialog box offers a Files Of Type list box. Click that box, and you'll find a whole bunch of programs whose files Works can read. Click one of those programs, and the File Name box lists files of that type in the directory you've selected. Choose the file to import, and Works converts it. Exporting a file works similarly: Use the Save As command and choose a file type in the Save As Type list box.

When you go to save an imported document, use the Save As command and delete the period and three-letter extension in the File Name area. Works supplies a proper extension and saves the document as a Works file.

Wrap Text in Small Windows

When you're working on a word-processor document in a tiny window, where lines extend beyond the window's edge, it's a pain to have to scroll left and right to be able to read. Instead, choose Tools➪Options; then choose the Editing tab in the dialog box that appears. Click the check box marked Wrap To Window. The document won't appear this way when you print; this just helps you read it.

Split a Window

To work on two different parts of a document at once, split the window. At the very top of the vertical scroll bar, above the up-pointing arrow, is a microscopic, obscure, shy little rectangle. Click that guy and drag him downward. This action splits the document into two windows that you can scroll independently. It's still only one document, though. To put the split away, drag the horizontal line that separates the two halves back up to the very top of the document window.

Use Computer Post-It Notes

If you're like me, you live in a small blizzard of those sticky 3M Post-it notes. And now you can even put the computerized equivalent in your word processor or database (Form view) documents. They're great for annotating your text with notes to yourself, because they don't print out.

Click where you want the note. Choose Insert➪Note-It from the menu bar. In the Note-It dialog box that appears, choose one of the adorable symbols in the Choose A Picture area (scroll to see more). Underneath that, where it says Type Your Caption Here, type a few words that will appear with the symbol in your document. To the right, where it suggests that you Type Your Note Here, do so.

Click the OK button, and you return to the document. Click and drag one of the corners of the frame around your symbol to shrink it to a reasonable size. Now, when you double-click the symbol, your note appears somewhere on your monitor. Click anywhere else to make it go away. To delete the Note-It altogether, click it and press the Delete key.

Use the Other Mouse Button

The *other* mouse button (the one on the right side of the mouse, unless you're a lefty and someone has configured your mouse for you) has a surprising amount of stuff behind it. Try highlighting (selecting) something — text or graphics — the usual way and then clicking with the *other* mouse button. You'll find editing commands such as Copy, Cut, and Paste, as well as formatting commands. Use them just as you would commands from the menu bar.

But wait, there's more! If a dialog box presents you with a thingy (check box, button, whatever) that you don't understand, click the right mouse button on that thingy. A brief explanation will appear, and it may even occasionally be helpful. (The explanation is the same one that appears if you click the "?" symbol in the upper right-hand corner of the dialog box and then the thingy.)

Chapter 23

Ten Things NOT to Do

*E*veryone has an idea about how things ought to work. Unfortunately, computers don't usually work that way. You can easily fall into old typewriter habits or form a mistaken impression that Works makes you do something that you don't really have to do. Here's my list of the top ten errors, misconceptions, or just plain boo-boos that you should avoid.

Do Not Use Extra Spaces, Lines, or Tabs

If you're using multiple, consecutive spaces or tabs in a word-processing document, you're probably making your life difficult. If you're using multiple tabs in every line, it's probably because you haven't set your tab stops or you've forgotten that you can indent a paragraph with a toolbar button. If you are using blank lines to separate paragraphs, try pressing Ctrl+0 (that's a zero, not the letter O) to put space above the paragraph instead. See Chapter 6 for additional better ways to do things.

Do Not Keep Pressing Enter to Begin a New Page

This trick may have worked nicely on your Royal typewriter, but in Works word-processing documents, it creates a royal mess. Press Ctrl+Enter to start a new page.

Do Not Press Enter at the End of Each Line

I know, I've said this before, but it pains me greatly to see people fighting their word processor. If you press Enter at the end of every line in a word-processing document, Works can't word-wrap for you. As a result, every time you edit a line, you have to manually readjust every line! AAAAAGGGH!! JUST DON'T DO IT, YOU HEAR ME?!! (Notice how annoying text is when it's all in capital letters? If you want to know why adults shouldn't shout at each other like this, see the tenth thing not to do in this chapter.)

Do Not Type Your Own File Extensions When Saving Files

When you save a file, just type the filename, not the .WKS or any other extension. Works automatically puts the proper extension on. If you use your own special extension, it's harder to get Works to display the file in the Open dialog box, and the file is therefore harder to open.

Do Not Number Your Pages Manually

Works can automagically number your word-processing pages, positioning the numbers where you want them. What more could you want? If you try to number your own pages by simply typing a number on each page, you'll be continually adjusting them as you edit the document.

Do Not Turn Off Your PC Before Exiting

Hey! It's time for dinner! But don't just flip the power switch on your PC. Exit Works and exit Windows first. (If your PC is one that suspends the state of all your programs — and of Windows — as you turn the PC off, you don't need to exit Works and Windows first. Some laptops also have a "suspend" feature.) If you don't exit before you turn off your computer, Windows and Works can become confused the next time you try to do things. At the very least, your hard disk fills up with little Windows temporary files.

Do Not Use Spaces for Blank Cells

In your spreadsheet documents, when you want to remove an entry, don't type a space; press the Delete key instead. If you put a space in the cell and use a COUNT, AVG, or other statistical function, the cell will be counted.

Do Not Work in Tiny Windows Unnecessarily

Just because Works starts out with a smallish window, you don't have to stay with it. Click and drag a corner or side of the Works window and enlarge Works. Do the same with your document windows. Better yet, maximize the Works or document window. See Chapter 2 for a refresher on doing this.

Do Not Stuff All Your Files in the Same Folder

See Chapter 2 for ways to make new folders. When you save files, put them in different folders. If you stuff them all in the same folder, you will eventually get very confused.

Do Not Type in ALL CAPITALS

Particularly when you're using the communications tool to send mail to somebody, don't type in all capital letters. It's considered shouting. In other tools, using all capitals (uppercase letters) makes your documents harder to read.

Appendix

Wisdom and Wizardry for Common Tasks

• •

• •

*T*hrough the magic of TaskWizards and templates, Works can create some amazing documents for you very quickly. Without the help of a template or TaskWizard, you would have to thoroughly study Works in order to create such delightful documents.

What are TaskWizards and templates? *TaskWizards* are automated programs that first ask you a series of questions by means of dialog boxes. Then, using one of Works' Big Four tools — such as the word processor — the TaskWizards create and format a custom document for you (letterhead stationery, for example) by using the name and address information that you supply. You finish that document by inserting or editing text or values and by adjusting the formatting. *Templates* are pre-built, general-purpose Works documents, like a game schedule for sports teams, from which you can create documents customized to your specific needs. Works comes with a bunch of pre-built templates, or you can create your own.

TaskWizards and templates present themselves on the Works Task Launcher that appears whenever you start Works or begin a new document (by choosing File⇨New, for instance). Chapter 1 shows you how to choose TaskWizards on the TaskWizard card of the Task Launcher. Templates don't have their own card on the Task Launcher, so they hang out with the TaskWizards. This Appendix tells you where to find them.

Some of the documents that TaskWizards and templates create can be a little overwhelming because they use advanced features and subtle tricks. This Appendix provides some instructions and hints to make things come out right. Works has too many TaskWizards and templates to cover thoroughly in this book, so this Appendix provides details on the most popular TaskWizards as well as general hints and tips for other TaskWizards and templates.

Tempting Templates

Dummies being who we are — intelligent people who would just as soon not do the same thing twice — templates are a fabulous Dummies feature. *Templates* are the bare bones of some type of document that you use over and over again.

For example, if you are a consultant, almost all your invoices look the same, except for the details of dates and charges and who the work is for. An invoice template supplies everything but those details, which you fill in. You can then save that invoice document as a file, and the original template remains untouched. (Some computer users simply modify their last invoice to create a new one, using Save As to save it with a new name. But a template is better because you don't run the risk of accidentally modifying the original.)

Works supplies more than 100 pre-built templates, complete with nice formatting, for a variety of uses. You can also create your own templates.

Using a template

Using a template is simply a way to start a new document with most of the work already done. Using the Task Launcher (choose File⇨New), click the TaskWizards tab. Way down at the bottom of the list of TaskWizard categories, you find User Defined Templates. Click User Defined Templates and then double-click the template of your choice, and a new document appears.

Your new document is just like any other document, except that it's already partly complete! Make edits and fill in the blanks. (Click at the beginning of a blank to fill it in. Blanks are actually underlined Tab characters, by the way.) Save your new document as you would any other document (by pressing Ctrl+S, for instance).

Creating a template

To create a template, begin by creating a document that has all the text and graphics that don't change (such as your address or logo). Format the document and set up the page layout. If you want the text that will be added later to have a particular format, put in *dummy,* or *placeholder,* text and format that. To later replace the dummy text, select it, type new text, and the new text will take on the same format.

To save the document as a template:

1. **Choose File⇨Save As.**

2. **Click the Template button on the lower right of the Save As dialog box. A Save As Template dialog box then requests a name.**

3. **Enter a name for the template.**

   If the only type of word-processing, database, spreadsheet, or commu-nications document you ever use is the one for which you created the template, click the Use This Template For New *whatever* Documents check box (with *whatever* being Word Processing, Database, and so on). This action turns your template into a *default* template. Now whenever you start a new document of that type — a word-processing document, for instance — your document automatically takes the form of that template. To turn this feature off, open the template by choosing File⇨Open, return to the Save As dialog box by using Steps 1 through 3, and click the check box again.

Works stores your template in the Template folder, within the MSWorks folder. If you need to modify the template in any way, choose File⇨Open and open that folder to find the template.

Creating an Address Book

Obviously Microsoft thinks that it's very important for you to have an address book. After all, Microsoft put an Address Book button on the toolbar. Because none of you wants to disappoint Microsoft, you should probably create an address book. Here are some other good reasons for creating an address book:

- ✔ You have lots of people whom you call often — usually while you are sitting next to your computer.

- ✔ You have lots of friends and want to keep track of their birthdays and anniversaries.

  - ✔ You are in charge of sending out letters or information to a lot of people on a regular basis.

  - ✔ You want to do your own junk mail: "Dear Mr. ___, I know you and others of the ___ family would love to send us your money."

  - ✔ You are a salesperson and need to keep a record of all your prospects and clients. When Ms. Steinway calls, you want to be able to say, "Oh, hi, Barbara, I was just thinking of you. How are, um, . . .," (brief pause while you look up her entry in the address book), "George and the kids? Isn't little . . . Sustenuto 12 now?"

Computerized address books make the preceding tasks easier because you can quickly search for people by name, by birthday, by company, or by other criteria. You can also reorganize your address book easily — for example, grouping together all the people who work for the same company.

You may want several address books — one for friends, another for clients, and another for members of the professional organization that you run. You can print out these address books as well as use them on the computer.

Address books are really database documents. Each entry (last name, first name, phone number, and so on) is a *field* in database lingo. For more information on creating, modifying, and using databases, see Part IV of this book.

Here's how to create an address book by using one of the cool TaskWizards that Works supplies:

1. **Choose File⇨New and click the TaskWizards tab in the Task Launcher.**

2. **In the Common Tasks category of the TaskWizards list, double-click Address Book.**

3. **If a Works Task Launcher dialog box appears, click the button marked Yes to run the TaskWizard.**

   The address book TaskWizard fires up and asks you to choose what type of address book you'd like.

4. **Choose a type of address book that sounds good; if the one you pick isn't perfect for your needs, you can go back and choose another one or modify this one.**

5. **Click the Next button to see what sort of information will be in this address book.**

   To go back and try another type of address book, click the Back button. To add other types of information to the address book you've chosen, hang on until you get to the next screen.

6. Click the Next button to add fields or specify *reports* (printed versions of your address book).

For each type of address book, Works has some standard additional fields it thinks you may like, such as extended phone numbers and an area for notes. (*Extended phone numbers* include fax, home/business phone, pager, cellular phone, and electronic mail addresses.) For these fields, choose Additional Fields. Click OK when you're done.

To add your own fields, such as a Dues Paid field, choose Your Own Fields. In the dialog box that appears, you can add up to four fields of your own choosing; click a field check box and enter a name for the field in the adjacent box. Click OK when you're done.

To create printed reports, click Reports. Works lets you choose between an alphabetized listing of people in your address book or a listing that is broken up into groups based on a "category" field. Click OK when you're done.

7. Click the Create It! button to check over your choices before creating the book.

To make this address book the one that pops up when you click the Address Book button on your toolbar (or when you choose Tools⇨ Address Book), click the option marked Yes, I Want This To Be My Default Address Book.

8. Click the Create Document button.

The address book TaskWizard, the world's fastest typist, tosses together a database document: your new address book.

9. Save your address book: Press Ctrl+S.

Give your file a name and folder to live in.

Of course, now you have to fill out your address book. Ugh. For more details on navigating around your address book database and entering information, see Chapter 12. But for now, here's the executive summary:

- ✔ You are looking at one page, or *record*, of your address book.
- ✔ To advance from one field to the next as you enter data, click the field you want or press the Tab key.
- ✔ Type to enter data, pressing the Enter or Tab key when you're done.
- ✔ To advance or go back one record, press Ctrl+Page Down or Ctrl+Page Up, respectively.
- ✔ If you requested a *category* report (when you specified your report back in Step 6 of the preceding steps), decide how you want people to be grouped (for example, members/nonmembers/prospects), and for each person, enter his or her group in the Category field.

✔ To edit an entry, click the entry, press the F2 key, and edit in the formula bar just under the toolbar. Press Enter when you are done.

✔ To find someone by name or other information, the easiest way is to choose Edit➪Find from the menu bar. In the Find dialog box, type the word or phrase you want in the Find What box, choose All Records, and then click OK. Choosing All Records hides records not containing your search word; press Ctrl+Page Down to step through them. When you're done, choose Record➪Show➪1 All Records to make all visible again.

To open your address book, you can use any of these methods:

✔ If you made this address book your default address book (in Step 7 of the preceding steps), just click the Address Book button (the last button on the right end).

✔ To open an address book other than your default book, open it like any other (database) document with File➪Open or the Task Launcher.

To change your default address book, choose Tools➪Options, click the Address Book tab, and double-click an address book in the list shown.

Creating Your Own Junk Mail

For that personal touch without actually being personal, there's nothing like junk mail. (Miss Manners, please call your office.) Yes, now you, too — *<your name here>*, of *<your address here>* — can send junk mail just like the pros!

This popular feature, also known as *mail-merge* or *form letters,* lets you write a single letter in the word processor, leave blanks in the text, and have Works automatically fill in the blanks *(merge)* from a database (such as an address book). Works prints out one letter for each lucky person in your database.

Of course, in addition to sending falsely personal letters, this feature can be used for more valid personalization, like:

✔ Sending a letter to members of your organization, telling them how much they have paid, and have left unpaid, of their annual dues or pledge.

✔ Welcoming each attendee to some event and telling the attendees what room they will be staying in.

In these examples, a piece of information that your database contains about that person appears in the letter.

Of course, you must have a database document with this information in it for the information to appear in a letter! You can use any database TaskWizard to create the database document, such as the address book TaskWizard described in the preceding section, "Creating an Address Book." In the Task Launcher, look through the various TaskWizard categories (such as Names and Addresses) for wizards with a database icon (a tiny picture of Rolodex-style cards). Or create a database from scratch — see Part IV of this book.

When you have a database, you need to create the letter. You have two alternatives:

✔ Write the letter from scratch, modifying it for mail-merge.

✔ Have Works write the letter with a TaskWizard, although this action typically doesn't do any more than begin the letter with the recipient's name and address.

If you are new to this mail-merge stuff, or if you just need some assistance in writing and properly formatting a letter, I suggest the second option: Use a TaskWizard to start the letter and then modify the letter to add any personal information you want in the body of the letter. By seeing how the TaskWizard handles the task, you can find out how to create your own form letters. See "Form letters using a letter TaskWizard," coming up soon in this Appendix.

Otherwise, you can create your own form letters from scratch fairly simply. Read on.

Form letters from scratch

Works has a tool for creating form letters, but it seems unnecessarily complicated to me for most purposes; you have to pop in and out of the tool to write the letter. Here's what I think is the simplest approach: Write your letter by using the word processor. Wherever you need to fill in some personal data for the addressee, do the following steps. (This strategy creates a document that prints a letter for every entry in your database. If you want to filter or exclude certain records, see the "Mailing to only a select few" section in this Appendix.)

1. **Choose Insert⇨Database Field.**

   If a First-Time Help dialog box appears, click To Write A Form Letter.

   An Insert Field dialog box appears. Click Use A Different Database, and in the Use Database dialog box that appears, double-click your chosen database.

2. **Click the field that contains the personal data you need (such as Child Name, a field you may have if you were writing an acceptance letter for summer camp using a database of applicants), and then click the Insert button.**

   You can enter several fields from this dialog box.

3. **Click Close when you're done.**

When you've finished composing your letter, you can best see the results of your work by using Print Preview. Choose File⇔Print Preview from the menu bar, click OK in the dialog box that mutters about "all records," and enjoy the view.

In Print Preview, you can see each of the many letters you are going to print! Just click the Next button to see the next letter. Continue editing the form letter if necessary and print for real when the form letter is ready. If the data is wrong, you need to edit the database, as Chapter 13 describes. To filter your data (select only certain records in your database), see the section "Mailing to only a select few," later in this Appendix.

Form letters using a letter TaskWizard

You can choose from several TaskWizards; just about any "letter" TaskWizard will do, but a good, basic one to use is the form letter TaskWizard in the Correspondence folder:

1. **Choose File⇔New and click the TaskWizards tab in the Task Launcher.**

2. **Click Correspondence in the TaskWizards list and double-click Form Letter.**

3. **If a Works Task Launcher dialog box appears, click the button marked Yes, Run The TaskWizard.**

   The Letter TaskWizard fires up and asks you to choose which layout of a letter you'd like.

4. **Choose the layout that sounds good to you (such as Professional) and click the Next button.**

   In the next Works TaskWizard dialog box that appears, you get to specify the details: Letterhead, Address, Content, Text Style, and Extras.

5. **Choose Letterhead.**

   Two choices appear: I Want To Design My Own and I Want To Use My Pre-Printed Letterhead Stationery. The first choice takes you to a letterhead design specialist; the second choice helps arrange body text around preprinted items if your letterhead is already preprinted on your paper.

Whichever choice you make, the TaskWizard presents a series of dialog boxes, one at a time. Just follow the steps provided by the TaskWizard, providing your own particular information in the blanks provided in the dialog boxes.

6. **Choose Address and then choose I Want To Use Addresses From A Works Database. Then click the Next button.**

7. **Select the database containing your names and addresses from the next dialog box.**

If the database you want isn't listed, click The File I Want Isn't In The List. Works tells you how you can continue to make the form letter and then go back and merge the database later.

8. **Build an address for the addressee area of the letter by using the Address dialog box shown in Figure A-1.**

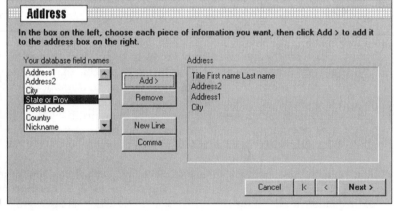

Figure A-1:
Select fields from your database for the Address area.

The task in this step is to choose which fields will be printed, the order in which they will appear, and on which line they will appear. The procedure goes like this:

a) Click a field on the left side of the Address dialog box; then click the Add button to copy it to the right side.

b) If you make a mistake, click the Remove button to remove the last field you added.

c) To begin a new line of the address, click the New Line button.

d) Click the Comma button to type a comma — for example, to separate city from state.

Don't use all the fields in your database! Use only the ones you want printed at the top of the letter. When you're done selecting the fields, click the Next button.

9. **Create a greeting or salutation line (Dear ____) in the Address dialog box by using the same method you just used for the addressee area in Step 7. Click the Next button when you're done creating the greeting.**

   For a formal letter, you can do Dear <Title> <Last name> for Dear Ms. ____ or Dear Mr. _____.

10. **Click OK in the next dialog box and . . . you're not done yet! Back to deciding the other features of your letter.**

11. **Choose Content and then click OK when you're done.**

    Wow! Works even provides prewritten letters! Use one if you like (although many of these are not particularly suited for bulk mailing — like the Acceptance Of Job Offer letter — unless you live a very interesting life!). I am occupationally predisposed toward writing, so I chose Blank Letter.

12. **All right, you get the idea. Finish up by choosing a Text Style and then Extras, if you like.**

13. **Click the Create It! button!! At last!!! How exciting!!!!**

    Check over the specifications for your form letter in the Checklist dialog box that appears, and if the letter needs changes, just click Return To Wizard. Otherwise, click the Create Document button.

When all the dust settles, you're left gazing at an ordinary Works word-processing document. Well, not entirely ordinary: As you can see in Figure A-2, there are some odd entries in it.

The items in << >> symbols are placeholders. Works will replace these with actual data from your database. The thing within the << >> symbols is the name of the field from which the data will come. (There are also paragraph and space symbols displayed that don't actually print, so don't fret about them.)

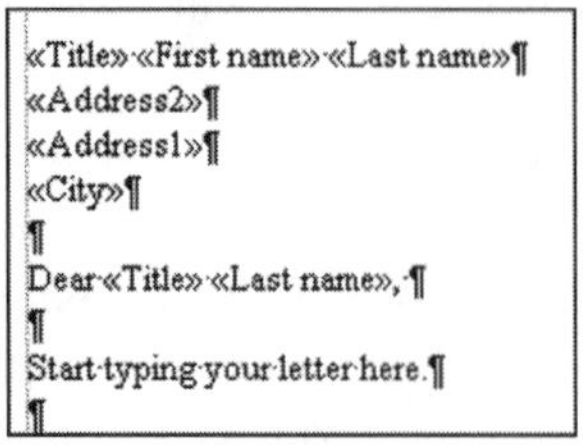

Figure A-2:
What you
end up with:
a letter with
odd text
in it.

```
«Title» «First name» «Last name»¶
«Address2»¶
«Address1»¶
«City»¶
¶
Dear «Title» «Last name», ¶
¶
Start typing your letter here.¶
¶
```

Finish your letter. Whenever you come to a place where you need to fill in some personal data for the addressee, do the following:

1. Choose Insert⊅Database Field.

If a First-time Help dialog box appears, click To Write A Form Letter.

An Insert Field dialog box appears.

2. Click the field that contains the personal data you need (such as Child Name, a field you may have if you are writing an acceptance letter for summer camp using a database of applicants) and then click the Insert button.

You can enter several fields from this dialog box.

3. Click Close when you're done.

When you've finished composing your letter, you can best see the results of your work by using Print Preview. Choose File⊅Print Preview from the menu bar, click OK in the dialog box that mutters about "all records," and enjoy the view.

In Print Preview you can see each of the many letters you are going to print! Just click the Next button to see the next one. Continue editing the form letter if necessary and print for real when the letter is ready. If the data is wrong, you need to edit the database.

Mailing to only a select few

You may not want to send mail to everyone in your database, so you need to *filter, hide,* or *mark* certain records. To do this, I suggest that you use the word-processor's Form Letter tool. This tool is actually designed to step you through the creation of a form letter. You can use the tool for that, but I think it's a bit confusing, so I suggest that you use the Form Letter tool only when you need to filter your records.

For information about filtering, hiding, and marking, see Chapter 14.

With your form letter open in Works word processor, here's how to specify exactly what records you want to use:

1. Choose Tools⊅Form Letters.

The Form Letter dialog box appears, in all its glory. You have already selected a database, so that task appears checked off on the Instructions card. Now it's time to make some changes in other cards.

2. Click the Recipients tab in the Form Letters dialog box.

This is the control center for what records are used from your database (see Figure A-3).

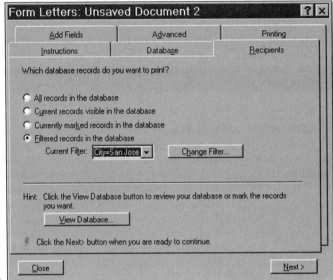

Figure A-3:
Controlling who gets a letter: the Recipients card of the Form Letters tool.

To use a filter, click Filtered records in the database and choose a filter from the drop-down list marked Current Filter. To modify the filter, click the Change Filter button.

To mark or hide records, you need to access the database document itself. The Form Letter tool manages this by letting you pop in and out of the database without exiting the Form Letter tool.

1. To pop into the database, click the button marked View Database near the bottom of the Form Letter dialog box.

(If a First-time Help dialog box appears, click To Mark Records.) Your database document appears, but it is partly obscured by a small Form Letters dialog box with a Return button on it. Drag that out of your way.

2. Mark the records you want to use, or hide the records you don't want to use (Record⇨Mark Record or Hide Record).

Switch views, if you need to.

3. Find the small Form Letters dialog box with the Go Back button on it, floating somewhere on your screen; click the Go Back button.

You return to the big Form Letters dialog box.

4. **To use marked records, click Currently Marked Records In The Database. Another one of those persistently helpful First-Time Help boxes may pop up. Click the To Show Or Hide Marked Records button.**

   To exclude using hidden records, click Current Records Visible In The Database.

To see the results of your efforts, click the Printing tab of the Form Letters dialog box and choose the Preview button. Click OK in the dialog box that pops up, and in Print Preview, see whether your filtering, marking, or hiding has had the desired effect. Click the Next or Previous button to move between records.

When you're all done, click the Close button in the Form Letters dialog box.

Envelopes and labels for mass mailing

Need to send out your form letter in an envelope or create mailing labels for your newsletter? Here are the Works tools that do the job for you. The first two work very much alike.

Works' envelope tool is specially designed to help you do mass mailings by using addresses from databases. Just choose Tools⇨Envelopes from the database menu bar.

Works' label tool is specifically designed to print on labels made by the Avery company. Choose an Avery label by its model number, and in Works choose Tools⇨Labels from the menu bar. Works automatically sets up the page size, layout, and printer settings to print precisely on the labels.

If you need to create only a page or so of labels and you don't mind typing in the addressee data by hand instead of using your address database, try Works' *Labels, Shipping* template. Take a look at the section "Using a template," earlier in this Appendix, for more information on where to find templates.

Make sure that you use Avery labels that are well suited to your printer. For example, for laser, inkjet, or bubble-jet printers, use the labels that come on $8^1/_2$ x 11-inch sheets. For laser printers, make sure that the labels are designed for laser printers, or you may end up with a gummy mess!

Both tools require you to have a database full of names and addresses. As with form letters, Works lets you write a document that is a normal word-processing document in nearly every way except that instead of regular text, it has placeholders for such database fields as Last name, First name, and Address.

Both tools present you with a set of cards. The top card is a checklist of things that have to be set up. These Works tools (I like to call them gnomes) are designed to take you through each item on this list. To do this, you can click the Next button on the lower right; the gnome moves you to the next item on the checklist, taking you to the next card. (Alternatively, you can click the button next to each step or on the card tabs.) The gnome will step you through the process, always returning to the Instructions card and showing you check marks for the steps that are now done.

If you are sending out form letters and want to save some time and effort, use envelopes with windows on them. Just lay out the addressee field so that it shows through the window!

These cards are pretty self-explanatory, except for a few items that I discuss a little later. Here's how to get started:

1. **If your document is a form letter and already has the placeholders for the recipient's name and mailing address in it, select the name and address portion.**

   Otherwise, move on to Step 2.

2. **Choose Tools⇨Envelopes or Tools⇨Labels.**

   If this is the first time you have printed an envelope since you started Works, you may get one of Works' First-time Help dialog boxes. This dialog box offers to help you 1) take a tour of envelopes and labels, 2) create an envelope or label, or 3) print an envelope or label. I suggest that you take the tour once, for fun: Click the Quick Tour Of Envelopes And Labels button and follow directions. When you return to the First-Time Help box, click Don't Display This Message In The Future, and First-Time Help will never bother you again. Then click the To Create Envelopes or To Create Labels button.

The gnome pops up the Instructions card for the dialog box. Click the Next button to move from card to card until you're done. Here are a few tips:

✔ **The Main Address or Label Layout card:** This card, shown in Figure A-4, is where the address information goes. If, in Step 1 of the preceding list, you initially highlighted the recipient's name and address in your letter, it appears here in a big text box (either Main Address or Label Layout). You can edit the name and address now if you like, in that box. If you didn't select an address, this text box will be blank, and you can fill it in as follows:

   • Click a field in Choose A Field and click the Add Field button to copy it to the address area. For example, to make your first address line, you may add Title, then First name, and then Last name from your database.

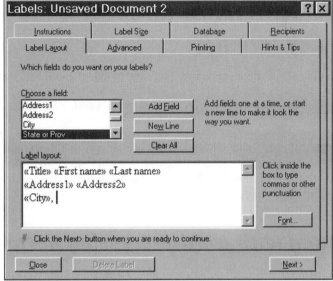

Figure A-4:
The Label
Layout card
in the Label
tool is just
like the
Main
Address
card in the
Envelope
tool.

- If you make a mistake or need to add a comma or other text, click in the big text box and edit.

- To add a new line, click the New Line button or press Enter in the text box.

✔ **The Recipients card:** This card allows you to trim out certain people from your mailing by specifying filters or marking or hiding certain records. If you want to mail to everyone in your database, just click the Next button and continue on. If you do need to select certain people, see the instructions in the section "Mailing to only a select few." Those instructions are for the Recipients card in the Form Letter tool, but this card works exactly the same.

✔ **To preview or print your envelope, click the Printing card.** I strongly suggest that you click the Preview button to see your envelope or labels in Print Preview. When you think that they look correct, click the Test button to actually try them out on paper.

✔ **For tips on labels, check out the Hints & Tips card in the labels tool.**

If you created an envelope while you had a form letter open, you end up with a properly formatted envelope page adhering to the top of your form letter. A special envelope/page break (the dotted line) separates it from your document.

Tips for Using Wizard and Template Documents

Works pulls out all the stops when it comes to Wizard and template documents. Works uses lots of advanced features in such clever ways that you may not recognize exactly what feature is being used.

Following are some tips for working with these clever wizard and template documents. To determine whether a document is a word-processing, database, spreadsheet, or communications document, check the icon to the left of the template name. See Figure 1-5 in Chapter 1 if you're unsure about the meaning of the icons.

Working with word-processing documents

Wizard and template word-processing documents are full of graphical and layout tricks. Here are a few of the most common tricks:

- ✔ In Newsletter documents, Works shows multiple columns, WordArt, charts, and graphics. (The Word NEWSLETTER, for example, is a WordArt box.) To change any of these features, double-click on what you want to change; whatever tool is responsible will appear.

- ✔ In Letterhead and other Wizard documents, Works uses paragraph formatting and borders extensively. Click some text and choose Format⇨Paragraph and Format⇨Borders And Shading to see what's going on.

- ✔ Works Wizard documents use tabs in creative ways. To see where tab characters appear, choose View⇨All Characters. Tab characters are represented by tiny arrows. Fill-in blanks are often created by using underlined tab characters.

Working with spreadsheet documents

Wizard and template spreadsheet documents use lots of tricks with borders, column widths, and gridlines. Here are tips for working around a few of those tricks:

- ✔ If a spreadsheet appears to have headings with text indented under them, this may be done by using a very narrow column for the heading text and then putting the indented text in the next column over.

✔ If you can't edit the text in a spreadsheet, select the area and choose Format⬌Protection. Click the Protect Data check box to clear the check mark.

✔ If a spreadsheet uses colored text that doesn't work well for you, remember that colors are an option in the Font card of the Format Cells dialog box.

Working with database documents

Wizard and template database documents come equipped with built-in reports and some tricky formulas, as well as fancy formatting. Here are a few tips for making sense of what you see:

✔ In label templates, you have to enter your name and address only once: in the upper left-hand corner. You don't have to enter it for every label. (Formulas automatically make copies.)

✔ Check out what reports are available by choosing View⬌Report; choose one from the list and then click Preview in the dialog box that appears.

✔ To pick up some advanced techniques with formulas, check out the built-in reports in Report view.

✔ To change the formatting, layout, or content of a database document, Form Design view generally works best.

✔ If you need to change a field, but Works won't let you, choose Format⬌ Protection and click to remove the Protect Field check mark.

Index

IDG BOOKS WORLDWIDE BOOK REGISTRATION

We want to hear from you!

Visit **http://my2cents.dummies.com** to register this book and tell us how you liked it!

- ✔ Get entered in our monthly prize giveaway.

- ✔ Give us feedback about this book — tell us what you like best, what you like least, or maybe what you'd like to ask the author and us to change!

- ✔ Let us know any other *...For Dummies*® topics that interest you.

Your feedback helps us determine what books to publish, tells us what coverage to add as we revise our books, and lets us know whether we're meeting your needs as a *...For Dummies* reader. You're our most valuable resource, and what you have to say is important to us!

Not on the Web yet? It's easy to get started with *Dummies 101*®: *The Internet For Windows*® *95* or *The Internet For Dummies*,® 5th Edition, at local retailers everywhere.

Or let us know what you think by sending us a letter at the following address:

...For Dummies Book Registration
Dummies Press
7260 Shadeland Station, Suite 100
Indianapolis, IN 46256-3945
Fax 317-596-5498

BUSINESS AND
GENERAL
REFERENCE
BOOK SERIES
FROM IDG

COMPUTER
BOOK SERIES
FROM IDG